# THE WRITER'S EXPRESS

## A Paragraph and Essay Text with Readings

SECOND EDITION

**Kathleen T. McWhorter**
*Niagara County Community College*

**HOUGHTON MIFFLIN COMPANY**   Boston   New York

Sponsoring Editor: Renée Deljon
Basic Book Editor: Martha Bustin
Senior Associate Editor: Ellen Darion
Associate Project Editor: Christina Lillios
Production/Design Coordinator: Jennifer Waddell
Manufacturing Coordinator: Marie Barnes
Marketing Manager: Nancy Lyman
Editorial Assistants: Kate O'Sullivan, Joy Park

**Cover illustration:** Cover design by Diana Coe; cover image by Celia Johnson.

**Art Credits:** Art Credits begin on page 489.

Acknowledgments for reprinted material appear on page 489.

Library of Congress Catalog Card Number: 96-76930
Student Text ISBN: 0-395-78292-9
Exam Copy ISBN: 0-395-78293-7

23456789-B-00 99 98 97

# Contents in Brief

# CONTENTS

## Part III   *Methods of Development*   93

CHAPTER **12**    **Summarizing and Synthesizing Sources**    218

CHAPTER **13**    **Writing Expository Essays**    247

# RHETORICAL CONTENTS

*Expository*

*Persuasive*

# THEMATIC CONTENTS

Note: Asterisks (*) designate paired readings.

# PREFACE

To succeed in college and beyond, today's students must be able to express their ideas clearly and correctly in written form and to read, think critically, interpret, and react to what they have read. Twenty-nine years of experience with developmental students have convinced me that these essential skills—writing, reading, and critical thinking—are most effectively taught when integrated. Many students flourish when given the opportunity to learn and practice these skills within a stimulating, non-threatening framework. My goals in writing *The Writer's Express* and in preparing the second edition have been to help students build a solid repertoire of strategies for writing, reading, and critical thinking—a repertoire that will stand them in good stead in freshman composition and in the rest of their college and work careers.

*The Writer's Express,* Second Edition, has retained its integrated writing-reading approach, step-by-step instruction, and supportive tone. It teaches developmental students the fundamentals of paragraph and essay writing through structured, sequential instruction; varied exercises that build upon each other; numerous pieces of student writing and examples; and high-interest, issue-oriented readings. In the second edition, I have given increased attention to essay-writing skills in a way that affords greater flexibility of use. Instructors can move earlier from a focus on the paragraph to a focus on the essay as the main unit of composition, with essay-writing instruction now in Chapter 11, Chapters 13–15, and in Chapters 6–10 (on the rhetorical modes) in the form of two new features, "Applying Your Skills to Essay Writing" and "Essay Option" assignments. I have also included a new chapter (Chapter 12) that helps students develop the important skills of annotating, paraphrasing, summarizing, and synthesizing. It contains a brief introductory look at finding and using appropriate sources, a skill students increasingly need. Complementing the enhanced essay coverage and new chapter are five pairs of readings that allow more comparative discussions and assignments and some beginning source-based writing. As in the first edition, sentence-level concerns are presented as integral to the clear expression of ideas; a handbook with exercises appears at the end of the text; and near the end of each chapter in Parts II–IV, a "Skill Refresher" box ties in with the handbook.

# Organization of the Text

The text is organized into six parts. Part I, "Getting Started," opens with a chapter that establishes the importance of effective writing, places writing within the context of the college experience, and offers five tips for writing success. Chapter 2 provides an overview of the writing process, with an emphasis on prewriting techniques. This chapter demonstrates many of its points by showing how a sample student paper (an ad analysis) develops through several stages and drafts.

Part II, "Paragraph Writing Strategies," covers paragraph structure and topic sentences (Chapter 3), developing a paragraph with details (Chapter 4), and the revision process (Chapter 5). Chapter 5 introduces a "Revision Checklist" feature that is further developed in each of the remaining chapters of the book. From Chapter 3 on, a reading or pair of readings appears at the end of each chapter, with accompanying opportunities for discussion, journal writing, critical thinking skills-building, and writing. Writing assignments are in two categories: "Writing About the Reading" and "Writing About Your Ideas."

In Part III, "Methods of Development," each chapter describes one of the rhetorical modes, gives examples, and provides practical advice for organizing, developing, and writing paragraphs and/or essays using that mode. The chapters in this part cover narration and process; description; example, classification, and definition; comparison and contrast; and cause and effect. As in other sections, writing assignments build sequentially. Students generate ideas about a topic, prepare a first draft, and revise using the "Revision Checklist" and "Proofreading Checklist."

Part IV, "Strategies for Writing Essays," concentrates on the short essay. Chapter 11, "Sharpening Your Essay-Writing Skills," emphasizes writing effective thesis statements, supporting them with evidence, and crafting strong introductions and conclusions. The new Chapter 12, "Summarizing and Synthesizing Sources," presents these basic academic skills, as well as annotating and paraphrasing, in an introductory way; it also provides simple guidelines for finding and using appropriate sources. Pairs of carefully selected readings appear at the end of this chapter and the next two to facilitate the teaching of these essay-related skills. Chapters 13–15 cover expository essays, persuasive essays, and essay exams. Topics include analyzing audience, selecting and organizing convincing evidence, and choosing a tone.

Part V, "Additional Readings," contains twelve selections on a range of stimulating topics. These readings offer instructors flexibility in choosing and assigning readings and further represent the rhetorical modes. Selections are accompanied by questions for discussion and by journal writing and writing assignments. Included in this part are two more pairs of readings; each pair explores a timely issue—encounters with strangers, and predators in the wild and in captivity. Part VI, "Reviewing the Basics," is a brief handbook with exercises. It reviews the principles of grammar, sentence structure, mechanics, and spelling and concludes with a set of error correction exercises.

## Features

The following features distinguish *The Writer's Express*, Second Edition, from other developmental writing texts and make its approach unique:

- *Readings*   Beginning with Chapter 3, each chapter includes an engaging reading around which prewriting, critical thinking, and writing assignments are structured. Readings touch on topics within the students' realm of experience, such as family relationships, the widening gap between rich and poor, gender differences, and the use of politically correct language. Each reading offers students a model for the writing skills taught in the particular chapter, as well as a source of ideas and a base for discussion and collaborative learning activities.
- *"Getting Ready to Write" Strategies*   After the first two introductory chapters, each chapter contains three activities that prepare students to write about the reading. In the first, "Examining the Reading," students are taught reading strategies including review techniques, underlining, and drawing idea maps to review and organize ideas. In the second, "Thinking Critically," students learn critical thinking strategies that enable them to analyze and evaluate the reading. Critical thinking skills include making inferences, understanding connotative language, and analyzing tone. In the third, "Reacting to Ideas: Discussion and Journal Writing," students are given a range of thought-provoking questions on which class discussions or collaborative learning activities may be built.
- *Writing Assignments*   Two types of writing assignments follow each chapter reading. "Writing About the Reading" involves students with ideas expressed in the reading. "Writing About Your Ideas" allows students to write about personal experiences related to the topic of the reading. In Chapters 6–10, Essay Options are included for instructors who choose to have their students write an essay rather than a paragraph.
- *Idea and Revision Maps*   Throughout the book, students are taught to use idea and revision maps and given opportunities to practice these techniques. Many developmental students are visual learners;

that is, they process information visually rather than verbally or through auditory means. Students learn to draw idea maps—visual representations of a paragraph's or essay's content and organization—in order to examine ideas. Students learn to draw revision maps of their own writing as a means of evaluating both content and organization.

- *Revision Checklists*    A "Revision Checklist" appears at the end of each chapter, starting with Chapter 5. This feature provides a review of writing strategies learned in the chapter as well as a cumulative review of strategies learned in previous chapters.
- *Skill Refreshers*    Each chapter after Chapter 2 offers a review of a topic related to sentence structure, grammar, or punctuation. The "Skill Refresher" begins with a brief section of instruction, followed by a ten-item self-assessment quiz. Students are directed to record their score on the "Skill Refresher Score Chart" at the back of the book. Students who miss more than two questions on the self-assessment quiz are directed to pages in Part VI, "Reviewing the Basics," that present a more detailed explanation of the topic.
- *Assessment Exercises*    Chapter 1 contains five assignments that will enable the student and instructor to assess the student's experience, attitude, and approach to writing. These assignments encourage writing early in the course and emphasize its importance as a vehicle of communication between instructor and student.
- *Student Writing Samples*    Each chapter features one or more pieces of student writing used as an example or a model of a particular writing strategy. The samples are motivational and enable students to establish realistic expectations for their own writing.

## Changes to the Second Edition

- *New Chapter*    A new chapter, "Summarizing and Synthesizing Sources" (Chapter 12), teaches the skills needed to use sources effectively: annotating, paraphrasing, summarizing, and synthesizing. The chapter also provides a brief and manageable introduction to finding and using appropriate sources.
- *Earlier Introduction of Essay-Writing Skills*    The revised text presents essay-writing skills earlier and allows instructors greater flexibility in terms of when they wish to focus on the essay. The skills covered in Part I, "Getting Started," may be applied to either paragraph or essay writing. Each chapter in Part III, "Methods of Development," introduces a rhetorical mode using paragraph

examples and concludes with a section titled "Applying Your Skills to Essay Writing." The writing assignments at the end of each chapter in Part III now include an "Essay Option."

- *Paired Readings*   Chapters 12, 13, and 14 each have two end-of-chapter readings. Two additional pairs are included in Part V, "Additional Readings." These paired readings offer students an opportunity to make comparisons, synthesize ideas, and begin to use other writers' ideas to support their own.
- *New Readings*   More than 50 percent of the readings (16 out of 28) are new to the second edition, while the most effective selections from the first edition have been retained. Readings are brief, high-interest, and issue-oriented.
- *New Design*   The updated design features a clear, easy-to-follow chapter format and organization.
- *Writing in Context Assignments*   Assignments that place writing tasks within an academic context have been added, beginning with Chapter 3. These options enable students to define concretely their audience and purpose and connect the writing skills they are learning in college with writing tasks they will encounter in other courses.
- *Increased Number of Journal Writing Opportunities*   Journal questions are placed earlier and have been expanded.
- *Improved Grammar Handbook*   Part VI has been extensively revised and now includes a brief section on documentation.
- *New Material on Writing and Supporting Thesis Statements*  Chapter 11 has been revised to focus on one of the most common essay-writing problems: developing and supporting thesis statements.
- *Student Essay Contest*   The "Call for Papers" invites students to send their work to the author to be considered for inclusion in an upcoming new ancillary, *The Student's Express: A Collection of Paragraphs and Essays.* This contest offers students the chance for their work to reach a wider audience and helps them see that writing really is about the communication of ideas.

## Ancillary Materials

- *Instructor's Resource Manual*   This manual provides a time-saving overview of the text, explains its pedagogical features, discusses the role of critical thinking in the writing class, describes the software ancillary *Expressways,* and offers practical suggestions for teaching writing. It also gives suggestions for using the readings and has notes on each chapter, including additional class activities, Overhead

Transparency Masters, a complete answer key to the text, and correlations to statewide writing competency tests (TASP and CLAST).

- *Expressways,* Second Edition   Available in DOS, Windows, and Macintosh versions, *Expressways,* Second Edition, software is an interactive program that provides a tutorial review of the key writing strategies presented in the text. Moving at their own pace, students complete a range of writing activities and exercises. Each unit models the pedagogical structure of the text, providing skill instruction, demonstration, practice, and a brief on-screen reading. The modules guide the student through the writing process and culminate in a writing assignment that may be printed and evaluated by the instructor or by peer reviewers.

- *The Student's Express: A Collection of Paragraphs and Essays*
This ancillary, to be published in 1997–98, will be created from student entries; see the "Call for Papers" contest announced in the front of *The Writer's Express,* Second Edition.

- *MicroLab,* Second Edition   Available in both IBM and Mac versions, this versatile software program teaches and reinforces the basics of grammar, punctuation, and mechanics.

- *Newsweek* Subscription   A 10-week subscription card may be shrink-wrapped with the text for a nominal fee.

- The Dictionary Deal   *The American Heritage College Dictionary* may be shrink-wrapped with the text at a substantial savings.

## Acknowledgments

I appreciate the excellent ideas, suggestions, and advice of my colleagues who served as reviewers:

Cathryn Amdahl, Harrisburg Area Community College, PA

Maryanne Felter, Cuyahuga Community College, NY

Cecelia Fiery, Northwest Community College, OH

Linda Houston, The Ohio State University Agricultural Technical Institute, OH

Pete Kinnas, Colorado Northwest Community College, CO

Randy Lawrence, Hocking College, OH

Michael Nolan, Monroe Community College, NY

Spencer Oleson, Mountain View College, TX

Kathleen Rice, IVY Tech, IN

Leslie Roberts, Oakland Community College, MI

David Rollison, College of Marin, CA

Bill Schikora, Bay State College, MA

Ben Thomerson, Crafton Hills College, CA

J-son Wooi-chin, Long Beach City College, CA

Eileen Zamora, Southwestern College, CA

The entire editorial staff with whom I have worked deserves praise and credit for their assistance throughout the writing of this text. In particular, I wish to thank Renée Deljon for her warm and generous support throughout the project and Martha Bustin for her creative talent and energy. I am also grateful to Beverly Ponzi for her most valuable assistance in typing and manuscript management. Finally, I thank my students, who continue to make teaching a challenging and rewarding profession.

*Kathleen T. McWhorter*
*Niagara County Community College*

# THE
# WRITER'S
# EXPRESS

# GETTING STARTED

# 1

# An Introduction to Writing

During the first week of classes Leon, a student who had just started college, was talking to his classmate Maria, who had completed two semesters. Leon had just learned that he had to write two three-page papers for his introduction sociology course and that they would count for thirty percent of his grade. "I've never been good at writing, and every time I try, I panic—I don't know what to say or how to begin," said Leon. "I'm worried about that course already." Maria smiled. "Leon, it'll be all right. Don't worry—you'll get lots of help in your writing course. I felt the same way last year, but my writing course really helped me. I don't panic about papers anymore—I know what to do."

Like it did for Leon and Maria, this course will give you the practical help that you need with writing. It is designed to make you feel more comfortable and confident about writing, and, let's face it, you will need to be. Both in college and on the job, you will need to write and to do so with skill and confidence.

## Why Is Writing Important?

Regardless of your curriculum or major, writing will be an important part of your college courses. Although not all introductory courses require writing, most advanced courses in your chosen discipline will demand a great deal of writing.

Here are a few examples of the kinds of writing you will do in your courses:

- short answers to questions
- essay exams
- research papers and reports
- reaction papers
- précis (summaries)
- logs and journals
- proposals
- reviews
- critiques

As you probably know, writing is also one of the keys to success in the workplace. No matter what career path you follow, it's likely that your job application and the job itself will require writing. People in business and industry rely on memos, letters, reports, directions, and logbooks to communicate with each other and to keep accurate records. Just as those students who write well tend to get the best grades in college, people who can write and communicate effectively usually get the best jobs and are most often promoted within their companies. In addition, knowing how to write well and being comfortable expressing yourself in writing have benefits in your private life. Writing well thus can add a whole new dimension to your life and your potential for success.

The exercises in this first chapter are designed to help both you and your instructor assess your writing skills: to identify those areas that require more attention and those skills that have already been mastered.

**EXERCISE** ▶ 1-1 | Write a paragraph describing the kinds of writing you have done over the past year for school, for a job, or in everyday life.

## Improving Your Writing Skills

### Resources

The following resources are available to help you improve your writing skills:

**1. Your writing instructor.** He or she is your most valuable resource. Be sure to work closely with your instructor by discussing topics, talking about writing problems, and seeking help with assignments. Do not be afraid to ask questions.

**2. Your classmates.** Classmates can offer support and friendly feedback. Get together informally to discuss assignments, compare notes, and react to each other's papers.

**3. Your textbook.** This text is designed to help you improve your writing skills by

- encouraging you to view writing not as a set of puzzling rules but as a satisfying way to develop and express ideas
- showing you how to generate ideas and organize them in paragraph and essay form
- helping you strengthen your writing by revising
- reviewing with you the basics of sentence structure, grammar, and punctuation

- showing you how other writers, both student and professional, express and organize their ideas
- presenting readings as springboards for developing your own thoughts on a subject.

**EXERCISE** ▶ **1-2** | Write a paragraph about your reading habits. Do you ever read for pleasure? If so, what do you like to read? If not, explain why you do not read frequently. When you read for assignments, how well do you understand and remember what you read?

## Practice: Sentences, Paragraphs, and Essays

Like any skill, such as guitar playing or carpentry, writing takes practice. The more you practice, the more successful you will be as a writer. To improve your writing, you need to practice these three basic building blocks in communicating your ideas: the sentence, the paragraph, and the essay. A *sentence* expresses one or more complete thoughts. A *paragraph* expresses one main idea and is usually made up of several sentences that explain or support that idea. An *essay* consists of multiple paragraphs that express and explain a series of related ideas, all of which support a larger, broader idea. The chart below shows how the parts of paragraphs are very much like those of essays. The emphasis in this text is on

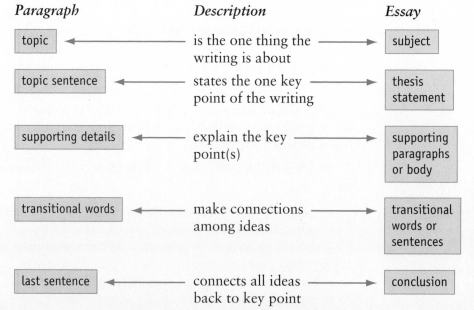

| *Paragraph* | *Description* | *Essay* |
|---|---|---|
| topic | is the one thing the writing is about | subject |
| topic sentence | states the one key point of the writing | thesis statement |
| supporting details | explain the key point(s) | supporting paragraphs or body |
| transitional words | make connections among ideas | transitional words or sentences |
| last sentence | connects all ideas back to key point | conclusion |

writing paragraphs and essays. However, the Skill Refreshers in each chapter and in Part VI, "Reviewing the Basics," will help you write more effective sentences by answering your questions about grammar, mechanics, and punctuation.

Throughout college you will write both paragraphs and essays. Some writing instructors prefer their students to write paragraphs first and then progress to writing essays. Other writing instructors prefer their students to write longer pieces such as essays almost immediately. Your other college instructors may ask you to write papers or take essay exams. Regardless of when you begin writing essays, this book will give you the opportunity to practice your writing and get the support and feedback you need to improve. With practice, you will develop writing skills that you can use and apply in any situation.

## What Is Good Writing?

To the question "What is good writing?" many students answer, "Correct grammar, spelling, and punctuation—no errors." Actually, writing is much more than not making errors. Think about pieces of writing that you have read or written that you found to be good. What made these satisfying?

 **EXERCISE 1-3**

Form groups of three or four students and make a list of the characteristics of good writing. Then compare your list with those of other groups. Here are a few ideas about what makes writing good. See how they compare with the ones you came up with.

### Good Writing Is Thinking

Good writing is a thinking process. As you read this book, you'll see that writers do a great deal of work before they actually begin writing. They think about their audience and topic, develop ideas and supporting material, and plan how best to say what they want to say. Once they have written a draft, they reevaluate their ideas carefully and see if there is a better way to express them.

### Good Writing Involves Change

Finding the best way to express your ideas involves experimentation and change. This process is called *revision*. When you revise, you rethink ideas and improve what you have said and how you have said it. All good writers revise, sometimes many times.

### Good Writing Expresses Ideas Clearly

The primary focus of this text is to help you express ideas clearly. Good writers communicate with their readers in a direct and understandable way, making their main points clearly and supporting these points with details, facts, reasons, or examples. To be clear, main points must be arranged logically. This book contains a variety of techniques to help you arrange ideas logically.

### Good Writing Is Directed Toward an Audience

Suppose you were going to an interview for a part-time job. You would probably dress differently for the interview than for lunch with a friend. You modify your appearance in keeping with the situation and the people you will be seeing. Similarly, when you write, you must consider the following: Who will be reading what I write? How should I express myself so that these readers will understand what I write? These imagined readers are your audience, and considering them is essential to good writing.

What is appropriate for one audience may be inappropriate for another. For example, if you were writing about a car accident in which you were involved, you would write one way to a close friend and another way to your professor. Because your friend knows you well, she would be interested in all of the details. Conversely, because you and your professor don't know each other well, she would want to know less about your feelings about the accident and more about how it would affect your course work. Study the following excerpts. What differences do you notice?

*Note to a friend:*

Jeff was driving the car. As we got to Cedar Road, the light turned red. Jeff was changing the radio station because Sue hates country music, and I guess he didn't notice. I yelled, "Stop!", but he went through the intersection, and a van hit the back of the car. I was terrified, and I felt sick. Fortunately, we were all O.K. Jeff felt really terrible, especially because by the time we got to school, I had missed my biology exam.

*Note to a professor:*

I missed the exam today because I was involved in a car accident. Although I was not injured, I didn't arrive on campus in time for class. Please allow me to make up the exam. I will stop by your office tomorrow during your office hours to talk.

While the letter to the friend is casual and personal, the letter to the professor is businesslike and direct. The writer included details and described his feelings when telling his friend about the car accident, but focused on missing the exam in his letter to his professor.

Writers make many decisions based on the audience they have in mind. As you write, consider

- how many and what kinds of details are appropriate
- what format is appropriate (for example, paragraph, essay, letter, or memo)
- how many and what types of examples should be used
- how formal the writing should be
- what kinds of words should be used (straightforward, technical, or emotional)
- what tone the writing should have; that is, how it should sound to readers (for example, friendly, distant, knowledgeable, or angry).

In later chapters you will learn more about adapting your writing to your audience and see how other writers address specific audiences.

## Good Writing Achieves a Purpose

When you call a friend on the phone, you have a reason for calling, even if it is just to stay in touch. When you ask a question in class, you have a purpose for asking. When you describe to a friend an incident involving you, you are relating the story to make a point or share an experience. These examples demonstrate that you use spoken communication to achieve specific purposes. Similarly, in written communication, you write for a specific reason or purpose. Sometimes in college you write for yourself: to record an assignment, take notes in class, or help you learn or remember information for an exam. Many other times, you write to communicate information, ideas, or feelings to a specific audience.

Good writing, then, must achieve your *intended purpose.* If you write a paragraph on how to change a flat tire, your reader should be able to change a flat tire after reading the paragraph. Likewise, if your purpose is to describe the sun rising over a misty mountaintop, your reader should be able to visualize the scene. If your purpose is to argue that the legal age for drinking alcohol should be twenty-five, your reader should be able to follow your reasoning, even if he or she is not won over to your view.

In later chapters, you will learn more about writing to achieve your purpose; working with the chapter readings will help you see how other writers accomplish their purpose.

**EXERCISE** ▷ **1-4** Think of a public event such as a concert or film showing you have attended recently.

1. Write a paragraph describing the event to a friend.
2. Write a paragraph describing the event to your English instructor.

## Ways to Think About Writing: Key Concepts

Attitude is important. Be open to experimenting, taking suggestions, and trying new strategies and techniques for writing. You have little to lose and much to gain by being open to learning. If you start off with a positive attitude, an open mind, and a basic understanding of the writing process, you too will become a good writer. Here are some key concepts for getting off to the right start in your writing course.

**1. Approach writing as a skill.** Just like driving a car, cooking a meal, or shooting a basketball, writing is a skill that can be learned. As with other skills, it requires practice and hard work and pays off with satisfaction, enjoyment, and success.

**2. Think of writing as a process of developing and explaining ideas.** Writing involves a series of steps you work through in order to produce an effective piece of writing. You certainly do not have to know everything you're going to say before you start.

**3. Consider writing as a way of telling people what you think.** A channel of communication between you and your reader, writing can add a new dimension to your relationships with others. You can share ideas with others through writing just as you do through talking.

**4. Apply new techniques.** Your writing will improve when you consciously apply the new approaches and techniques you learn in this book, from your instructor and classmates, and by reading other writers.

**5. Plan on making changes.** The most important steps in the writing process are rethinking and revising. Professional writers change what they write several times before they are satisfied with what they have produced.

**EXERCISE  1-5** | Write a paragraph on one of the following topics:

1. Why people watch accidents or fires when their help is not needed.
2. What you imagine yourself doing five or ten years from now.
3. What you do to relax when you feel tense.
4. What you would change, if possible, in your family, school, or job.
5. What life would be like if blue jeans did not exist.

## Tips for Writing Success

In the previous section, we looked at ways to think about writing. In this section, you will find practical tips that will lead to successful college writing.

## Tip #1: Organize a Place and Time to Write

Time and quiet—few people these days have much of either one. However, when it comes to writing, it is worthwhile to *create* them for yourself.

### Organizing a Place to Write

1. **Find a quiet area that you can reserve for writing.** If possible, avoid areas used for other purposes, such as the dining room or kitchen table, because you'll have to move or reorganize your materials frequently. If you live in a dorm, your desk is an ideal place to write, unless the dorm is too noisy. If it is, find a quiet place elsewhere on campus, such as the library, or invest in earplugs.

2. **Work at a table or desk.** Don't try to write on an arm of a comfortable chair. Choose a space where you can spread out your papers and other writing materials.

3. **Eliminate distractions from your writing area.** Photos or stacks of unpaid bills will take your mind off your writing.

4. **Collect and organize supplies:** paper, pens, pencils, erasers, tape, stapler, correction fluid, and so on.

5. **Keep papers, quizzes, and class handouts in separate folders or sections in binders.**

6. **Keep a good college dictionary nearby** (*The American Heritage Dictionary of the English Language* or *Webster's Collegiate Dictionary,* for example). Also have other reference materials recommended by your instructor nearby (a thesaurus or a one-volume encyclopedia for instance).

### Organize Time to Write

1. **Reserve a block of time each day for reading this book and working on writing exercises and assignments.** Make time to write in your journal.

2. **Work at the same time each day.** You will end up with a schedule that is easy to follow.

3. **Choose a time during the day when you are at the peak of your concentration.** Do not try to write when you are likely to be interrupted or are very tired or hungry. Avoid times when you may be distracted by other activities (your favorite soap opera or Monday-night football, for example).

4. **Begin assignments well ahead of their due date.** This allows you enough time to plan, organize, write a draft, ask questions, revise, and proofread. It's best to leave at least a day between finishing your draft and beginning to revise.

5. **If you get stuck and cannot think clearly or write, take a break.** Walk around, get a snack, or study a different subject for a time. Discuss your ideas about your assignment with a classmate. In addition to clearing your mind, taking a break will enable you to discover new ideas or clarify old ones. To get started again, reread what you've written. If you are still stuck, try one of the prewriting techniques—freewriting, brainstorming, branching, and questioning—described in Chapter 2, "The Writing Process: An Overview."

## Tip #2: Build Your Concentration

Consider the following suggestions to improve your ability to stick with a writing task.

### Eliminate Distractions

1. **Identify distractions.** As you are working, make a list of what bothers you. When you have finished working, study your list and try to find solutions.

2. **Write down bothersome details.** When you think of an errand you need to do or a call you need to make, jot it down on a separate pad on your desk. In all probability, you'll stop thinking about it.

3. **Enlist the cooperation of family or roommates.** Make sure they know when and where you plan to write.

### Build Your Motivation and Interest

No one has trouble concentrating on tasks he or she wants to do or is interested in. You can motivate yourself and stay interested in your writing task if you do the following:

1. **Choose a topic that genuinely interests you.** Although it might seem faster to use the first topic that pops into your head, take the time to discover a topic that you truly feel like writing about.

2. **Give yourself deadlines.** It is tempting to procrastinate or to work on another course assignment instead of writing. When you have a paper due, make a list of deadlines for yourself. For example, plan that you will complete a first draft by Tuesday, complete revisions by Thursday, and do a careful proofreading on Friday.

3. **Use psychological rewards.** After you complete a writing task, reward yourself by doing something enjoyable, like calling a friend or taking a walk.

### Tip #3: Consider Using a Word Processor

A computer word processing program enables you to type your paper onto a computer disk, print it using a printer connected to the computer, and revise your text and correct errors without retyping your entire paper. Some basic information that will help you decide whether to use a word processor follows.

### Advantages

1. Word processors produce neat, easy-to-read, printed copy. Most instructors prefer to read printed rather than handwritten copy.

2. Word processors make revising text and correcting errors much easier. If you want to add, delete, or change a sentence, for example, you don't have to rewrite the entire paragraph or page. You simply make the change on the computer screen and then reprint your paper.

3. Word processing makes it easy to experiment with different arrangements of ideas without tiresome recopying. Word processors have a copy function that allows you to make a copy of your writing. Once you've copied it, you can revise the text and compare it with your original.

4. Word processing allows you to store your paper on disk, so you always have duplicates of papers you've submitted without having to use a photocopier.

5. By saving time, you'll have more time to spend on revising and will be more likely to make necessary revisions.

6. When you recopy a final draft by hand, you can introduce new errors, such as leaving out a comma or misspelling a word. With word processing, your text stays intact.

### Disadvantages

1. You have to write where and when a computer is available, unless you own one.

2. You need some basic typing skills. You need not type fast, but you do need to be familiar with the keyboard. (Many colleges offer workshops or credit courses that teach basic computer use.)

### Availability

Many colleges have labs with computers and computer software available for your use. Usually, an assistant is present who can help you become familiar with their use. Other colleges offer workshops on how to use a specific word processing program. Many public libraries also have computers available for your use.

### Advice

Give it a try! The hours you'll save over the course of your years in college will be substantial, and it is likely that you will have some instructors who require typed work. The extra time it will take to learn word processing will be saved many times over. In addition, because most businesses and offices use computers, your familiarity with them will be an asset when you apply for jobs.

### Tip #4: Keep a Writing Journal

A journal can be a fun, exciting, and meaningful way to improve your writing, keep track of your thoughts and ideas, and develop ideas to write about. Writing in your journal daily can also add a new dimension to the way you think about events in your life and can make you a more confident writer.

### How It Works

1. Buy an 8-1/2-by-11-inch spiral-bound notebook and use it exclusively for journal writing.

2. Take ten to fifteen minutes a day to write in your journal. You can do this during "dead time"—waiting for a bus or for class to begin, for example. Some students prefer to write at the end of each day.

3. Record your ideas, feelings, and impressions of the day. Don't just record events; analyze what they mean to you.

4. To get started, ask yourself thought-provoking questions such as the following:

   - What new ideas did you encounter today? Perhaps you started thinking about world hunger or the value of religion. Describe your thoughts.
   - What interesting conversations did you have? Jot down some of your dialogue.
   - What are you worrying about? Describe the problem and suggest possible solutions.
   - What are your interests? Sometimes you may want to write about an event, person, or subject that interests you. You might write about a movie you have seen or a book you have read.
   - What was a particularly pleasurable experience? Maybe it was smelling a chocolate cake baking or feeling your dog's wet nose nudging you to wake up.
   - What was the best/worst/most unusual thing that happened today? Describe how you feel about it.
   - What interesting person did you meet? Think about what type of relationship might develop between you.

**Sample Journal Entries**

*Sample 1*

Today in my biology class we talked about animal organ transplants. I was surprised that research is going on about this. My instructor told us that scientists have experimented with putting pigs' hearts into baboons. It didn't work because the baboons' immune systems rejected the hearts. The reason for doing this is the shortage of human organs. I wonder why more people don't donate . . .

*Sample 2*

Today Dad and I took his boat out and went fishing in the river. It's been three years since I've gone fishing with him. I guess the last time was before I moved out of the house. We had a chance to talk like we used to when I saw more of him. He told me some stuff about my sisters and problems they were having with Mom. He seemed depressed about it and was glad to talk about it. I probably should spend more time with him but . . .

### Why It Works

An obvious benefit of keeping a journal is that it gives you practice writing, and the more you write the better you become. However, the journal has many other benefits as well.

1. Journal writing allows you to write for yourself. Class assignments and papers are written for someone else to read. You will begin to see writing as a means of personal expression. Writing can release pent-up feelings about your problems and make you feel better.

2. Journal writing gives you experience in using writing to think about ideas, react to problems, and discover solutions. You'll learn to use writing to discover and sort out ideas, adding a new dimension to the way you think.

3. Your journal will become a valuable source of ideas. When you are asked to write a paragraph or essay on a topic of your choice, you will be able to refer to your journal.

4. Many students find that they enjoy journal writing, so they continue it long after they complete their writing course. A journal provides a valuable record of a person's ideas and experiences. Rereading a journal written several years ago is like looking at old photographs—it brings back memories and preserves the past.

## Tip #5: Use Peer Review

Many students have found that their peers—classmates or friends—can offer valuable suggestions for revision. Peer review is an excellent way to find out what is good and what needs to be improved in your draft. Often your classmates will see things you don't because you are too involved with the topic. Here are some tips on using peer review.

### How to Find a Reviewer

A good source of reviewers is your writing class. These students are familiar with what you are learning and are working on the same skills themselves. Friends who have already taken a writing course also make good reviewers. Get the opinion of more than one reviewer, if possible.

### What to Ask Your Reviewer

1. Give your reviewer a copy of your draft that is easy to read, one that he or she also can write on. Ask him or her to mark any parts that are unclear or confusing.

2. Ask your reviewer to define your audience and purpose for writing. If the answer does not match what you intended, revise so that your audience and purpose are clearer.

3. Give the reviewer a copy of the revision questions found in later chapters (see p. 80). Ask the reviewer to focus on these questions.

4. Don't accept everything your reviewers say. Weigh their comments carefully.

5. If you are uncertain about advice you've been given, talk with your instructor.

**How to Be a Good Reviewer**

If you're asked to be a reviewer, use these suggestions:

1. **Read the draft through completely at least once before making any judgments.**

2. **Offer positive comments first.** Tell the writer what is good about the paper.

3. **Avoid general comments.** Don't just say that the topic sentence is unclear; also explain how it could be improved or what it lacks.

4. **Offer specific revision suggestions.** For instance, if you feel a paragraph needs further development, tell the writer what type of information to include.

## CHAPTER SUMMARY

1. Writing is an important part of many college courses and is essential for many careers.

2. Resources for improving your writing skills include
   - your writing instructor
   - your classmates
   - your textbook.

3. Practice is the key to becoming a successful writer.

4. Good writing is more than not making errors. Good writing
   - is thinking

- involves change
- expresses ideas clearly
- is directed toward an audience
- achieves a purpose.

5. You can improve your writing by experimenting, taking suggestions, and trying out new strategies.

6. Tips for writing success are
   - organize a place and time to write
   - build your concentration
   - consider using a word processor
   - keep a writing journal
   - use peer review.

# The Writing Process: An Overview

I n the third week of the semester, Mo was given a writing assignment by his sociology instructor. This was the assignment:

> Visit the local zoo and spend at least one hour in the monkey house. Write a description of what you see, and explain how it relates to our introductory unit on group behavior.

This assignment did not make much sense to Mo, but on Sunday afternoon he and a friend went to the monkey house and found that he actually had fun watching the monkeys' antics. Because the assignment was due Tuesday, he decided that he would begin writing later that day. He pulled out several sheets of paper, said to himself, "Well, here goes nothing," and started his assignment with the following sentence.

> I visited the monkey house over the weekend and saw many interesting things.

At that point Mo was in trouble; he didn't know what to say next. He stared at the blank paper awhile. Realizing that he *had* to write something, he tried to describe some of what three individual monkeys did while he was there. When he finished writing a page or so of description, Mo put the assignment in his notebook and handed it in on Tuesday. The next week, when the professor returned the papers, Mo was angry and disappointed when he saw his grade of C–. The instructor's note said, "This should really be a D, but I know you tried." Mo thought, "You bet I tried, but this is all I get!"

## The Five Steps

Where did Mo go wrong? Actually, he made several mistakes, but they all stem from a larger problem. He was viewing writing as a single-step

**CHAPTER OBJECTIVES**

*In this chapter you will learn to*

1. understand writing as a process.
2. follow the steps in the process.

activity instead of a multi-step *process*. Writing is a series of steps in which you *generate ideas* on what to say, *plan* how you will organize your ideas, and then *write, revise,* and *proofread.* Mo neither thought nor planned before he began writing; consequently, he had trouble knowing what to say. Then, in desperation, he resorted to simply reporting events, without placing his observations into a unifying framework. Once he finished writing, he put the assignment away and did not look at it again. When he handed in his paragraph, he hadn't reread it to see how he could improve it, nor had he proofread for errors.

In this chapter you will begin to approach writing as a process and learn to avoid making Mo's mistakes. Don't be concerned if this process is not entirely clear by the end of this chapter; the rest of the book will go into more detail on each step. You'll understand more and more as you work through each chapter and apply each step to your own writing. The five steps you will learn are

1. generating ideas
2. organizing your ideas
3. writing a first draft
4. revising and rewriting drafts
5. proofreading your final draft.

In the course of writing, people frequently find that some of these steps overlap or that some circling back to earlier steps is necessary. For example, you may continue to organize your ideas while writing your first draft, or you may need to generate more ideas while revising. This circling back is fine; the writing process does not always go in a straight line. If you use each of these steps, however, and are aware of their general progression, you will find that writing will be easier and more successful for you than it was for Mo. You will not find yourself frustrated, staring at a blank sheet of paper, or writing something that doesn't seem to hang together or say much. Instead, you will feel as if you are developing and focusing your ideas, shaping them into words, and making a point that will hold and interest your reader. You will be well on your way to producing a good paper.

## Generating Ideas

Before you begin to write your paper, the first step is to generate ideas about your topic. Although Mo spent time in the monkey house, he did not spend time thinking about what he saw or how it related to what he had learned in his course. He did not develop any ideas to write about.

Four good techniques you can use to generate ideas are: (1) freewriting, (2) brainstorming, (3) branching, and (4) questioning. Each of these techniques can help you overcome the common problem of feeling as if you have nothing to say. They can unlock ideas you already have and help you discover new ones. Each of these four techniques provides a different way to generate ideas. Feel free to choose from among them; at times you may use several at different points in the writing process, or you may need to use only one of them for a particular writing assignment. Experiment to see what works best for you.

## Freewriting

Freewriting involves writing nonstop for a limited period, usually around five or ten minutes. Write whatever comes into your mind, regardless of whether it is about the topic or not. If nothing comes to mind, you can just write, "I'm not thinking of anything." As you write, don't be concerned with grammar, punctuation, or spelling, or with writing in complete sentences. Words and phrases are fine. Focus on recording your thoughts as they come to you. The most important thing is to keep writing without stopping. Write fast; don't think about whether what you are writing is worthwhile or makes sense. You can do freewriting by hand on paper or using a word processor. After you finish, reread what you have written. Start to think of what your main point could be, a point that would unify various details and observations and fit them into an interesting framework. Underline everything that you might be able to use in your paper.

Mo discussed his sociology assignment with his writing instructor, who explained how to use freewriting to generate ideas. He suggested that Mo redo the assignment to see how freewriting works.

*Mo's Freewriting*

The monkeys are behind bars like prisoners. They leap and jump and play but seem to know they can't get out. They eat with their hands—they look like impolite humans. There's an <u>old monkey who has been there forever and he's crabby and nasty to the others.</u> People like to go there during feeding time. Monkeys eat bananas. It smells in the monkey house. The monkeys seemed to enjoy being watched by us. <u>They seemed to be showing off for us.</u> The monkey house is located next to the reptile house. I hate going there. <u>Some monkeys threw things at us and at other monkeys and they looked angry. One monkey stole another's food but the monkey whose food was stolen didn't fight back.</u> Most people go to the zoo during the summer. Sometimes I wonder if the zoo is really humane. <u>Monkeys were</u>

grooming each other by picking each other's hair. Monkeys in the zoo don't act like they would in the wild though either. I felt sorry for some of them they looked so confused. Sometimes they seemed to compete with each other to see who could do the most antics.

Mo reviewed what he had written and zeroed in on all the points having to do with his topic, group behavior: that is, how the monkeys interacted with each other and with zoo visitors. The other topics in his freewriting—zoos as depressing places, how zoos differ from the wild, the eating habits of monkeys—did not relate to group behavior.

Freewriting is a creative way to begin translating ideas and feelings into words without being concerned about their value or worrying about correctness. You will often be pleasantly surprised, as Mo was, by the number of usable ideas this technique uncovers. The other ideas will be too broad or too personal or will stray from the topic. Still, once you have some ideas down on paper, you can begin to shape your material and select what you need. You can also do additional freewriting—or use another technique for generating ideas—once your topic or direction has become clear.

**EXERCISE** ▸ 2-1

Choose three of the following topics and then, using a clock or timer, freewrite on your chosen topics for at least five minutes each. Be sure to write without stopping. After you finish each freewriting, reread carefully. Underline ideas that seem connected by a common thread, looking for a group of usable ideas that would be a good focus for a paper.

1. the athletic-shoe craze
2. rap music—its influence on attitudes and behavior, if any
3. the problem of obsolete (out-dated) entertainment equipment
4. a friend's annoying or bad habit you wish you could break
5. the physical environment of your campus—what it is like, how it makes you feel

### Brainstorming

Brainstorming is a way of developing ideas by making a list of everything you can think of about the topic. You might list feelings, ideas, facts, examples, or problems. There is no need to write in sentences; instead, list words and phrases. Don't try to organize your ideas; just list them as you think of them. Give yourself a time limit. You'll find ideas come faster that way. As with freewriting, you can brainstorm by hand on paper or by using a word processor. You can brainstorm alone or with friends.

With your friends you will discover a lot more ideas, because their ideas will help trigger more of your own. When you've finished, reread your list and mark usable ideas. One group of students came up with the following list on the topic of sports fans.

| | |
|---|---|
| sit in bleachers | baseball card collections |
| stadiums and ball parks | beer |
| have tailgate parties | betting |
| do the "wave" | cost of tickets |
| excitement and shouting | parking |
| disappointment | traffic jams in and out |
| restrooms, long lines | dress funny |
| food costs | chanting |
| bored | cold and snow |
| fanatical | hotseats |
| radio sports talk show | |

The topic of sports fans is too broad for a paragraph or short essay, but there are several groups of usable ideas here: the behavior and attitude of fans at games, the costs and conveniences of being a fan, tailgate parties, and radio sports talk shows. A student could develop a good paper on any one of these ideas, doing more brainstorming as necessary.

**EXERCISE**  **2-2**

For two of the following topics, brainstorm for about five minutes each. When you finish, review your list and mark ideas that seem closely connected enough to use in writing a paragraph.

1. How do male and female television-news anchors differ?
2. Why is talking to strangers sometimes fun (or not fun)?
3. Why are cellular phones so popular?
4. Why are some people always late and what consequences does this have?
5. Why do people visit zoos (or aquariums)?

## Branching

Branching is a visual way of generating ideas. To begin, write your topic in the middle of a whole sheet of paper and draw a circle around it. Next, think of related ideas and write them near the circle. Connect each to the circle with a line. These ideas are called the primary branches. Your topic is like a tree trunk, and your ideas are like primary limbs that branch out from it. Here is an example of a branching diagram that one student did for the topic shopping at convenience stores.

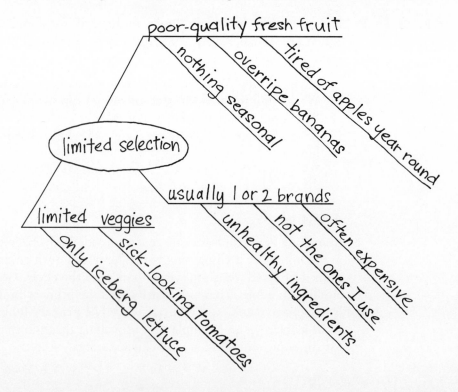

You can connect other related ideas to the primary branches with smaller, or secondary, branches. In the example below, the student looked at his first branching diagram and decided to focus on one of the narrower topics (the limited selection at convenience stores) on a primary branch.

The student used "limited selection" as the trunk, then created three primary branches: poor fruit, limited vegetables, and limited brand selection.

He drew secondary branches onto each of these primary ones and could have kept going. If you use this technique, you can branch from your branches almost indefinitely. If you run out of room, you can attach extra sheets of paper. On the other hand, it is not always necessary to develop branches for every one of your main branches. It is often fine to choose one branch and to ignore all the other possibilities.

When you have finished branching, use a highlighter or colored pencil to mark those branches that seem like good possibilities to write about.

**EXERCISE 2-3** Draw branching diagrams for two of the following topics. Then use a highlighter or colored pencil to mark those branches that you could use to form the basis of a paragraph or essay.

1. the lives of professional athletes (choose one sport to focus on)
2. homeless people's rights
3. tourists (sightseers) who litter or display a lack of respect for the site they are visiting
4. outdoor wedding receptions
5. waiting in hospital emergency rooms (or somewhere else of your choice)

## Questioning

Another way to generate ideas about a given topic is to write down questions about it. As with freewriting and brainstorming, write any question that comes to mind, on paper or using a word processor. Don't worry if it seems silly, and don't stop to evaluate if it is related to the topic. If you can think of answers, include them as well, but don't limit yourself to questions for which you know the answers. The key words *Who? What? When? Where?* and *How?* can help you get started in your questioning of a topic. When you have finished, reread carefully. Underline questions or answers that seem to bring out interesting angles on a topic and that you might be able to use in writing a paragraph or essay. Here are the questions one student wrote on the topic of dreams.

| | |
|---|---|
| Why do we dream? | Do I remember all of my dreams? |
| Do dreams have meaning in our everyday life? | Are dreams predictions? |
| How do you interpret a dream? | Are dreams warnings? |
| Why are they so frightening when they hardly make sense? | What are the most common dreams? |
| When at night do we dream? | How are dreams studied? |

| | |
|---|---|
| Can we control our dreams? | Do men and women have different dreams? |
| How long do dreams last? | Do children have different dreams? |
| What do our bodies do while we are dreaming? | What scary dreams can I remember? |
| Why do people sleepwalk? Do they remember it? | |

**EXERCISE** ▶ 2-4   Use questioning to generate ideas on two of the following topics. Afterward underline the questions or answers that you could see forming the basis of an interesting paragraph or essay.

1. giving candy for Valentine's Day
2. fringe benefits (medical insurance, paid vacation, and sick days) for people with part-time jobs
3. an incident of sexual harassment you have experienced, observed, or heard about
4. smoking in public places
5. the importance of music in your life

## When to Use Which Technique

Now that you have tried freewriting, brainstorming, branching, and questioning, you are probably wondering when to use each technique. In general, there are no rules to follow. The best advice is to give them all a good chance and use the technique that you are most comfortable with. You may find that for certain topics one technique works better than the others. For example, suppose you decide to write a paragraph about your mother's sense of humor. While it might be difficult to think of questions, freewriting might help you remember important, humorous events from your life with her. Suppose, however, that you are studying religious institutions in your sociology class. Your instructor has assigned a paper that requires you to explain your personal religious beliefs. Asking questions is likely to produce useful ideas to include in your paper.

## Sorting Usable Ideas

Remember, freewriting, brainstorming, branching, and questioning each produce a wide range of usable ideas. You will need to sort through them to decide which ones you can put together and expand upon to produce a paper that is unified and interesting to your reader. You will read more about this process in the upcoming section "Organizing Your Ideas," and more on narrowing topics in Chapter 3, "Writing Topic Sentences."

| TABLE 2-1 | **Techniques for Generating Ideas** |
|---|---|

| Technique | How to Do It |
|---|---|
| *Freewriting* | 1. Write nonstop about your topic.<br>2. Write whatever comes to mind without concern for correctness.<br>3. Give yourself a time limit; then stop, review, and repeat as necessary. |
| *Brainstorming* | 1. List all ideas about your topic that come to mind.<br>2. List words and phrases, observations, and thoughts without attention to correctness.<br>3. Give yourself a time limit; then stop, review, and repeat as necessary. |
| *Branching* | 1. Write and circle your topic in the middle of your page.<br>2. As you think of related ideas, write them down around the circle. Connect with lines.<br>3. Draw additional branches as you think of additional ideas. |
| *Questioning* | 1. Ask *What? Why? Where? How? When? Who?* questions about your topic.<br>2. Ask any other questions that come to mind.<br>3. Include answers, if you know them. |

### What If I Am Not Given an Assigned Topic?

When an instructor assigns a topic or provides a choice of topics, part of your paper, in a sense, has been done for you. You may not like the topic(s), or you may need to narrow the topic, but at least you have a point from which to start. If your instructor directs you to choose a topic, you have great freedom, but sometimes your first reaction may be "I don't know what to write about!"

Although you may be tempted to grab any topic to get on with writing, remember that the most important element in clear writing is clear thinking. Invest your time in thinking about what you want to write. Choose a topic that interests you and one you either know something about or are willing to read about. You will feel more like writing and will find that you have more to say, and what you write will be engaging and memorable to your reader.

If you become involved with and react to the world around you, you'll never run out of topics to write about. For example, you can generate ideas if you do the following:

1. **Think of an interesting topic that was discussed in one of your classes or a topic that relates to your major.** Nursing students might, for example, think of genetic engineering, and accounting students of new computer software.

2. **Think of activities you have participated in over the past week.** Going to work or to church, playing softball, taking your child to the playground, shopping at a mall, or seeing a horror film could produce the following topics: communication patterns among co-workers; why attendance at church is rising (or falling); the problem with pitchers; how toddlers develop language skills; the mall as adult playground; the redeeming value of horror films.

3. **Look around you or out the window.** What do you see? Perhaps it is the television, a dog lying at your feet, traffic, or children playing tag. Possible topics are the influence of television on what we buy, pets as companions, passing cars as noise polluters (or entertainment), and play as a form of learning.

4. **Think of the time of year.** Think about what you do on holidays or vacation, what is happening around you in the environment, or what this season's sports or upcoming events might mean to you.

5. **Consult your writing journal (see p. 12).** It can be an excellent source of topics.

6. **Think of a controversial topic you have read about, heard about on radio or television, or argued over with a friend.** A political candidate up for reelection, a terminally ill patient's right to euthanasia, and reforms in public education are examples.

7. **As you read, listen to the news, or go about your daily life, be alert for possible topics, and write them down.** Keep the list, and refer to it when your next paper is assigned.

**EXERCISE** ▶ 2-5

Select one of the topics listed below or one of your own. Try all four techniques—freewriting, brainstorming, branching, and questioning—on the same topic.

*Topics*
1. Is violence a necessary part of sports?
2. What do you think of people who bring babies to adult-oriented concerts and why?
3. How can we eat well without spending a lot of money?

4. What should one do (or not do) upon losing a job or being laid off?
5. Why is it so difficult to save money?

When you have tried all four techniques, read the list of ideas produced using each one and mark the usable ideas. Then write short answers to the following questions.

### Questions

1. Which technique produced the most usable ideas?
2. Which technique were you most comfortable using?
3. Which technique were you least comfortable using? Why?

## Organizing Your Ideas

Once you have generated ideas about your topic, the next step is to decide how to organize them. Ideas in a paragraph or essay should progress logically from one to another. Group or arrange your ideas in a way that makes them clear and understandable to your reader. Imagine someone picking up what you have written and reading it for the first time: will that person be able to follow your train of thought easily? That is the goal.

Assume you are studying advertising in a business class. Your instructor gives you the following writing assignment: How does this magazine ad sell its product? Spend a few moments looking at the ad and brainstorming how you might respond to the assignment.

THIS is you.

THIS is the creep who stole your wallet.

A CITIBANK PHOTOCARD gives you the security of knowing that only one unique face is on the front of your card. Yours. It's one more reason to carry The Citibank Card. To apply, call 1-800-CITIBANK. THE CITI NEVER SLEEPS.

Got your Citibank Card?

Here are the ideas that resulted from the brainstorming that one student, Lucia, did.

first reaction—humor
it's funny because it's not what you expect
most people don't look like the "You" character
the "Creep" looks average, trustworthy
the "You" person (victim) looks unusual, possibly dangerous
"You" person looks tough, not easily fooled
the "You" person does not seem up–to–date
"Creep" seems clean-cut, friendly, intelligent (glasses)
"Creep" seems a typical credit card user, "You" person doesn't
models for good guys/bad guys turned upside down
encourages trust-no-one attitude
some people more honest than they look, others less so
photocard less likely to get used if stolen—too risky for thief
Citibank would benefit too—less fraud
card would put you more in control
you wouldn't have to worry as much about losing it
both ad and card use photos

As Lucia reviewed her brainstorming ideas, she realized that many of them seemed to make the same point: appearances can fool you. The ad seemed to be saying that people may not be what they seem to be, even to themselves; you might see yourself as worldly wise, in control, and able to trust your judgment and protect yourself, but you could be taken advantage of at any minute because nowadays who knows who can be trusted.

Lucia decided to focus on how both the ad and the product use photos to raise, then calm, people's fear that they cannot deal with today's confusing and dangerous world. She next realized that it would be good strategy to explain that appeal of the ad first and then discuss the appeal of the product, the card. That way she would be laying out her points in a way readers could follow: grouping similar ideas together.

1. The ad
   The humor
   "You" person
   "Creep" person
   What the ad shows
   How the ad uses photos

2. The card
   Safety
   Security—thief can't use the card
   Uses photo

**EXERCISE  2-6** ▶ Select one of the topics you developed in Exercises 2-1, 2-2, 2-3, 2-4, or 2-5. Determine which ideas are usable and interrelated, and arrange them in a logical order.

## Writing a First Draft

Suppose you are taking a weekend trip and are about to pack your suitcase. You have in mind what you'll be doing and whom you'll see. You look through your entire closet, then narrow your choices to several outfits. You mix and match the outfits, figure out how much will fit in the suitcase, and finally decide what to take.

Writing a draft of a paragraph or essay is similar to packing for a trip. You have to try out different ideas, see how they work together, express them in different ways, and, after several versions, settle upon what your paper will include. Drafting is a way of trying out ideas to see if and how they work.

A first draft expresses your ideas in sentence form. Work from your list of ideas, and don't be concerned with grammar, spelling, or punctuation at this point. Instead, focus on expressing and developing each idea fully. The following suggestions will help you write effective first drafts.

**1. After you have thought carefully about the ideas on your list, try to write one sentence that expresses the main point of your paragraph (working topic sentence) or essay (thesis statement).**

**2. Concentrate on developing and explaining your topic sentence or thesis statement, using ideas from your list.** Focus first on those ideas you like best or those that you think will be most effective in expressing your main point. Later in the writing process, you may find you need to add more ideas from your list.

**3. Think of a first draft as a chance to experiment with different ideas and ways of organizing them.** While you are working, if you think of a better way to organize or express your ideas or if you think of new ideas, make changes. Be flexible. Do not be overly concerned about getting your exact wording at this point.

**4. As your draft develops, feel free to change your focus or even your topic, unless it has been assigned.** If you decide to change your topic, you might want to develop new ideas using freewriting, brainstorming, branching, or questioning. If your draft is not working out, don't hesitate to start over completely. Go back to generating ideas. It is always all right to go back and forth among the steps in the writing process.  Most writers have many "false starts" before they produce a draft with which they are satisfied.

5. **When you finish your first draft, you should feel as if you have the** *beginnings* **of a paper you will be happy with.**

Lucia, the student writing about the Citibank ad, wrote the following first draft. Shading indicates the main point that she develops as she writes.

*First Draft*

The ad for the Citibank photocard and the photocard both work on the same notion: "You can't trust anyone." At first glance, the ad is funny. The ad shows the opposite of what the reader expects. The way the "You" and "The Creep" photos are labeled is switched from what the reader expects. Readers do not expect victims to look hard, tough, and unfriendly; they expect victims to look honest and trustworthy. The "Creep," who does look honest and trustworthy, is a thief. The "You" person, who does not look honest and trustworthy, turns out to be a victim. The ad, then, sends the messages that things are not the way they may appear at first and that today's world is more dangerous than we might be realizing.

Because the world is full of people you can't trust, a Citibank photocard is appealing. Everybody worries about having his or her credit card stolen. Once mine actually was stolen, but I reported it soon enough, so I did not have to pay what the thief charged on my card. It was a headache anyway. The card is appealing because if someone steals it, they cannot easily use it because of the picture. So people feel more safe and secure with the card. Because people know a thief cannot use the card, they don't worry about carrying it. Without worry, they probably would carry it more often, and if you're carrying it, you're more likely to use it, which is what Citibank wants you to do. The Citibank ad and photocard both use photos to appeal to our need to be safe and our fear that nowadays it is harder to be safe.

**EXERCISE**  2-7 ▶ | Write the first draft of a paragraph (or two) using the topic you chose in Exercise 2-6 and the ideas you put in logical order in that exercise.

# Revising and Rewriting Drafts

Let's think again about the process of packing a suitcase. At first you may think you have included everything you need and are ready to go. Then, a while later, you think of other things that would be good to take. Because your suitcase is full, you have to reorganize everything. When you repack, you take everything out and rethink your selections and their relationships to each other. You might eliminate some items, add others, and switch around still others.

A similar thing often happens as you revise first drafts. When you finish a first draft, you are more or less satisfied with it. Then you reread it later and see you have more work to do. When you revise, you have to rethink your entire paper, reexamining every part and idea. Revising is more than changing a word or rearranging a few sentences, and it is not concerned with correcting punctuation, spelling errors, or grammar. Make these editing changes later, when you are satisfied that you have presented your ideas in the optimal way. Revision is your chance to make significant improvements to your draft. It might mean changing, adding, deleting, or rearranging whole sections.

Here is a later draft of the paragraph shown on page 30. In this draft, Lucia clarifies and expands her ideas and organizes them more effectively. You can see she's moved her main point up to the beginning, for example.

### Revision

The Citibank photocard ad works the same way the photo-card product does: it uses photos to express the point "You can't trust anyone these days," then to calm that fear. The ad first gets your attention with humor and surprise. It shows two pictures, a victim ("You") and a thief ("Creep"), labeled in a surprising way. Readers do not expect victims to look hard, tough, and unfriendly, like the one in the ad does. They do not expect thieves to look honest, open, and maybe a little wimpy, but in the ad that is how the thief looks. By reversing things, the ad gets you to think about how, even if you don't feel like you could be a target for crime, you could be. It does this by showing that people are not the way they may look at first and it is hard to know whom to trust.

The ad works even better when you realize that the product it is selling, the Citibank photocard, is also built on this lack of trust and idea of appearances as deceiving. The ad is saying that these days you can't trust anyone, so now you need a credit card with your photo on it, for extra protection. Everyone worries about having his or her wallet and credit card stolen. It is well known to be a headache when it happens. However, if this card gets stolen, it would be harder for the thief to use because of the picture. So the product answers the nervousness and worry that the ad brings out in the reader. Although the ad uses humor and exaggeration, both it and the photocard product appeal to our need for safety and security and to our fear that nowadays these things are harder to find than ever.

The following suggestions will help you revise effectively.

**1. Reread the sentence that expresses your main point.** It must be clear, direct, and complete. Experiment with ways to improve it.

**2. Reread each of your other sentences.** Does each relate directly to your main point? If not, cross it out or rewrite it to clarify its connection to the main point. If all of your sentences suggest a main point that is different from the one you've written, rewrite the topic sentence or thesis statement.

**3. Make sure your writing has a beginning and an end.** A paragraph should have a clear topic sentence and concluding statement. An essay should have introductory and concluding portions, their length depending on the length of your essay.

**4. Replace words that are vague or unclear with more specific or descriptive words.**

**5. Seek advice.** If you are unsure about how to revise, visit your instructor during office hours and ask for advice or have a friend read your paper and mark ideas that are unclear or need further explanation.

**6. When you have finished revising, you should feel satisfied with what you have said and with the way you have said it.**

Refer to Chapter 5, "Strategies for Revising," for additional suggestions and strategies for revising.

**EXERCISE** ▶ 2-8 │ Revise the first draft you wrote for Exercise 2-7 following steps 1 through 6 above.

## Proofreading Your Final Draft

Proofreading is a final reading of your paper to check for errors. In this final polishing of your work, you need to be concerned with correctness, so don't proofread until all your rethinking of ideas and revision are done. Check for each of these errors:

- run-on sentences
- fragments
- spelling
- punctuation
- grammar
- capitalization

The Skill Refreshers at the ends of the remaining chapters provide a quick review of these topics. Part VI, "Reviewing the Basics," gives more detailed information on each.

The following tips will ensure you don't miss any errors.

**1. Review your paper once for each type of error.** First, read it for run-on sentences and fragments. Take a short break, and then read it four more times, each time paying attention to one of the following: spelling, punctuation, grammar, and capitalization.

**2. To spot spelling errors, read your paper from last sentence to first sentence and from last word to first word.** Reading in this way, you will not get distracted by the flow of ideas, so you can focus on spotting errors. If you are working with a word processing program, use the spell-check function, but be sure to proofread for errors the program cannot catch, such as missing words or errors that are themselves words, such as "of" for "or."

**3. Read each sentence aloud, slowly and deliberately.** This technique will help you catch such errors as endings you have left off of verbs or missing plurals.

**4. Check for errors again as you rewrite or type your paper in final form.** Don't do this when you are tired; you might introduce new mistakes. Ask a classmate or friend to read your paper to catch any mistakes you missed.

Chapter 5, p. 82, will show you how to keep a proofreading error log and includes a proofreading checklist. See also the proofreading checklist printed inside this book's back cover.

**EXERCISE 2-9** ▶ Proofread and prepare the final version for the paper you have developed throughout this chapter.

## CHAPTER SUMMARY

Important steps in the writing process are as follows:

1. **Generating ideas.** Use freewriting, brainstorming, branching, and questioning to develop ideas on your topic.

2. **Organizing your ideas.** Look for relationships among ideas and work to present ideas logically, so they build upon one another.

3. **Writing a first draft.** Express your ideas in sentence form. Focus on ideas, not correct grammar, spelling, or punctuation.

4. **Revising and rewriting drafts.** Rethink your ideas and evaluate how effectively you have expressed them. Rewrite your draft by adding, deleting, changing, and reorganizing your ideas.

5. **Proofreading your final draft.** Check your paper for errors in sentence structure, grammar, spelling, and punctuation.

# PARAGRAPH WRITING STRATEGIES

# Writing Topic Sentences

**CHAPTER OBJECTIVES**

*In this chapter you will learn to*

1. understand the structure of a paragraph.
2. write effective topic sentences.

## What Is a Paragraph?

Writing, in many ways, mirrors speech. The way we organize and present ideas in writing is similar to the way we present them orally. When we speak, we speak in groups of sentences. Seldom does our conversation consist of isolated statements or a series of unrelated statements. For example, you probably would *not* simply say to a friend, "I think you are making a mistake if you decide to marry Sam." Rather, you would support your general remark by offering reasons or by giving an example of someone else who made the same mistake. Similarly, in writing we group ideas together into paragraphs. A *paragraph* is a group of related sentences that develops one main thought about a single topic. The structure of most paragraphs, however, is not complex. There are usually two basic elements: (1) a topic sentence and (2) supporting details.

The *topic sentence* states your main point or controlling idea. The sentences that explain this main point are called *supporting details*. These details may be facts, reasons, or examples that provide further information about or support for the topic sentence. If you were to write a paragraph based on the example above, "I think you are making a mistake if you decide to marry Sam" would be the topic sentence and all of your reasons and examples would be supporting details.

A paragraph is, therefore, a unit of thought that deals with a single main idea in a unified way. The first sentence of a paragraph is indented five letter spaces from the left margin to signal the reader that a new idea is about to begin. In general, a paragraph should stay focused on this idea, not switch from topic to topic. It should also be a manageable length for your reader to digest. Short paragraphs can seem skimpy and underdeveloped. Overly long ones can become hard for a reader to follow.

Read the following paragraph, noticing how the details explain the topic sentence, which is shaded.

Acupuncture is an ancient and still widely used treatment in Oriental medicine that is alleged to relieve pain and other maladies. The method is based on the idea that body energy flows along lines called channels or meridians. There are fourteen main channels, and a person's health supposedly depends on the balance of energy flowing in them. Stimulating channels by inserting very fine needles into the skin and twirling them is said to restore a balanced flow of energy. The important spots to stimulate are called *Ho-Ku points*. Modern practitioners of acupuncture also use electrical stimulation through needles at the same points. The needles produce an aching and tingling sensation called *Teh-ch'i* at the site of stimulation, but relieve pain at distant, seemingly unrelated parts of the body.

Douglas A. Bernstein et al., *Psychology*

In this paragraph, the topic sentence identifies the topic as acupuncture and states that its primary use is to relieve pain. The remaining sentences provide further information about how acupuncture works.

You can visualize a paragraph as follows:

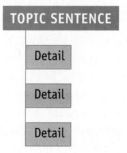

You might visualize the paragraph on acupuncture as follows:

**ACUPUNCTURE IS AN ORIENTAL TREATMENT TO RELIEVE PAIN.**

It is based on the idea of energy flow lines.

A person's health depends on energy flow through 14 channels.

Needles are used to stimulate flow of energy.

Points of stimulation are called Ho-Ku.

Electrical stimulation can be used.

etc.

Notice how well the topic sentence and details in the acupuncture paragraph work together to develop a main idea. The more general topic sentence is expanded upon and explained by the more specific details. You might ask, "How can I tell what is 'general' and what is 'specific' when I am writing?" Here are a few examples. The first three use one-word topics and details; the last two use topic sentences and detail sentences.

| | |
|---|---|
| GENERAL: | fruit |
| SPECIFIC: | apples, oranges, bananas |
| GENERAL: | emotions |
| SPECIFIC: | love, fear, anger |
| GENERAL: | music |
| SPECIFIC: | rhythm, beat, tempo |
| GENERAL: | My sister-in-law is selfish and self-centered. |
| SPECIFIC: | She talks about herself constantly.<br>She shows no interest in the opinions of others.<br>She focuses attention on herself by dressing boldly. |
| GENERAL: | Newspapers include a wide variety of information. |
| SPECIFIC: | Newspapers contain advertisements for products and services.<br>Newspapers report world and local news events. |

Notice that in each of these examples, the specific point explains or describes the general by giving examples, reasons, component parts, or further information. In the same way, supporting details in your paragraph explain or support your topic sentence.

**EXERCISE** ▶ 3-1

Complete the following sets by supplying specific information that supports the more general statement.

1. GENERAL:  Advertisements are often misleading.
   SPECIFIC:  1. Products often appear larger than they really are.

   2. _____

   3. _____

2. GENERAL:  Television provides several types of entertainment.

   SPECIFIC:  1. _____

   2. _____

   3. _____

3. GENERAL: Many careers require specialized training.
   SPECIFIC: 1. Nurses must learn anatomy and physiology.

   2. _____

   3. _____

   _____

4. GENERAL: _____
   SPECIFIC: 1. Some television commercials use humor to sell their product.
   2. Other commercials use celebrities to convince the audience to buy the product.
   3. Some commercials use the message "everyone's buying it, so why don't you?"

5. GENERAL: _____
   SPECIFIC: 1. Newspapers provide news of local and regional interest.
   2. Newspapers offer news of statewide policies and regulations as they affect the local community.
   3. Newspapers contain advertising by local businesses.

## Writing Effective Topic Sentences

### Purpose of a Topic Sentence

An effective topic sentence does two things. First, it makes clear what the paragraph is about—the topic. Second, it expresses a view or makes a point about the topic. In the following examples, the topic is circled and the point about the topic is underlined.

1. The (first week of college) is a frustrating experience.
2. (Fanny's) serves the best hamburgers in town.
3. (State-operated lotteries) are growing in popularity in America.
4. (Time management) is a vital skill for college students.

**EXERCISE** 3-2 ▶ For the following topic sentences, circle the topic and underline the view the writer takes toward the topic.

1. (Sunday morning) is a time for reading and relaxing.
2. My (part-time job) at a department store is providing me with valuable sales experience.
3. Publicly funded FM (radio stations) need your financial support.
4. (Time, a weekly newsmagazine,) presents thorough coverage of world events.

5. Danny Everett, my favorite morning-radio personality, gets my day off to a bright and humorous start.

**EXERCISE  3-3**

Complete the following topic sentences by supplying a view about each topic.

1. Cigarette advertisements _____ .

2. Most fast-food restaurants _____ .

3. Monday morning _____ .

4. Violence on television _____ .

5. College professors _____ .

## Choosing a Manageable Topic

To write a good paragraph, you need a manageable topic, one that is the right size. Your topic must be general enough to allow you to bring together interesting details that will engage your reader. It must also be specific or narrow enough so that you can cover it adequately in a few sentences. If your topic is too general, you'll end up with a few unrelated details that do not add up to a specific point. If your topic is too narrow, you will not have enough to say.

Suppose you have decided to write a paragraph about sports. You write the following topic sentence:

Sports is a favorite activity for many people.

The topic of sports as a popular activity is too broad to cover in one paragraph. Think of all the different aspects you could write about. Which sports would you consider? Would you write about both playing sports and watching them? Would you write about both professional and amateur sports? Would you write about the reasons people enjoy sports? Because you cannot include all of this in one paragraph, you could revise the topic sentence to be more specific:

Watching professional football on Sunday afternoons is a form of relaxation for my family.

Here you have limited your topic to a specific sport (football), a specific time (Sunday afternoon), and some specific fans (your family).

Here are a few other examples of sentences that are too general. Each has been revised to be more specific.

| | |
|---|---|
| Too General: | My parents have influenced my life. |
| Revised: | My parents helped me make the decision to attend college. |
| Too General: | Sex education is worthwhile. |
| Revised: | Sex-education courses offered in high school allow students to discuss sex openly. |

If your topic is *too* specific (narrow), you will run out of details to use in the paragraph. Or you may include details that do not relate directly to the topic. Suppose you decide to write a paragraph about using a computer for word processing and come up with the following topic sentence:

**Using the word processor for my paper allowed me to correct spelling errors without retyping.**

What else would your paragraph say? Beyond saying that the computer corrects your mistakes, you may have little else to say. This sentence is too specific. It might work as a detail, but not as a main idea. To correct this problem, ask, "What else does the word processor allow me to do?" You might say it allows you to change the order of paragraphs, correct punctuation, and replace words. Your revised topic sentence could be:

**The word processor has several features that save time and make revision easy.**

Here are a few other examples of topic sentences that are too narrow, along with revisions for each one.

| | |
|---|---|
| Too Narrow: | Only 36 percent of Americans voted in the 1994 election. |
| Revised: | Many Americans do not exercise their right to vote. |
| Too Narrow: | The television commercial that shows talking cereal boxes is annoying. |
| Revised: | Television commercials that use gimmicks are annoying. |
| Too Narrow: | A yearly subscription to *With the Grain* costs $20. |
| Revised: | *With the Grain,* a magazine devoted to environmental issues, is a bargain considering the information it provides. |

Suppose you used brainstorming or branching to generate ideas. If you find you can develop the topic in many different directions, or if you have trouble choosing details from a wide range of choices, your topic is probably too general. You will know your topic sentence is too specific if you cannot think of anything to explain or support it.

**EXERCISE** 3-4 ▶ Evaluate the following ineffective topic sentences. Label each "G" for too general or "S" for too specific.

_____ 1. Learning foreign languages is difficult.

_____ 2. Dinner for two at my favorite Italian restaurant costs $15.

_____ 3. Attending graduate school is worth the time and money.

_____ 4. Many rules of etiquette have changed over the past 25 years.

_____ 5. Passive cigarette smoke makes me feel sick.

## Tips for Writing Effective Topic Sentences

Use the following suggestions to write clear topic sentences.

**1. Your topic sentence should state the main point of your paragraph.** It should identify your topic and express a view toward it.

**2. Be sure to choose a manageable topic**—one that is neither too general nor too specific.

**3. Make sure your topic sentence is a complete thought.** Be sure your topic sentence is not a fragment or run-on sentence. (Refer to section C in Part VI, "Reviewing the Basics," for a review of sentence errors.)

**4. Place your topic sentence first in the paragraph.** Topic sentences often appear in other places in paragraphs or their controlling idea is implied, not stated. For now, it will be easier for you to put yours at the beginning. That way, as you write, you can make sure you stick to your point, and your readers will immediately be alerted to that point.

**5. Avoid announcing your topic.** Sentences that sound like announcements are usually unnecessary. Avoid such sentences as "This paragraph will discuss how to change a flat tire," or "I will explain why I object to legalized abortion." Instead, directly state your main point: "Changing a flat tire involves many steps," or "I object to abortion on religious grounds."

Not all expert or professional writers follow all of these suggestions. Sometimes, a writer may use one-sentence paragraphs or include topic sentences that are fragments to achieve a special effect. You will find these paragraphs in news and magazine articles and other sources. Although professional writers can use these variations effectively, you probably should not experiment with them too early. It is best while you are polishing your skills to use a more standard style of writing.

**EXERCISE** 3-5 ▶ Evaluate each of the following topic sentences and mark them as follows:

E = effective          G = too general
A = announcement       N = not complete thought
S = too specific

_____ 1. This paper will discuss the life and politics of Alexander Hamilton.

_____ 2. Japanese culture is fascinating to study because its family traditions are so different from American traditions.

_____ 3. A large box of my favorite breakfast cereal costs $3.19.

_____ 4. The discovery of penicillin was a great step in the advancement of modern medicine.

_____ 5. I will talk about the reasons for the removal of the Berlin Wall.

_____ 6. Poor habits may lead to weight gain.

_____ 7. Oranges and lemons are a good source of vitamin C.

_____ 8. The White House has many famous rooms and an exciting history.

_____ 9. There are three factors to consider when buying a CD player.

_____ 10. Iraq has a long and interesting history.

**EXERCISE** 3-6 ▶ Analyze the following topic sentences. If a sentence is too general or too specific, or if it makes a direct announcement or is not a complete thought, revise it to make it more effective.

1. World hunger is a crime.

   REVISED: _____

   _____

2. Freud, a founder of a school of psychotherapy in which patients talk about their problems and past.

   REVISED: _____

   _____

3. I will point out the many ways energy can be conserved in the home.

   REVISED: _____

   _____

4. Congress is very important in the United States.

   REVISED: _____

   _____

5. Pollution is a serious problem.

   REVISED: _____

   _____

**EXERCISE 3-7**  Write a topic sentence for four of the following topics, using the tips given above. Then select one of your topic sentences and use it to develop a paragraph.

1. Should suicide be legal under certain circumstances?
2. Who deserves college scholarships?
3. Do children learn better with computers?
4. Why are baseball games fun to watch?
5. Is space exploration valuable or a waste of money?
6. Does the news coverage of presidential campaigns unfairly influence voters?

**EXERCISE 3-8**  Suppose you are taking a sociology course this semester. In preparation for class discussions that will focus on issues, your instructor has assigned the following topics. Choose *one* topic and write a one-paragraph response.

1. Educational reform: If you could make one significant change in the public education system, what would it be?

2. Gender differences: Describe one way in which the behavior of men is different from that of women.

3. The family: What do you think is the most important function of a family? That is, why do we live in family groups? What is one key advantage? Support your answer with examples from your own experience.

4. Discrimination: Describe one instance of discrimination (sexual, racial, religious, class, or age) that you have witnessed or experienced.

# Thinking Before Reading

Just as you must think about writing before you actually put words down on paper, thinking before you read will help you get the most from your reading. Following are two strategies designed to get you thinking before you begin reading.

## Previewing

Previewing is like looking at a map before driving in an unfamiliar city. It is a way of learning what a reading is about before you actually read it. By reading selected portions of an essay, you can discover a great deal about its content and its organization. You become familiar with its layout so that you can understand it more easily as you read. Previewing is not time consuming. You can preview a brief essay in two or three minutes by following these basic steps.

**1. Read and think about the title.** What does it tell you about the subject? Does it offer any clues about how the author feels about the subject or how he or she will approach it?

**2. Check the author.** Read any biographical information about him or her that is provided with the article. Is the author's name familiar? If so, what do you know about him or her?

**3. Read the first paragraph.** Here the author introduces the subject. Look for a statement of the main point of the entire reading.

**4. Read all bold headings.** Headings divide up the reading into pieces and announce the topic of each section.

**5. Read the first sentence under each heading.** This sentence often states the main point of the section.

**6. Read the first sentence of each paragraph.** You will discover many of the main ideas of the article. If the reading consists of very short paragraphs, read the first sentence of every third or fourth paragraph.

**7. Read the last paragraph.** Often this paragraph summarizes or concludes the reading.

The more you practice previewing, the more effectively you will find it works. Use it for all of your college textbooks and course reading.

**EXERCISE** ▶ 3-9 │ Preview the reading, "Divorce: Sometimes a Bad Notion," pp. 46–49, using the steps just described.

## Making Connections

Reading is always easier if you are interested in the subject and feel it has something to do with you. Before you begin to read, take a minute to discover what you already know about the subject or what connection it may have to your life or experience.

For example, the reading in this chapter discusses the negative effects of divorce on the couple as well as on the children. You might ask yourself the following questions about the topic:

- What effects has divorce had on a couple you know? How has their divorce changed them?
- What effects of divorce have you noticed among children?
- What problems would you expect a married couple you know well to have if they decided to divorce?

The next section of this chapter contains an article, "Divorce: Sometimes a Bad Notion," written by Seattle newspaper columnist, Fred Moody. As you read it, watch how he constructs paragraphs and how the writing moves from general to specific thoughts in each paragraph.

**R E A D I N G**

## Divorce: Sometimes a Bad Notion
### Fred Moody

Divorce, along with high-school graduation, marriage, and death, is now an established American rite of passage. Everyone, either directly or indirectly, is touched by it. A first marriage undertaken today stands (avert your eyes, squeamish reader) a 66 percent chance of ending in divorce. For the first time in history, an American marrying now is more likely to lose a spouse through divorce than through death.

When no-fault divorce was ushered in 20 years ago, it was hailed as a quick and easy solution to relationships gone sour. Now, a generation later, legions of divorced parents and their children are emerging to paint a far different picture: one of financial travail, psychological devastation, and endless emotional turmoil. Study after study documents so much discontent surrounding divorce that it now appears to be an even greater source of disillusionment than marriage is.

1

2

There's no question that the fundamental right to divorce should be [3]
available to anyone; the ability to divorce a monster or an addict, or to
get out of a marriage that is an incurable mistake, is a humane and civilized right. But the notion that every unhappy marriage is a bad one, or
that individuals are morally as well as legally entitled to place their own
pursuit of happiness above the well-being of their offspring, is *ruinous.*[1]
Opting for divorce before having exhausted every effort at preserving a
relationship is self-destructive.

The emotional fallout of divorce is easy to see. Legions of divorced [4]
people, their attorneys, their therapists, their children, and their children's therapists have learned that divorce is shattering.

"Quite often, divorce is much more devastating than people who go [5]
into the process anticipate," says Seattle psychiatrist Dr. Herbert
Wimberger. "They are surprised by how painful it is, by how long the
pain lasts. Divorce very often is a serious loss, bringing on a severe grief
reaction." Adds Seattle psychotherapist Diane Zerbe, "Everybody knows
somebody five years later who is still emotionally invested in their failed
marriage, still angry at their ex-spouse, and their bitterness is a major
part of their life. They haven't been able somehow to come to terms with
what happened and go on to find a more satisfying relationship."

The evidence also seems to suggest that second marriages are no [6]
happier, with even less likelihood of working than first marriages (for
some reason, third ones have better odds).

In many divorces, the rage that formerly came out during the debate [7]
over grounds for divorce now is redirected into interminable custody
disputes and negotiations over child support. In one recent case, the husband, being divorced by his wife, was determined to get sole custody of
their children, even though he had had little to do with them during his
marriage. He made extravagant accusations against his wife—of aban-
donment, child abuse, and incest—all of which were dutifully investi-
gated and dismissed by the court.

As all this suggests, no-fault also failed to deliver on its promise of [8]
convenience and lower cost. "People are spending more time and money
on divorce than ever before," says Seattle family-law attorney Nancy
Hawkins.

Worst of all has been the disastrous impact of no-fault divorce on [9]
women and children. In Washington state, for example, property is
divided equally between divorcing spouses, regardless of who is primarily responsible for the failure of the marriage. Before 1973, the wounded
party—usually the wife—was awarded a greater share of a couple's

1. causing ruin; destructive

property as a form of compensation for pain and suffering. No-fault's attempts to make divorce law gender-neutral, and therefore more fair, have created a raw deal for women. It has led to the virtual elimination of alimony payments to wronged or financially disadvantaged wives, and to drastic reductions in the amount and duration of maintenance payments to wives who gave up career goals for their families.

Consequently, divorced women who win custody of their children now suffer, on the average, a 33 percent decline in their standard of living, while their ex-husbands enjoy a corresponding rise in theirs. This is largely due to the dismal complexities of court-ordered child support. In Washington, research shows that court orders for child support are almost always too low to cover the actual costs of raising children. Further, only 50 percent of divorced dads in Washington pay the full amount of their child-support judgment; 25 percent pay part of what they're ordered, and the remaining 25 percent simply ignore the order and pay nothing at all.    10

The effect on children is enormous. According to University of Washington sociologist Diane Lye, more than 70 percent of America's black children and 50 percent of its white children will live in single-parent homes by the time they are 16 years old. "There are 18 million poor children in our country now," she says, "and over half of them are living in single-parent homes caused by divorce." . . .    11

Clearly, far more sweeping reforms are called for. At the very least, courts need enough time and money to study divorce decrees and determine whether they adequately provide for women and children. As things stand now, they simply rubber-stamp agreements reached between people who are in no shape to keep their children's best interests in mind.    12

There should also be lawyers representing children in divorce hearings, as they do in child-abuse hearings. A child's lawyer should be able to argue on behalf of the child's best interests—that the divorce be denied, that parents undergo further counseling, that children be compensated for the emotional and material damage divorce will bring down on them.    13

Young people need to be made aware of the dire consequences of marriages carelessly undertaken: Marriage and divorce education is as critical to our society's health as sex education. Divorce's romanticized[2] image as a harmless quick fix is a lie. That fantasy has led legions of naive and discontented people into even greater unhappiness than they had suffered in their marriages.    14

Since the advent of no-fault, one of the fundamental truths about divorce has been discounted: that love or marriage may be fleeting, but    15

2. not based on fact; imaginary

divorce is forever. Those contemplating divorce should understand that it often affords not a new beginning, but only a new form of anguish. "You never get divorced for real," says one woman, who left her husband six years ago. "You never get rid of that person." Another woman concurs: "I thought divorce would be like jumping through a hoop," she says. "But it's not a hoop—it's a tunnel."

*Seattle Weekly*, Nov. 22, 1989

## Getting Ready to Write

■ **Examining the Reading: Immediate Review and Underlining Topic Sentences**

When you have read anything once, you probably can remember many of the key points and some of the supporting details, but there will be ideas you cannot recall. Also, your level of understanding may be literal—that is, you can recall facts and details, but you're not ready to interpret and react to the ideas expressed.

### Immediate Review

A quick review of the reading will improve both your comprehension and retention. The review will also help you identify portions that need to be reread; questions may also come to mind.

An easy way to review the selection is to follow the same steps for previewing (see p. 45). The best time to do this is *immediately* after you've finished reading, while the content is still fresh in your mind.

**EXERCISE**  3-10 | Review the reading "Divorce: Sometimes a Bad Notion" now by following the previewing steps on p. 45.

### Underlining Topic Sentences

Another valuable way to review is to underline the topic sentence of each paragraph. This activity forces you to decide what each paragraph is about and, at the same time, helps you to remember it. You can also reread the underlined text to refresh your memory for a class discussion and to locate specific sections quickly.

**EXERCISE**  3-11 | Underline the topic sentence of each paragraph in "Divorce: Sometimes a Bad Notion." *Helpful hint:* If you have difficulty identifying the topic sentence, ask yourself, "What one key, general idea do all the sentences in the paragraph discuss or explain?"

■ Thinking Critically: **Discovering the Author's Purpose**

A writer always has a purpose for writing. A writer may write to defend an action or policy (drug testing, gun control, or mercy killing). A writer may write to present information on a topic (the increased risk of skin cancer). Other times, a writer may intend to entertain, express emotions, or describe an event or person. As a reader, it is your job to recognize the author's purpose and to judge whether he or she accomplishes it effectively.

To discover the author's purpose, do the following:

1. Answer the questions "What is the writer trying to tell me? What does he or she want me to do or think?"

2. Pay close attention to the title of the piece and the source of the material because these may offer clues. Suppose an article is titled "Twenty-six Reasons to Vote in National Elections." The title suggests the author's purpose is to urge citizens to vote. If an essay on the lumber industry appears in *Eco-Ideas,* a magazine devoted to environmental preservation and improvement, you might predict that the author's purpose is to call for restrictions on the industry.

3. Look for clues or statements about purpose in the beginning and concluding paragraphs of the material. Suppose an essay concluded with a statement such as "The above evidence clearly suggests that gun-control laws have little effect on reducing crime." This statement reveals that the author's purpose is to persuade readers and win them over to a certain view.

■ Reacting to Ideas: **Discussion and Journal Writing**

1. Summarize Fred Moody's attitude toward divorce.

2. Do you agree or disagree with the statement in paragraph 3, "But the notion that every unhappy marriage is a bad one, or that individuals are morally as well as legally entitled to place their own pursuit of happiness above the well-being of their offspring, is *ruinous*"?

3. Must all divorces involve anger, frustration, and bitterness?

4. Discuss the idea that children should have their own attorneys in divorce disputes.

5. Do you agree that divorce has been "romanticized" as a "quick fix" for couples with problems?

# Writing Assignments

## Writing About the Reading

1. Write a paragraph to explain how you think Moody wanted his audience to react to this article. Start your paragraph with a topic sentence that begins, "Moody wanted the people who read 'Divorce: Sometimes a Bad Notion' to . . ." Complete your paragraph by explaining your topic sentence or giving examples to support it.

## Writing About Your Ideas

2. Write a paragraph explaining whether or not you feel divorce is sometimes a bad notion. Include details to support why you feel as you do.

3. Moody states that divorce has the most disastrous effects on women and children. Write a paragraph explaining why you agree or disagree with this statement.

**Essay Option**

4. Write an essay describing the positive or negative effects of divorce that you have observed. Support each topic sentence with examples.

# SKILL REFRESHER

## Sentence Fragments

A sentence fragment is a group of words that (1) lacks a subject, (2) lacks a verb, or (3) is a dependent (subordinate) clause unattached to a complete sentence. It therefore fails to express a complete thought.

NOTE: A **subject** is the noun or pronoun that performs the action of the sentence. A **verb** is a word that conveys the action or state of being of the subject. A **dependent clause** is a group of words beginning with a subordinating conjunction like *although, because, if, since, unless, wherever,* or *while* or with a relative pronoun like *which, that, what, who,* or *whoever.*

In the examples below, the fragments are underlined.

My friend Anita called me last night. Calls me every night. [The second group of words lacks a subject.]

Anita, a friend I have known all my life, and excellent at math. She asked if I had finished doing my taxes. [The first group of words lacks a verb.]

I planned to fill out the tax forms that evening. Because the deadline was approaching. [The second group of words is a dependent clause unattached to a complete sentence.]

## How to Spot Fragments

A fragment begins with a capital letter and ends with a period, like a complete sentence, but it is not complete. To identify fragments in your writing, ask the following questions of each sentence.

**1. Is there a subject?** To find the subject, ask who or what is performing the action of the sentence.

FRAGMENT:    Asked Mr. Gomez how he grew rhubarb. [Who asked Mr. Gomez?]

CORRECT:     Gail asked Mr. Gomez how he grew rhubarb.

**2. Is there a verb?** To find the verb, look for a word that conveys what is happening, what has happened, or what will happen. Do not confuse a verb with verbals (*-ing, -ed,* or infinitive *"to"* forms of verbs that are used as nouns or modifiers). A true verb changes form to communicate a time change. A verbal does not.

FRAGMENT:    A nervous, pressured feeling and a headache.

CORRECT:     A nervous, pressured feeling and a headache struck me.

## SKILL REFRESHER CONTINUED

FRAGMENT: The express train leaving the station at four.
CORRECT: The express train will leave the station at four.

FRAGMENT: To get a taxi and hurry downtown.
CORRECT: I need to get a taxi and hurry downtown.

**3. If the dependent clause—a group of words starting with a subordinating conjunction or relative pronoun—attached to a complete sentence?** A dependent clause cannot stand alone.

FRAGMENT: Although we wanted to go to the softball game.
CORRECT: Although we wanted to go to the softball game, we could not find the right park.

FRAGMENT: If we had asked directions or bought a map.
CORRECT: We might have found the park if we had asked directions or bought a map.

### How to Correct Fragments

1. Add the missing subject or verb.
   FRAGMENT: Waiting for my paycheck to be delivered.
   REVISED: I was waiting for my paycheck to be delivered.

2. Revise by combining the fragment with an appropriate existing complete sentence.
   FRAGMENT: My sister loved her job at the jewelry store. Until she got a new boss.
   REVISED: Until she got a new boss, my sister loved her job at the jewelry store.

3. Remove the word or phrase that makes the statement incomplete.
   FRAGMENT: While I was waiting for class to begin.
   REVISED: I was waiting for class to begin.

### Rate Your Ability to Spot and Correct Fragments

Place a check mark in front of each sentence fragment, then correct it so it is a complete sentence.

1. Leaving the room, she turned and smiled.

2. Until the exam was over, the professor paced in the front of the room.

3. I remembered her birthday. Because we're good friends.

4. I realized I forgot my book. After I left the classroom.

5. Jason asked a question about centrifugal force. Before the professor moved on to the next topic.

6. Until the phone rang and the answering machine answered.

7. Hoping I would do well on the test.

8. Scheduling a conference with her art-history professor to discuss the topic for her final paper.

9. I got a B on the quiz. Because I reread my notes.

10. Marcus was interested in the course. Focused on the rise of communism.

Score_____

Check your answers using the Answer Key on page 481. If you missed more than two, you need additional review and practice recognizing and correcting fragments. Refer to section C.1 of Part VI, "Reviewing the Basics."

## CHAPTER SUMMARY

**Writing Skills**

1. A topic sentence states the main point of your paragraph. Be sure that your topic sentence
   - identifies the topic you are writing about.
   - expresses a view or makes a point about the topic.

2. To write an effective paragraph, choose a manageable topic. Your topic must be
   - specific enough so that you can cover it adequately in a single paragraph.
   - general enough to allow you to bring together interesting details that explain it.

1. Previewing is a useful way to become familiar with an article or essay before reading it.

2. Use immediate review—a quick review after reading—to increase your recall of what you have read.

3. Underlining topic sentences builds comprehension and retention.

4. Be sure to analyze the author's purpose for writing by considering the source and looking for clues in the title and introductory and concluding paragraphs.

# Developing and Arranging Details

## CHAPTER OBJECTIVES

*In this chapter you will learn to*

1. use details to develop your topic sentence.
2. select relevant and sufficient details.
3. arrange details in a paragraph.
4. use specific words.
5. use transitional words.

I magine that you have decided to request a raise from the manager at your part-time job. You walk into her office and say, "Based on my performance over the past year, I feel I deserve a raise." Of course, your manager's response would be "Why?" She would expect you to explain exactly what you have done to deserve a raise. When you state your main point in the topic sentence of a paragraph, your reader, too, will ask "Why?" You must provide supporting details so that he or she will accept your main point.

## Using Relevant and Sufficient Details

The details you choose to support your topic sentence must be both relevant and sufficient. *Relevant* means that such detail must directly explain and support your topic sentence. For example, if you were to write a paragraph explaining why you deserve the raise, it would not be relevant to mention that you plan to use the money to go to Florida next spring. A vacation has nothing to do with—is not relevant to—your job performance.

*Sufficient* means that you must provide enough information to make your topic sentence understandable and convincing. In your paragraph explaining why you deserve a raise, it would probably not be sufficient to say that you are always on time. You would need to provide more information, for example, that you always volunteer to work holidays, improvements you've suggested, or instances of customer satisfaction.

### Selecting Relevant Details

Relevant details help to clarify and strengthen your ideas, whereas irrelevant details make your ideas unclear and confusing. Here is the first draft of a paragraph written by a student named Edward to explain why he decided to attend college. Can you locate the detail that is not relevant?

> (1) I decided to attend college to further my education and achieve my goals in life.  (2) I am attempting to build a future for myself.  (3) When I get married and have kids, I want to be able to offer them the same opportunities my parents gave me.  (4) I want to have a comfortable style of living and a good job.  (5) As for my wife, I don't want her to work because I believe a married woman should not work.  (6) I believe college is the way to begin a successful life.

Sentence 5 does not belong in the paragraph. The fact that Edward does not want his wife to work is not a reason for attending college.

Use the following simple test to be sure each detail you include belongs in your paragraph.

1. Read your topic sentence in combination with each of the other sentences in your paragraph. For example,

   read topic sentence + last sentence

   read topic sentence + second-to-last sentence

   read topic sentence + third-to-last sentence

2. For each pair of sentences ask yourself, "Do these two ideas fit together?" If your answer is "No," then you have found a detail that is not relevant to your topic. Delete it from your paragraph.

Another student wrote the following paragraph on the subject of the legal drinking age. As you read it, cross out the details that are not relevant.

> (1) The legal drinking age should be raised to age twenty-five. (2) Those who drink should be old enough to determine whether or not it is safe to drive after drinking.  (3) Bartenders and others who serve drinks should also have to be twenty-five.  (4) In general, teenagers and young adults are not responsible enough to limit how much they drink.  (5) The party atmosphere enjoyed by so many young people encourages crazy acts, so we should limit who can drink.  (6) Younger people think drinking is a game, but it is a dangerous game that affects the lives of others.

Did you delete the third sentence? It does not belong in the paragraph because the age of those who bartend or serve drinks is not relevant to the topic. Sentence 5, about partying, should also be eliminated or explained because the connection between partying and drinking is not clear.

**EXERCISE 4-1**   For each of the topic sentences listed, place a check mark by those statements that provide relevant supporting details.

1. Magazines are published about hundreds of different subjects.

_____ a. Fashion magazines are popular among women in their twenties.

_____ b. Advertising in specialty magazines is very reader specific.

_____ c. There is a magazine for almost every sport.

2. Water can exist in three forms, which vary with temperature.

_____ a. At a high temperature, water becomes steam; it is a gas.

_____ b. Drinking water often contains mineral traces.

_____ c. At cold temperatures, ice is water in its solid state.

3. Outlining is one of the easiest ways to organize facts.

_____ a. Formal outlines use Roman numerals and Arabic letters and numerals to show different levels of importance.

_____ b. Outlining emphasizes the relationships among facts.

_____ c. Outlines make it easier to focus on important points.

**EXERCISE 4-2**   Write a paragraph beginning with one of the topic sentences listed below. Complete the paragraph by including at least three relevant details. When you've finished, use the test described on page 57 to make certain each detail is relevant.

1. Hunting wild animals should (should not) be allowed.
2. My hometown (city) has (has not) changed in the past five years.
3. Religion is (is not) important in my life.
4. White parents should (should not) be allowed to adopt black children.
5. Medical doctors are (are not) sensitive to their patients' feelings.

## Including Sufficient Detail

After reading your paragraph, your reader should have a sufficient amount of specific information to understand your main idea. Your supporting details must thoroughly and clearly explain why you believe your topic sentence is true.

Let's look at a paragraph a student wrote on the topic of billboard advertising.

> There is a national movement to oppose billboard advertising. Many people don't like billboards and are taking action to change what products are advertised and what companies use them. Community activists are destroying billboard advertisements at an increasing rate. As a result of their actions, numerous changes have been made.

Notice that this paragraph is filled with general statements. It does not explain who dislikes billboards or why they dislike them. It does not say what products are advertised or name the companies that make them. No detail is given about how the billboards are destroyed, and the resulting changes are not described. Here is the student's revised version. Notice the addition of numerous details.

> Among residents of inner-city neighborhoods, a national movement is growing to oppose billboard advertising. Residents oppose billboards that glamorize cigarettes and alcohol and target people of color as consumers. Community activists have organized and are taking action. They carry paint, rollers, shovels, and brooms to an offending billboard. Within a few minutes the billboard is painted over, covering the damaging advertisement. Results have been dramatic. Many tobacco and liquor companies have reduced their inner-city billboard advertising. In place of these ads, some billboard companies have placed public-service announcements and ads to improve community health.

If you have trouble thinking of enough details to include in a paragraph, try brainstorming or one of the other prewriting techniques described in Chapter 2, "The Writing Process: An Overview." Write your topic sentence at the top of a sheet of paper. Then list anything that comes to mind about that topic. Include examples, events, incidents, facts, and reasons. You will be surprised at how many useful details you think of.

Once you have finished, read over your list and cross out details that are not relevant. (If you still don't have enough, your topic may be too specific. See pp. 40–42.) The next section will help you decide in what order you will write about the details on your list.

**EXERCISE 4-3**

Reread the paragraph you wrote for Exercise 4-2 to see if it includes sufficient detail. If necessary, revise your paragraph to include more details, always making sure the details you add are relevant ones. Use a prewriting technique, if necessary, to generate additional details.

## Methods of Arranging Details

Nan had an assignment to write a paragraph about travel. She drafted the paragraph and then revised it. As you read each version, pay particular attention to the order in which she arranged the details.

*Version 1*

This summer I had the opportunity to travel extensively. Over Labor Day weekend I backpacked with a group of friends in the Allegheny mountains. When spring semester was over, I visited my seven cousins in Florida. My friends and I went to New York City over the Fourth of July to see fireworks and explore the city. During June I worked as a wildlife-preservation volunteer in an Ohio state park. On July 15 I celebrated my twenty-fifth birthday by visiting my parents in Syracuse.

*Version 2*

This summer I had the opportunity to travel extensively in the United States. When the spring semester ended, I went to my cousins' home in Florida to relax. When I returned, I worked during the month of June as a wildlife-preservation volunteer in an Ohio state park. Then my friends and I went to New York City to see fireworks and look around the city over the Fourth of July weekend. On July 15th, I celebrated my twenty-fifth birthday by visiting my parents in Syracuse. Finally, over Labor Day weekend, my friends and I backpacked in the Allegheny mountains, looking forward to the upcoming school year.

Did you find Nan's revision easier to read? In the first version, Nan recorded details as she thought of them. There is no arrangement of or connection among them. In the second version, she arranged the details in the order in which they happened. Nan chose this arrangement because it fit her details logically. The three common methods for arranging details are as follows:

1. time sequence
2. spatial arrangement
3. least/most arrangement

We will discuss each of these methods below. In Part III of this book, "Methods of Development," additional methods of arranging ideas are discussed.

## Time Sequence

When you write about an event or a series of events that took place over a long period, it is often easiest to describe things in the order in which they happened. For example, if you were to write about a particularly bad day in which everything went wrong, you might begin with waking up in the morning and end with going to bed that night. If you were describing a busy or exciting weekend, you might begin with what you did on Friday night and end with the last activity on Sunday. (You will learn more about this method of arrangement in Chapter 6, "Narration and Process.")

## Spatial Arrangement

Suppose you have an assignment to describe the room in which you are sitting. You want your reader, who has never been in the room, to visualize it. You need to describe, in an orderly way, where items are positioned in the room. You could describe the room from left to right, from ceiling to floor, or from door to window. In other situations, your choices might include front to back, inside to outside, near to far, east to west, and so on. This method of presentation is called spatial arrangement. Notice how one student arranged her details from front to back in the following paragraph.

> Keith's antique car was gloriously decorated for the Fourth of July parade. Red, white, and blue streamers hung in front from the headlights and bumper. The hood was covered with small American flags. The windshield had gold stars pasted on it, arranged to form an outline of our state. On the sides, the doors displayed red plastic-tape stripes on them. The convertible top was down, and Mary sat on the trunk dressed up like the Statue of Liberty. In the rear, a neon sign blinked "God Bless America." His car was not only a show-stopper but the highlight of the parade.

The topic you are writing about will often determine the arrangement you choose. In writing about a town, you might choose to begin with the center and then move to each surrounding area. In describing a building, you might go from top to bottom.

**EXERCISE 4-4** | Indicate which spatial arrangement you would use to describe the following topics. Then write a paragraph on one of the topics.

1. a local market or favorite store
2. a photograph you value
3. a prized possession
4. a car or ——————— you'd like to own
5. your campus snackbar, bookstore, or lounge

## The Least/Most Arrangement

Another method of arranging details is to present them in order from least to most or most to least, according to some quality or characteristic. For example, you might arrange details from least to most *expensive,* least to most *serious,* or least to most *important.*

By arranging the details from least to most frustrating in the following paragraph, a student describes the events of a day that went wrong.

> Have you ever had a day when everything seemed to go wrong? Yesterday ranks as a disaster for me! Everything I tried to accomplish seemed to take twice as long as it should. For example, I picked the wrong line in the cafeteria and had to wait while the cashier checked prices on everything. When driving to work, I got caught at all nine traffic lights. Even worse, if there was a mistake to be made, I made it. I made careless mistakes preparing breakfast, and at work I fed the register tape in backwards and made errors counting change. The day's worst episode happened when I was driving home. While waiting at still another red light, a car hit me from behind and damaged my taillights and bumper.

Notice that the writer wrote more about the minor annoyances first and progressed to more serious mishaps.

You can also arrange details from most to least. This structure allows you to present your strongest point first. Many writers use this method to construct a case or an argument. For example, if you were writing a business letter requesting a refund for damaged mail-order merchandise, you would want to begin with the most serious damage and put the minor complaints at the end, as follows:

> I am returning this merchandise because it is damaged. The white sneakers have dark streaks across both toes. One of the shoes has a red mark on the heel. The laces also have some specks of dirt on them. I trust you will refund my money promptly.

**EXERCISE** ▶ 4-5   Write a paragraph supporting one of the following topics. Organize your details using the most-to-least or least-to-most arrangement.

1. reasons why you enjoy a particular sport or hobby
2. five special items in your closet
3. three favorite musicians or musical groups
4. things to remember when renting an apartment
5. why you like city (or small-town or country) living

# Using Specific Words

When you are writing a paragraph, use specific words to give your reader as much information as possible. You can think of words the way an artist thinks of colors on her palette. Vague words are brown and muddy; specific words are brightly colored and lively. Try to paint pictures for your reader with specific, vivid words. Here are a few examples of vague words along with more specific words or phrases for the same idea.

VAGUE: fun
SPECIFIC: thrilling, relaxing, enjoyable, pleasurable

VAGUE: dark
SPECIFIC: hidden in gray-green shadows

VAGUE: good
SPECIFIC: appetizing

VAGUE: tree
SPECIFIC: red maple

The following suggestions will help you develop your details.

**1. Use specific verbs.** Choose verbs (action words) that help your reader picture the action.

VAGUE: The woman left the restaurant.
SPECIFIC: The woman stormed out of the restaurant.

**2. Give exact names.** Include the names of people, places, objects, and brands.

VAGUE: A man was eating outside.
SPECIFIC: Anthony Hargeaves lounged on the deck of his yacht *Penelope*, spearing Heinz dill pickles out of a jar.

**3. Use adjectives before nouns to convey details.**

VAGUE: Mary had a dog on a leash.
SPECIFIC: A short, bushy-tailed dog strained at the end of the leash in Mary's hand.

**4. Use words that appeal to the senses.** Choose words that suggest touch, taste, smell, sound, and sight.

VAGUE: The garden was lovely.
SPECIFIC: The brilliant red, pink, and yellow roses filled the air with their heady fragrance.

To summarize, use words that help your readers create mental pictures.

VAGUE:    Al was handsome.

SPECIFIC: Al had a slim frame, curly brown hair, deep brown almond-
shaped eyes, and perfectly ordered, glittering white teeth.

EXERCISE  4-6    Reread the paragraph you wrote and revised in Exercises 4-2 and 4-3. As
you read, underline any vague or general words. Then replace the underlined words with more specific ones.

## Using Transitional Words

Transitional words allow readers to move easily from one detail to another.
They show how details relate to one another. You might think of them as
words that guide and signal. They guide the reader through the paragraph
and signal what is to follow. As you read the following paragraph, notice
the transitional words and phrases (underlined) that this student used.

> I have so many things to do when I get home today. <u>First,</u> I have
> to take my dog, Othello, for a walk. <u>Next,</u> I should do my home-
> work for my sociology class and study the chapter on franchises
> for Business. <u>After that</u> I should do some laundry, since my sock
> drawer is empty. <u>Then</u> my brother is coming over to fix the
> tailpipe on my car. <u>Afterward</u>, we will probably order a pizza
> for a speedy dinner.

Here are some commonly used transitional words and phrases for
each method of arranging details discussed on pages 60–62.

| *Arrangement* | *Transition* |
| --- | --- |
| Time Sequence | first, next, during, eventually, finally, later, meanwhile, soon, then, suddenly, currently, after, afterward, before, now, until |
| Spatial | above, below, behind, in front of, beside, next to, inside, outside, to the west (north, etc.) of, beneath, nearby, on the other side of |
| Least/Most | most, above all, especially, even more |

To understand how these transitional words and phrases work, review
the sample paragraphs for each of these arrangements (pp. 60–62).
Underline each transitional word or phrase.

EXERCISE 4-7    Review the paragraphs you wrote for Exercises 4-4 and 4-5. Underline
any transitions you used. Revise each paragraph by adding transitional
words or phrases to clarify your details.

## Thinking Before Reading

The following article, "Politically Correct Language," describes how insensitive language can offend others. The essay was taken from a book titled *Television and Radio Announcing,* by Stuart W. Hyde. As you read, notice how the author uses clear topic sentences and supports each using relevant and sufficient details.

1. Preview the reading using the steps listed on page 45.
2. Discover what you already know about political correctness by answering the questions below.
    a. In what situations have you heard the term "political correctness" used?
    b. What kind of language do you think is politically incorrect?

**READING**

## Politically Correct Language
### Stuart W. Hyde

A friend of mine once told me that, when his mother was in her 1
80s and living in a retirement home, she always introduced him to her friends as her "baby." Despite the fact that he was any-thing but a "baby," he *was* her youngest child. He was embarrassed by this introduction until he realized that this usage was common in that setting, and was acceptable and amusing to his mother's friends. They understood the intent and the context of the words she used. It was acceptable to use *this* expression in *this* environment, and within *this* group of people. At the same time, it is important to understand that usage appropriate to one setting often is out of place and resented in other contexts.

As you most likely know, it is common for members of "closed" 2
groups to use words and names that would be unacceptable if used outside the group. Perhaps you belong to a closed group where good-natured banter, including insults, is common. Some groups are ethnically related; others are ethnically diverse, as in social groups called "cliques." (Pronounced "KLEEKS" by my generation, and most likely "KLICKS" by yours.) The banter of the "locker room" often is paralleled by that of professors at a university luncheon table—but only if those present have formed a distinct "closed" group. Within such groupings, it is common for very blunt statements to be made and nasty names to be

used, all directed toward joviality; such behavior is most likely natural and will never change. It has to do with bonding, testing, and camaraderie. Insults in such a context seldom hurt because they come from friends. But, it is quite a different matter to be called an offensive name by an *outsider,* or to use derogatory terms when speaking *to* an outsider; *or, even more to the point, when speaking in public, as during a broadcast.*

**Political correctness (PC)** is a recently coined term to describe a movement that actually began some time ago. The move was motivated by a conviction that some names and words are offensive or exclusionary and should be used with caution or dropped altogether. Despite some excesses committed in the name of political correctness, the movement is long overdue in sensitizing us to language that is noninclusive and inconsiderate of the feelings of others.    3

The term "political correctness" is not well chosen because the movement has little to do with politics; at the same time, the term *does* have the virtue of being widely used and, therefore, widely understood. What this term really means is that we should be ever sensitive to the feelings of others, and we should incorporate this sensitivity into our speech and our actions. As talk-show host Michael Krasny states:    4

> Political correctness is less the appropriate phrase than *civility* and *kindness,* expressions that should be an integral part of rational—or even *irrational*—discourse. Whatever the nature of the discussion, we all need to be mindful and sensitive (without getting carried away) to that which can hurt or wound or undermine.

The desire to avoid hurtful terminology and demeaning statements predates the "politically correct" movement by several years, if not decades. One example from the past is the change made several years ago by Stanford University in renaming its mascot "Cardinal," dropping the term "Indians." The Atlanta Braves, the Cleveland Indians, and the Washington Redskins, among many others, have been criticized for using Native American designations for their mascots. Other mascot names have been criticized, including "Minutemen" (excludes women) and "Norsemen" (too Aryan and too masculine). A great many hymns, carols, creeds, and prayers of the Christian church have been undergoing review and revision to eliminate a long-standing male orientation— "God Rest Ye Merry Gentlemen," is one example.    5

In addition to terms of ethnicity and gender, political correctness asks us to consider our use of language in other contexts that might be offensive or hurtful. PC suggests we use the term "international students" instead of "foreign students," because the word *foreign* is, in some constructions, negative. ("She had a *foreign* object in her eye." And, one definition of foreign is "*not natural; alien.*")    6

PC also asks us to be careful in choosing words to describe those with physical or mental deviations from the norm. "Norm" is a relative term, not a standard by which those who differ from it should be negatively judged. In times past, jokes were told (and laughed at) that ridiculed alcoholics, as well as those who were obese, stuttered, had regional or national accents, or differed in some other way from the majority of the citizens in a community or a nation. The concept of the "superiority" of the majority and the "inferiority" of the minority goes back to ancient times, when people born with red hair (in some societies) were considered evil, and where mothers of twins were harassed as adulterers because twins were thought to require two different fathers. And, left-handedness was considered by many societies to be a defect. The French for "left-handed" is *gauche,* meaning "clumsy," but the Italian version is even harsher—*sinistra,* which gave us the word "sinister."

Words, carelessly or insensitively used, can hurt others. Perhaps *you* were referred to as a *child* for some time after you felt grown up; people in their sixties—or even in their seventies—can also feel demeaned if they are described as *old* or *elderly.* Perhaps you suffered from schoolyard taunts about your appearance or your behavior when you were younger. If so, you know how much such actions can hurt. The old expression "Sticks and stones may break my bones, but names will never hurt me" is totally false. Derogatory names can be devastating! Additionally, slang terms for mental or physical conditions can be very hurtful, as in calling someone a *retard* or a *blimp.*

Finally, to call a woman a *girl* or a *gal* may be resented by many who see it as demeaning—much as adult African American men and women are upset when called "boys" and "girls" by insensitive persons. It might be added that many women do call one another "girl" or "gal," and, of course, there is nothing wrong with this practice when there is agreement within the group that the words are acceptable and even slightly humorous.

You should always be aware of the feelings of your listeners. Comments that exclude or hurt others in our society are used only by those who are unaware of the offense, and by a number of talk-show demagogues who *intentionally* insult and offend others. If you truly care about people, your feelings will be reflected in the words you choose. Using in-group language outside the group is always dangerous, and the likelihood that your remarks will cause some people to feel degraded is great. When in doubt, play it safe by following the rules of sensitive and considerate usage! Make sure that the language you use outside a group is "politically correct."

From Stuart W. Hyde, *Television and Radio Announcing*

## Getting Ready to Write

■ **Examining the Reading: Recognizing Types of Supporting Details**

Before you can write about an author's ideas, you must understand how that author supports and explains his or her main points. Hyde uses a variety of details. Specifically, Hyde uses examples, anecdotes, definitions, reasons, and quotations to support his ideas. He also uses lively verbs, exact names, and descriptive words and phrases to make his writing interesting.

EXERCISE  4-8   Analyze Hyde's use of supporting detail by indicating in which paragraphs and sentences he uses

1. anecdotes _____

2. examples _____

3. quotations _____

4. reasons _____

5. comparisons _____

6. specific verbs _____

7. exact names _____

8. adjectives to add detail _____

■ **Thinking Critically: Analyzing Tone**

Often you can tell from a speaker's tone of voice how he or she feels. For example, you may be able to tell whether he or she is angry, serious, sincere, concerned, hostile, amused, or sympathetic. Although you cannot hear a writer's voice, you can sense how a writer feels about his or her subject. In other words, you can detect a *tone*. Tone is the writer's attitude toward the subject. Recognizing an author's tone is often important in understanding, interpreting, and evaluating a piece of writing because tone often reveals feelings, attitudes, or viewpoints not directly expressed by the author. Can you sense the tone in each of the following statements?

• Rude or indifferent waiters and waitresses should be fired. Nothing can ruin a meal in a restaurant like a nasty or indifferent server.
• People who abuse alcohol should know better than to get involved with a substance that has such detrimental effects on the human body.
• Many dogs spend their last few days confined in dark, dank shelters waiting for someone to adopt them; when no one comes, they are euthanized.

Do you sense the first author to be angry, the second to be disapproving, and the third to be concerned and sympathetic? Tone is not always as obvious as in the above statements. You often can detect tone, however, by studying how the author approaches his or her topic. In particular, look at the language he or she uses to describe the subject.

In the reading "Politically Correct Language," the tone is instructive. You can sense that the writer is trying to explain and give advice about political correctness.

## ■ Reacting to Ideas: Discussion and Journal Writing

1. Give some examples of "closed groups" or cliques.

2. Can things other than language and actions be politically incorrect? Can foods or clothing, for example, be politically incorrect?

3. Who decides what is and is not politically correct? Who should decide?

## Writing Assignments

### Writing About the Reading

1. Hyde says we should incorporate sensitivity to others in both our speech and actions, yet the article is mostly about speech. What actions might be politically incorrect? Write a paragraph answering this question.

2. Hyde states that usage can be appropriate in one setting and out of place in another. Write a paragraph giving examples that illustrate this statement.

Essay Option  3. Write an essay explaining the term "political correctness" to someone who is unfamiliar with it. Use examples from your own experience.

### Writing About Your Ideas

4. The article mentions the use of Indian names and terms in conjunction with sports and sports teams. Write a paragraph presenting your position on this issue.

5. Hyde mentions that many hymns, carols, and prayers are being revised to eliminate male orientation. A recent best-selling book titled *Politically Correct Bedtime Stories* poked fun at applying present-day language to the past. Do you think songs, myths, and fairy tales from the past should be revised to be politically correct? Write an essay discussing this issue.

### Run-on Sentences

A run-on sentence (also known as a fused sentence) consists of two complete thoughts placed within the same sentence, without any punctuation to separate them. Each thought could stand alone as a separate sentence.

RUN-ON:  Political science is a difficult course I am thinking of dropping it and taking it next semester.

RUN-ON:  My younger sister will visit us this weekend I probably will not have much time to study.

### How to Spot Run-Ons

You can often spot run-ons by reading them aloud. Listen for a break or change in your voice midway through the sentence. Read the two examples above to see if you can hear the break.

### How to Correct Run-Ons

Simply adding a comma to correct a run-on sentence does *not* work. Doing so leads to an error known as a comma splice. There are four basic ways to correct a run-on sentence.

1. Create two separate sentences. End the first thought with a period and begin the next with a capital letter.

   My younger sister will visit us this weekend. I probably will not have much time to study.

2. Connect the two thoughts using a semicolon.

   My younger sister will visit us this weekend; I probably will not have much time to study.

3. Join the two thoughts by using a comma and a coordinating conjunction (*and, or, but, for, nor, so,* or *yet*).

   My younger sister will visit us this weekend, so I probably will not have much time to study.

4. Subordinate one thought to the other. To do this, make one thought into a dependent clause (a subordinate clause) by adding a subordinating conjunction (such as *although, because, since,* or *unless*) or a relative pronoun (such as *which, that, what, who,* or *whoever*). Then connect the dependent clause to an independent clause (a group of words with a subject and a verb that expresses a complete thought and that can stand alone as a complete sentence).

## SKILL REFRESHER CONTINUED

Since my younger sister will visit us this weekend, I probably will not have much time to study.

### Rate Your Ability to Spot and Correct Run-Ons

Read the following sentences and place a check mark in front of the ones that are run-ons. Then correct each run-on using one of the methods described above.

1. The Civil War ended in 1865 the period of Reconstruction followed.

2. Although light and sound both emit waves they do so in very different ways.

3. The Constitution forms the basis of our federal system of government and divides the government into the executive, legislative, and judiciary branches.

4. Archaeologists study the physical remains of cultures anthropologists study the cultures themselves.

5. The body's nervous system carries electrical and chemical messages these messages tell parts of the body how to react and what to do.

6. Neil Armstrong was the first human to walk on the moon this event occurred in 1969.

7. Robert Frost is a well-known American poet his most famous poem is "The Road Not Taken."

8. Algebra and geometry are areas of study of mathematics calculus and trigonometry are other branches.

9. There are two parts of the British parliamentary system, the House of Lords and the House of Commons; the American Congress also has two parts, the Senate and the House of Representatives.

10. It is easy to become distracted by other thoughts and responsibilities while studying it helps to make a list of these distractions.

Score _____

Check your answers using the Answer Key on page 481. If you missed more than two, you need additional review and practice recognizing and correcting run-on sentences. Refer to section C.2 of Part VI, "Reviewing the Basics."

# CHAPTER SUMMARY

**Writing Skills**

1. Use details to support and explain your topic sentence. The details you include must be

   - relevant—each detail must directly explain and support your topic sentence.
   - sufficient—you must provide enough detail to make your topic sentence clear and understandable.

2. Arrange your details in a logical order. Three common methods of arrangement are

   - time sequence—events are presented in the order in which they happen.
   - spatial arrangement—objects or places are described by their location in relation to one another.
   - least/most arrangement—ideas are arranged from most to least or least to most according to a particular quality or characteristic.

3. Present your details using specific words—words that help your reader create mental pictures.

4. Use transitional words or phrases to relate your details to one another.

**Reading and Critical Thinking Skills**

1. Writers emphasize their main points using exact words and vivid details.

2. Tone is the author's attitude toward his or her subject.

# Strategies for Revising

Suppose you are planning a special picnic for the weekend. Since it's June and it has been hot all month, you decide on cold fried chicken, cold salads, melon, and ice-cold soda. The day of the picnic, a sudden weather change drops the temperature to 50 degrees, and you realize that your warm-weather menu won't work. You have to rethink and revise your menu, substituting hot soup, chili, and grilled chicken and eliminating the soda and adding coffee.

A similar situation occurs in writing. Planning and organizing are useful and important steps, but they do not produce a finished product right away. Often you need to rethink and rewrite to express your ideas more clearly and vividly.

This chapter suggests strategies to help you with this kind of revising and editing. Revising involves looking at every idea and sentence again and often making major changes. Editing is a part of the revision process that involves adding or deleting words and sentences, as well as correcting your grammar, spelling, and punctuation. As you saw in the overview of the writing process (p. 17), revision is an essential part of the process.

**CHAPTER OBJECTIVES**

*In this chapter you will learn to*

1. revise your ideas.
2. correct your errors.

## Using Revision Maps to Examine Your Ideas

The most important part of revision is reevaluating your ideas. Think of revision as an opportunity to reassess and change your ideas to make them work as effectively as possible. One of the best ways to revise is to use a revision map. A revision map is a visual display of your ideas in a paragraph or essay. Think of it as similar to a road map. A road map allows you to see how towns and cities connect to one another. A revision map allows you to see how ideas relate and connect to one another. A revision map can help you check two important features of your writing:

- your use of relevant and sufficient detail
- the logical organization of your ideas

To draw a paragraph revision map, use the following steps:

1. Write a shortened topic sentence at the top of your paper, as shown in the diagram below.
2. As you work through your paragraph sentence-by-sentence, list underneath the topic sentence each detail that directly supports the topic sentence.
3. If you spot a detail that is an example of one of the details already listed, or a further explanation of a detail, write it underneath the detail it relates to and indent it.
4. If you spot a detail that does not support or is not related to anything else, write it to the right of your list, as in the sample below.

*Sample Revision Map*

**Relevant and Sufficient Detail**

As you revise, you want to be sure you have provided enough information and that all your details directly support your topic sentence. Drawing a revision map will allow you to see if you have explained each detail adequately. You will also see immediately any details that are not relevant.

Here is the first draft of a paragraph written by a student named Joe. His revision map follows.

*Draft 1*

Currently, Herbalife is one of the top companies in the world for rate of growth and also for leading the industry in research and development of nutritional products. You may begin your own distributorship as I did with as little as fifty dollars. The potential of your income depends on the effort you put forth. Herbalife stands alone because it deals with overall health and is backed by a team of doctors and scientists who are the leaders in weight-loss research and maintenance on a daily basis. Herbalife will continue to be a leader because its products are of high quality and it cares about the health of the entire world. My involvement with Herbalife is just beginning, and I look forward to a profitable future.

*Sample Revision Map*

**HERBALIFE IS TOP COMPANY.**

- growth
- R & D of nutritional products
- deal with overall health
- backed by doctors and scientists
- leaders in weight-loss research
- high-quality products
- care about health of entire world

Unrelated Details

1. begin distributorship— $50
2. income potential depends on effort
3. involvement is just beginning

Joe's map shows him how he structured his paragraph. It allows him to see whether his ideas connect and whether he has enough detail to support his main ideas. By studying this map, he can spot details that do not fit and ideas that need further development or explanation. Joe found three details (see right side of map) that did not support his original topic sentence. He realized that these details related instead to why he felt Herbalife was a good company with which to begin his own business. Joe rewrote his topic sentence to include this idea and added more explanation in his revision.

*Draft 2*

Because Herbalife is one of the top companies in the world for nutrition and health, it may be a good opportunity for me to start my own business. It is a company that is not only growing rapidly but also becoming a leader in the research and development of nutritional products. Herbalife products are easy to sell because they are backed by medical doctors and scientists. The products are appealing because they are of high quality and the company demonstrates its concern for worldwide health through its advertising. You can start your own distributorship for only fifty dollars. There are no other hidden costs, and you are not required to maintain a large inventory. I'm expecting my Herbalife distributorship to be the start of a business that will help me pay for college.

This second draft focuses more directly on the newly sharpened topic and includes relevant and sufficient detail. Further decisions might focus on improving sentence structure, strengthening the connection among details, and adding transitional words and phrases.

**EXERCISE** ▶ 5-1 Read the following student paragraph and draw a revision map for it. Use your map to identify details that are not relevant to the topic, and underline these.

Labor unions are valuable to employees of large companies. They represent workers' rights that would not seem as important to employers if workers were not organized and represented by leaders. Being a union leader is a difficult but important job. Unions are also important because they make sure that all employees are treated equally and fairly. Before unions were created, each employee had to make his or her own deal with an employer, and some workers ended up doing the same job as others for less pay. Employers listen to unions because they can organize strikes and contact federal agencies about violations. Sometimes strikes don't work and people are out of work for long periods. Many times this is on the news. Labor unions also make sure that work sites are safe and that there are no health hazards.

**EXERCISE** ▶ 5-2 Assume that you are taking a course in computer literacy and that your instructor has given you a choice of the following topics as your first assignment. Choose a topic and write a first draft. Then draw a revision map that will help you evaluate whether you have relevant and sufficient detail.

1. Describe one important convenience or service you would miss if computers did not exist, and imagine life without it.

2. Give three reasons the Internet is useful (or is not useful).

3. Describe one of your first experiences using a computer.

4. Make a list of everyday products, activities, or services that do not require a computer in any way. Write a paragraph summarizing your findings.

5. Can computers and the personal information stored in them jeopardize our right to privacy?

6. A computer-controlled robot has been developed to perform specialized types of surgery. Discuss the advantages and disadvantages of this innovation.

## Logical Organization of Ideas

Another major issue to consider as you revise is whether you have arranged your ideas in a way your readers can follow. As we saw in Chapter 4, "Developing and Arranging Details," even if you have plenty of detail, the wrong organization can throw your readers off track. In addition, you need to make sure you use transitional words and phrases to help readers follow your thoughts.

Revision maps are also useful for checking your organization. By listing the ideas in the order in which they appear in your paragraph, you will be able to see if they are arranged logically. Study the following student paragraph and then its revision map.

*Draft 1*

The women's movement has produced important changes in women's lifestyles. Women started the movement with rallies and marches. The Nineteenth Amendment to the Constitution gave women the vote. A lot of men were not happy about that. Women never used to be able to vote, and they were not supposed to drink or swear or wear pants. That was ridiculous. Women now have more rights and freedoms. But women still don't get paid as much as men. Many women have jobs plus families that they take care of. Women do a lot more than men. Women now have a choice about what they want to do for a career but are not rewarded as much as men.

The map shows that the details are not arranged in any specific order. Since most of them relate to changes in women's rights, these details could be arranged from past to present. The writer arranged the details in chronological order in her second draft.

*Revision Map*

**WOMEN'S MOVEMENT PRODUCED CHANGES IN WOMEN'S LIFESTYLES.**

Unrelated Details

1. started with marches
2. men not happy
3. ridiculous

19th amendment—voting

couldn't vote, smoke, wear pants

women now have more freedoms

but not as much pay

jobs and families now

do more than men

have choice, but less reward

*Draft 2*

The women's movement has produced important changes in women's lifestyles. Before 1900, women could not vote, hold certain jobs, or wear pants. They were oppressed. The Nineteenth Amendment to the Constitution, passed in 1920, allowed women to vote. Other rights have come gradually over the years. Now women have a wide variety of job possibilities. They are not prohibited from wearing pants. Women have more freedom now, but they still do not earn as much as men. Today women have more choices, but they are still short on rewards.

Notice the added transitional words and phrases in Draft 2. The writer added the phrase "Before 1900" to signal the reader that she was going to review the early status of women.

Revision maps are also useful in identifying several other common writing problems.

• First, if you strayed from your topic, you will see it happening on your revision map.

- If your paragraph is repetitious, you will realize as you study your revision map that you are saying the same thing more than once.
- If your paragraph is unbalanced because you have emphasized some ideas and not others that are equally important, a revision map will show it.

**EXERCISE** 5-3 ▶    Study the revision map of the paragraph you wrote for Exercise 5-2. Evaluate your arrangement of details. If they are not arranged logically, number them on your map and revise your paragraph.

## Examining Your Language

After you have examined your ideas, the next step is to be sure that you have expressed them effectively and appropriately. Specifically, you should determine whether the language you have chosen is specific and vivid and whether it is suited to your audience and achieves your purpose for writing.

### Specific and Vivid Language

In Chapter 4, "Developing and Arranging Details," we discussed using specific and vivid words and phrases to provide accurate and interesting detail. As you revise, look for drab, nondescriptive words and phrases. Replace them with lively words that enable your reader to create a mental picture of your topic.

Here is a paragraph, with revisions, that a student wrote on the topic of aerobic dancing. Notice how she changed and replaced words to make her details more specific and vivid.

Aerobic dancing is ~~great~~ *energizing and enjoyable* exercise. It makes you ~~use a lot of~~ *stretch and exert* muscles *from nearly all muscle groups*. It also gives your cardiovascular system a good workout because ~~it gets~~ your heart *starts* pumping and (increases) your rate of breathing. You maintain the pace for ~~awhile~~ *twenty or thirty minutes*, which is also beneficial. Aerobic dancing builds endurance and stamina, which make you ~~feel as if you are in good physical condition.~~ *r body come alive and scream, "I'm in shape!"* In aerobics the risk of injury is slight since there is no intense strain on any one part of the body.

**EXERCISE**  **5-4** | Evaluate your use of specific and vivid language in the paragraph you wrote for Exercise 5-2. Revise the paragraph to make your language livelier and more descriptive.

### Purpose and Audience

As we mentioned in Chapter 1, "An Introduction to Writing," good writing achieves your purpose and is directed toward a specific audience. When you are ready to revise, read your draft through once or twice to get an overall impression of it. Then decide if the paragraph accomplishes what you want it to. If it doesn't, try to identify what went wrong, using the remaining questions in this section. Sometimes, however, it is difficult to identify the reasons a draft doesn't achieve its purpose. When this happens, ask a friend or classmate to read your writing and to summarize what it does accomplish. This information will often give you clues about how to improve the piece.

To evaluate whether your writing is suited to your audience, read it from the viewpoint of your audience. Try to anticipate what ideas they might find unclear, what additional information they might need, and whether the overall reaction will be positive or negative. Imagine that someone else had written the piece and you are reading it for the first time. Does it keep your interest and make some fresh and original points? If not, consider how you could frame or treat your subject in a more engaging or challenging way.

**EXERCISE** **5-5** | Evaluate whether the paragraph you wrote for Exercise 5-2 is suited to your purpose and audience. Revise your paragraph if it is not well suited.

## REVISION CHECKLIST

During revision, there is a lot to think about. The following Revision Checklist will help you keep in mind important questions to ask about your writing.

1. Who is your audience? How interested are they in your subject, and how much do they know about it? Is your paragraph suited to your audience?

2. What is your purpose? Will your paragraph accomplish your purpose?

3. Is your main point clearly expressed in your topic sentence?

4. Is each detail relevant? Does each explain or support the topic sentence directly?

5. Have you supported your topic sentence with sufficient detail to make it understandable and believable?

6. Do you use specific and vivid words to explain each detail?

7. Do you connect your ideas with transitional words and phrases?

## Editing for Errors

Errors in grammar, spelling, and punctuation can make your writing less effective. Many readers are less likely to believe what a writer says if he or she makes careless errors. Making corrections, then, is an important *final step* to writing a good paragraph. Of course, if you notice an error while you are drafting or revising, you should correct it. In general, however, focus on looking for errors only after you are satisfied with the content and organization of your paragraph.

### What Errors to Look For

Many students wonder how they will ever learn enough to spot all the errors in their writing. The job is easier than you think! Most students' serious errors fall into a manageable list. If you master the items on the list, you will have taken a big step toward writing an error-free paper. The Skill Refreshers contained in Chapters 3 through 15 address the most common errors students make. These errors and the pages on which you can find help with them are as follows:

- sentence fragments (p. 52)
- run-on sentences (p. 70)
- subject-verb agreement (p. 90)
- pronoun-antecedent agreement (p. 110)
- pronoun reference (p. 128)
- dangling modifiers (p. 152)
- misplaced modifiers (p. 173)
- coordinate sentences (p. 190)
- subordinate clauses (p. 215)
- parallelism (p. 244)

- comma usage (p. 264)
- colon and semicolon usage (p. 286)
- capital-letter usage (p. 309)

The following Proofreading Checklist will remind you to check for spelling, punctuation, and other mechanical errors. It is also reprinted inside the back cover for easy reference.

## PROOFREADING CHECKLIST

1. Does each sentence end with appropriate punctuation (period, question mark, exclamation point, or quotation marks)?

2. Is all punctuation within each sentence correct (commas, colons, semicolons, apostrophes, dashes, and quotation marks)?

3. Is each word spelled correctly?

4. Have you used capital letters where needed?

5. Are numbers and abbreviations used correctly?

6. Are any words omitted?

7. If your paper is typed, have you corrected all typographical errors?

8. If your paper is handwritten, is your handwriting legible throughout?

9. Are your pages in the correct order and numbered?

### Keeping an Error Log

Many students consistently make certain types of errors and not others. You can identify and learn to avoid yours by keeping a record of your mistakes. Use the form shown in the sample error log on page 83. Each time your instructor returns a paper, count how many errors you made of each type, and enter that number in the log. Soon you will see a pattern. You can then review your final drafts to locate those specific errors.

If you make frequent spelling errors, keep a separate list of the words you misspell. Study them and practice writing them correctly.

**EXERCISE** 5-6 | Check the paragraph you wrote for Exercise 5-2 for errors and correct any you find. Enter them in an error log.

**Sample Error Log**

| Type of Error | Assignment | | |
|---|---|---|---|
| | #1 | #2 | #3 |
| Sentences | | | |
| run-ons | one | two | one |
| fragments | one | 0 | 0 |
| Grammar | subject–verb agreement | — | subject–verb agreement |
| | verb tense | verb tense | verb tense |
| | pronoun reference | | pronoun reference |
| Punctuation | comma | comma | comma |
| | | quotation mark | semicolon |
| Misspelled Words | favorite | chemicals | necessary |
| | relies | majority | hoping |
| | knowledge | especially | definitely |
| | | leisure | |

## Thinking Before Reading

This reading demonstrates how a professional writer, E. B. White, revised his work. The reading contains three drafts of a paragraph describing Neil Armstrong and Edwin Aldrin Jr. as they make the first human contact with the moon. After White watched Armstrong and Aldrin plant the U.S. flag on the moon's surface, he describes his thoughts in "Moon-walk."

1. Preview "Moon-walk" by reading Draft 3 *completely.* Be sure to read it again, more thoroughly, after you have studied the first two drafts.
2. Connect the topic of the moon to your own experience by answering the following:
   a. What meanings does the moon have for you? Use brainstorming to compile a list.
   b. If outerspace travel became commonplace, would you consider traveling to the moon?
   c. What do you think it would be like to step out of a spaceship onto the moon?

**READING**

## Moon-walk

### E. B. White

(DRAFT 1)

white

comment

Planning a trip to the moon differs in no essential respect from planning a trip to the beach. You have to decide what to take along, what to leave behind. Should the thermos jug go? The child's rubber horse? The dill pickles? These are sometimes fateful decisions on which the success or failure of the whole outing turns. Something goes along that spoils everything because it is always in the way. Something gets left behind that is desperately needed for comfort or for safety. The men who drew up the moon list for the astronauts planned long and hard and well. (Should the vacuum cleaner go? to suck up moondust and save the world?) Among the items they sent along, of course, was the little jointed flagpole and the flag that could be stiffened to the breeze that didn't blow. (It is traditional among explorers to plant the flag.) Yet the two men who stepped out on the surface of the moon were in a class by themselves: they were of the new race of men, those who had seen the earth whole. When, following instructions, they colored the moon red, white, and blue, they were stepping out of character---or so it seemed to us who watched, trembling with awe and admiration and pride. This was the last scene in the long book of nationalism, and they followed the book. But the moon still holds the key to madness, which is universal, still controls the tides, that lap on every shore everywhere, and blesses lovers that kiss in every land, under no particular banner. What a pity we couldn't have played the scene as it should been played planting, perhaps, a simple white handkerchief, symbol of the common cold, that belongs to mankind universally and knows no borders

is and troubles

**(DRAFT 2)**

white

comment

      Planning a trip to the moon differs in no
essential respect from planning a trip to the beach. You have to
decide what to take along, what to leave behind.  Should the thermos
jug go?  The child's rubber horse?  The dill pickles?  These are
sometimes fateful decisions on which the success or failure of the
whole outing turns.  Something goes along that spoils everything
because it is always in the way;  something gets left behind that
is desperately needed for comfort or for safety.  The men who drew
up the moon list for the astronauts planned long and hard and well.
(Should the vacuum cleaner go, to suck up moondust?)  Among the _inevitable_
items they sent along, of course, was the little jointed flagpole
and the flag that could be stiffened to the breeze that did not
blow.  (It is traditional among explorers to plant the flag.) Yet
the two men who stepped out on the surface of the moon were in a
class by themselves and should have been equipped accordingly:
they were of the new breed of men, those who had seen the earth
whole.  When, following instructions, they colored the moon red,
white, and blue, they were fumbling with the past---or so it seemed
to us, who watched, trembling with awe and admiration and pride.
This moon plant was the last _chapter_ scene in the long book of nationalism,
one that could well have been omitted. The moon still holds the
key to madness, which is universal, still controls the tides
that lap on shores everywhere, still guards lovers that kiss in
every land under no banner but the sky.  What a pity we
couldn't have forsworn our little Iwo Jima scene and planted instead
a banner acceptable to all---a simple white handkerchief, perhaps,
symbol of the common cold, which, like the moon, affects us all.

(DRAFT 3)

it tu~s~n out;

~that~

The moon is a great place for men, and when

~did Von Rocking little~
Armstrong and Aldrin danced from sheer exuberance, it was

a poor place for
a sight to see. But the moon is ~no place for banners~ flags.

~a flag~
for the breeze doesn't blow     a flag is out
~They~ cannot float on the breeze, and ~they cannot~ belong there

of place on the moon anyway.
anyway.  Like every great river, every great sea, the moon

~none~
belongs to ~no one~ and belongs to all.  What a pity we

couldn't have forsworn our little Iwo Jima flag-lanting

scene and planted instead a universal banner acceptable

to all---a limp white handkerchief, perhaps, symbol of the

common cold, which, like the moon, affects us all.


Of course, it is traditional that explorers plant the flag,

and it was inevitable that our astronauts should follow thw

as we nothd
custom.  But the act was the last chapter in the long book

of nationalism, one that could well have been omitted---or

~so it seemed to us.~ \The moon still holds the key to madness,

still controls the tides that lap on shores everywhere, still

guards the lovers that kiss in every land under no banner but th

the sky.  What a pity ~we couldn't~ that, in our triumph, we

instead
couldn't have forsworn the little Iwo Jima scene  and planted

limp
a banner acceptable to all---a ~simple~ white handkerchief,

perhaps, symbo l of the common cold, whcih, like the moon, affects
us all.

## Getting Ready to Write

### ■ Examining the Reading: **Drawing Idea Maps**

Earlier in this chapter you learned to draw revision maps to check the content and organization of your own writing. Maps can also help you analyze someone else's writing. They can help you understand how the writer's ideas relate to one another and discover how the piece is organized. You will also find that by expressing the writer's ideas briefly in your own words, you'll remember the material better.

**EXERCISE**  **5-7**    To see the revision process White went through, construct an idea map of each of his three drafts of "Moon-walk."

### ■ Thinking Critically: **Understanding Symbols**

A symbol is an object that stands for something else. Usually a symbol stands for something abstract, often an idea or belief. For example, a dove is a symbol of peace, a cross is a symbol of Christianity, a wedding band is a symbol of marriage vows, an eagle is a symbol of the United States. Here are a few other common symbols. Think about what each represents:

a. swastika
b. skull and crossbones
c. Uncle Sam
d. shamrock

In "Moon-walk," E. B. White discusses several symbols. First, he describes the act of planting a flag—a symbol of ownership or conquest. Then he discusses the U.S. flag, a symbol of American patriotism and nationalism. White suggests that Armstrong and Aldrin should have been equipped with a universal symbol, instead of a national one. White concludes the paragraph by suggesting that the men should have planted a limp white handkerchief, the symbol of the common cold. However, the white handkerchief has other symbolic meanings as well. The color white symbolizes something pure and unspoiled. A white flag is used during battle to symbolize truce or surrender. Hence, the white handkerchief would suggest other meanings as well.

Here are a few questions to think about:

1. Was White creating a new symbol when he said the white handkerchief could stand for the common cold?

2. Is the common cold itself a symbol? Could it be a symbol of shared human misery or universal man?

3. Does White mention any other symbol?

### ■ Reacting to Ideas: **Discussion and Journal Writing**

Get ready to write about the reading by discussing the following questions:

1. How do you imagine Armstrong and Aldrin felt when they touched down on the moon?

2. Do you think Armstrong and Aldrin should have planted an international flag instead of the U.S. flag?

3. Is space exploration worth the costs and risks?

## Writing Assignments

### Writing About the Reading

1. Write a paragraph describing the types of changes White made to produce his final draft.

**Essay Option**

2. Write an essay explaining what symbols other than flags might have been appropriate to place on the moon during the first moon-walk.

### Writing About Your Ideas

3. Write a paragraph describing what you think it would be like to land and walk on the moon or to travel in outerspace.

**Essay Option**

4. Landing on the moon was a first for Armstrong and Aldrin, for the United States, and for the world. Write an essay describing a first experience of your own of which you are proud.

S KILL R EFRESHER

## Subject-Verb Agreement

A verb must agree with its subject in number. A subject that refers to one person, place, or thing is called a *singular subject*. A subject that refers to more than one thing is called a *plural subject*.

## Guidelines

1. A singular subject must be used with a singular verb.

   The <u>dog wants</u> to go jogging with me.

2. A plural subject must be used with a plural verb.

   The <u>dogs want</u> to go jogging with me.

## Mistakes to Watch For

Subject-verb agreement errors often occur in the following situations:

1. With compound subjects (two or more subjects).
   INCORRECT:   <u>Yolanda</u> and <u>Lion wants</u> to lead the way.
   CORRECT:   <u>Yolanda</u> and <u>Lion want</u> to lead the way.

2. When the verb comes before the subject.
   INCORRECT:   There <u>is</u> four gas <u>stations</u> on Main Street.
   CORRECT:   There <u>are</u> four gas <u>stations</u> on Main Street.

3. When a word or phrase comes between the subject and the verb.
   INCORRECT:   The <u>woman</u> standing in the waves with the other swimmers <u>win</u> a prize for her endurance.
   CORRECT:   The <u>woman</u> standing in the waves with the other swimmers <u>wins</u> a prize for her endurance.

4. With indefinite pronouns (pronouns like *someone* or *everybody,* which do not refer to a specific person). Some indefinite pronouns (*everyone, each, neither, such as*) take a singular verb; others (*both* or *many*) always take a plural verb. Some indefinite pronouns may take either a singular or a plural verb (*all, any, none*). Treat the pronoun as singular if it refers to something that cannot be counted. Treat the pronoun as plural if it refers to more than one of something that can be counted.
   INCORRECT:   <u>Everybody wish</u> to become a millionaire.
   CORRECT:   <u>Everybody wishes</u> to become a millionaire.

## S K I L L   R E F R E S H E R   CONTINUED

### Rate Your Ability to Use Subject-Verb Agreement

Circle the word or phrase that correctly completes each sentence.

1. Someone (want, wants) to make a left turn.

2. Chalkboards (is, are) not always black.

3. The sheriff, together with three deputies, (agree, agrees) to establish a roadblock.

4. Trisha and I (swim, swims) together every morning.

5. Neither Bo nor Jeff (know, knows) the answer.

6. Here (is, are) your lottery tickets.

7. Pizza and chicken wings (is, are) my favorite takeout foods.

8. (Candy, Candies) harms teeth because of its high sugar content.

9. (Sabrina, Sabrina and Mary) is going to the fireworks display tonight.

10. On my front lawn (was, were) two discarded soda cans.

Score _____

Check your answers using the Answer Key on page 482. If you missed more than two, you need additional review and practice recognizing and correcting errors in subject-verb agreement. Refer to section C.7 of Part VI, "Reviewing the Basics."

## CHAPTER SUMMARY

1. Revising involves examining what you have written and carefully considering how you could improve it. To revise effectively,

   • use revision maps to be sure that your ideas are relevant, that you have relevant and sufficient detail, and that your ideas are logically arranged.

- examine the language you have used. Make certain that your language is vivid, specific, and well suited to your audience and purpose.

- use the Revision Checklist to guide you as you revise.

2. Editing involves correcting errors in grammar, spelling, and punctuation. Refer to the Skill Refreshers in Chapters 3 through 15 to identify common errors (see list on pp. 81–82). Use an error log to keep track of your error patterns.

**Reading and Critical Thinking Skills**

1. Mapping a reading is a useful way to analyze the writer's ideas and to discover how the piece is organized.

2. A symbol is an object that stands for something else, usually an idea or belief.

# METHODS OF DEVELOPMENT

# 6

# Narration and Process

## CHAPTER OBJECTIVES

*In this chapter you will learn to*

1. organize events in a narrative sequence.
2. explain processes and procedures.

Imagine that you are describing to a friend a recent disagreement you had with a sales clerk when attempting to return a defective CD player. Probably you would repeat the conversation in the order in which it occurred: "I said . . . , then he said . . ." and so on. Now suppose you were explaining to a family member how to program your VCR. The easiest way to explain this is to describe each step in the order it is to be done: "First you . . . , and then you . . ."

In each of these instances, you organize ideas in the order in which they occur in time—that is, in time sequence. Organizing ideas using time sequence is a common and effective writing technique. Describing events that have already occurred using time sequence is called *narration*. Such writing is often referred to as a *narrative*. Describing how something is done using time sequence is called *process*. There are many everyday and academic situations in which you will find narration or process to be a clear and useful way to organize your ideas. Here are a few examples.

## Narration

*Everyday Examples*

- telling a friend how you spent the weekend
- describing a frightening or humorous occurrence

*Academic Examples*

- summarizing the plot of a short story
- describing a series of historical events

## Process

*Everyday Examples*

- giving directions to a shopping mall
- explaining how to file a health-insurance claim

*Academic Examples*

- explaining how to do an experiment or research project
- explaining how to solve a math problem

# Writing Narratives

Writing a narrative is similar to telling a story—one of the oldest, most appealing, and most enjoyable ways of communicating ideas. Throughout history, ideas have been communicated and recorded through stories, myths, fables, and legends. Stories remain popular today: movies, television shows, soap operas, and even many jokes involve a series of events organized and presented in story form.

A narrative is different from a simple recounting of events, however. A narrative makes a point through the story. By recounting what happens, you communicate an idea about the topic. The following narrative explains a Native American legend.

> Face Rock, a striking arrangement of rocks off the coast of Oregon near Bandon, gets its name from a Native American legend. A princess, the daughter of Chief Siskiyou, was warned by her father not to wade too far into the dangerous coastal waters. She disobeyed and walked far into the pounding surf. Her dog and two kittens followed her. The Princess was unaware that an evil spirit, Seatka, lurked in the waves. Seatka willed the Princess to look at him so he could place her within his power. She refused, and instead, stared directly at the moon, set high in the sky. To this day, the Princess and her faithful animals stand in the water, stonily determined not to succumb to evil. Seatka is there too, still awaiting her glance.

This narrative makes the point that it is dangerous for children to disobey their parents and to play by water.

## Selecting a Topic and Generating Ideas

For shorter pieces of writing, such as paragraphs and short essays, it is usually best to concentrate on a single event or experience. Otherwise, you will have too much information to cover, and you will not be able to include sufficient detail. To generate ideas for a narrative, make a list of events. Don't worry, at this point, about expressing each in sentence form or listing them in the order in which they occurred. Record in the margin any feelings you have about the events. Although you may not include them in the paragraph, they will be helpful in writing your topic sentence.

**EXERCISE** ▶ 6-1 ▏ Assume you are taking an introductory psychology class this semester and your instructor has asked you to describe one of the following. Begin by making a list of events that occurred.

1. a situation in which you observed or benefited from altruistic behavior (someone helping another person unselfishly, out of concern and compassion)
2. a vivid childhood memory
3. an experience in which you felt stress
4. a time when you were in danger and how you reacted
5. a situation in which you either rejected or gave in to peer pressure

## Writing Your Topic Sentence

Your topic sentence should accomplish two things. First, it should identify your topic—the experience you are writing about. Second, it should indicate your view or attitude toward that experience. For example, suppose you are writing a paragraph about your first college registration. Your view might be that it was confusing and frustrating or that it required you to make decisions for which you felt unprepared. Here are a few possible topic sentences that indicate a view.

Registration was a frustrating experience because course selection was limited.

Registration was an endless stream of paperwork to complete and procedures to follow.

Registration was simpler than I expected because the system is now computerized.

Sometimes you may discover your view toward the experience as you are writing about it. For example, a student drafted the following paragraph about her first college registration.

I was overwhelmed by the number of human bodies crammed into one room and didn't realize that I would be there for almost four hours! I was terribly late for work, and my boss was pretty annoyed. I didn't think I would have to fill out so many forms and wished they had planned for more available seating. The crowded room was so noisy and warm that I had trouble thinking. I almost cursed when I learned that the courses I wanted were closed, and I didn't know where to go to ask for advice about what to do next.

As she was writing she wished she had known more about the registration process before she began. Then she wrote the following topic sentence:

My first registration at college might not have been so frustrating if someone had explained the process to me ahead of time.

**EXERCISE 6-2** | For the experience or situation you chose in Exercise 6-1, write a topic sentence that expresses your attitude toward it.

### Sequencing and Developing Your Ideas

The events in a narrative paragraph should usually be arranged in chronological order—the order in which they happened. Sometimes you may want to rearrange events to emphasize a point. If you do, make sure the sequence of events is clear enough for the reader to follow.

You can visualize a narrative paragraph as follows:

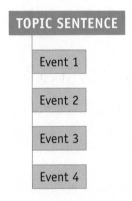

To place the events in the correct sequence, review and number your list of events.

A clear, well-written narrative should provide sufficient detail to allow your reader to understand fully the situation you are writing about. Try to answer for your reader most of the following questions:

*When* did it happen?      *What* events occurred?

*Where* did it happen?      *Why* did they happen?

*Who* was involved?      *How* did they happen?

Be sure to include only essential and relevant details. Other details will distract readers from the events you are describing.

 **EXERCISE 6-3** | For the experience or situation you selected for Exercises 6-1 and 6-2, draft a paragraph in which you present the events in the order in which they occurred.

### Useful Transitions

Transitions are especially useful in narratives to lead your reader from one event to another. Here are some frequently used transitional words and phrases:

| TABLE 6-1 | Frequently Used Transitional Words and Phrases for Narratives |
|-----------|---------------------------------------------------------------|

| | | | |
|---|---|---|---|
| first | then | in the beginning | next |
| second | later | after | during |
| third | at last | following | after that |
| finally | | | |

**EXERCISE**  6-4  Revise the paragraph you wrote for Exercise 6-3. Check it for transitional words and phrases and add them, as necessary, to make your ideas clearer.

## Writing Process Descriptions

A process paragraph describes how something is done or how something works. A "how-to" paragraph, for example, may explain how to change a flat tire, aid a choking victim, or locate a reference source in the library. A "how-it-works" paragraph may explain the operation of a pump, how the human body regulates temperature, or how children acquire speech. Here are examples of both. The first explains how to eat an ice cream cone. The second describes how hibernation works.

*"How-to" Paragraph*

In trying to make wise and correct decisions about the ice-cream cone in your hand, you should always keep the objectives in mind. The main objective, of course, is to get the cone under control. Secondarily, one will want to eat the cone calmly and with pleasure. Real pleasure lies not simply in eating the cone but in eating it right. Let us assume that you have darted to your open space and made your necessary emergency repairs. The cone is still dangerous—still, so to speak, "live." But you can now proceed with it in an orderly fashion. First, revolve the cone through the full three hundred and sixty degrees, snapping at the loose gobs of ice cream; turn the cone by moving the thumb away from you and the forefinger toward you, so the cone moves counterclockwise. Then, with the cone still "wound," which will require the wrist to be bent at the full right angle toward you, apply pressure with the mouth and tongue to accomplish overall realignment, straightening and settling the whole mess. Then, unwinding the cone back through the full three hundred and sixty degrees, remove any trickles of ice cream. From here on, some supplementary repairs may be necessary, but the cone is now defused.

> L. Rust Hills, *How to Do Things Right: Revelations of a Fussy Man*

*"How-It-Works" Paragraph*

Hibernation is a biological process that occurs most frequently in small animals. The process enables animals to adjust to a diminishing food supply. When the outdoor temperature drops, the animal's internal thermostat senses the change. Then bodily changes begin to occur. First, the animal's heartbeat slows, and oxygen intake is reduced by slowed breathing. Metabolism is then reduced. Food requirements become minimal. Finally, the animal falls into a sleep-like state during which it relies on stored body fat to support life functions.

### Selecting a Topic and Generating Ideas

When you are describing a process, write about one that you are familiar with, preferably something you have done often or have a complete understanding of. Both "how-to" and "how-it-works" paragraphs describe steps that occur *only* in a specified order. Begin developing your paragraph by listing these steps in the order in which they must occur. It is helpful to visualize the process. For "how-to" paragraphs imagine yourself actually performing the task. For complicated "how-it-works" descriptions, draw diagrams and use them as guides in identifying the steps and putting them in the proper order.

**EXERCISE** ▶ **6-5** Think of a process or procedure you are familiar with, or select one from the following list, and make a list of the steps it involves.

1. how to read a map
2. how to waste time

3. how to learn to like _____
4. how the NFL football draft works

5. how to win at _____
6. how to make a marriage or relationship work
7. how to protect your right to privacy
8. how to improve your skill at a particular sport or pastime
9. how to select a movie that is worth seeing

### Writing Your Topic Sentence

For a process paragraph, your topic sentence should (1) identify the process or procedure and (2) explain to your reader why familiarity with it is useful or important (*why* he or she should learn about the process). Your topic sentence should state a goal, offer a reason, or indicate what can be accomplished by using the process. Here are a few examples of topic sentences that contain both of these important elements.

Reading maps, a vital skill for vacations by car, is a simple process, except for the final refolding.

Because leisure reading encourages a positive attitude toward reading, every parent should know how to select worthwhile children's books.

To locate books in the library, you must know how to use the computerized card catalog.

**EXERCISE**  **6-6**  Revise the following topic sentences so that the reason the topic is important or relevant is clear.

1. Making pizza at home involves five steps.
2. Taking notes in a lecture class requires good listening and writing skills.
3. Bloodhounds that can locate criminals are remarkable creatures.
4. Have you ever wondered how to use dental floss?
5. Here's how to change a flat tire.

**EXERCISE** **6-7**  Write a topic sentence for the process you selected in Exercise 6-5.

### Sequencing and Developing Your Ideas

Use the following tips to develop an effective process paragraph.

1. **Present the steps in a process in the order in which they happen.**

2. **Include only essential, necessary steps.** Avoid comments, opinions, or unnecessary information because it may confuse your reader.

3. **Assume that your reader is unfamiliar with your topic** (unless you know otherwise). Be sure to define unfamiliar terms and describe clearly any technical or specialized tools, procedures, or objects.

4. **Use a consistent point of view.** Use either the first person ("I") or the second person ("you") throughout. Don't switch between them.

5. **Place your topic sentence first.** This position provides your reader with a purpose for reading.

6. **Use transitional words** (like those in Table 6-1, p. 98) to help your reader follow the process.

7. If the process is long, complicated, or unfamiliar to your audience, give an overview of the process before describing specific steps.

**EXERCISE** **6-8**  Draft a paragraph for the process you chose in Exercise 6-5.

**EXERCISE** **6-9**  Revise the draft you wrote for Exercise 6-8. Check transitional words and phrases and add them, as necessary, to make your ideas clearer.

# Applying Your Skills to Essay Writing: Narration and Process

Although this chapter has focused on writing narrative and process paragraphs, you can use many of the same skills for writing narrative and process essays.

## Writing Narrative Essays

Here are a few guidelines to follow in writing narrative essays:

**1. Tell your story from a consistent point of view.** That is, choose one person involved in the story and tell it from his or her perspective. When explaining a complicated series of events over the course of several paragraphs, it is easy to switch from one person's perspective to another's. Before you begin writing, decide whose point of view you will use. Once you've made this decision, you are more likely to be conscious of point of view and to use it consistently.

**2. Use the same tense throughout.** Unless you have a specific reason for doing otherwise, write in one tense—past or present. That is, tell the story as it did happen (past) or as if it is happening now (present).

**3. Focus on the most important elements of your story.** Do not distract your reader by including insignificant facts, events, people, or descriptions.

**4. Use vivid language.** Help your reader visualize the action in your narrative by using descriptive detail (see p. 116) about sights, people, places, and so forth.

**EXERCISE**  **6-10** Assume you are taking a health and nutrition course. Your instructor has given you the following assignment: Write a one- to two-page essay that illustrates one of the following situations:

1. the relationship between sleep and effective functioning
2. the consequences of alcohol or drug abuse
3. the dispute between smokers and nonsmokers over a smoke-free environment
4. the appeal and health dangers of salty, fatty, or sweet snacks
5. the difficulty (or ease) of regular exercise

## Writing Process Essays

Use the following guidelines for writing process essays:

**1. Before writing, list or outline the steps.** Decide how to arrange the steps and how to group them logically into paragraphs. For example, if you were writing about how to plan a wedding, you might group your steps into things to do many months ahead, things to do several weeks ahead, and things to do several days ahead.

**2. For a difficult process, devote one paragraph to each step.** Help your reader by giving a thorough, detailed explanation of each step. By separating them into individual paragraphs you will also help your reader distinguish one step from another.

**3. For a difficult or unfamiliar process, offer examples and make comparisons to a simpler or more familiar process.**

**4. Use the same verb tense throughout your essay.** Generally, processes are described in the present tense. There may be times, however, when you want to use the past tense; for instance, you may want to use the past tense to describe how you fixed your car this morning before leaving for school.

**EXERCISE** ▶ 6-11 ▶ Write an essay describing one of the following processes:

1. You have inherited a large sum of money but are required to award $5,000 to each of five homeless people. Explain how you would go about choosing those five people.

2. Suppose you learn you have a serious disease, but one that with the proper treatment is completely curable. Without proper treatment, it could be fatal. Write an essay describing the process of finding the right doctor to treat you.

3. Suppose you are shopping for a used car. You find two cars in the same price range with nearly equal numbers of miles. How would you decide which one to buy? Write an essay describing your decision-making process.

## Thinking Before Reading

The following reading, "The Charwoman," is taken from the autobiography of Gordon Parks, *Voices in the Mirror.* Parks is a famous photographer, well known for his work in *Life* magazine. In this narrative Parks relates an experience early in his career as a photographer and describes the racial discrimination and bigotry he faced in Washington, D.C.

1. Preview the reading using the steps described in Chapter 3, page 45.
2. Connect the reading to your own experience by answering the following questions:
   a. Can photographs capture and communicate feelings?
   b. Can photographs communicate ideas?
   c. Do discrimination and racism still exist today? In what forms?

READING

# The Charwoman
## Gordon Parks

I have one formidable, overwhelming and justifiable hatred, and that is for racists. Thorn-wielding is their occupation and I can attest to their proficiency. Throughout my childhood they kept their eyes glued to my tenderest parts, striking me, impaling me, leaving me bloodied and confused—without my knowing what had provoked their hostility. I came at last to think of them as beasts with cold hearts; of lost souls impassioned with hatred, slithering about in misery, their feelings severed of all humaneness and spreading over the universe like prickly cloth. Rancor[1] seems to have been their master, and any good that befalls the targets of their grudges sets them to brooding. And though the wind sings with change they remain deaf to it; change to them is the unbearable music of imaginary monsters, which they resist. Their actions and attitudes easily identify them. Their smiles have a curl. Their voices, no matter how gentle, are bedded in loathing. At times I can only look at them in a curious silence, wondering about their feelings, and the climates that bred them. I recall having a sort of innocence about the source of their bigotry,[2] but naïveté was no antidote for the bleeding. Washington, D.C., in 1942, bulged with racism.

I arrived there in January of that year with scant knowledge of the place, knowing only that beneath the gleaming monuments and gravestones lay men who had distinguished themselves. What I had learned along the way had little to do with this sprawling city where Washington and Lincoln had been empowered. Sensing this, Roy Stryker, the photographic mentor at FSA [Farm Security Administration], sent me out to get acquainted with the rituals of the nation's capital. I went in a hurry and with enthusiasm. The big blue sky was without clouds and everything seemed so pure, clean and unruffled. It appeared that the entire universe was pleasured in peace.

My contentment was short-lived. Within the hour the day began opening up like a bad dream; even here in this radiant, high-hearted place racism was busy with its dirty work. Eating houses shooed me to the back door; theaters refused me a seat, and the scissoring voices of white clerks at Julius Garfinckel's prestigious department store riled me with curtness. Some clothing I had hoped to buy there went unbought. They just didn't have my size—no matter what I wanted.

1. bitter hate
2. narrow-minded intolerance

In a very short time Washington was showing me its real character.     4
It was a hate-drenched city, honoring my ignorance and smugly creating
bad memories for me. During that afternoon my entire childhood rushed
back to greet me, to remind me that the racism it poured on me had not
called it quits.

Not only was I humiliated, I was also deeply hurt and angered to a     5
boiling point. It suddenly seemed that all of America was finding grim
pleasure in expressing its intolerance to me personally. Washington had
turned ugly, and my angry past came back to speak with me as I walked
along, assuring me that, even here in the nation's capital, the walls of
bigotry and discrimination stood high and formidable. In all innocence,
I had gone to a restaurant to eat, to a store to buy clothing and a movie
theater for enjoyment. And Washington was telling me, in no uncertain
terms, that I shouldn't have done it. Now I was hurrying back to Roy
Stryker's office like an angry wind.

When I reached there he looked at me for a few moments without     6
speaking. He didn't have to. The gloom shadowing my face told him
everything. "Well," he finally asked, "tell me—how did it go?"

I answered him with a question. "What's to be done about this hor-     7
rible place? I've never been so humiliated in my life. Mississippi couldn't
be much worse."

"It's bad—very bad. That's why I was hesitant about taking you on     8
here. The laboratory technicians here are all from the Deep South.
You're not going to have an easy time. Their attitude about photographers is not the best. To them they are a glorified lot who roam the
world while they slave away in the back rooms doing the dirty work.
And slaving for a black photographer isn't going to improve that attitude. You're on your own here, and you'll have to prove yourself to
them—with superior work." He rubbed his chin, thinking. "As for that
city out there, well—it's been here for a long time, full of bigotry and
hatred for black people. You brought a camera to town with you. If you
use it intelligently, you might help turn things around. It's a powerful
instrument in the right hands." He paused, thinking things through for
me. "Obviously you ran into some bigots out there this afternoon. Well,
it's not enough to photograph one of them and label his photograph
*bigot*. Bigots have a way of looking like everyone else. You have to get
at the source of their bigotry. And that's not easy. That's what you'll
have to work at, and that's why I took you on. Read. Read a lot. Talk
to other black people who have spent their lives here. They might help
to give you some direction. Go through these picture files. They have a
lot to say about what's happening here and other places throughout this
country. They are an education in themselves. The photographers who
produced those files learned through understanding what our country's

problems are. Now they are out there trying to do something about those problems. That's what you must do eventually."

Eventually. All well and good—but I was still burning with a need to hit back at the agony of the afternoon. I sat for an hour mulling over his advice and the humiliation I had suffered. It had grown late; the office had emptied and Stryker had left for the day. Only a black charwoman remained but she was mopping the floor in an adjoining office. "Talk to other black people who have spent their lives here," he had said. She was black, and I eased into conversation with her. Hardly an hour had gone by when we finished, but she had taken me through a lifetime of drudgery and despair in that hour. She was turning back to her mopping when I asked, "Would you allow me to photograph you?"     9

"I don't mind."     10

There was a huge American flag hanging from a standard near the wall. I asked her to stand before it, then placed the mop in one hand and the broom in the other. "Now think of what you just told me and look straight into this camera." Eagerly I began clicking the shutter. It was done and I went home to supper. Washington could now have a conversation with her portrait.     11

Gordon Parks, *Voices in the Mirror*

## Getting Ready to Write

■ **Examining the Reading: Using Sequence Maps**

To understand a narrative or process paragraph or essay, you must have a clear understanding of the sequence of events. A sequence map—a visual representation of key events or steps in the order in which they occur—can help you keep these straight. A sequence map looks like this:

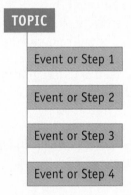

For complicated narratives or processes, you can include key details about each step, as shown here:

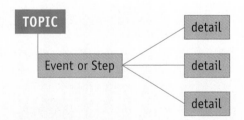

You'll find sequence maps useful in understanding a variety of materials. Plots of novels and short stories, for example, frequently switch back and forth in time; a sequence map can help you follow events. Sequence maps are also useful to draw when studying events in history and processes and procedures in the sciences.

**EXERCISE** ▶ 6-12 | Complete the following sequence map for "The Charwoman" by filling in the blank boxes.

## PARKS'S DAY IN WASHINGTON

Parks recalls past experience with racism

Stryker sends Parks out to learn about city

Got shooed out of resturants

Theaters refused Him a seat

Dept stores made him leave

Parks storms into Stryker's office

Stryker calms down Parks / talks sense

talks to black womans life story

takes portrait of woman

Parks goes home to supper

### ■ Thinking Critically: **Point of View**

Narratives are always told from a point of view—that is, from a particular perspective. Think of point of view as the eyes through which the story is seen. The point of view of "The Charwoman" is that of the photographer. His impressions, feelings, and reactions are conveyed.

A writer's point of view is important to recognize and evaluate as you read and write about narratives (or any other type of writing that expresses attitudes and feelings). Point of view often allows you to look beyond events to see how they are perceived by the people involved. The same event, from a different person's perspective, can be described quite differently.

**EXERCISE**  **6-13**   "The Charwoman" could be told from points of view other than that of the photographer. For example, the story could be told from the viewpoint of Roy Stryker, the author's mentor, from the charwoman's viewpoint, or even from the viewpoint of the clerks at Garfinckel's department store. Each story would, necessarily, include a different series of events and feelings. Write a paragraph telling the story from Roy Stryker's viewpoint.

■ **Reacting to Ideas: Discussion and Journal Writing**

Get ready to write about the reading by discussing the following questions.

1. Do you think Roy Stryker knew what Parks would experience when he sent Parks out to get acquainted with the city?

2. Describe Parks's feelings as he rushed back to Stryker's office.

3. Describe your reaction to the photograph of the charwoman.

4. How does the photograph of the charwoman address bigotry and racism?

5. Stryker told Parks he must eventually "do something" about "our country's problems." Do you think the charwoman photograph did something?

## Writing Assignments

### Writing About the Reading

1. The narrative is told from Parks's point of view: he relates how he met, spoke with, posed, and photographed the charwoman. Write a narrative paragraph relating these same events from the point of view of the charwoman. Feel free to add details, including those that reveal how you think the charwoman felt toward Parks.

*Essay Option*    2. Write an essay explaining what Stryker meant when he said that a camera is "a powerful instrument in the right hands" and how Parks proved that statement to be correct.

### Writing About Your Ideas

3. Stryker told Parks that he must prove himself through superior work. Write a narrative paragraph describing a situation in which you had to prove yourself.

*Essay Option*    4. In order to accomplish his goal, Parks followed a process in posing the charwoman. Think of a goal you have accomplished, and write an essay describing how you accomplished it and how you felt when you did.

## REVISION CHECKLIST

1. Is your paragraph or essay appropriate for your audience? Does it give them the background information they need? Will it interest them?

2. Will your paragraph or essay accomplish your purpose?

3. Is your main point clearly expressed in a topic sentence?

4. Is each detail relevant? In other words, does each directly explain or support the topic sentence?

5. Have you supported your topic sentence with sufficient detail to make it understandable and believable?

6. Do you use specific and vivid words to explain each detail?

For Narrative and Process Writing:

7. Have you made a point about your narrative? Have you told the reader why the process you describe is important?

8. Are the events or steps arranged in the order in which they occurred? If not, will your reader be able to follow the sequence?

9. Have you used transitional words and phrases to help the reader follow the events or steps?

10. Have you written your narrative from a consistent point of view?

11. Have you proofread? (See the inside back cover of this book for a proofreading checklist.)

### Pronoun-Antecedent Agreement

A pronoun (*he, she, it*) substitutes for a noun and must agree in person, number, and gender (male, female) with its antecedent (the word it replaces).

### Rules to Follow

1. If the noun is singular, the pronoun replacing it must also be singular.

   Robert wanted to lend me his class notes.

2. If the noun is plural, the pronoun substitute must be plural.

   Mark wrote lyrics for songs; many were depressing and sad.

3. Some indefinite pronouns are singular; others are plural. Use a singular pronoun to replace a singular noun and a plural pronoun to replace a plural noun.

   One of the team members could not find his keys.

   Both of the instructors said they planned to vacation in Maine.

4. Some indefinite pronouns are either singular or plural, depending on how they are used. If the pronoun refers to something that cannot be counted, use a singular pronoun to refer to it. If the pronoun refers to something that can be counted, use a plural pronoun to refer to it.

   Too much ice on airplane wings is dangerous, so it is removed before take-off.

   Many students think they will register for an economics course.

5. Use a plural pronoun to refer to two or more nouns linked by *and*.

   Sam and Mark lost their keys.

6. If a pronoun substitutes for two or more nouns joined by *or* or *nor*, the pronoun agrees with the noun it is nearer to.

   Either Mrs. Marcus or her sons will drive their car.

### Rate Your Ability to Use Pronoun-Antecedent Agreement

Circle the word or phrase that correctly completes each sentence.

## S K I L L   R E F R E S H E R   CONTINUED

1. Ellen and I are going to pool (their, our) money to buy a couch.

2. Gene or Bo brought (his, their) drumsticks for the practice session.

3. Each student received (his or her, their) transcripts by mail.

4. Either the sweater or the turtleneck will be returned to the store (it, they) came from because I don't need both.

5. Everyone opened (his or her, their) book to page 50.

6. When the play was over, the audience rose from (its, their) seats to give a standing ovation.

7. When a speaker makes a joke, (he or she, they) is trying to maintain audience interest.

8. No one handed in (his or her, their) exam before the time was up.

9. At some point in (their, his or her) lives, men and women will stop to evaluate their goals and accomplishments.

10. Every foreigner must master Portuguese if (they, he or she) expects to succeed in Brazil.

Score _____

Check your answers using the Answer Key on page 483. If you missed more than two, you need additional review and practice recognizing and correcting errors in pronoun-antecedent agreement. Refer to section C.8 of Part VI, "Reviewing the Basics."

## CHAPTER SUMMARY

**Writing Skills**

1. Narration is a method of describing events using time sequence. To write effective narratives
   • focus your writing on a single event or experience.
   • identify your topic and express your view or attitude in the topic sentence or thesis statement.
   • arrange your details in chronological order.

- use transitional words and phrases to lead your reader from one event to the next.

2. A process paragraph or essay describes how something is done or how something works. To write an effective process paragraph or essay

- write about a topic that is familiar.
- be sure your topic sentence or thesis statement identifies the process or procedure you are writing about.
- be sure your topic sentence or thesis statement explains why your topic is useful or important.
- arrange your details in the order in which they should occur.
- use transitional words and phrases to connect your details.

**Reading and Critical Thinking Skills**

1. Sequence maps are useful for recalling, identifying, and clarifying events or steps in a process.

2. Point of view refers to the perspective from which a story is told.

# Description

## 7

Imagine that you are searching through a newspaper's classified-ads section for a cottage to rent for a week during the summer. You find two cottages listed that meet your basic requirements and fall into your price range. The ad for each is shown below. Which would you be more interested in viewing? Which cottage would you be more interested in renting?

> *Ad A*  Two-bedroom cottage on Lake Simon. Kitchen, living room, full bath. Deck and fireplace. $375/week.

> *Ad B*  Comfortable, secluded, shore-front cottage on Lake Simon. Two large bedrooms, modern kitchen and bath. Living room with lake view. Wood-burning fireplace and redwood deck. $375/week.

Each cottage has the same basic features and the same price and location, but you are probably drawn to the cottage described in Ad B. Why? Ad B offers descriptive details to help you visualize the apartment. You begin to imagine what it looks like and to "get a feel for it." Ad A, on the other hand, contains only factual information. When you have finished reading it, no real impression of the cottage emerges.

Descriptive writing, then, creates an impression. It helps the reader visualize the topic. Now suppose summer is over and you just spent a week at the cottage in Ad B. You might write the following paragraph describing it.

The rented cottage was charming because it was old-fashioned and modern at the same time. The bedrooms had colorful patchwork quilts on the beds and antique pictures on the walls, but the mattresses were brand new and extremely comfortable. The reading lights were of the same, efficient, up-to-date style I have at home. On entering the living room, one's immediate desire was to fling oneself onto the huge sofa. An old-fashioned radio, hooked rugs, and a handmade checkerboard combined with the wood-burning fireplace to create a rustic atmosphere. From the modern

## CHAPTER OBJECTIVES

*In this chapter you will learn to*

1. establish a dominant impression in your descriptive writing.
2. choose details that support your dominant impression.
3. choose details that vividly describe your topic.
4. organize details to convey your topic clearly.

redwood deck I had a peaceful view of the quiet, secluded lake. The cottage took me back in time in the best ways.

Your paragraph begins with a topic sentence that identifies your topic (the cottage) and indicates how you feel about it. This feeling or attitude toward the topic is called the *dominant impression*. The remainder of the paragraph offers details that help the reader visualize the cottage and help explain the dominant impression. Each sentence contains vivid and descriptive words and phrases. In this chapter you will learn to write descriptive paragraphs that convey a dominant impression and contain descriptive details.

## Establishing a Dominant Impression

The dominant impression of a descriptive paragraph is the overall sense you want to convey about your topic or the main idea you want to convey about it. It is expressed in your topic sentence, usually at the beginning of the paragraph. Suppose your topic is the audience at a recent concert. If you felt the audience was appreciative, you might write the following topic sentence:

> The audience at the recent Laura Love concert was appreciative and responsive to both the old and new songs she and her band performed.

Different dominant impressions of the audience are created by the following topic sentences:

> The antics and immature behavior of the audience at the Laura Love concert ruined the event for me.

> Because many in the audience at the recent Laura Love concert were international students, I realized that her music has broad appeal.

The dominant impression often reflects your first reaction to a topic. Let's say you are writing about your bedroom. Think of a word or two that sums up how you feel about it. Is it comfortable? Messy? Organized? Your own territory? A place to escape? Any one of these could be developed into a paragraph. For example, your topic sentence might be

> My bedroom is an orderly place where I am surrounded by things that are of personal value.

The details that follow would then describe objects on which you place personal value. If you have difficulty deciding or thinking of a dominant impression for a topic, brainstorm a list of words to sum up your observations and reactions. For example, for the topic of your college health office you might write things such as "friendly," "helpful," "smells like a doctor's office," or "antiseptic and clean." This brainstorming eventually could lead you to write about the health office as a place of impersonal, sterile sights and sounds that houses a warm and caring staff.

**EXERCISE 7-1**

For two of the following topics, write three topic sentences that each express a different dominant impression.

1. professional athletes

   a. _____

   b. _____

   c. _____

2. a favorite food

   a. _____

   b. _____

   c. _____

3. recent film or television show you have seen

   a. _____

   b. _____

   c. _____

**EXERCISE 7-2**

Suppose you are taking a business course and are currently studying advertising. Your instructor has asked you to write a paragraph on one of the following topics. For the topic you select, use prewriting techniques to generate ideas and details. Then write a topic sentence that establishes a dominant impression.

1. Find an ad in a newspaper or magazine that contains a detailed scene. Describe the ad, and explain whether or not it is effective. Make note of what props have been placed in the scene, what the models are wearing, and whatever else helps to support your answer.

2. Choose an ad you think is effective. Write a paragraph describing the person you imagine is likely to buy the product. Explain how the ad would appeal to him or her.

3. Suppose you have developed a new product (frozen gourmet pizza or a long-lasting, multicolored highlighter, for example). Write a paragraph

describing the product to a company that is interested in distributing it. Be sure to describe your product in a positive, appealing way.

## Developing and Selecting Descriptive Details

All the details in a descriptive paragraph must be relevant to and helpful in creating your dominant impression. Begin by brainstorming a list of all the details you can think of that describe your topic or support your dominant impression. Try to visualize the person, place, or experience and write down what you see. Your details should enable your reader to paint his or her own mental picture of the topic. Here's a list of details a student produced about movie theaters:

| | |
|---|---|
| fold-up seats | greasy smell of popcorn |
| big screen | kids running up the aisle |
| previews | squishy seats you sink into |
| people whispering | ushers with flashlights |
| trash on floor | "Excuse me" |
| ticket stubs | "Sshh" |
| sticky floors | lines at the box office |
| dim lights | always crowded—sit next to others |
| popcorn—salty | |

If you have not formed a dominant impression, review your list looking for a pattern to your details. What feeling or impression do many of them suggest? In the above list, many of the details convey the feeling of annoyance or dislike. After you have decided upon an impression, eliminate those details that do not support that impression. For example, the details about the screen, ticket stubs, and lighting should be eliminated because they do not support the impression of annoyance.

Now read the following student paragraph on the topic of movie theaters. Notice how the student developed ideas from the above list. The paragraph still contains some details that do not directly support the dominant impression. Watch for them as you read.

Movie theaters are crowded, annoying places. I don't enjoy sitting next to strangers, especially rude or noisy ones. I don't appreciate practically arm wrestling with them for the privilege of using the arm rest. Ticket takers are usually people I know. People talk during the film, and others say "Sshh." Waiting in line at the concession stand irritates me because the prices are always outrageous and service is poor. The air smells like popcorn, and usually you want to buy some, although it's always too salty and greasy and you get thirsty. I wish theaters would show more previews. I am convinced that they make their popcorn overly salty on purpose. I think they should serve pizza, since it is such a popular food. It's annoying when people eat this salty stuff and make such loud crunching noises. People trash the floors and spill so much soda that my feet stick to the floor.

The details about ticket takers and serving pizza should be deleted because they do not explain the writer's annoyance.

**EXERCISE**  **7-3**

For the following topic sentences, circle the letters of the details that are not relevant to the dominant impression.

1. You don't need a lot of equipment to enjoy fishing.
   a. The only necessary items are a rod and reel.
   b. There are many different types of rods.
   c. A net is helpful if you're fishing from a boat.
   d. Take a picnic lunch if you're fishing from a boat.

2. Gambling is addictive and can lead to financial disaster.
   a. Some people are unable to stop because they want to win just one more time.
   b. Money is exchanged for gambling chips at casinos.
   c. Las Vegas is a place where many people go to gamble.
   d. I know a gambler who often bets his entire paycheck on one horse race.

3. Officials at sporting events must be knowledgeable and skillful and have strong personalities.
   a. Officials must be able to withstand crowd reactions to unpopular calls.
   b. Officials must know the technicalities of the game.
   c. Officials must exert authority and win the respect of the players.
   d. The pay that officials receive is not commensurate with their responsibilities.

**EXERCISE**  **7-4**

Select one of the topic sentences you wrote for Exercise 7-1 or 7-2, and develop a descriptive paragraph for it, revising it if necessary.

## Using Descriptive Language

Descriptive language is exact, colorful, and appealing. It enables the reader to envision what the writer has seen. Here are two sentences about a day at the beach. The first presents lifeless, factual information; the second describes what the writer saw and felt.

> I went to the beach today, lay on the sand, and read a book.
>
> At Rexham beach this morning, I spread my soft plaid blanket on the white sand, got out the latest John Grisham novel, and settled down to enjoy the sun's warming rays.

You might think of descriptive language as the way the reader sees the world through the eyes of the writer. A section of Chapter 4, "Developing and Arranging Details," pp. 63–64, discusses the use of descriptive language. Review that section before continuing with this chapter.

One of the best ways to help your reader see, as you'll remember from Chapter 4, is to use specific words that draw on your reader's five senses—sight, hearing, smell, touch, and taste. The student whose paragraph appeared on page 116 used details like the touch of sticky floors from spilled soda and the sound of the audience's whispers to make you see why she dislikes movie theaters.

Use vivid verbs, adjectives, and adverbs to help your readers see what you are describing. When you can, use exact names of people, places, and objects ("a red Toyota," not "a car").

**EXERCISE  7-5** ▶  For each of the following items, write a sentence that provides a vivid description. The first one is done for you.

1. an old coat
   Mr. Busby wore a tattered, faded, stained-around-the-neck, deep burgundy leather coat.
2. a fast-food meal

   _____

3. a bride (or groom)

   _____

4. a sidewalk

   _____

5. the dog behind a sign that warns "Guard Dog on Premises"

   _____

**EXERCISE  7-6** ▶  Revise the paragraph you wrote for Exercise 7-4, adding descriptive words and phrases.

**EXERCISE  7-7** ▶  Write a paragraph describing what you think is happening in one of the following photographs. Be sure that your paragraph conveys a dominant impression and that you use descriptive language to make your details vivid.

## Organizing Details and Using Transitions

The arrangement of details in a description is determined by your topic and by the dominant impression you want to convey. You want to emphasize the most important details, making sure your readers can follow your description.

One of the most common arrangements is a spatial organization (which we discussed in Chapter 4, p. 61). If you were describing your college campus, for example, you might start at one end and work toward the other. You might describe a stage set from left to right or a building from bottom to top.

Transitional words and phrases help your reader follow a spatial arrangement and see how details relate to each other. Some common transitional words for such an organization include *above, below, behind, in front of, beside, next to, inside, outside, to the west (north,* etc.), *beneath, nearby,* and *on the other side.*

If you were describing a person, you might work from head to toe. But you might prefer to follow another common organization: from least to most important. If the dominant impression you want to convey about the person's appearance is messiness, you might start with some characteristics that are only slightly messy (an untied shoe, perhaps) and work toward the most messy (a blue-jean jacket missing one sleeve, stained with paint, and covered with burrs).

Again, transitional words and phrases will help your reader see how details relate to each other and where you are going. Common transitional words and phrases for a least-to-most-important organization include *most, above all, especially, particularly,* and *even more.*

**EXERCISE** ▶ 7-8 Evaluate the arrangement of details in the paragraph you wrote for Exercise 7-6 or 7-7. Does it support your dominant impression? Revise it and add transitional words and phrases, if needed.

## Applying Your Skills to Essay Writing: Description

Both descriptive paragraphs and descriptive essays share a similar purpose: to convey an impression. Consequently, the skills that you have learned for writing paragraphs will help you write effective essays. An essay also offers the opportunity to expand your ideas and provide greater detail. Use the following guidelines in writing descriptive essays:

**1. Your thesis statement should express your dominant impression.** Be sure it is specific and well focused.

2. **Consider your purpose for writing.** If your purpose is to present information, then offer plenty of factual detail. If you are writing to create a feeling or emotional response, choose details that evoke those responses.

3. **Organize your essay logically.** Divide your topic into parts, and devote one paragraph to each part. For example, if you are describing the claustrophobic experience of being trapped in a crowded elevator, devote one paragraph to background details (how, when, where), another to sights, another to smells, another to thoughts that run through your mind, and a final one to the resolution of the situation.

4. **Use vivid language.** In an essay, you have the opportunity to paint detailed, exacting descriptions. As one step in the revision process, focus on improving your use of descriptive language.

**EXERCISE** **7-9**  Choose one of the following assignments:

1. Go outside for approximately ten minutes and carefully observe and take notes on what you see. Write an essay that describes the scene to someone who has never been to this place. Create a dominant impression by organizing your details into a vivid word picture.

2. Select one of the topics listed in Exercise 7-2 (p. 115) that you have not written on, and write an essay on it. Note the way that the essay format gives you more room for development of ideas and details than a paragraph does.

3. Suppose you have an important job interview next week. You want to appear studious, serious, and trustworthy. Write a paragraph describing how you would dress and what you would do or say during the interview to create that impression.

4. A student group on your campus has decided to publish a directory of college courses that will describe what each course is about, how it is taught, and what is required of students. The directory is intended to be a guide that will help students select courses and instructors, so the group is asking students to submit descriptions of courses that they have taken. Choose one of your courses, and write a description of it that could be included in the guide.

## Thinking Before Reading

The following reading, "Obāchan" by Gail Y. Miyasaki, is a good example of a descriptive essay that uses vivid, sensory detail to capture the reader's interest. The author describes her Japanese family heritage as revealed through the life of her grandmother.

1. Preview the reading using the steps provided on page 45.
2. Connect the reading to your own experience:
   a. Brainstorm a list of details that describe your grandmother, grandfather, or other close relative. Next, review your list. What feelings does the list reveal?
   b. Do older members of your family have different ideas and values than younger members? If so, think of and describe several situations that demonstrate these differences.

**READING**

# Obāchan[1]
## Gail Y. Miyasaki

Her hands are now rough and gnarled from working in the cane-fields. But they are still quick and lively as she sews the "futon" cover. And she would sit like that for hours Japanese-style with legs under her, on the floor steadily sewing.

She came to Hawaii as a "picture bride." In one of her rare self-reflecting moments, she told me in her broken English-Japanese that her mother had told her that the streets of Honolulu in Hawaii were paved with gold coins, and so encouraged her to go to Hawaii to marry a strange man she had never seen. Shaking her head slowly in amazement, she smiled as she recalled her shocked reaction on seeing "Ojitchan's" (grandfather's) ill-kept room with only lauhala mats as bedding. She grew silent after that, and her eyes had a faraway look.

She took her place, along with the other picture brides from Japan, beside her husband on the plantation's canefields along the Hamakua coast on the island of Hawaii. The Hawaiian sun had tanned her deep brown. But the sun had been cruel too. It helped age her. Deep wrinkles lined her face and made her skin look tough, dry, and leathery. Her bright eyes peered out from narrow slits, as if she were constantly squinting into the sun. Her brown arms, though, were strong and firm, like those of a much younger woman, and so different from the soft, white, and plump-dangling arms of so many old teachers I had had. And those arms of hers were always moving—scrubbing clothes on a wooden washboard with neat even strokes, cutting vegetables with the

1. grandmother

big knife I was never supposed to touch, or pulling the minute weeds of her garden.

I remember her best in her working days, coming home from the canefields at "pauhana" time. She wore a pair of faded blue jeans and an equally faded navy-blue and white checked work shirt. A Japanese towel was wrapped carefully around her head, and a large straw "papale" or hat covered that. Her sickle and other tools, and her "bento-bako" or lunchbox, were carried in a khaki bag she had made on her back.

I would be sitting, waiting for her, on the back steps of her plantation-owned home, with my elbows on my knees. Upon seeing me, she would smile and say, "Tadaima" (I come home). And I would smile and say in return, "Okaeri" (Welcome home). Somehow I always felt as if she waited for that. Then I would watch her in silent fascination as she scraped the thick red dirt off her heavy black rubber boots. Once, when no one was around, I had put those boots on, and deliberately flopped around in a mud puddle, just so I could scrape off the mud on the back steps too.

Having retired from the plantation, she now wore only dresses. She called them "makule-men doresu," Hawaiian for old person's dress. They were always gray or navy-blue with buttons down the front and a belt at the waistline. Her hair, which once must have been long and black like mine, was now streaked with gray and cut short and permanent-waved.

The only time she wore a kimono was for the "Bon"[2] dance. She looked so much older in a kimono and almost foreign. It seemed as if she were going somewhere, all dressed up. I often felt very far away from her when we all walked together to the Bon dance, even if I too was wearing a kimono. She seemed almost a stranger to me, with her bent figure and her short pigeon-toed steps. She appeared so distantly Japanese. All of a sudden, I would notice her age; there seemed something so old in being Japanese.

She once surprised me by sending a beautiful "yūkata" or summer kimono for me to wear to represent the Japanese in our school's annual May Day festival. My mother had taken pictures of me that day to send to her. I have often wondered, whenever I look at that kimono, whether she had ever worn it when she was a young girl. I have wondered too what she was thinking when she looked at those pictures of me.

My mother was the oldest daughter and the second child of the six children Obāchan bore, two boys and four girls. One of her daughters,

2. the Lantern Festival, the Buddhist All Soul's Day

given the name of Mary by one of her school teachers, had been dis-
owned by her for marrying a "haole" or Caucasian. Mary was different
from the others, my mother once told me, much more rebellious and
independent. She had refused to attend Honokaa and Hilo High Schools
on the Big Island of Hawaii, but chose instead to go to Honolulu to
attend McKinley High School. She smoked cigarettes and drove a car,
shocking her sisters with such unheard of behavior. And then, after
graduation, instead of returning home, Mary took a job in Honolulu.
Then she met a haole sailor. Mary wrote home, telling of her love for
this man. She was met with harsh admonishings from her mother.

"You go with haole, you no come home!" was her mother's                10
ultimatum.

Then Mary wrote back, saying that the sailor had gone home to         11
America, and would send her money to join him, and get married. Mary
said she was going to go.

"Soon he leave you alone. He no care," she told her independent       12
daughter. Her other daughters, hearing her say this, turned against her,
accusing her of narrow-minded, prejudiced thinking. She could not
understand the words that her children had learned in the American
schools; all she knew was what she felt. She must have been so terribly
alone then.

So Mary left, leaving a silent, unwavering old woman behind. Who       13
could tell if her old heart was broken? It certainly was enough of a
shock that Honolulu did not have gold-paved streets. Then, as now,
the emotionless face bore no sign of the grief she must have felt.

But the haole man did not leave Mary. They got married and had         14
three children. Mary often sends pictures of them to her. Watching her
study the picture of Mary's daughter, her other daughters know she
sees the likeness to Mary. The years and the pictures have softened the
emotionless face. She was wrong about this man. She was wrong. But
how can she tell herself so, when in her heart, she only feels what is right?

"I was one of the first to condemn her for her treatment of Mary,"     15
my mother told me, "I was one of the first to question how she could be
so prejudiced and narrow-minded." My mother looked at me sadly and
turned away.

"But now, being a mother myself, and being a Japanese mother           16
above all, I *know* how she must have felt. I just don't know how to say
I'm sorry for those things I said to her."

Whenever I see an old Oriental woman bent with age and walking         17
with short steps, whenever I hear a child being talked to in broken
English-Japanese, I think of her. She is my grandmother. I call her
"Obāchan."

*Asian Women's Journal,* 1971

## Getting Ready to Write

■ **Examining the Reading: Marking Revealing Actions, Descriptions, and Statements**

Writers often reveal how they feel and what they think through description rather than through direct statements. For example, Miyasaki never directly states her feelings for Obāchan, but the details demonstrate that she loved and respected her.

As you read descriptive writing, it is helpful to highlight words, phrases, or bits of conversation that are particularly revealing about the writer's attitudes toward the subject. For example, in paragraph 7 the following passages reveal Miyasaki's attitude toward her grandmother dressed in a kimono: "She seemed almost a stranger to me. . . . She appeared so distantly Japanese. . . . there seemed something so old in being Japanese."

Actions, too, may reveal an author's feelings. In paragraph 5, the author describes wearing her grandmother's boots. This action suggests Miyasaki admired Obāchan and wanted to be like her.

**EXERCISE 7-10** ▶ Review the reading, underlining particularly revealing actions, descriptions, and statements.

■ **Thinking Critically: Understanding Connotative Language**

Many words have two levels of meanings—denotative and connotative. A word's denotative meaning is its precise dictionary meaning. For example, the denotative meaning of the word *mother* is "female parent." A word's connotative meaning is the collection of feelings and attitudes that come along with that word. These are sometimes called emotional colorings or shades of meaning. The common connotation of *mother* is a warm, caring person. Connotative meanings vary, of course, among individuals.

Think of the word *rock*. The dictionary defines it as "a large mass of stone." But doesn't *rock* also suggest hardness, inability to penetrate, and permanence? Now think of the words *bony* and *skinny*. Their connotations are somewhat negative. The word *slender*, although similar in denotative meaning, has a more positive connotative meaning.

Here are several groups of words. Decide how each word differs from the others in the group.

1. fake, synthetic, artificial (they all mean "not real," but how are they different?)
2. difficult, challenging, tough
3. inspect, examine, study
4. expose, reveal, show, display

Now look at these words from the reading and consider their connotative meanings:

paved with gold coins (para. 2)

haole (para. 9, 10)

independent daughter (para. 12)

silent, unwavering old woman (para. 13)

Connotative meanings, then, can provide additional clues about the writer's purpose.

■ Reacting to Ideas: **Discussion and Journal Writing**

1. What was Obāchan's reaction when she first met her husband?

2. Describe the life that Obāchan led in her early years in Hawaii.

3. Why did Obāchan object to the marriage of Mary to a Caucasian?

4. How would you describe Mary?

5. Why does the author's mother regret accusing Obāchan of prejudice and narrow-mindedness?

## Writing Assignments

### Writing About the Reading

1. Write a paragraph describing Obāchan's feelings and reactions when Mary married the Caucasian. Use details from the reading to support your dominant impression.

**Essay Option**    2. Write an essay describing how Obāchan's attitudes changed as she got older. Support your essay with details from the reading.

### Writing About Your Ideas

3. Write a paragraph describing your grandmother, grandfather, or other close family relative. Reveal your attitude toward him or her through your choice of detail and connotative language.

**Essay Option**    4. Write an essay describing a belief, custom, or attitude within your family that has changed from one generation to another.

## REVISION CHECKLIST

1. Is your paragraph or essay for your audience? Does it give them the background information they need? Will it interest them?

2. Will your paragraph or essay accomplish your purpose?

3. Is your main point clearly expressed in a topic sentence or thesis statement?

4. Is each detail relevant? Does each explain or support your main point?

5. Have you supported your topic sentence or thesis statement with sufficient details to make it understandable and believable?

For Descriptive Writing

6. Have you created a dominant impression in your description? Do your details support this impression?

7. Have you used vivid and specific language to convey your details?

8. Is your organization appropriate to your topic and the dominant impression you want to create? Have you used transitional words and phrases to help your reader follow your description?

9. Have you proofread? (See the inside back cover of this book for a proofreading checklist.)

# SKILL REFRESHER

## Pronoun Reference

A pronoun refers to a specific noun and is used to replace that noun. It must always be clear to which noun a pronoun refers.

## Rules to Follow

1. A pronoun must refer to a specific word or words. Avoid vague or unclear references.

   INCORRECT:   They said on the evening news that the President would visit France.

   CORRECT:   The evening news commentator reported that the President would visit France.

2. If more than one noun is present, it must be clear to which noun the pronoun refers.

   INCORRECT:   Jackie told Amber that she passed the exam.

   CORRECT:   Jackie told Amber, "You passed the exam."

3. Use the relative pronouns *who, whom, which,* and *that* with the appropriate antecedent.

   INCORRECT:   Sam, whom is the captain of the team, accepted the award.

   CORRECT:   Sam, who is the captain of the team, accepted the award.

## Rate Your Ability to Use Pronouns Correctly

Evaluate each of the following sentences. If there is an error in pronoun reference, revise the sentence so that each pronoun is used correctly.

1. Marissa told Kristin that her car wouldn't start.

2. Brian found a book in the trunk his mother owned.

3. Naomi put the cake on the table, and Roberta moved it to the counter after she noticed it was still hot.

4. The professor asked the student about a book he wanted to borrow.

5. Our waiter, which was named Burt, described the restaurant's specials.

6. Aaron's sister was injured in a car accident, but it would heal.

7. In the professor's lecture, he described the process of photosynthesis.

8. Another car hit mine, which was swerving crazily.

9. In hockey games, they frequently injure each other in fights.

## SKILL REFRESHER CONTINUED

10. The hunting lodge had lots of deer and moose antlers hanging on its wall, and Ryan said he had killed some of them.

Score_____

Check your answers using the Answer Key on page 483. If you missed more than two, you need additional review and practice recognizing the correct usage of pronouns. Refer to section C.9 of Part VI, "Reviewing the Basics."

## CHAPTER SUMMARY

**Writing Skills**

Descriptive paragraphs create an impression and enable your reader to visualize your topic. To write effective descriptions

- establish a dominant impression—an attitude or feeling about your topic. Express this impression in your topic sentence or thesis statement.
- select relevant and sufficient details to support your dominant impression
- use descriptive language: exact and vivid words that appeal to the senses.
- organize your details logically.
- use transitional words and phrases to link your details.

**Reading and Critical Thinking**

1. As you read, highlight actions, descriptions, and statements that reveal the writer's attitude toward the subject.

2. Connotative language expresses feelings and attitudes as well as basic meaning. Studying connotative language can help you discover the writer's purpose.

# 8

# Example, Classification, and Definition

Suppose you have become friends with an international student in one of your classes. During class your professor mentions bumper stickers; after class your friend asks you what bumper stickers are. There are several ways you could explain. First, you could give examples: "You know, signs like 'I Brake for Animals,' 'Vote No on Question 3,' and 'Ugly, but Paid For,' that people put on the back of cars." Second, you could explain by giving several types or categories of bumper stickers: "You know, signs that state the values of the driver or urge action. Some are intended simply to be humorous." Or you could define the term by focusing on essential qualities: "Bumper stickers are adhesive signs placed on the back of cars. They express a message the car owner wants to convey to other drivers." Finally, you might use a combination of these techniques; for instance, you might provide a definition and then give several examples.

As this situation illustrates, example, classification, and definition are three useful ways to explain a topic. Examples are particular, representative instances that illustrate something. Classification is a way of grouping or arranging parts of a topic into categories. Definition makes the precise meaning and importance of a word, phrase, topic, or term clear and distinct. In this chapter you will learn to use all three of these approaches to develop effective paragraphs and essays.

## Using Examples to Explain

Examples are specific details that explain a general idea or statement. You already use them to describe daily situations to your friends. Textbooks and instructors also use them to make abstract, general

130

statements more real and understandable. Here are a few sample general statements along with specific examples.

## Everyday

| *General Statement* | *Examples* |
|---|---|
| I had an exhausting day. | 1. had two exams<br>2. worked four hours<br>3. swam 20 laps at the pool<br>4. did three loads of laundry |

| *General Statement* | *Examples* |
|---|---|
| The food in the hotel is expensive. | 1. french fries cost $3.00<br>2. a hamburger costs $6.00<br>3. yogurt costs $2.50 |

## Academic

| *General Statement* | *Examples* |
|---|---|
| Aggressive behavior can be triggered by small annoyances. | 1. smashing a malfunctioning soda machine<br>2. shouting and honking at a slow driver<br>3. shoving someone who accidentally steps too close |

| *General Statement* | *Examples* |
|---|---|
| Snowshoe rabbits are well adapted to their environment. | 1. thick fur provides warmth in subzero temperatures<br>2. white in winter, brown in summer to blend in with background and fool predators<br>3. powerful hind legs for crossing broad areas quickly |

In each case, the examples make the general statement clear, understandable, and believable by giving specific illustrations or supporting details.

## Writing Your Topic Sentence

To write a paragraph in which you use examples to explain a general statement, you follow the same process described in Chapter 6, "Narration and Process," and Chapter 7, "Description." Use freewriting, brainstorming, branching, or questioning to generate ideas. Consider what you want to say about your topic and what your main point or fresh insight is. From this main idea, compose a first draft of a topic sentence. Be sure it states your topic and your view toward it. (See Chapter 3, pp. 39–44, if necessary, for a review of developing a viewpoint.) You will probably want to revise this topic sentence once you've written the paragraph, but for now, use it as the basis for gathering examples.

## Selecting Appropriate and Sufficient Examples

Use brainstorming again to create a list of as many examples as you can think of. Suppose your topic is dog training. Your tentative topic sentence is, "You must be firm and consistent when training dogs; otherwise, they will not respond to your commands." You might produce the following list of examples:

> My sister's dog jumps on people; sometimes she disciplines him and sometimes she doesn't.
>
> Every time I want my dog to heel, I give the same command and use a firm tone of voice.
>
> If my dog does not obey the command to sit, I repeat it, this time saying it firmly while pushing on his back.
>
> The dog trainer at obedience class used a set of hand signals to give commands to his dogs.

Now review your list and select between two and four examples to support your topic sentence. Use the following guidelines.

**1. Each example should illustrate the idea stated in your topic sentence.** Sometimes you may find that your examples do not clarify your main point or that each example you think of seems to illustrate something slightly different. If your topic is too broad, narrow your topic using the suggestions in Chapter 3, pp. 40–41.

**2. Each example should be as specific and vivid as possible, accurately describing an incident or situation.** Suppose your topic sentence is, "Celebrities are not reliable sources of information about a product because they are getting paid to praise it." For your first example you write: "Many sports stars are paid to appear in TV commercials." "Many sports stars" is too general. To be convincing, your example has to name specific athletes and products or sponsors: "Michael Jordan is paid to tell us how good Nike Air Jordan sneakers are; Chris Evert promotes tennis shoes."

**3. Choose a sufficient number of examples to make your point under-standable.** The number you need depends on the complexity of the topic and your reader's familiarity with it. One example is sufficient only if it is well developed. The more difficult and unfamiliar the topic, the more examples you will need. For instance, if you are writing about how poor service at a restaurant can be viewed as an exercise in patience, two examples may be sufficient. Your paragraph could describe your long wait and your rude waiter and make its point quite powerfully. However, if you are writing about test anxiety as a symptom of poor study habits, you probably would need more than two examples. In this case, you might discuss the need to organize one's time, set realistic goals, practice relaxation techniques, and work on self-esteem.

**4. Draw the connection for your reader between your example and your main point.** The following student paragraph illustrates this principle well.

> My dad always remains calm, even in emergency situations. One night my husband cut his hand badly on a knife, and blood was everywhere. I felt so frightened that I couldn't look at the wound, and I didn't know if I should call 911. Instead, I called my dad, who lives next door. He came right over. He looked at the cut, applied direct pressure to stop the bleeding, washed and bandaged it, and then decided we should go to the emergency room. He was calm and knew what to do even though, as I could tell, he was worried, too.

**EXERCISE 8-1**

Select one of the topics listed below, write a topic sentence for it, and develop a paragraph on it using examples.

1. slang language
2. daily hassles or aggravations
3. the needs of infants or young children
4. over-commercialization of holidays
5. irresponsible behavior of crowds or individuals at public events

## Using Classification to Explain

Classification is a method of explaining or examining a topic by organizing its parts into categories. For instance, a good way to discuss reptiles is to arrange them into categories: crocodiles, alligators, snakes, turtles, tortoises, and lizards. You can explain the defensive line of a football team by classifying players as nose tackles, cornerbacks, safeties, linebackers, and defensive ends. If you wanted to explain the people who make up your school's orchestra, you could classify the various musicians by type of instrument played (or, alternatively, by age, level of skill, or some other factor). You can visualize the process of classification as follows:

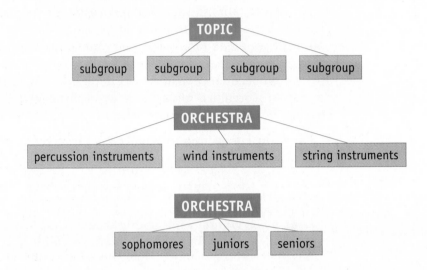

Note that subgroups in a classification system should be at the same level of detail and should be similar in terms of type. In other words, subgroups need to be distinct, but also comparable and matching. If your topic is the school orchestra, a series of subgroups such as "sophomores, violin soloists, wind instruments, and drummers" would not work because they represent different categories: class level, ability, general class of instrument, and specific instruments. When classifying reptiles, you would not include garter snakes as a subgroup in a series with crocodiles and alligators. Garter snakes is a more specific and detailed category than the other subgroups.

Classification is a common and useful way to organize complex information. Restaurant menu items are classified as appetizers, main courses, and desserts. Airline TV monitors classify flights by arrivals and departures. Grocery stores classify and arrange items by product type: paper products, canned foods, frozen foods, dairy, produce, and so on. Biologists classify plants by genus and species. Psychologists classify people by behavior (normal, neurotic, psychotic), and mathematicians classify equations by complexity (binomials, trinomials). In each of these situations, the classification system makes information more understandable and usable.

### Deciding on What Basis to Classify

To write a paper using classification, you must first decide the basis on which you will break your topic down into subgroups. As the two charts for the orchestra on page 134 show, subjects can be organized in any number of ways, depending on what you want to emphasize. Suppose you are given an assignment to write about some aspect of community life. You decide to classify the recreational facilities in your town into groups. You could classify them by cost, location, or facilities depending on what you wanted the focus of your writing to be and what would best bring out community issues.

The best way to lay the groundwork for your classification paper is to find a good general topic, then brainstorm different ways to break it down into subgroups or categories. As we have seen, a subject can be classified or organized into subgroups in any number of ways, depending on what factor you want to emphasize. In considering the topic of her friends, for example, one student realized she could sort or classify them by:

| | |
|---|---|
| age | personality type |
| length of friendship | occupation |
| closeness of friendship | marital status |
| gender | status as parent |

Each of these factors could be used to classify friends into subgroups and therefore be the subject of a paper.

EXERCISE  8-2

Choose one of the following topics: jobs, mail, relatives, or exercise. List ways to fill in the blank: "I could classify this topic by _____."

EXERCISE 8-3

For each of the following topics, brainstorm to discover different ways you might classify them.

1. Topic: criminals
   Ways to classify:

   _____

   _____

2. Topic: college courses
   Ways to classify:

   _____

   _____

3. Topic: entertainment
Ways to classify:

_____

_____

Once you have brainstormed to discover possible ways of classifying, select the one that best represents or describes the topic and best fulfills your purpose for writing. Assume your topic is college professors. You could classify them according to personality, teaching style, style of dress, or age. Teaching style would be a good choice because it focuses on their job responsibility and would allow you to describe the various teaching styles that you observe. Age, however, would not be particularly useful, unless your purpose is to explore some connection between age and the teaching profession, for example.

Once you decide how you will classify, the next step is to divide your topic into subgroups. If you've decided to classify college professors according to teaching style, you could use the following subgroups:

**EXERCISE 8-4**    For each of the following topics, brainstorm to discover ways of classifying. Choose one way, underline it, and list the subgroups into which you could classify the topic.

1. Topic: machines for communication
Ways of classifying:

_____

Subgroups:

_____

_____

2. Topic: environmental pollutants
Ways of classifying:

_____

Subgroups:

_____

_____

3. Topic: books
   Ways of classifying:

   _____

   Subgroups:

   _____

   _____

## Developing Your Topic Sentence

Once you have chosen a way to classify and have identified the subgroups, you are ready to write a topic sentence. Your topic sentence should not only identify your topic but also indicate the way in which you will classify items within your topic. The topic sentence also may mention the number of subgroups you will use. Here are a few examples:

> An automobile exhaust system has four main sections.

> Clocks come in many sizes, from watches and alarm clocks to grandfather clocks and huge outdoor digital displays.

> Three common types of advertising media are radio, television, and newspaper.

> By working at Denny's, I've discovered that there are three main types of customers.

## Explaining Each Subgroup

The details of your paragraph should explain and provide further information about each subgroup. Depending on your topic and/or your audience, it may be necessary to define each subgroup. For instance, suppose you are given an essay-exam question that asks you to discuss how psychologists classify behavior. In your answer, you would want to thoroughly explain the terms *normal, neurotic,* and *psychotic.* It is often helpful to include examples as well as definitions. Examples of normal, neurotic, and psychotic behavior would demonstrate your grasp of these concepts and improve your answer.

If possible, provide an equal amount of detail for each subgroup. If you define or offer an example for one subgroup, you should do the same for each of the others, as one student did in the following paragraph.

Parents discipline their children in different ways. Some use physical punishment, but this can hurt the child and make for an angry, resentful child. Others yell constantly, yet this approach does not work well because the children get used to it and it can destroy their feelings of self-esteem. Other parents make their children feel guilty if they do something bad. This works, but is not direct and the child can suffer from guilt and confusion for his or her entire life. Some parents talk to their children, explain how to act, and ask for the child's ideas. When the child misbehaves, the parents explain why the action is wrong and talk about it with the child. This seems to work pretty well because the children grow up to understand right from wrong and to feel involved with solving problems.

**EXERCISE** ▶ 8-5 | For one of the topics in Exercise 8-4, write a paragraph classifying it into the subgroups you identified.

### Testing the Effectiveness of Your Classification

In order to test the effectiveness of your groups or categories, try to think of exceptions (items or situations that don't fit into any one of your established categories). In the example mentioned earlier—orchestras—you could consider possible exceptions. Hammered dulcimers, for example, are both string *and* percussive instruments; electronic synthesizers are neither string, percussion, nor wind instruments. If you discover many exceptions, you might need to redefine your groups or expand their number so that you can accommodate the exceptions. You can also revise your topic sentence to indicate that you will discuss only several large or common categories, or you can restrict your topic by adding a limiting word like *most* or *common*. Here are two examples:

> Most childhood temper tantrums stem from one of the following . . .

> Several common varieties of wine are . . .

## Using Definition to Explain

All of us have had to explain the meaning of a term or concept at one time or another. Perhaps you've had to define your new favorite hobby or sport for a friend. You may have explained new slang terms to older adults or grandparents. Maybe you defined the functions or features of a word processor to a friend who was learning to use one. In some cases, people may ask you to explain vague or relative terms. If you said, "The movie was so *great,* I've seen it three times," your listener might have asked what you meant by "great." Relative terms (those that imply a comparison with something else) require definition. For example, you might say a coat is expensive and a car is expensive. But your listener would not assume that the coat and the car had the same dollar value. Instead, he or she would want to know what "expensive" means for each item. Clear, crisp definitions are as important in college as they are in everyday life. All disciplines contain specialized vocabulary terms. When you take short-answer and essay exams for your college courses, you will sometimes be asked to define the terms that have been discussed in class or used in assigned readings.

## Writing Your Topic Sentence

The topic sentence of a definition paragraph should identify the term you are explaining. It should also place the term in a general group or class and offer one or more distinguishing characteristics.

In the example below, the term being defined is *mythomaniac,* the general group or class is "person," and the distinguishing feature is "abnormal tendency to exaggerate."

A *mythomaniac* is a person who has an abnormal tendency to exaggerate.

Here are two other examples:

A *kuchen* is a German coffeecake that is made with yeast dough and often contains raisins.

A relative of the monkey, the *lemur* is an animal that lives in Madagascar and has a long, slim muzzle.

The class places the term in a general group or category. In this example, it tells the reader that a lemur is an animal—*not* a person, plant, or object— and that the lemur is in the general category of "monkey." The distinguishing characteristic tells how the term is different from others in the same class. The lemur is distinguishable from other animals and monkeys because it lives in Madagascar and has a distinctive snout. You can distinguish a kuchen from other coffeecakes by the fact that it contains yeast and raisins.

In writing about any term, especially an unfamiliar one, it is helpful to do some research. If possible, talk to others about their understanding of the term. Check the meaning of the term in a dictionary or glossary. Don't copy what you find. Instead, express its meaning in your own words.

**EXERCISE** ▶ 8-6 | Write a topic sentence that includes a class and distinguishing characteristic for each of the following terms.

1. generation gap
2. affirmative action
3. sex appeal
4. age discrimination
5. gay rights

## Developing Your Paragraph

Usually your topic sentence will not be sufficient to give your reader a complete understanding of the term you are defining. For instance, when asked to define the term *discrimination*, one student wrote the following topic sentence:

> Discrimination is the unfair treatment of people because they belong to a particular group.

This sentence is not enough to explain the term completely to your reader. Discrimination can be explained further in the following ways.

**1. Give examples.** Examples can make a definition more vivid and interesting to your reader.

> Discrimination is the unfair treatment of people because they belong to a particular group. When my parents didn't talk to a new family in the neighborhood because they were of a different religion, it was discrimination. When my cousin Joan interviewed for a job and it went to a man, even though she had more experience, it was discrimination.

**2. Classify the term.** Breaking down your subject into subcategories helps to organize your definition. For example, you might explain discrimination by classifying some of the types: racial, gender, and age.

> Discrimination is the unfair treatment of people because they belong to a particular group. One kind of discrimination is racial, as when someone is treated differently because of his or her ethnic background. When a person is treated differently because of his or her sex, it is gender discrimination. A third kind of discrimination is age discrimination. That occurs when people are treated differently because of how old or young they are.

**3. Explain what the term is not.** To bring the meaning of a term into focus for your reader, it is sometimes helpful to give counter examples, or to discuss ways that the term means something different from what one might expect.

> Discrimination is the unfair treatment of people because they
> belong to a particular group. Discrimination is not rare in
> America, even though America is committed to equal opportu-
> nity for all. Most people experience discrimination in some form
> at some time in their lives. People are discriminated against
> because of their race, age, religion, handicap, gender, appear-
> ance, national origin, family background, or other factors that
> have nothing to do with their qualifications or abilities.

**4. Trace the term's meaning over time.** If the term has changed or expanded in meaning over time, this development may be a useful means of explanation.

> Discrimination is the unfair treatment of people because they
> belong to a particular group. In the past, discrimination meant
> the ability to tell the difference between things. People were
> said to have discriminating taste in food or fashion. The ability
> to discriminate was considered a positive trait. More recently,
> discrimination has come to have a negative meaning. The term
> now refers to prejudice against certain people. At first, it was
> used to mean only racial discrimination. Then there was sexual
> discrimination against women and homosexuals. Now we have
> age discrimination, too. Some businesses and organizations
> discriminate against teenagers and senior citizens because of
> their age.

**5. Use descriptive language.** Depending on the term you are defining, you may also want to describe it or explain its function. If you are defin- ing a centrifugal pump, you might describe what it looks like and then explain how it works. (Refer to Chapter 6, "Narration and Process," and Chapter 7, "Description," for suggestions on these types of development.)

**EXERCISE**  | Select one of the topic sentences you wrote for Exercise 8-6. Develop a paragraph defining that topic.

**EXERCISE**  | Revise the paragraph you wrote for Exercise 8-7. In particular, consider your organization, use of examples, and the clarity of your explanation.

## Helpful Transitional Words and Phrases

When you use example, classification, or definition to explain your topic, use strong transitional words and phrases to help your reader follow your presentation of ideas. The table on page 142 offers useful transitional words and phrases for each method of organization.

| TABLE 8-1 | Useful Transitional Words and Phrases for Each Method of Organization |
|-----------|----------------------------------------------------------------------|

| Method of Organization | Transitional Word or Phrase |
|------------------------|------------------------------|
| Example | for example, for instance to illustrate, an example is |
| Classification | one, another, first, second, third, last, finally |
| Definition | also, in addition, too, first, second, third |

# Applying Your Skills to Essay Writing

This chapter has focused on explaining ideas using example, classification, and definition. These methods are effective for both paragraphs and essays. In writing some essays, you may decide to use classification only—for example, as a means of development. Other times, you may want to combine classification with other methods to explain your thesis statement.

Here are some additional guidelines for using these three methods of development when writing essays.

## Using Examples to Develop Essays

Since giving examples is one of the best ways to explain an unfamiliar or difficult topic, you will often use examples in essay writing. Sometimes you will use examples as a primary means of development; other times you will use them in combination with another method. For example, you might use examples from your personal experience as a primary means of development for an essay that discusses how attending preschool contributes to a child's intellectual and social development. You might use examples to support an essay (see Chapter 10, "Cause and Effect") that explains the effects of excessive television watching.

## Using Classification to Develop Essays

1. **Use paragraphing to separate subgroups.** Devote at least one paragraph to each type or subgroup.

2. **Maintain a balance among subgroups.** Unless you have a specific reason for doing otherwise, provide similar amounts of explanation, detail, and examples for each subgroup.

**3. Emphasize differences.** Make it clear how each subgroup differs from all the others. Use examples and definitions to help you make these distinctions.

**4. Consider your audience.** The type and amount of detail you provide throughout should depend on how much your reader knows about your topic.

**5. Use transitional words and phrases.** Transitions cue your reader that you are moving from one subgroup to another.

## Using Definition to Develop Essays

When your topic is difficult, abstract, complicated, or confusing, you may need to write an essay rather than a single paragraph to explain it. Suppose, for example, your purpose is to define *democracy*—an abstract, important concept with wide-ranging applications. For an audience unfamiliar with the term, an essay, not a single paragraph, would be needed to define it fully. Here are some ways to develop ideas using definition.

**1. Explain the term's etymology (origin).** For example, explain that *democracy* comes from two Greek words: *demos* (common people) and *kratia* (strength or power).

**2. Trace the term's use or history.** For example, you might discuss the first democracy and summarize the term's use throughout history.

**3. Provide realistic examples.** To make your definition clear and understandable, use examples to which your audience can relate.

**4. Draw upon other methods of development.** You might also use classification, comparison and contrast (discussed in Chapter 9, "Comparison and Contrast"), or cause and effect (discussed in Chapter 10, "Cause and Effect"). For example, you could describe types of democracy, contrast democracy and monarchy, or explain what it is about democracy that causes it to be the preferred form of government in the United States.

**EXERCISE** ▶ 8-9

Assume you are taking a course in mass media this semester and must choose one of the media listed below. Define the medium, classify it into three to five subgroups, and supply at least one example of each subgroup.

1. television
2. popular magazines
3. radio
4. film

## Thinking Before Reading

This selection consists of excerpts from "The Ways We Lie," an essay by Stephanie Ericsson first published in the *Utne Reader*. In this skillful demonstration of classification, Ericsson presents common types of lies we all engage in. Note: Ellipses marks (. . . .) show where portions of original article have been left out due to length considerations.

1. Preview the reading using the steps listed on page 45.
2. Discover what you already know about lying by doing the following.

   a. Make a list of all the ways to deceive people that you can think of.
   b. Think about those times when you have lied to avoid hurting other people's feelings. Describe the circumstances.

**R E A D I N G**

## The Ways We Lie
### Stephanie Ericsson

The bank called today and I told them my deposit was in the mail, even though I hadn't written a check yet. It'd been a rough day. The baby I'm pregnant with decided to do aerobics on my lungs for two hours, our three-year-old daughter painted the living-room couch with lipstick, the IRS put me on hold for an hour, and I was late to a business meeting because I was tired.    1

I told my client that traffic had been bad. When my partner came home, his haggard face told me his day hadn't gone any better than mine, so when he asked, "How was your day?" I said, "Oh, fine," knowing that one more straw might break his back. A friend called and wanted to take me to lunch. I said I was busy. Four lies in the course of a day, none of which I felt the least bit guilty about.    2

We lie. We all do. We exaggerate, we minimize, we avoid confrontation, we spare people's feelings, we conveniently forget, we keep secrets, we justify lying to the big-guy institutions. Like most people, I indulge in small falsehoods and still think of myself as an honest person. Sure I lie, but it doesn't hurt anything. Or does it?. . . .    3

What far-reaching consequences will I, or others, pay as a result of my lie? Will someone's trust be destroyed? Will someone else pay *my* penance because I ducked out? We must consider the *meaning of our*    4 *actions.* Deception, lies, capital crimes, and misdemeanors all carry meanings. *Webster's* definition of *lie* is specific:

> 1: a false statement or action especially made with the intent to deceive;
> 2: anything that gives or is meant to give a false impression.

A definition like this implies that there are many, many ways to tell a lie. Here are just a few.

### The White Lie

The white lie assumes that the truth will cause more damage than a simple, harmless untruth. Telling a friend he looks great when he looks like hell can be based on a decision that the friend needs a compliment more than a frank opinion. But, in effect, it is the liar deciding what is best for the lied to. Ultimately, it is a vote of no confidence. It is an act of subtle arrogance for anyone to decide what is best for someone else.

Yet not all circumstances are quite so cut-and-dried. Take, for instance, the sergeant in Vietnam who knew one of his men was killed in action but listed him as missing so that the man's family would receive indefinite compensation instead of the lump-sum pittance the military gives widows and children. His intent was honorable. Yet for twenty years this family kept their hopes alive, unable to move on to a new life. . . .

### Ignoring the Plain Facts

In the '60s, the Catholic Church in Massachusetts began hearing complaints that Father James Porter was sexually molesting children. Rather than relieving him of his duties, the ecclesiastical authorities simply moved him from one parish to another between 1960 and 1967, actually providing him with a fresh supply of unsuspecting families and innocent children to abuse. After treatment in 1967 for pedophilia, he went back to work, this time in Minnesota. The new diocese was aware of Father Porter's obsession with children, but they needed priests and recklessly believed treatment had cured him. More children were abused until he was relieved of his duties a year later. By his own admission, Porter may have abused as many as a hundred children.

Ignoring the facts may not in and of itself be a form of lying, but consider the context of this situation. If a lie is *a false action done with the intent to deceive,* then the Catholic Church's conscious covering for Porter created irreparable consequences. The church became a co-perpetrator with Porter. . . .

## Omission

Omission involves telling most of the truth minus one or two key facts 10
whose absence changes the story completely. You break a pair of glasses
that are guaranteed under normal use and get a new pair, without mentioning that the first pair broke during a rowdy game of basketball. Who
hasn't tried something like that? But what about omission of information
that could make a difference in how a person lives his or her life?

For instance, one day I found out that rabbinical legends tell of 11
another woman in the Garden of Eden before Eve. I was stunned. The
omission of the Sumerian goddess Lilith from Genesis felt like spiritual
robbery. I felt like I'd just found out my mother was really my step-
mother. To take seriously the tradition that Adam was created out of the
same mud as his equal counterpart, Lilith, redefines all of Judeo-
Christian history.

Lilith was a proud goddess who defied Adam's need to control her, 12
attempted negotiations, and when this failed, said adios and left the
Garden of Eden. This omission of Lilith from the Bible was a patriar-
chal strategy to keep women weak. Omitting the strong-woman archetype of Lilith from Western religions and starting the story with Eve the
Rib has helped keep Christian and Jewish women believing they were
the lesser sex for thousands of years.

## Stereotypes and Clichés

Stereotype and cliché serve a purpose as a form of shorthand. Our need 13
for vast amounts of information in nanoseconds has made the stereotype vital to modern communication. Unfortunately, it often shuts down
original thinking, giving those hungry for the truth a candy bar of misinformation instead of a balanced meal. The stereotype explains a situation with just enough truth to seem unquestionable.

All the "isms"—racism, sexism, ageism, et al.—are founded on and 14
fueled by the stereotype and the cliché, which are lies of exaggeration,
omission, and ignorance. They are always dangerous. They take a single
tree and make it a landscape. They destroy curiosity. They close minds
and separate people. The single mother on welfare is assumed to be
cheating. Any black male could tell you how much of his identity is
obliterated daily by stereotypes. Fat people, ugly people, beautiful people, old people, large-breasted women, short men, the mentally ill, and
the homeless all could tell you how much more they are like us than we
want to think. I once admitted to a group of people that I had a mouth
like a truck driver. Much to my surprise, a man stood up and said, "I'm
a truck driver, and I never cuss." Needless to say, I was humbled. . . .

#### Out-and-Out Lies

Of all the ways to lie, I like this one the best, probably because I get    15
tired of trying to figure out the real meanings behind things. At least I
can trust the bald-faced lie. I once asked my five-year-old nephew,
"Who broke the fence?" (I had seen him do it.) He answered, "The
murderers." Who could argue?

At least when this sort of lie is told it can be easily confronted. As    16
the person who is lied to, I know where I stand. The bald-faced lie
doesn't toy with my perceptions—it argues with them. It doesn't try to
refashion reality, it tries to refute it. *Read my lips . . .* No sleight of
hand. No guessing. If this were the only form of lying, there would be
no such things as floating anxiety or the adult-children-of-alcoholics
movement.

---

*The liar's punishment . . . is that he cannot believe anyone else.*    17

—George Bernard Shaw

These are only a few of the ways we lie. Or are lied to. As I said ear-    18
lier, it's not easy to entirely eliminate lies from our lives. No matter how
pious we may try to be, we will still embellish, hedge, and omit to lubri-
cate the daily machinery of living. But there is a world of difference
between telling functional lies and living a lie. Our acceptance of lies
becomes a cultural cancer that eventually shrouds and reorders reality
until moral garbage becomes as invisible to us as water is to a fish.

Maybe if I don't tell the bank the check's in the mail I'll be less    19
tolerant of the lies told me every day. A country song I once heard
said it all for me: "You've got to stand for something or you'll fall for
anything."

*Utne Reader,* Nov./Dec. 1992

## Getting Ready to Write

### ■ Examining the Reading: **Using Idea Mapping to Review and Organize Ideas**

Your knowledge of classification, definition, and example provides you
with a useful way to organize the information that you read. By summarizing a reading's main points in chart form (see p. 148), you will find the
material easier to remember and review.

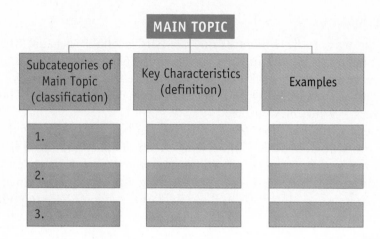

**EXERCISE** 8-10 ▶ | Complete the following map for "The Ways We Lie."

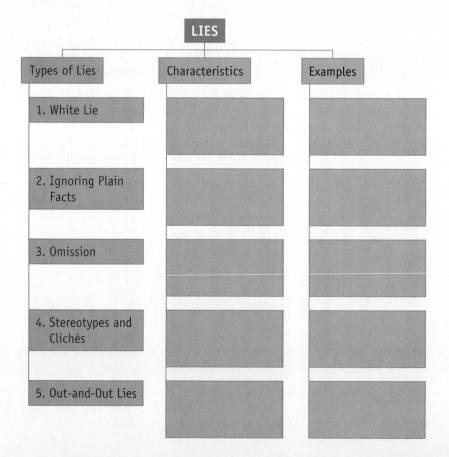

■ Thinking Critically: **Applying and Transferring Information**

The purpose of the reading is to make you aware of the various types of lies we tell and are told. On your map, you've recorded each type of lie and its characteristics. However, this information, like much information, is of little practical value to you unless you can use and apply it in new situations. For example, being able to list the types of lying is of little value if you cannot recognize when you or someone else is using these types of lies and cannot anticipate the consequences.

A critical thinker, then, is concerned with how ideas and information can be applied in or transferred to real situations. Because college instructors will expect you to be able to use what you are learning, many of their assignments and test questions will require this level of thinking.

Develop the habit of applying new information that you hear in lectures and read in textbooks. Ask yourself such questions as *How can I use this? To what situations does this information apply? Where have I observed this? What are some examples of this?* When you think of an application, make a note of it. You'll find, too, that this type of thinking will help you remember the information. Applications connect new ideas to what you already know or have experienced, thereby, increasing your retention.

**EXERCISE  8-11**  ▶ Apply the information in "The Ways We Lie" by identifying and giving some examples of how lies are used in television commercials or other forms of advertising.

■ Reacting to Ideas: **Discussion and Journal Writing**

1. What types of lies do you feel are the most common? Why?

2. Which lie is the most destructive? Which is least destructive? Why?

3. Can we eliminate lies from our daily life? If so, how?

4. Can lies ever have positive consequences? Give examples.

5. Do you think that the types of lies we tell change as we get older? If so, how? If not, why not?

## Writing Assignments

### Writing About the Reading

1. Write a paragraph explaining what Ericsson means when she says of stereotypes and clichés: "They take a single tree and make it a landscape."

**Essay Option**     2. The concluding section of this essay begins with one quotation and ends with another. Write an essay explaining how each describes a logical outcome of lying and accepting lies.

### Writing About Your Ideas

3. Ericsson views stereotyping as a form of lying. Write a paragraph describing a stereotype you most object to and explaining why.

**Essay Option**     4. Ericsson opens her essay by describing several lies she told over the course of a day. Write an essay in which you describe lies you recently have told or been told and how you felt about telling or hearing them.

## REVISION CHECKLIST

1. Is your paragraph or essay appropriate for your audience? Does it give them the background information they need? Will it interest them?

2. Will your paragraph or essay accomplish your purpose?

3. Is your main point clearly expressed?

4. Is each detail relevant? Does each explain or support your main point?

5. Have you supported your main point with sufficient detail to make it understandable and believable?

6. Did you use specific words to explain each detail?

**For Example Writing**

7. Does the topic sentence or thesis statement express a viewpoint toward the topic?

8. Is each example understandable by itself?

9. Are there sufficient examples to explain your main point to the intended audience?

10. Are the examples arranged in a logical order?

11. Are ideas connected with transitional words and phrases?

**For Classification Writing**

7. Does the topic sentence or thesis statement identify the topic and method of classification?

8. Is each subgroup adequately explained?

9. Is equal detail provided for each subgroup?

10. Are the subgroups presented in a logical order?

11. Are ideas connected with transitional words and phrases?

| | |
|---|---|
| For Definition Writing | 7. Does the topic sentence or thesis statement identify the term to be defined? |
| | 8. Do you identify the class to which the term belongs and include a distinguishing characteristic? |
| | 9. Does the paragraph or essay include sufficient detail (examples, classification, explaining what the term is not, tracing its origin, or description) arranged in an easily understandable order? |
| | 10. Are specific words and phrases used? |
| | 11. Are ideas connected with transitional words and phrases? |
| For All Writing | 12. Have you proofread? (See the inside back cover of this book for a proofreading checklist.) |

**Dangling Modifiers**

A modifier is a word or group of words that describes another word or qualifies or limits the meaning of another word. When a modifier appears at the beginning of the sentence, it must be followed immediately by the word it describes. Dangling modifiers are *not* followed by the word they describe. Dangling modifiers either modify nothing or do not clearly refer to the correct word or word group.

DANGLING:    After getting off the bus, the driver pulled away.
CORRECT:    After I got off the bus, the driver pulled away.

**How to Correct Dangling Modifiers**

There are two ways to correct dangling modifiers:

1.  Add a word or words so that the modifier describes the word or words it is intended to describe. Place the new word(s) just after the modifier.

    DANGLING:    While sitting under the maple tree, ants started to attack.
    CORRECT:    While sitting under the maple tree, I was attacked by ants.

2.  Change the modifier to a dependent clause. (You may need to change the verb in the modifier.)

    DANGLING:    After giving the dog a flea bath, the dog hid under the bed.
    CORRECT:    After I gave the dog a flea bath, she hid under the bed.

**Rate Your Ability to Spot and Correct Dangling Modifiers**

Correct any dangling modifiers used in the following sentences. If the sentence is correct, mark **C** in front of the sentence.

_____   1. While standing on the ladder with tar paper, Harvey patched the roof.

_____   2. Being nervous, the test seemed more difficult than it was.

_____   3. Waiting to drop a class at the Records Office, the line seemed to go on forever.

_____   4. After many years, Joan had received her degree in engineering.

_____   5. Moving the couch, the elevator was, of course, out of order.

## SKILL REFRESHER CONTINUED

_____  6. Watching the evening news, the power went out.

_____  7. After deciding to mow the lawn, it began to rain.

_____  8. Being very tired, the long wait was unbearable.

_____  9. Skiing downhill, the wind picked up.

_____  10. At the age of eighteen, the phone company hired me.

Score _____

Check your answers using the Answer Key on page 484. If you missed more than two, you need additional review and practice recognizing and correcting dangling modifiers. Refer to page 433 of Part VI, "Reviewing the Basics."

## CHAPTER SUMMARY

**Writing Skills**

1. Examples are specific details that explain a general idea or statement. To develop a paragraph or essay using examples, be sure that
   • your examples are relevant and sufficient.
   • each example is as specific as possible.
   • it is clear how each example illustrates your main point.
   • you use transitional words and phrases to connect your ideas.

2. Classification is a way of explaining by dividing the topic into groups or parts. To explain a topic using classification,
   • decide how you will divide the topic into groups.
   • develop a topic sentence or thesis statement that identifies your topic as well as your method of classification.
   • explain each subgroup by giving adequate detail.
   • use transitional words and phrases to connect your ideas.

3. Definition is a method of explaining a word's meaning. When using definition to explain, be sure to
   • identify the term you are defining.
   • place the term in a general group and offer a distinguishing characteristic.

- use one or more examples, classify the term, explain what the term is not, trace the term's meaning over time, or use descriptive language to develop your definition.
- use transitional words and phrases to connect your ideas.

1. With your knowledge of classification, definition, and example, you can summarize the main points of a reading by making a map or chart. Include subcategories, key characteristics, and examples.

2. Be sure to apply and transfer ideas and information to new situations. Use what you have learned, connecting it to your own experience.

# Comparison and Contrast

Shopping for a used car? Imagine that you eventually narrow your choices to two cars—a Nissan and a Chevrolet. Each meets your basic requirements in terms of cost, mileage, and mechanical soundness. Which do you buy? How do you choose? Or suppose you are thinking of changing your major from accounting, but you can't decide whether to switch to marketing or business administration. Again, how do you decide? In each situation, you find similarities and differences among your options. When you consider similarities, you are comparing. When you consider differences, you are contrasting.

In your course work, instructors will ask you to compare and contrast a variety of different people, ideas, events, or things. For example, your biology instructor may want you to compare the early biologists Mendel and Darwin; your psychology instructor may ask you to analyze the differences between two (or more) theories of motivation. In some instances you will be asked to discuss only similarities or only differences, but in many instances you will need to write about both. In this chapter you will learn how to analyze similarities and differences and use different methods of organization to present the results of your analysis.

Comparing and contrasting ideas can get complicated. It requires excellent planning and organization. Consequently, a major portion of this chapter is devoted to strategies for organizing your material and planning your writing.

## Identifying Similarities and Differences

If you have two items to compare or contrast, the first step is to figure out how they are similar and how they are different. Be sure to select subjects that are neither too similar nor too different. If they are,

## CHAPTER OBJECTIVES

*In this chapter you will learn to*

1. analyze similarities and differences.
2. develop paragraphs and essays using comparison and contrast.

155

you will have either too little or too much to say. Follow this effective two-step approach: (1) brainstorm to produce a two-column list of characteristics, and (2) match up the items and identify points of comparison and contrast.

### Brainstorming to Produce a Two-Column List

Let's say you want to write about two friends—Rhonda and Maria. Here is how to identify their similarities and differences.

1.  Brainstorm and list the characteristics of each person.

    | *Rhonda* | *Maria* |
    |---|---|
    | reserved, quiet | age, 27 |
    | age, 22 | single parent, two children |
    | private person | outgoing |
    | friends since childhood | loves to be center of |
    | married, no children | attention |
    | hates parties | loves sports and competition |
    | fun to shop with | plays softball and tennis |
    | tells me everything about | often |
    | her life | |

2.  When you have finished your list, match up items that share the same feature or characteristic—age, personality type, marital status—as shown below.

    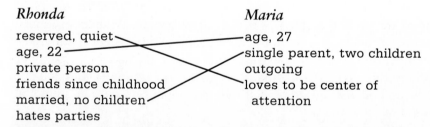

    *Rhonda*

    reserved, quiet
    age, 22
    private person
    friends since childhood
    married, no children
    hates parties

    *Maria*

    age, 27
    single parent, two children
    outgoing
    loves to be center of
    attention

3.  When you have listed an item in a certain category for one person but not for the other, try to think of a corresponding detail that will balance the lists. For instance, you listed "friends since childhood" for Rhonda, so you could indicate how long you have known Maria.

**EXERCISE**  **9-1**  Make a two-column list of similarities and differences for two of the following topics.

1.  two courses you are taking
2.  two tasks (one difficult, one easy)

3. two forms of communication
4. two decisions you made recently
5. two businesses
6. two types of entertainment

### Identifying Points of Comparison and Contrast

The next step is to add a column to the right side of your list and reorganize the list so that the items you have matched up appear next to each other. In the new column, write the term that describes or categorizes each set of items on your two lists. These are general categories we will call "Points of Comparison/Contrast." As you reorganize, you may find it easier to group several items together. For example, you might group some details about Rhonda and Maria together under the category of personality. Study the following list, noticing the points of comparison and contrast that have been added in the left-hand column.

| *Points of Comparison/Contrast* | *Rhonda* | *Maria* |
|---|---|---|
| personality | quiet, reserved, private person | outgoing, loves to be center of attention |
| marital status | married, no children | single parent, two children |
| length of friendship | friends since childhood | met at work last year |
| shared activities | go shopping | play softball together, go to parties |

**EXERCISE** 9-2 ▶ For the two topics you chose in Exercise 9-1, match up the items and identify points of comparison/contrast.

This two-step process can work in reverse order as well. You can decide points of comparison/contrast first and then brainstorm characteristics for each point. For example, suppose you are comparing and contrasting two restaurants. Points of comparison/contrast might be location, price, speed of service, menu variety, and quality of food. If you are comparing or contrasting Professors Rodriquez and Meyer, you might do so on the following points.

| Points of Comparison/Contrast | Professor Meyer | Professor Rodriquez |
|---|---|---|
| amount of homework | | |
| type of exams | | |
| class organization | | |
| how easy to talk to | | |
| grading system | | |
| style of teaching | | |

You could then fill in columns 2 and 3 with appropriate details, as shown below.

| Points of Comparison/Contrast | Professor Meyer | Professor Rodriquez |
|---|---|---|
| amount of homework | assignment due for every class | hardly any |
| type of exams | essay | multiple choice and essay |
| class organization | well organized | free and easy |
| how easy to talk to | always around, approachable | approachable, but talks a lot |
| grading system | 50% quizzes, 50% essay exams | 100% exams |
| style of teaching | lecture | class discussion, questions |

Once you have completed your three-column list, the next step is to study your list and decide whether to write about similarities or differences, or both. It is usually easier to concentrate on one or the other. If you deem similarities to be more significant, you might need to omit or deemphasize differences—and vice versa if you decide to write about differences.

**EXERCISE  9-3**

List at least three points of comparison/contrast for each of the following topics. Then choose one topic and make a three-column list on a separate sheet of paper.

1. Two films you have seen recently
   Points of comparison/contrast:

   a. _____

   b. _____

c. _____

d. _____

e. _____

2. Hard rock and soft rock music
   Points of comparison/contrast:

   a. _____

   b. _____

   c. _____

   d. _____

   e. _____

3. Baseball and football players
   Points of comparison/contrast:

   a. _____

   b. _____

   c. _____

   d. _____

   e. _____

## Developing Your Topic Sentence

Your topic sentence should identify the two subjects that you will compare or contrast and state whether you will focus on similarities, differences, or both. It may also indicate what points you will compare or contrast. Suppose you compare two former U.S. presidents—Reagan and Ford. Obviously, you could not cover every aspect of their presidencies in a single paragraph. Instead, you could limit your comparison to their personalities, administrative style, or popularity.

Here are a few sample topic sentences that meet the above requirements:

1. Former presidents Reagan and Ford have vastly different personalities.
2. Both Ford and Reagan used a hands-off administrative style, allowing their staffs to make important decisions.
3. Reagan was much more popular with the press while in office than was Ford.

Be sure to avoid topic sentences that announce what you plan to do. Here's an example: "I'll compare network news and local news and show why I prefer local news."

**EXERCISE  9-4**   For the two topics you worked with in Exercises 9-1 and 9-2, write a topic sentence for a paragraph that develops the topic.

## Organizing Your Paragraph

Once you have identified similarities and differences and drafted a topic sentence, you are ready to organize your paragraph. There are two ways you can organize a comparison or contrast paragraph: (1) subject by subject or (2) point by point.

### Subject-by-Subject Organization

Subjects are the two entities you are comparing or contrasting. In the subject-by-subject method, you write first about one of your subjects, covering it completely, and then you write about the other, covering it completely. Ideally, you cover the same points of comparison and contrast for both and in the same order. Let's return to the comparison between Professors Meyer and Rodriquez. With subject-by-subject organization, you first discuss Professor Meyer—his class organization, exams, and grading system; you then discuss Professor Rodriquez—her class organization, exams, and grading system. You can visualize this arrangement as follows:

| *Subject* | *Points of Comparison/Contrast* |
|---|---|
| 1. Professor Meyer | a. class organization |
| 2. Professor Rodriquez | b. exams |
| | c. grading system |

To develop each subject, focus on the same kinds of details and discuss the same points of comparison in the same order. If you are discussing only similarities or only differences, then organize your points within each topic using a most-to-least or least-to-most arrangement. If you are discussing both similarities and differences, then you might discuss points of similarity first and then points of difference, or vice versa.

Here is a sample paragraph using subject-by-subject organization.

Two excellent teachers, Professor Meyer and Professor Rodriquez, present a study in contrasting teaching styles. Professor Meyer is extremely organized. He conducts each class the same way. He reviews the assignment, lectures about the new chapter, and explains the next assignment. He gives essay exams, and they are always based on important lecture topics. Because the topics are predictable, you know you are not wasting your time when you study. Professor Meyer's grading depends half on class participation and half on the essay exams. Professor Rodriquez, on the other hand, has an easy-going style. Each class is different and seems to reflect whatever she thinks will help us understand what she's teaching. Her classes are fun because you never know what to expect. Professor Rodriquez gives both multiple-choice and essay exams. These are difficult to study for because they are unpredictable. Our final grade is based entirely on the exams, so each exam requires a lot of studying beforehand. Although each professor teaches very differently, I am figuring out how to learn from each particular style.

**EXERCISE** 9-5 | Using the subject-by-subject method of organization, write a comparison and contrast paragraph on one of the topics you worked with in Exercises 9-1 and 9-2.

### Point-by-Point Organization

In the point-by-point method of organization, you discuss both of your subjects together for each point of comparison and contrast. For the paragraph on Professors Meyer and Rodriquez, you would talk about how each organizes his or her class, then what kinds of exams each gives, and then the grading system, and so on.

You can visualize this organization as follows:

| *Points of Comparison/Contrast* | *Subject* |
|---|---|
| a. class organization | 1. Professor Meyer |
| | 2. Professor Rodriquez |
| b. exams | 1. Professor Meyer |
| | 2. Professor Rodriquez |
| c. grading system | 1. Professor Meyer |
| | 2. Professor Rodriquez |

When using this organization, maintain consistency by discussing the same subject first for each point. (That is, always discuss Professor Meyer first and Professor Rodriquez second for each point.)

If your paragraph focuses only on similarities or only on differences, then arrange your points in a least-to-most or most-to-least pattern.

Here is a sample paragraph using point-by-point organization.

Professor Meyer and Professor Rodriquez demonstrate very different teaching styles in how they operate their classes, how they give exams, and how they grade us. Professor Meyer's classes are highly organized; we work through the lesson every day in the same order. Professor Rodriquez uses an opposite approach. She creates a lesson to fit the material, which enables us to learn the most. Their exams differ too. Professor Meyer gives standard, predictable essay exams that are based on his lectures. Professor Rodriquez gives both multiple-choice and essay exams, so we never know what to expect. In addition, each professor grades differently. Professor Meyer counts class participation as half of our grade, so if you talk in class and do reasonably well on the exams, you will probably pass the course. Professor Rodriquez, on the other hand, counts the exams 100 percent, so you *have* to do well on them to pass the course. Each professor has a unique, enjoyable teaching style, and I am learning a great deal from each.

**EXERCISE** ▶ 9-6 | Using the point-by-point method of organization, write a comparison and contrast paragraph on the topic you chose for Exercise 9-5.

### Developing Your Points of Comparison and Contrast

As you discuss each point, don't feel as if you must compare or contrast in every sentence. Your paragraph should not just list similarities and/or differences. For every point, provide explanation, descriptive details, and examples.

Try to maintain a balance in your treatment of each subject and each point of comparison and contrast. Give equal attention to each point and each subject. If you give an example for one subject, try to do so for the other as well.

## Useful Transitional Words and Phrases

Transitions are particularly important in comparison and contrast writing. Because you are discussing two subjects and covering similar points for each, your readers can easily become confused. Table 9-1 lists commonly used transitional words and phrases.

| TABLE 9-1 | **Transitional Words and Phrases for Comparison and Contrast Writing** |
|---|---|
| To show similarities | likewise, similarly, in the same way, too, also |
| To show differences | however, on the contrary, unlike, on the other hand |

Each method of organization uses different transitions in different places. If you choose a subject-by-subject organization, you'll need the strongest transition in the middle of the paragraph, when you switch from one subject to another. You will also need a transition each time you move from one point to another while still on the same subject. In the following paragraph, notice the underlined transitional sentence.

> Two dogs of the same breed may look similar, but they can have completely different personalities. My two golden retrievers, Meg and Dude, are good examples. Meg is shy and is afraid of her own shadow. When guests arrive, she quivers and whines and runs to hide in the basement. Dude, on the other hand, is completely the opposite. He is forward and pushy. He eagerly greets guests and lets them know whether he likes them. Dude is alert and protective. He occupies a good part of each day watching cars pass the house, growling at any that drive by too slowly. Despite their differences, Meg and Dude are both lovable companions.

This paragraph uses a subject-by-subject organization. A strong transition emphasizes the switch from Meg to Dude.

If you choose point-by-point organization, use transitions as you move from one subject to the other. On each point, your reader needs to know quickly whether the two subjects are similar or different. Here is an example:

> Although colds and hay fever are both annoying, their symptoms and causes differ. Hay fever causes my eyes to itch and water. I sneeze excessively, bothering those around me. Colds, on the other hand, make me feel stuffy, with a runny nose and a cough. For me, hay fever arrives in the summer, but colds linger on through late fall, winter, and early spring. Their causes differ, too. Pollens produce hay fever. I am most sensitive to pollen from wildflowers and corn tassels. Unlike hay fever, viruses, which are passed from person to person by air or body contact, cause colds.

Notice that each time the writer switched from hay fever to colds, a transition was used.

**EXERCISE 9-7** Reread the paragraph you wrote for Exercises 9-5 and 9-6. Add transitions to make your organization clearer.

## Applying Your Skills to Essay Writing

When comparing or contrasting in much detail, you will often find an essay, rather than a single paragraph, is needed. Use the following suggestions for writing comparison and contrast essays.

**1. Be sure your essay has a concise thesis statement.** Your thesis statement, like your paragraph's topic sentence, should identify your subjects, indicate whether you will focus on similarities, differences, or both, and express a viewpoint toward your subjects.

**2. Focus on your purpose for writing.** Often, your primary purpose is not to show how one thing is similar to or different from another. Instead, your purpose usually is to make a point or reach a conclusion through comparison or contrast. In comparing two poems, for example, you may want to examine how two poets from different centuries and different parts of the world describe the same human dilemma.

**3. Choose meaningful points of comparison.** With many topics, there are many possible points of comparison. Be sure to choose points of comparison that will support your purpose in writing and your thesis statement. For example, when you compare two friends, your points of comparison might be hats, jewelry, shoes, and so forth if your purpose in writing is to discuss fashion. If, however, your purpose in writing is to discuss qualities of friendship, then your points of comparison might be helpfulness, generosity, and trust.

**4. Be sure to follow the organization you have chosen (subject by subject or point by point) consistently throughout your essay.**

**5. Use transitions to guide your reader.** Transitions are even more important in essays than in paragraphs. With longer and oftentimes more complicated comparisons or contrasts, essays must have transitions to enable readers to follow your train of thought.

**EXERCISE** ▶ **9-8**

Suppose you are taking a course titled "Marriage and Family" and are studying the social role of families and the customs of dating and marrying in Western culture. Your instructor has asked you to complete one of the following assignments. Choose one topic and draft an essay.

1. The functions of a family include emotional support, economic support, and socialization (the sharing of beliefs, attitudes, and values). Choose two families you know, and compare and/or contrast how they function using one or more of these points of comparison, as well as any of your own choosing.

2. The functions of dating include entertainment, learning to get along with others, development of companionship and intimacy, and opportunity

to choose a spouse. Think of two dates you have had, and compare and/or contrast them using some or all of these points of comparison.

3. The functions of weddings are to make a public announcement, to provide a celebration, to make a marriage legal, and to serve as a marker or milestone for the beginning of a new life. Think of two weddings you have attended, and compare and/or contrast how well each fulfilled some or all of these functions.

## Thinking Before Reading

This reading, "Are There Sex Differences in Emotion?" was taken from a psychology textbook by Saul Kassin. The selection presents the results of research that examined differences between men's and women's emotions. This reading is a good example of comparison and contrast organization, so as you read, notice how the writer organizes his ideas.

1. Preview the reading using the steps described on page 45.
2. Activate your thinking by answering the following:
   a. Do you think men and women differ in how they express their emotions? If so, why?
   b. In your own home, have you observed differences in the ways men and women express their emotions? If so, what are they?
   c. Do you think one gender is more aware of other people's feelings than the other? If so, why?

**READING**

## Are There Sex Differences in Emotion?
### Saul Kassin

When people are asked to describe the typical man and woman, they consistently say that women are more emotional than men are (or, to put it another way, that men are less emotional than women are). This belief is found in many different cultures and among young children as well as adults (Fabes & Martin, 1991; Williams & Best, 1982). In a study that illustrates just how deeply ingrained this stereotype is, adult subjects were shown a videotape of a nine-month-old baby. Half were told that they were watching a boy; the other half thought the baby was a girl. In fact, everyone saw the same tape. Yet when the baby burst into tears over a jack-in-the-box, subjects were gender-biased in their interpretations of the child's emotional state: *he* was *angry, she* was *frightened* (Condry & Condry, 1976).

Are there sex differences in emotion, or is this perception a mere illusion? The research is mixed, but certain differences do seem to emerge with regularity (Brody & Hall, 1993; Grossman & Wood, 1993; LaFrance & Banaji, 1992). On the one hand, women describe themselves as more emotional—or men describe themselves as less emotional—when asked direct questions about their emotionality. On the other hand, there is little support for the conclusion that the sexes differ in their actual feelings. Both men and women become happy when they achieve something that they have strived for. Similarly, both sexes experience sadness over the loss of a loved one, anger when frustrated, fearful when in danger, embarrassed when they slip up in front of others. Men and women also exhibit the same facial expressions and autonomic reactions to emotion-triggering events. People surely differ in their propensity for happiness, sadness, anger, embarrassment, fear, and other emotions, but these differences say more about us as individuals than as men or women.

So, in what ways are women more emotional than men? One clear finding is that regardless of how men and women actually feel, the sexes do often differ in their public expressions of emotion, or *self-disclosure*. Based on a review of 205 studies involving more than 23,000 subjects, Kathryn Dindia and Mike Allen (1992) concluded that women self-disclose to friends, parents, spouses, and others more than men do (in turn, people in general self-disclose more to women than to men). Women are also more likely to wear emotions on the face and show more muscle activity on the facial EMG (Dimberg, 1990). The result is that people in general can "read" women better than they can men. In one study, for example, male and female subjects saw slides that evoked feelings of joy, sadness, fear, surprise, anger, or disgust. As they watched, their facial reactions were recorded with a hidden camera, and the videotapes were later shown to observers. Observers were better at judging the emotions felt by the expressive female subjects (Wagner et al., 1986).

Why are women more open and expressive than men? One easy explanation is that girls more than boys are socialized at an early age to talk about their feelings. Researchers who analyze parent-child conversations in the home find that parents talk more about the emotional aspect of events with their daughters than with their sons ("That music was scary, wasn't it?" "You were happy, weren't you?")—even when the children are only two or three years old (Dunn et al., 1987; Kuebli & Fivush, 1992). Another reason, at least in our culture, is that although women are permitted if not encouraged to be expressive (except when it comes to rage and anger, emotions that men are allowed to express and women are supposed to contain), men are taught to be stoic—to fulfill the ideal of the strong, silent type. Masculinity norms demand that men publicly suppress their own fears, sorrows, and weaknesses. As the saying goes, "big boys don't cry" (Tavris, 1992).

Another possible basis for the perceived sex differences in emotion is *5* that women outperform men at using nonverbal cues to make judgments about how *others* are feeling. In a series of studies, Robert Rosenthal and his colleagues (1979) showed subjects 220 two-second film clips of an actor revealing various emotions in her face, body, and/or voice. After each film, the subjects were asked to make a social judgment: Was she expressing love or trying to seduce someone? Was she saying a prayer or talking to a lost child? Research shows that women outscore men—not only in this test but in others like it (Hall, 1984). For example, Mark Costanzo and Dane Archer (1989) presented subjects with thirty videotaped scenes, each depicting a natural, spontaneous behavior and followed by a multiple-choice question. In one scene, for example, subjects saw two women interacting with an eleven-year-old boy and were asked to determine which woman was the boy's mother. In another scene, subjects watched a female student talking on the phone and were asked to determine whether she was talking to her mother, her boyfriend, or to a close female friend. Once again, sex differences were found, again suggesting that women are more attuned than men to the emotional state of others.

In conclusion, there is some basis for the widespread belief that *6* women are more emotional than men, even though the sexes do not differ significantly in their actual feelings. Research has shown that men and women differ in how they publicly express their emotions and in their awareness of the emotional state of other people. This fact may be largely due to differences in how boys and girls are socialized in regard to their emotions.

*Psychology, 1995*

## Getting Ready to Write

■ **Examining the Reading: Using the Three-Column List for Review**

The three-column list that you constructed to organize your ideas before writing also may be used as an effective study and review technique. As you read other writers' comparison and contrast pieces, organize your notes on their ideas into a three-column format. A three-column list for "Are There Sex Differences in Emotion?" would be organized as follows:

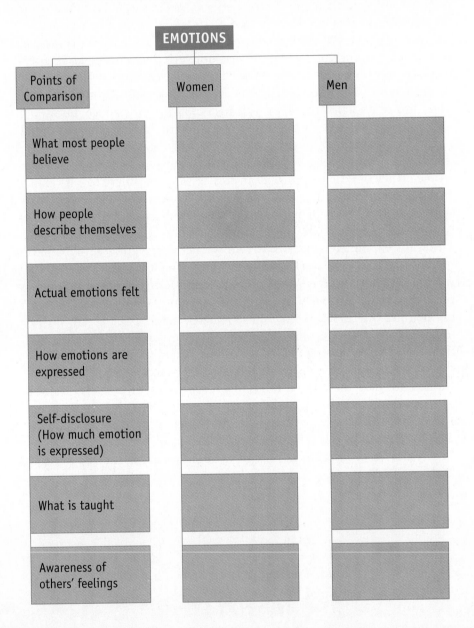

**EXERCISE 9-9** | Complete the above three-column list by supplying details from the reading.

## ■ Thinking Critically: **Identifying and Examining Supporting Evidence**

Most writers who express their opinions, state viewpoints, make generalizations, or offer hypotheses also provide data or evidence in support of their ideas. Your task as a critical reader is twofold: first, identify the evidence; and second, weigh and evaluate the quality of this evidence.

In assessing the adequacy of evidence, you must be concerned with the type of evidence being presented and the relevance of that evidence. The following types of evidence are commonly used:

- personal experience or observation
- statistical data
- examples, particular events, or situations that illustrate
- analogies (comparisons with similar situations)
- informed opinion (the opinions of experts and authorities)
- historical documentation
- experimental evidence
- reports of research

Evaluating the evidence an author uses to support his or her main statement on a subject is important because this evidence can help you determine if the statement is accurate and believable.

Ask the following questions:

1. Is the evidence relevant?
2. How does the evidence support the main statement?
3. Is there a sufficient amount of evidence?
4. Did the author provide representative evidence? That is, is the evidence representative of the body of information that is available—or did the author find an exceptional piece of evidence to support his or her statement?
5. Is there evidence available that the author did not report and that does not support his or her statement?

Not all of these questions are easily answered. In some situations you may have to do additional research. With most textbooks, you can be confident that the author, a scholar and expert in the discipline, has provided you with relevant, representative evidence. However, when reading other sources, approach evidence with a questioning, critical viewpoint.

**EXERCISE**  9-10 | List general statements for which the author gives supporting evidence in "Are There Sex Differences in Emotion?" After each, indicate what supporting evidence is provided. The first one is done for you.

|  | *Statement* | *Supporting Evidence* |
|---|---|---|
| 1. | People consistently say that women are more emotional than men. | • found in many different cultures<br>• believed by both adults and children<br>• gender-biased interpretations of child's emotional state in experiment |
| 2. | _____ | _____ |
| 3. | _____ | _____ |
| 4. | _____ | _____ |

■ **Reacting to Ideas: Discussion and Journal Writing**

Use the following questions to generate ideas about the reading:

1. Did the author use point-by-point or subject-by-subject organization?

2. What in the reading did you particularly agree or disagree with? Explain using evidence from your own experience.

3. Should boys be raised to be more open about their emotions? If your answer is yes, why do you think so?

4. Do you agree that men feel emotions as deeply as women? If so, why?

5. If you were viewing the videotape of two women interacting with an eleven-year-old boy, what would you look for to determine which woman was the boy's mother?

# Writing Assignments

## Writing About the Reading

1. Drawing from the information contained in the reading, write a paragraph that compares how men and women deal with emotions. Use a point-by-point organization.

**Essay Option**
2. Write an essay defending the author's generalization that "people in general can read women better than they can men." Develop your essay through examples from your personal experience.

## Writing About Your Ideas

3. Write a paragraph comparing your mother's emotional profile with that of your father—or compare the profiles of some other couple you know.

**Essay Option**
4. Write a paragraph comparing men and women on some other characteristic, such as use of language, aggressiveness, or nurturing ability.

5. Write an essay on how emotional differences between men and women can lead to miscommunication or failed relationships. Support your statements with evidence.

## REVISION CHECKLIST

1. Is your paragraph or essay appropriate for your audience? Does it give them the background information they need? Will it interest them?

2. Will your paragraph or essay accomplish your purpose?

3. Is your main point clearly expressed?

4. Is each detail relevant? Does each explain or support your main point?

5. Have you supported your main point with sufficient detail to make it understandable and believable?

6. Do you use specific words to explain each detail?

For Comparison
and Contrast
Writing

7. Does your topic sentence or thesis statement identify the two sub-jects that you compare or contrast?

8. Does your topic sentence or thesis statement indicate whether you will focus on similarities, differences, or both?

9. Is your comparison and contrast writing organized using a subject-by-subject or point-by-point arrangement?

10. For each point of comparison, have you provided sufficient expla-nation, descriptive details, and examples?

11. Have you used transitions to indicate changes in subject or point of comparison?

12. Have you proofread? (See the inside back cover of this book for a proofreading checklist.)

# SKILL REFRESHER

## Misplaced Modifiers

Misplaced modifiers are words or phrases that do not modify or explain other words the way the writer intended.

MISPLACED:   Crispy and spicy, the waitress served the chicken wings to our table. [Was the waitress crispy and spicy, or were the wings?]

CORRECT:   The waitress served the crispy, spicy chicken wings to our table.

MISPLACED:   I saw a dress in a magazine that cost $1200. [Did the magazine or the dress cost $1200?]

CORRECT:   In a magazine, I saw a dress that cost $1200.

MISPLACED:   Already late for class, the red light delayed Joe even longer. [Was the light or Joe late for class?]

CORRECT:   The red light delayed Joe, already late for class, even longer.

## How to Avoid Misplaced Modifiers

To avoid misplaced modifiers, be sure to place the modifier immediately before or after the word or words it modifies.

## Rate Your Ability to Spot and Correct Misplaced Modifiers

Identify and correct the sentences containing misplaced modifiers.

1. Studiously, the test was previewed by Marietta before she began answering the questions.

2. The book was checked out by a student that Mark had returned late.

3. Keshim proudly turned in his research paper that had taken two months to complete.

4. Shocked, the article about the large donations political candidates receive from interest groups caused Lily to reconsider how she viewed candidates and their campaign promises.

5. The student-loan check was cashed by Bryant that was desperately needed.

6. Angry with the delay, the referee finally arrived and the crowd booed.

7. Called aboriginals, the native people of Australia have a culture rich with hunting skills and legends.

8. Young, unhappy, and lovelorn, the poetry of Emily Dickinson reveals a particular kind of misery and pain.

9. A national problem, the governors of all the states met to discuss homelessness.

## SKILL REFRESHER CONTINUED

10. Concerned about the risk of being exposed to the virus, many AIDS patients are refused treatment by health-care workers.

Score_____

Check your answers using the Answer Key on page 484. If you missed more than two, you need additional review and practice in recognizing and correcting misplaced modifiers. Refer to page 432 of Part VI, "Reviewing the Basics."

## CHAPTER SUMMARY

**Writing Skills**

1. Comparison and contrast writing explains similarities and/or differences between two subjects.

2. To develop ideas
   • use a two-column chart to identify and list similarities and differences.
   • add a third column, "Points of Comparison and Contrast," to categorize items on your list.

3. Your topic sentence or thesis statement should
   • identify the two subjects that you will compare or contrast.
   • indicate whether you will focus on similarities, differences, or both.

4. Organize your paragraph or essay using either
   • subject-by-subject organization, or
   • point-by-point organization.

5. For each point of comparison, be sure to provide sufficient explanation, details, and examples.

6. Use transitions to indicate changes in subject or point of comparison.

**Reading and Critical Thinking Skills**

1. For study and review, use the three-column list to organize and summarize an author's ideas.

2. Be sure to identify and examine the evidence an author provides to support his or her main statement.

# Cause and Effect

Each day we face situations that require cause-and-effect analysis. Some are daily events; others mark important life decisions. Why won't my car start? Why didn't I get my student loan check? What will happen if I skip class today? How will my family react if I decide to get married? We seek to make sense of and control our lives by understanding why things happen (causes) and what will happen as a result (effects).

Cause and effect is a common method of organizing and discussing ideas. Cause-and-effect thinking is used in many courses of study. In psychology, for example, you might study

| | |
|---|---|
| why children are self-centered | (causes) |
| what causes phobias (fears) | (causes) |
| the effects of depression | (effects) |
| how people react to stress | (effects) |

You will also find yourself writing in the cause-and-effect mode or pattern in both personal and academic situations, as illustrated below.

### Personal Examples

- a letter to a bank explaining why a loan payment is late
- a car-accident report to an insurance company explaining how an accident occurred
- a letter to your parents explaining why you need money

### Academic Examples

- essay exams that begin with "Explain why" or "Discuss the causes of"
- assignments that ask you to agree or disagree with a statement and explain your reasons
- exercises that ask you to predict the consequences of a recent political event

CHAPTER OBJECTIVES

*In this chapter you will learn to*

1. understand cause-and-effect relationships.
2. plan and organize cause-and-effect paragraphs and essays.

## Distinguishing Between Cause and Effect

How do we distinguish between causes and effects? To determine causes, ask, "Why did this happen?" To identify effects, ask, "What happened because of this?" Let's consider an everyday situation: you turn the ignition key, but your car won't start because it's out of gas. This is a simple case in which one cause produces one effect. You can visualize this situation as follows:

*Cause*       *Effect*

You are out of gas.⟶Your car won't start.

Here are a few other examples of one cause producing one effect:

*Cause*       *Effect*

You forgot to mail your ⟶ You receive a notice of cancellation.
car-insurance payment.

Chemical wastes are ⟶ The stream is polluted.
dumped in a stream.

You wrote your paper ⟶ You can revise without retyping.
using a word processor.

Most situations, however, are much more complicated than those shown above, and even a simple cause-and-effect sequence may contain hidden complexities. Perhaps your car was out of gas because you forgot to buy gas, and you forgot because you were making other preparations for the upcoming visit of a good friend. Suppose you missed your math class because the car would not start, and an exam was scheduled for that day. Missing the exam lowered your average, and, as a result, you failed the course. You can see, then, that cause and effect often works like a chain reaction: one cause triggers an effect, which in turn becomes the cause of another effect. In a chain reaction, each event in a series influences the next, as shown below.

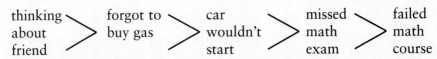

thinking about friend > forgot to buy gas > car wouldn't start > missed math exam > failed math course

Other times, many causes may contribute to a single effect or many effects may result from a single cause. For example, there may be several reasons why you decided to major in accounting:

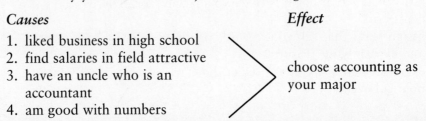

*Causes*       *Effect*

1. liked business in high school
2. find salaries in field attractive
3. have an uncle who is an accountant
4. am good with numbers

> choose accounting as your major

There may be several effects of your decision to reduce your hours at your part-time job.

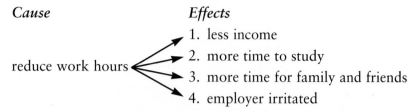

*Cause*                                    *Effects*

                                           1. less income

reduce work hours                          2. more time to study

                                           3. more time for family and friends

                                           4. employer irritated

Multiple causes and multiple effects, then, are common. When analyzing a cause-and-effect situation that you plan to write about, ask yourself the following questions:

1. What are the causes? What are the effects? (To help answer these questions, draw a diagram of the situation.)
2. Which should be emphasized—cause or effect?
3. Are there single or multiple causes? Single or multiple effects?
4. Is a chain reaction involved?

**EXERCISE 10-1** ▶ Complete each of the following diagrams by adding a cause or effect, as needed. The first one is done for you.

*Cause* ——————————————▶ *Effect*

1.

watching too much TV

  a. not enough time to study

  b. get "hooked"–can't stop watching

  c. feel as if I got nothing accomplished

2. a. _____

  b. _____ ——▶ popularity of radio talk shows

  c. _____

3. a. _____

  b. _____ ——▶ children who misbehave

  c. _____

4.

alcoholism among teenagers

  a. _____

  b. _____

  c. _____

5.  a. _____

    b. _____  ⟶ the popularity of horror films

    c. _____

6.

    employee theft  ◁  a. _____

                        b. _____

                        c. _____

## Developing Your Topic Sentence

To write effective topic sentences for cause-and-effect paragraphs, do the following:

**1. Clarify the cause-and-effect relationship.** Before you write, carefully identify the causes and the effects. If you are uncertain, divide a sheet of paper into two columns. Label one column "Causes" and the other "Effects." Brainstorm about your topic, placing your ideas in the appropriate column.

**2. Decide whether to emphasize causes or effects.** In a single paragraph, it is best to focus on either causes or effects—not both. For example, suppose you are writing about students who drop out of college. You need to decide whether to discuss why they drop out (causes) or what happens to students who drop out (effects). Your topic sentence should indicate whether you are going to emphasize causes or effects. (In essays, you may consider both causes and effects.)

**3. Determine if the events are related or independent.** Analyze the causes or effects to discover if they occurred as part of a chain reaction or are not related to one another. Your topic sentence should suggest the type of relationship you are writing about.

If you are writing about a chain of events, your topic sentence should reflect this—for example, "A series of events led up to my sister's decision to drop out of college." If the causes or effects are independent, then your sentence should indicate that—for example, "Students drop out of college for a number of different reasons."

Now read the following paragraph a student wrote on the topic of advertising for children. Notice that the topic sentence makes it clear that she is focusing on reasons and that they are independent of one another.

Advertising intended for children should be limited to facts for three reasons. First, because parents teach children to obey and respect adults, children tend to accept as truth whatever an adult on a commercial tells them. Second, children do not have the ability to sort out accurate claims from misleading ones. They do not have enough experience or sophistication to question the claims advertisers make. Finally, because children are not emotionally mature, they tend to overreact to emotional appeals. Therefore, it is unfair to appeal to and to manipulate them in the same way in which advertisers treat adults.

**EXERCISE**  **10-2** | Review the lists you made for Exercise 10-1. For each situation, write a topic sentence for a paragraph that will explain either causes *or* effects.

## Organizing Supporting Details

Providing supporting details for cause-and-effect paragraphs requires careful thought and planning. You must provide relevant and sufficient details and organize them effectively.

### Providing Relevant and Sufficient Details

Each cause or effect you describe must be relevant to the situation introduced in your topic sentence. Suppose you are writing a paragraph explaining why you are attending college. Each sentence must explain this topic. You could not include ideas, for example, about how college is different from what you expected.

If, while writing, you discover you have more ideas about how college is different from what you expected, then you need to revise your topic sentence in order to refocus your paragraph.

Each cause or reason requires explanation, particularly if it is *not* completely clear or obvious. For example, it is not sufficient to write, "One reason I decided to attend college was to advance my position in life." This sentence needs further explanation. For example, you could discuss the types of advancement (financial, job security, job satisfaction) you hope to attain.

Jot down a list of the causes or reasons you plan to include. This process may help you think of additional ones and will give you a chance to consider how to explain or support each cause or reason. You might decide to eliminate one or to combine several. Here is a list of reasons for deciding to attend college that one student produced:

| *Causes* | *Effect* |
|---|---|
| 1. get a better job | |
| 2. make new friends | |
| 3. get higher salary | decision to attend college |
| 4. get more respect from family | |
| 5. get interesting job I enjoy | |

By listing his reasons, this student realized that the first reason—to get a better job—was too general and was covered more specifically later in the list, so he eliminated it. He also realized that "get higher salary" and "get interesting job" could be combined. He then wrote the following paragraph.

> There are three main reasons I decided to attend Ambrose Community College. First, and most important to me, I want to get a high-paying, interesting job that I will enjoy. Right now, the only jobs I can get pay minimum wage, and as a result, I'm working in a fast-food restaurant. This kind of job doesn't make me proud of myself, and I get bored with routine tasks. Second, my parents have always wanted me to have a better job than they do, and I know my father will not respect me until I do. A college degree would make them proud of me. A third reason for attending school is to make new friends. It is hard to meet people, and everyone in my neighborhood seems stuck in a rut. I want to meet other people who are interested in improving themselves like I am.

## Organizing Your Details

There are several ways to arrange the details in a cause-and-effect paragraph. The method you choose depends on your purpose in writing, as well as your topic. Suppose you are writing a paragraph about the effects of a hurricane on a coastal town. Several different arrangements of details are possible:

**1. Chronological.** A chronological organization arranges your details in the order in which situations or events happened. The order in which the hurricane damage occurred becomes the order for your details. This arrangement is similar to the arrangement you learned in Chapter 6, "Narration and Process." A chronological arrangement works for situations and events that occurred in a specific order.

**2. Order of importance.** In an order-of-importance organization, the details are arranged from least to most important or from most to least important. In describing the effects of the hurricane, you could discuss the most severe damage first and then describe damage of lesser importance. Alternatively, you could build up to the most important for dramatic effect.

**3. Spatial.** Spatial arrangement of details uses physical or geographical position as a means of organization. In describing the hurricane damage, you could start by describing damage to the beach and work toward the center of town.

**4. Categorical.** This form of arrangement divides the topic into parts or categories. To describe hurricane damage using this arrangement, you could recount what the storm did to businesses, roads, city services, and homes.

As you can see from the example of hurricane damage, there are many ways to organize cause-and-effect details. Each has a different emphasis and achieves a different purpose. The organization you choose, then, depends on the point you want to make.

Once you have chosen which method of organization to use, return to your preliminary list of causes or reasons. Study your list again, make changes, eliminate, or combine. Then rearrange or number the items on your list to indicate the order in which you will include them in your paragraph.

**EXERCISE**  Write a paragraph developing one of the topic sentences you wrote for Exercise 10-2. Be sure to include relevant and sufficient details. Organize your paragraph using one of the methods described above.

**EXERCISE**  Choose one of the following topic sentences and develop a paragraph using it. Organize your paragraph using one of the methods described above.

1. Exercise has several positive (or negative) effects on the body.
2. Professional athletes deserve (or do not deserve) the high salaries they are paid.
3. There are several reasons why parents should reserve time each day to spend with their children.
4. Video (or computer) games are popular among teenagers for several reasons.

## Helpful Transitional Words and Phrases

To blend your details smoothly, use the transitional words and phrases listed below.

| TABLE 10-1 | Useful Transitional Words and Phrases for Cause-and-Effect Writing | |
|---|---|---|
| | For causes | For effects |
| | because, due to, one cause is . . . , another is . . . , since, for, first, second | consequently, as a result, thus, resulted in, one result is . . . , another is . . . , therefore |

The student paragraph on page 180 is a good example of how transitional words and phrases are used. Notice how these function as markers and help you to locate each separate reason.

**EXERCISE 10-5**  In each blank provided, supply a transitional word or phrase that strengthens the connection between the two ideas.

1. No known cure exists for the common cold _____ it is a virus.

2. Computers provide an easy way to store and process information quickly. _____ computers have permeated every aspect of society.

3. Animal skins are warm and very durable; _____ almost every culture has made use of them for clothing or shelter.

4. _____ some people refused to accept his views and beliefs, Martin Luther King Jr. was brutally murdered.

**EXERCISE 10-6**  Reread the paragraphs you wrote for Exercises 10-3 and 10-4. Add transitional words and phrases, if needed, to connect your details.

## Applying Your Skills to Essay Writing

When writing cause-and-effect essays, keep the following suggestions in mind:

**1. Remember your purpose for writing as you plan your essay.** The two main purposes for writing cause-and-effect essays are to inform and to persuade. For example, you may be writing to explain the effects of cigarette smoking or to convince your reader that smoking's effects are harmful. Focus your essay to suit your purpose.

**2. Focus on primary—immediate and direct—causes or effects.** Unless you are writing a lengthy paper, it is best to limit yourself to primary causes or effects. Secondary causes or effects—those that occur later or are indirectly related—may confuse and distract your reader. For example, immediate effects of cigarette smoking would include physical effects on smokers and those around them. Secondary effects might include higher medical-insurance rates due to the costs of treating smoking-related illnesses.

**3. Strengthen your essay using supporting evidence.** In explaining causes and/or effects, you may need to define terms, offer facts and statistics, or provide examples, anecdotes, or personal observations that support your ideas.

**4. Be cautious in determining cause-and-effect relationships.** Many logical-reasoning errors can occur with cause-and-effect relationships. Do not assume that because one event occurs close in time to another that it caused the other or that they are related.

**5. Qualify or limit your statements about cause-and-effect relationships.** Unless there is clear, indisputable evidence that one event is related to another, qualify your statements by using such phrases as "It appears that the cause was" or "Available evidence suggests."

**EXERCISE** ▶ 10-7

Suppose you are taking a course in education and have been assigned a paper. Select one of the following topics, and write a one-page paper on it.

1. Watch a television show or movie that contains violence, and consider what a young child watching it alone might learn from it about what is right and wrong and about how people behave and should behave. Summarize your findings.

2. Talk to or think of someone who has dropped out of high school. What problems facing that person seem to be related to dropping out? Summarize your findings.

3. What are the effects of the course registration system used at your school? Answer this question using examples to support your points.

## Thinking Before Reading

The following reading, "Light in Montana" by Jo Clare Hartsig and Walter Wink, was originally published as an article in *Fellowship* magazine. It describes what residents of Billings, Montana, did to combat hate crimes against a minority group in their community.

1. Preview the reading using the steps listed on page 45.
2. Activate your thinking by answering the following:
   a. What does the term *hate crime* mean to you? What ideas and experiences do you associate with that term?
   b. Are hate crimes a problem in your community? If so, what is being done to counteract them?
   c. What hate crimes, if any, have you read about, in either the past or present, in the United States or elsewhere?

# Light in Montana
## Jo Clare Hartsig and Walter Wink

### How One Town Said No to Hate

Darkness cannot drive out darkness; only light can do that. Hate cannot      1
drive out hate; only love can do that.

—Martin Luther King Jr.

Montana, long known as "big sky" territory, is vast and beauti-      2
ful, like all its Northwestern neighbors. One might assume that
there is room enough for everyone. Yet over the past decade the
five-state area of Washington, Oregon, Wyoming, Idaho, and Montana
has been designated a "white homeland" for the Aryan Nation and growing numbers of kindred skinheads, Klan members, and other white
supremacists. These groups have targeted nonwhites, Jews, gays, and lesbians for harassment, vandalism, and injury, which in some cases has led
to murder.

In Billings, Montana (pop. 83,000), there have been a number of      3
hate crimes: desecration of a Jewish cemetery, threatening phone calls to
Jewish citizens, swastikas painted on the home of an interracial couple.
But it was something else that activated the people of faith and goodwill
throughout the entire community.

On December 2, 1993, a brick was thrown through 5-year-old Isaac      4
Schnitzer's bedroom window. The brick and shards of glass were strewn
all over the child's bed. The reason? A menorah[1] and other symbols of
Jewish faith were stenciled on the glass as part of the family's Hanukkah
celebration. The account of the incident in the *Billings Gazette* the next
day reported that Issac's mother, Tammie Schnitzer, was troubled by the
advice she got from the investigating officer. He suggested that she
remove the symbols. How would she explain this to her son?

Another mother in Billings was deeply touched by that question. She      5
tried to imagine explaining to her children that they couldn't have a
Christmas tree in the window or a wreath on the door because it wasn't
safe. She remembered what happened when Hitler ordered the king of
Denmark to force Danish Jews to wear the Star of David. The order
was never carried out because the king himself and many other Danes

---

1. a seven-branched candleholder used in Jewish religion to symbolize the seven days of creation

chose to wear the yellow stars. The Nazis lost the ability to find their "enemies."

There are several dozen Jewish families in Billings. This kind of tactic could effectively deter violence if enough people got involved. So Margaret McDonald phoned her pastor, Rev. Keith Torney at First Congregational United Church of Christ, and asked what he thought of having Sunday school children make paper cut-out menorahs for their own windows. He got on the phone with his clergy colleagues around town, and the following week menorahs appeared in the windows of hundreds of Christian homes. Asked about the danger of this action, police chief Wayne Inman told callers, "There's greater risk in not doing it."

Five days after the brick was thrown at the Schnitzer home, the *Gazette* published a full-page drawing of a menorah, along with a general invitation for people to put it up. By the end of the week at least six thousand homes (some accounts estimate up to ten thousand) were decorated with menorahs.

A sporting goods store got involved by displaying "Not in our town! No hate. No violence. Peace on earth" on its large billboard. Someone shot at it. Townspeople organized a vigil outside the synagogue during Sabbath services. That same night bricks and bullets shattered windows at Central Catholic High School, where an electric marquee read "Happy Hanukkah to our Jewish Friends." The cat of a family with a menorah was killed with an arrow. Windows were broken at a United Methodist church because of its menorah display. The car and house windows of six non-Jewish families were shattered. A note that said "Jew lover" was left on a car.

Eventually these incidents waned, but people continued in their efforts to support one another against hate crimes. After being visited at home and threatened by one of the local skinhead leaders, Tammie Schnitzer is now always accompanied by friends when she goes on her morning run. During the Passover holiday the following spring, 250 Christians joined their Jewish brothers and sisters in a traditional Seder meal. New friendships have formed, new traditions have started, and greater mutual understanding and respect have been achieved.

Last winter families all over Billings took out their menorahs to reaffirm their commitment to peace and religious tolerance. The light they shared in their community must be continuously rekindled until hatred has been overcome.

## Getting Ready to Write

■ **Examining the Reading: Reviewing and Organizing Ideas**

"Light in Montana" presents a chain of causes and effects. By describing a series of events, each of which led to the next, Hartsig and Wink tell us how one town is combating hatred. They show what happened as the result of a hate crime and how this caused another action, which, in turn, led to another and another.

As you have discovered in previous chapters, an idea map is a useful way to record, organize, and review ideas. Since cause-and-effect relationships are often complex, this kind of diagramming can clarify relationships, simplify them, and reduce them to a basic form. The ideas in this reading can be organized as shown below.

### CHAIN OF EVENTS STARTED BY HATE CRIME

**Event 1**

brick thrown through Isaac Schnitzer's window

**Event 2**

_____

**Event 3**

_____

**Event 4**

_____

**Event 5**

_____

**Event 6**

_____

> **Event 7**
>
> another rash of hate crimes occurs

> **Event 8**
>
> people continue to support each other; new friendships formed

> **Event 9**
>
> _____

**EXERCISE 10-8** ▶ Complete the above idea map by supplying key events from "Light in Montana."

### ■ Thinking Critically: **Evaluating Cause-and-Effect Relationships**

You should not accept everything you read as true. Instead, you should evaluate the author's claim and make a decision about whether or not to accept or agree with the ideas presented. In this selection the author reasons that a community's reaction to hate crimes brought people closer together. Do you accept this reasoning?

To answer, you will need to analyze the cause-and-effect relationships and the evidence the author offers to support them. Cause-and-effect relationships will establish that one thing is the cause of another. The author, for example, asserts that a brick was thrown through the Schnitzers' window because they displayed a menorah. Your task as a critical thinker is to question or evaluate this assertion. You might ask the following:

1. What evidence does the author offer in support of this assertion? Is it relevant and sufficient?
2. Can you think of other situations that support this assertion?
3. Is the connection logical? Plausible?
4. Can you think of situations in which this connection does not hold true?
5. Might there be other causes the author has not thought of?

In "Light in Montana," there is strong evidence that the brick was thrown through the Schnitzers' window as an expression of hatred against Jews. The incidents that occurred prior to the brick throwing and the continuation of crimes after it serve as substantial evidence.

**EXERCISE**  **10-9**   For each cause and effect you listed in your idea map for Exercise 10-8, review the reading to determine if the cause-and-effect relationship is supported with evidence.

■ **Reacting to Ideas: Discussion and Journal Writing**

1. Do you think the actions taken by citizens in Billings, Montana, will be sufficient to counteract the hatred of hate groups? Why or why not?

2. Have you ever been singled out by an individual or group because you were unique or different from others? If so, what were your feelings about the situation?

3. Can you think of situations in which the actions of one person can initiate a big change in our society?

4. What activities, other than the ones engaged in by the Billings citizens, could be used to combat hate crimes?

## Writing Assignments

### Writing About the Reading

1. Write a paragraph explaining how the quotation at the beginning of this reading applies to the situation in Billings.

**Essay Option**  2. Write an essay stating whether or not you think the actions taken in Billings will eventually solve the problem the city has with hate crimes. Be sure to give reasons based on the information in the article.

### Writing About Your Ideas

1. Write a paragraph explaining why you think hate groups target non-whites, Jews, gays, and lesbians.

2. Write a paragraph describing an actual situation in which you and others stood up to a bully. Also describe the outcome of your actions. Try to organize your ideas in the cause-and-effect pattern.

**Essay Option**  3. Do you think actions like those taken in Billings could be effective against other crimes? Can you think of other situations in which a community has worked together to combat problems or initiate change? Write an essay in which you support your viewpoint with reasons and examples.

**Essay Option**  4. In what ways, other than acts of violence, do people show their hatred of certain groups? Write an essay answering this question.

## REVISION CHECKLIST

1. Is your paragraph or essay appropriate for your audience? Does it give them the background information they need? Will it interest them?

2. Will your paragraph or essay accomplish your purpose?

3. Is your main point clearly expressed?

4. Is each detail relevant? Does each explain or support your main point?

5. Have you supported your main point with sufficient detail to make it understandable and believable?

6. Do you use specific and vivid words to explain each detail?

For Cause-and-Effect Writing

7. Does your topic sentence or thesis statement indicate whether you will emphasize causes or effects?

8. Does your topic sentence or thesis statement indicate whether the events you are describing are related or independent?

9. Are your details arranged using one of the following arrangements: chronological, order of importance, spatial, or categorical?

10. Have you used transitional words and phrases to blend your details smoothly?

11. Have you proofread? (See the inside back cover of this book for a proofreading checklist.)

# SKILL REFRESHER

## Coordinate Sentences

Two or more equally important ideas can be combined into one sentence. (Each idea must be an independent clause, which is a group of related words that contains a subject and a predicate and that can grammatically stand alone as a sentence.) This type of sentence is called a *coordinate sentence*.

## How to Combine Ideas of Equal Importance

There are three ways to combine ideas of equal importance.

1. Join the two independent clauses with a comma and a coordinating conjunction (*and, so, for, but, yet, or, nor*).

   EXAMPLE: 1. Russell recommended that we try the Mexican restaurant down the street.
   2. The restaurant turned out to be excellent.

   COMBINED: Russell recommended that we try the Mexican restaurant down the street, and it turned out to be excellent.

2. Join the two clauses using a semicolon.

   EXAMPLE: 1. The candidates for mayor made negative comments about each other.
   2. Many people disapproved of the candidates' tactics.

   COMBINED: The candidates for mayor made negative comments about each other; many people disapproved of their tactics.

3. Join the clauses using a semicolon and a conjunctive adverb (words such as *however, therefore, thus*) followed by a comma.

   EXAMPLE: 1. Professor Sullivan did not discuss the chapter on polar winds.
   2. The exam included several questions on polar winds.

   COMBINED: Professor Sullivan did not discuss the chapter on polar winds; however, the exam included several questions of the topic.

## Rate Your Ability to Write Coordinate Sentences

Combine each of the following pairs of sentences to form coordinate sentences.

## SKILL REFRESHER  CONTINUED

1. A field study observes subjects in their natural settings. Only a small number of subjects can be studied at one time.

2. The Grand Canyon is an incredible sight. It was formed less than ten million years ago.

3. Many anthropologists believe that Native Americans migrated to North and South America from Asia. Alaska and Siberia used to be connected twenty-five thousand years ago.

4. Neon, argon, and helium are called inert gases. They are never found in stable chemical compounds.

5. The professor returned the tests. He did not comment on them.

6. Ponce de Leon was successful because he was the first European to "discover" Florida. He did not succeed in finding the fountain of youth he was searching for.

7. The lecture focused on the cardiopulmonary system. The students needed to draw diagrams in their notes.

8. Rudy had never read *Hamlet*. Rufus had never read *Hamlet*.

9. Presidents Lincoln and Kennedy did not survive assassination attempts. President Ford escaped two assassination attempts.

10. Marguerite might write her paper about *Moll Flanders*. She might write her paper about its author, Daniel Defoe.

Score_____

Check your answers using the Answer Key on page 485. If you missed more than two, you need additional review and practice in working with coordinate sentences. Refer to page 436 of Part VI, "Reviewing the Basics".

## CHAPTER SUMMARY

**Writing Skills**

1.  Cause-and-effect paragraphs and essays are concerned with why events and actions occur and what happens as a result.

2.  To write an effective topic sentence or thesis statement
    - clarify the cause-and-effect relationship.
    - decide whether to emphasize causes or effects.
    - determine if the events are related or independent.

3.  Four useful ways to organize your details are
    - chronological.
    - order of importance.
    - spatial.
    - categorical.

4.  Use transitional words and phrases to blend your details.

**Reading and Critical Thinking Skills**

1.  Mapping is a useful way to organize and review cause-and-effect relationships.

2.  Evaluate cause-and-effect relationships by considering supporting evidence, plausibility, and alternative explanations.

# STRATEGIES FOR WRITING ESSAYS

# 11

# Sharpening Your Essay-Writing Skills

## CHAPTER OBJECTIVES

*In this chapter you will learn to*

1. write effective thesis statements.

2. support your thesis with evidence.

3. write more effective introductions and conclusions.

4. use revision maps to revise

We have all used a dull knife, a dull saw, or a dull pencil. It is possible, of course, to go through the motions of using these tools, but not very satisfying in the end. Sometimes you might feel, similarly, "I'm doing what I'm supposed to be doing when I write an essay—generating good ideas and organizing them as best I can—but something is missing from the end result." This chapter is all about sharpening your essay-writing skills so that the end result— your papers—will be more interesting, more effective, and more satisfying to write and to read. Specifically, this chapter will help you polish your thesis statement, support it with substantial evidence, show connections among your ideas, write effective introductions, conclusions, and titles, and use revision maps to revise.

## Write Strong Thesis Statements

One way to be sure that you develop a sound essay is to begin with a well-focused thesis statement. A thesis statement explains to your reader what your essay is about and gives clues about how the essay will unfold. The thesis statement should not only identify your topic but also express the main point about your topic that you will explain or prove in your essay. Some students think they should be able to just sit down and write a thesis statement. They do not realize that a thesis statement very rarely just springs into a writer's mind: it evolves and, in fact, may change throughout the writing process of prewriting, grouping ideas, drafting, and revising. This section will show you how to draft a thesis statement and how to polish it into a more focused statement.

## Group Your Ideas to Discover a Thesis Statement

The first step in developing a thesis statement is to generate ideas to write about. Use one of the four prewriting methods that we have studied: (1) freewriting, (2) brainstorming, (3) questioning, and (4) branching. Refer to page 18 of Chapter 2, "The Writing Process: An Overview," for a review of these strategies. Once you have ideas to work with, the next step is to group or connect your ideas to form a thesis. Let's see how one student produced a thesis following these steps.

Ernie was taking a sociology course in which he was studying the public-education system. His instructor assigned a short (one to two pages) paper on educational reform. The instructor directed students to propose a particular educational change and to write a paper explaining why this change is needed. After brainstorming on educational reforms he could write about, Ernie finally decided to write about lengthening the school year. He decided to do a second brainstorming to discover good reasons for lengthening the school year. This time he came up with the following list of ideas:

kids get bored in the summer
would spend more time practicing skills
kids spend day watching TV
don't see much of other kids unless they live nearby
kids who are weak in skills could catch up
others could accelerate
school buildings are empty, wasting valuable space
many teachers who are unemployed for the summer want
  to work
daycare or day camps are expensive

Ernie's next step in essay writing was to select usable ideas and try to group or organize them in an orderly, logical fashion. In the above brainstorming list, Ernie saw three main ideas: behavioral or social skills, academic skills, and financial considerations. He sorted his list into the following categories:

### Social

kids get bored in the summer
kids spend the day watching TV
don't see much of other kids unless they live nearby

### Academic

would spend more time practicing skills
kids who are weak could catch up
others could accelerate

*Financial*
school buildings are empty, wasting valuable space
many teachers want to work in the summer
daycare or day camps are expensive

Once Ernie had grouped his ideas into these categories, he could write a thesis statement:

> Lengthening the school year is a good idea for social, academic, and financial reasons.

This thesis statement identifies his topic—lengthening the school year—and suggests three primary reasons why it is a good idea. You can see that this thesis statement grew out of the idea grouping that he had done. Furthermore, this thesis statement gives readers clues as to how the essay will be organized. A reader knows from this preview that each type of reason will be discussed in this order.

The following suggestions for grouping ideas will help you discover connections and relationships among ideas that you generate during prewriting.

**1. Look for categories.** Try to discover ways your ideas can be classified or subdivided. Think of categories as titles or slots under which ideas can be placed. Look for a general term that is broad enough to cover several of your ideas. For example, Ernie discovered that academic achievement was a broad term that could include the following topics: time for learning, practicing skills, and acceleration. Suppose you are writing a paper on where sexual discrimination occurs. You could break down the topic by location.

SAMPLE THESIS STATEMENT:    Sexual discrimination exists in the workplace, in social situations, and in politics.

**2. Consider organizing your ideas chronologically.** Group your ideas according to the clock or calendar.

SAMPLE THESIS STATEMENT:    When prostitution is traced from its early beginnings in history to modern times, a social and economic pattern is evident.

**3. Look for similarities and differences.** When working with two or more topics, see if they can be approached by looking at how similar or different they are.

SAMPLE THESIS STATEMENT:    Two early biologists, Darwin and Mendel, held similar views about evolution.

**4. Separate your ideas into causes and effects or problems and solutions.** Events and issues can often be analyzed in this way.

> SAMPLE THESIS STATEMENT: The problem of increased teenage smoking should be addressed by parents and politicians.

**5. Divide your ideas into advantages and disadvantages or pros and cons.** When you are evaluating a proposal, product, or service, this approach may work.

> SAMPLE THESIS STATEMENT: Playing on a college sports team has many advantages, but also several serious drawbacks.

**6. Consider several different ways to approach your topic or organize and develop your ideas.** As you consider what your thesis statement is going to be, push yourself to see your topic from a number of different angles or a fresh perspective. For example, Ernie could have considered what the regular school year lacks that school during the summer could provide (field trips, hands-on learning, tutoring, and so on). He could have examined his brainstorming list and decided to focus only on financial aspects of the issue, looking more deeply at salaries, taxes, and cost of building maintenance. In other words, within every topic lie many possible thesis statements.

**EXERCISE** ▶ **11-1** Assume you are taking the course "Interpersonal Communication Skills." In addition to tests and quizzes, your instructor requires two papers. Your first assignment is to write a paper of one or two pages on one of the following topics.

1. Watch a portion of a television program with the sound turned off. If you could understand what was happening, write a paper explaining how you knew.

2. Analyze a recent phone conversation. What feelings and emotions were expressed by you and the other person? Write a paper describing how these feelings were communicated.

3. If you were applying for a full-time job today and your potential employer asked you to describe what "people skills" you have to offer and how well you work with other people, what would you say? Write an essay answering the employer's question.

4. We encounter conflict in our daily lives. Write a paper describing a recent conflict you had and how you and the other person handled the situation.

5. Describe a communication breakdown between you and another person. Why did it happen and, if possible, how could it have been prevented?

6. Describe a situation in which a person's body language (gestures, posture, facial expressions) allowed you to understand what he or she was really saying. Describe the body language and what it told you.

## How to Write More Effective Thesis Statements

A thesis statement should explain what your essay is about and also give your readers clues about its organization. Think of your thesis statement as a promise; it promises your reader what your paper will deliver. Here are some guidelines to follow for writing more effective thesis statements.

**1. It should state the main point of your essay.** It should not focus on details; it should give an overview of your approach to your topic.

> TOO DETAILED:    The human face has eighty muscles.
>
> REVISED:    The human face has eighty muscles with which to communicate a wide range of facial expressions.

**2. It should assert an idea about your topic.** Your thesis should express a viewpoint or state an approach to the topic.

> LACKS AN ASSERTION:    Advertising contains images of both men and women.
>
> REVISED:    In general, advertising presents men more favorably than women.

**3. It should be as specific and detailed as possible.** For this reason, it is important to review and rework your thesis *after* you have written and revised drafts.

> TOO GENERAL:    Advertisers can influence readers' attitudes toward competing products.
>
> REVISED:    Athletic shoe advertisers focus more on attitude and image than on the actual physical differences between their product and those of their competitors.

**4. It may suggest the organization of your essay.** Mentioning key points that will be discussed in the essay is one way to do this. The order in which you mention them should be the order in which you discuss them in your essay.

> DOES NOT SUGGEST ORGANIZATION:    Public-school budget cuts will have negative effects on education.
>
> REVISED:    Public-school budget cuts will have negative effects on academic achievement, student motivation, and the drop-out rate.

**5. It should not be a direct announcement.** Do not begin with phrases such as "In this paper I will" or "My assignment was to discuss."

DIRECT ANNOUNCEMENT:   The purpose of my paper is to show that businesses lose money due to inefficiency, competition, and inflated labor costs.

REVISED:   Businesses lose money due to inefficiency, competition, and inflated labor costs.

**6. It should offer a fresh, interesting, and original perspective on the topic.** A thesis statement can follow the guidelines above, but if it seems dull or predictable, it needs more work.

PREDICTABLE:   Circus acts fall into three categories: animal, clown, and acrobatic.

REVISED:   Each of the three categories of circus acts—animal, clown, and acrobatic—are exciting because of the risks they involve.

## How to Revise Your Thesis Statement

The best time to evaluate and, if necessary, revise your thesis statement is after you have written a first draft. Once your draft is written, examine your thesis statement and check that your essay accurately represents it. When evaluating your thesis statement, ask the following questions:

**1. Does my essay develop and explain my thesis statement?** Often as you write an essay, its focus and direction may change. Revise your thesis statement to reflect any changes. If you discover that you drifted away from your thesis and want to maintain your original thesis, work on revising your paper so that it delivers what your thesis promises.

**2. Is my thesis statement broad enough to cover all the points made in the essay?** Check to see that all ideas in your essay fit into your thesis. For example, suppose your thesis statement is "Media coverage of national political events shapes public attitudes toward politicians." If, in your essay, you discuss media coverage of international events as well as national ones, then you need to broaden your thesis statement.

**3. Does my thesis statement use vague or unclear words that do not provide my reader with a focus on the topic?** For example, in the thesis statement "The possibility of animal-organ transplants for humans is interesting," the word *interesting* is vague and does not suggest how your essay will approach the topic. Instead, if your paper discusses both the risks and benefits of these transplants, then this approach should be reflected in your thesis: "Animal-organ transplants for humans offer both risks and potential benefits."

**EXERCISE** ▶ 11-2   Identify what is wrong with each of the following thesis statements, and revise each to make it more effective.

1. Jogging has a lot of benefits.
2. Counseling can help people with problems.
3. Getting involved in campus activities has really helped me.
4. Budgeting your time is important.
5. Commuting to college presents problems.

**EXERCISE**  **11-3** Using the topic you chose in Exercise 11-1, develop a tentative thesis statement.

## Support Your Thesis with Substantial Evidence

Every essay you write should offer substantial evidence in support of your thesis statement. This evidence makes up the body of your essay. There are many types of evidence, the most common being personal experience, anecdotes (stories that illustrate a point), examples, reasons, descriptions, facts, statistics, and quotations (taken from sources). Many students have trouble locating concrete, specific evidence to support their thesis. While prewriting yields plenty of good ideas and helps you focus your thesis, at times prewriting ideas are not sufficient evidence. Often you need to brainstorm for additional ideas; other times, you may need to consult one or more sources to obtain further information on your topic (see Chapter 12, "Summarizing and Synthesizing Sources," pp. 218–236).

Ernie realized that he did not have enough ideas for his essay on lengthening the school year. The chart below lists ways to explain a thesis statement and gives an example of how Ernie could use each in his essay.

**TABLE 11-1    Ways to Add Evidence**
**Topic: Lengthening the School Year**

| Explain Your Thesis by | Example |
| --- | --- |
| Telling a story (narration) | Relate a story about a student who needed extra time to practice skills |
| Explaining how something works (process) | Explain how the length of the school year is determined |
| Adding descriptive detail (description) | Add description that allows your reader to visualize how a child with too much unstructured time behaves |
| Giving an example | Discuss specific instances of children who are falling behind academically |
| Discussing types or kinds (classification) | Discuss types of accelerated programs that could be offered |

| | |
|---|---|
| Giving a definition | Discuss the meaning of the terms *vacation*, *learning*, or *practice* |
| Making comparisons | Compare unstructured activities to structured school activities |
| Making distinctions (contrast) | Contrast the length of the school year in the United States with that of other countries |
| Giving reasons (causes) | Explain why too much free time is not beneficial |
| Analyzing effects | Explain how too much free time affects a child's behavior |

The above chart offers a variety of ways Ernie could add evidence to his essay. He would not need to use all of them; instead he could choose the ones that he feels would be most appropriate for his audience and purpose. Ernie could use these types of evidence in combination as well. For example, he could *tell a story* that illustrates the *effects* of children having too much free time.

Use the following guidelines in selecting evidence to support your thesis:

**1. Be sure your evidence is relevant.** That is, it must directly support or explain your thesis.

**2. Make your evidence as specific as possible.** Help your readers see the point you are making by offering detailed, concrete information. For example, if you are explaining the effects of right-to-privacy violations on an individual, include details that make the situation come alive: names of people and places, types of violations, and so forth.

**3. Be sure your information is accurate.** It may be necessary to check facts, verify stories you have heard, and ask questions of individuals who may have provided information.

**4. Locate sources that provide evidence.** Because you may not know enough about your topic and lack personal experience, you may be unable to provide strong evidence. When this happens, locate several sources on your topic. Consult Chapter 12 for information on synthesizing and summarizing sources.

**5. Be sure to document any information that you borrow from other sources.** See Chapter 12, p. 230, for further information on crediting sources.

Now let's take a look at how Ernie developed his essay on lengthening the school year. As you read, notice, in particular, the types of evidence he uses and how his thesis statement promises what his essay delivers.

## Lengthening the School Year

If I were given eight weeks of vacation each year, I know exactly what I would do. I would visit my family in Arizona, do household chores, and catch up on projects I have not had time to do in three years. Schoolchildren do get eight weeks of vacation each year, but they haven't any idea of how to use it. In fact, they don't need it. There has been a lot of talk lately about lengthening the school year, and this talk deserves consideration. Extending the school year from 180 to 220 days is a good idea for a number of reasons: academic, social, and financial.

The most important reason for lengthening the school year is to improve our children's academic skills. Compared with the children in many other countries, our children are falling behind, especially in math and science. In other countries, parents are much stricter with children than we are. News stories report increasing illiteracy and declining SAT scores as well. Increased time in school will give children more time to receive instruction and to practice. Kids who are weak in skills could catch up, while others could accelerate. Consider also that without two months' vacation each year, students are less likely to forget what they have learned.

A second reason for extending the school year has to do with social skills: how kids behave and get along with each other. With two months' vacation, kids have time on their hands; they get bored and don't know what to do. My son stays up late each night watching television and sleeps late in the mornings. He says, "There's nothing to do in the morning, so I kill it by sleeping." Other kids spend day and night in front of the television. They don't see other kids unless they live nearby. If they do play, their play is not supervised, since many parents must work during the summer. Year-round school would occupy daytime hours and offer sports and worthwhile social activities.

Finally, financial reasons indicate that year-round school would be a good idea. As it is, school buildings sit empty and teachers are unemployed or must find part-time jobs. The buildings could be put to good use and teachers who need money could work. Some teachers paint houses or work on construction during the summer. In addition, parents would save money, since now they have to pay for babysitting, daycare, or day camps to care for their children while they work.

Extending the school year has many advantages. Those opposed to lengthening the school year say it would be a struggle to get kids to give up their summers. Others say it would cost too much. What could we possibly buy that would be worth more than the education of our children?

**EXERCISE** ▶ 11-4 ▶ | Write a first draft for the thesis statement you wrote in Exercise 11-3. Support your thesis statement with at least three types of evidence.

## Make Connections Among Your Ideas Clear

To produce a well-written essay, be sure to make it clear how your ideas relate to one another. There are several ways to do this:

**1. Use transitional words and phrases.** The transitional words and phrases that you learned for connecting ideas in Chapters 6 through 10 are helpful for making your essay flow smoothly and communicate clearly. Table 11-2 lists useful transitions for each method of organization. Notice the use of these transitional words and phrases in Ernie's essay: *most important, also, a second reason, finally,* and *in addition.*

| TABLE 11-2 | Useful Transitional Words And Phrases |
|---|---|
| **Method of Development** | **Transitional Words and Phrases** |
| Most-Least/Least-Most | most important, above all, especially, particularly important |
| Spatial | above, below, behind, beside, next to, inside, outside, to the west (north, etc.), beneath, near, nearby, next to |
| Time Sequence | first, next, now, before, during, after, eventually, finally, at last, later, meanwhile, soon, then, suddenly, currently, after, afterward, after a while, as soon as, until |
| Narration/Process | first, second, then, later, in the beginning, when, after, following, next, during, again, after that, at last, finally |
| Description | see Spatial and Most-Least/Least-Most above |
| Example | for example, for instance, to illustrate |
| Classification | one, another, second, third |
| Definition | means, can be defined as, refers to, is |
| Comparison | likewise, similarly, in the same way, too, also |
| Contrast | however, on the contrary, unlike, on the other hand, although, even though, but, in contrast, yet |
| Cause and Effect | because, consequently, since, as a result, for this reason, therefore, thus |

**2. Write a transitional sentence.** This sentence is usually the first sentence in the paragraph. It might come before the topic sentence or it might *be* the topic sentence. Its purpose is to link the paragraph in which it appears with the paragraph before it. In Ernie's essay on page 202, the first sentences of paragraphs 2, 3, and 4 function as transitional sentences.

**3. Repeat key words.** Repeating key words from either the thesis statement or the preceding paragraph helps your reader see connections among ideas. In Ernie's essay, notice the repetition of key words and phrases such as *lengthening the school year, vacation,* and *reasons.*

EXERCISE  11-5  Review the draft you wrote for Exercise 11-4. Analyze how effectively you have connected your ideas. Add key words or transitional words, phrases, or sentences, as needed.

## Writing the Introduction, Conclusion, and Title

The introduction, conclusion, and title each serves a specific function. Each strengthens your essay and helps your reader understand your ideas.

### The Introduction

An introductory paragraph has three main purposes:

- It presents your thesis statement.
- It interests your reader in your topic.
- It provides any necessary background information.

Although your introductory paragraph appears first in your essay, it does *not* need to be written first. In fact, it is sometimes best to write it last, after you have developed your ideas, written your thesis statement, and drafted your essay.

We have already discussed writing thesis statements earlier in the chapter (see pp. 194–199). Here are some suggestions on how to interest your reader in your topic:

| *Technique* | *Example* |
| --- | --- |
| Ask a provocative or controversial question | What would you do if you were sound asleep and woke to find a burglar in your bedroom? |
| State a startling fact or statistic | Did you know that the federal government recently spent $687,000 on a research project that studied the influence of Valium on monkeys? |

| Begin with a story or anecdote | Mark Brown, a 14-year-old convicted auto thief, has spent the past two months riding in a police cruiser assigned to a high-crime neighborhood. |
|---|---|
| Use a quotation | Oscar Wilde once said, "Always forgive your enemies—nothing annoys them so much." |
| State a little-known fact, a myth, or a misconception | It's hard to lose weight and even harder to keep it off. Right? Wrong! A sensible eating program will help you. |

A straightforward, dramatic thesis statement can also capture your reader's interest, as in the following example:

My dream vacation that I spent two years saving for was a complete disaster.

An introduction should also provide the reader with any necessary background information. Consider what types of information your reader would need to understand your essay. You may, for example, need to define the term *genetic engineering* for a paper on that topic. Other times, you might need to provide a brief history or give an overview of a controversial issue.

Now reread the introduction to Ernie's essay on page 202. Ernie interests his reader by raising the possibility of eight weeks of vacation, something most of us would like to have. He also provides essential background information: that schoolchildren do get eight weeks of vacation, that the school year now consists of 180 days, and that lengthening the year is an issue many people are discussing.

**EXERCISE**  11-6 | Revise your introduction to the essay you wrote for Exercise 11-4.

### Writing the Conclusion

The final paragraph of your essay has two functions. It should reemphasize your thesis statement and draw the essay to a close. It should not be a direct announcement, such as "This essay has been about" or "In this paper I hoped to show that." It's usually best to revise your essay at least once *before* working on the conclusion. During your first or second revision, you often make numerous changes in both content and organization, which may, in turn, change your conclusion.

Here are a few effective ways to write a conclusion. Choose one that will work for your essay.

**1. Suggest a new direction for further thought.** Raise a related issue that you did not address in your essay, or ask a series of questions. Ernie's essay uses this strategy.

**2. Look ahead.** Project into the future. Consider outcomes or effects.

**3. Return to your thesis.** If your essay is written to prove a point or convince your reader of the need for action, it may be effective to end with a sentence that recalls your main point or calls for action. If you choose this way to conclude, be sure not to merely repeat your first paragraph. Be sure to reflect on the thoughts you developed in the body of your essay.

**4. Summarize key points.** Especially for longer essays, briefly review your key supporting ideas. In shorter essays, this tends to be unnecessary.

Ernie's essay might have ended with the following restatement:

Extending the school year will have important advantages. Children will learn to handle their time in meaningful ways and become better educated.

If you have trouble writing your conclusion, it's probably a tip-off that you need to work further on your thesis or organization. In the next section, we discuss how to reexamine your work to strengthen your message.

**EXERCISE**  **11-7** | Write or revise a conclusion for the essay you wrote for Exercise 11-4.

## Selecting a Title

Although the title appears first in your essay, it is often the last thing you should write. The title of your essay should identify the topic in an interesting way, and it may also suggest the focus. To select a title, reread your final draft, paying particular attention to your thesis statement and your overall method of development. Here are a few examples of effective titles:

"Surprise in the Vegetable Bin" (for an essay on vegetables and their effects on cholesterol and cancer)

"Denim Goes High Fashion" (for an essay describing the uses of denim for clothing other than jeans)

To write accurate and interesting titles, try the following tips:

1. Write a question that your essay answers, for example: Why Change the Minimum Wage?

2. Use key words that appear in your thesis statement. If your thesis statement is "The new international trade ruling threatens the safety of the dolphin, one of our most intelligent mammals," your title could be "New Threat to Dolphins."

3. Use brainstorming techniques to generate options. Don't necessarily go with the first title that pops into your mind. If in doubt, try out some options on friends to see which is most effective.

**EXERCISE** 11-8 ▶ | Select a title for the essay you wrote for Exercise 11-4.

## Using Revision Maps to Revise

In Chapter 5, "Strategies for Revising," p. 73, you learned to draw revision maps to evaluate paragraphs. The same strategy works well for essays, too. The revision map will enable you to evaluate the overall flow of ideas as well as the effectiveness of individual paragraphs. To draw an essay revision map, work through each paragraph, recording your ideas in abbreviated form, as shown below. Then write the key words of your conclusion. If you find details that do not support the topic sentence, record that detail to the left of the map.

**INTEREST AND BACKGROUND**

**THESIS STATEMENT**

**TRANSITION**

Unrelated details

1. _____
2. _____
3. _____

| Topic Sentence 1 | Topic Sentence 2 | Topic Sentence 3 | Conclusion |

detail · detail · detail

detail · detail · detail

detail · detail

A sample revision map for the essay on page 202 is shown below.

**Sample Revision Map**

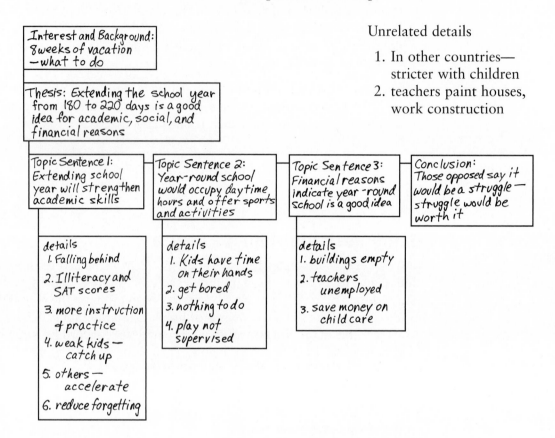

Unrelated details

1. In other countries—
   stricter with children
2. teachers paint houses,
   work construction

*Interest and Background:*
*8 weeks of vacation*
*—what to do*

*Thesis: Extending the school year*
*from 180 to 220 days is a good*
*idea for academic, social, and*
*financial reasons*

*Topic Sentence 1:*
*Extending school*
*year will strengthen*
*academic skills*

*Topic Sentence 2:*
*Year-round school*
*would occupy daytime*
*hours and offer sports*
*and activities*

*Topic Sentence 3:*
*Financial reasons*
*indicate year-round*
*school is a good idea*

*Conclusion:*
*Those opposed say it*
*would be a struggle—*
*struggle would be*
*worth it*

*details*
*1. Falling behind*
*2. Illiteracy and*
*   SAT scores*
*3. more instruction*
*   + practice*
*4. weak kids —*
*   catch up*
*5. others —*
*   accelerate*
*6. reduce forgetting*

*details*
*1. Kids have time*
*   on their hands*
*2. get bored*
*3. nothing to do*
*4. play not*
*   supervised*

*details*
*1. buildings empty*
*2. teachers*
*   unemployed*
*3. save money on*
*   child care*

When you've completed your revision map, conduct the following tests:

**1. Read your thesis statement along with your first topic sentence.** Does the topic sentence clearly support your thesis? If not, revise to make relationship clearer. Repeat this step for each topic sentence.

**2. Read your topic sentences, one after the other, without corresponding details.** Is there a logical connection between them? Are they arranged in the most effective way? If not, revise to make the connection clearer or to improve your organization.

**3. Examine each individual paragraph.** Are there enough relevant, specific details to support the topic sentence?

**4. Read your introduction and then look at your topic sentences.** Does the essay deliver what the introduction promises?

**5. Read your thesis statement and then your conclusion.** Are they compatible and consistent? Does the conclusion agree with and support the thesis statement?

EXERCISE  11-9 | Draw a revision map for the essay you wrote for Exercises 11-4 through 11-8 and revise accordingly.

## Thinking Before Reading

This reading, "The End of the Golden Era" by John Cassidy, first appeared in *The New Yorker* magazine in a longer form. It serves as an excellent example of how an essay is organized. As you read, notice how the author presents and develops his thesis statement and how he introduces and concludes his essay.

1. Preview the reading using the steps listed on page 45.
2. Activate your thinking by answering the following:
   a. Are you or your family doing as well economically today as you were three or four years ago?
   b. Are you spending more now on necessities than you were a few years ago?
   c. In what economic class would you place yourself?

**READING**

## The End of the Golden Era
### John Cassidy

In the three decades after the Second World War, the American dream of moving to the suburbs, buying a house, and even sending the kids to college was no mere election slogan. Home-ownership soared, and the living standards of the middle class—idealized in television sitcoms like "The Adventures of Ozzie and Harriet," "Leave It to Beaver," and "The Donna Reed Show"—were the envy of the world. Whereas an English workingman might aspire to own a small row house on a grim city street, his American counterpart could look forward to acquiring a split-level house in the sprawling suburbs, with a backyard and a barbecue—and maybe even a summer cabin on a lake. From 1945 until 1973—a period that economic historians now refer to as the Golden Era—the rich got richer, but almost everybody else got richer with them, and at roughly the same pace. The spoils of economic growth were divided remarkably evenly. Broadly speaking, all Americans' incomes doubled—secretaries', factory workers', bank executives'. Today, that image is as dated as the television shows it spawned. Falling wages—and, of course, rising real-estate prices—have transformed the home economics of tens of millions of American families.

The country has now split into four groups. At the top, there is an immensely wealthy élite, which has never had it so good. At the bottom, there is an underclass, which is increasingly divorced from the rest of society. And between these extremes there are, instead of a unified middle class, two distinct groups: an upper echelon of highly skilled, highly educated professionals, who are doing pretty well; and a vast swath of unskilled and semiskilled workers, who are experiencing falling wages, stagnant or declining living standards, and increased economic uncertainty. To label this group "middle class" doesn't make sense. The phrase implies two things—rising living standards and a high degree of economic security—that no longer apply.

Few politicians are willing to admit this publicly. Prime-time sitcom producers, however, have long been aware of the truth that the politicians dare not utter. As a result, the Simpsons, the Bundys, and the Conners have replaced the Cleavers, the Stones, and the Nelsons as the archetypal American families. These shows are well grounded in reality. They all feature nuclear families, which are still the typical living arrangement, despite the growth of single-parent households. (In 1993, according to the Census Bureau, there were 53.2 million families headed by married couples and 12.4 million headed by females, with no male present.)

Homer Simpson, Al Bundy, and Dan Conner are excellent examples of the seventy-five per cent of American men who do not have a college degree and are feeling the pinch. Between 1979 and 1995, according to the Labor Department, the median male worker saw his annual earnings tumble 11.5 per cent, from $31,317 to $27,716. Those who didn't go to college fared even worse. Lawrence Mishel and Jared Bernstein point out that between 1973 and 1993 the hourly wages of high-school graduates and high-school dropouts fell by 14.7 per cent and 22.5 per cent, respectively.

With men's wages plummeting during those two decades, married women came under increasing pressure to enter the workforce, and that development was also picked up in Hollywood. While Harriet Nelson stayed at home and looked after the family, Roseanne Conner has held at least six jobs in eight seasons. There are millions of women like Roseanne. In 1979, the proportion of families with children under eighteen in which both parents worked year-round was less than one in five. By 1993, it had grown to almost one in three. Women with very young children were also increasingly likely to work. Twenty years ago, only thirty-one per cent of all women with children under two years of age were in the labor force. Earlier this year [1995], that figure was found to be more than fifty-five per cent.

The big squeeze was reflected in changed spending patterns. Middle-income families, with their incomes stagnating, were forced to spend an ever-expanding share of their income on three of the basic necessities: housing, utilities, and health care. The typical American household is now spending almost half its income—46.1 per cent—on these three necessities. A generation ago, only a third—33.3 per cent—of the family's income went for these expenses. (The percentage spent on another necessity—food—has remained relatively stable, at about sixteen per cent.)

4

5

6

At some point both parties will have to level with the voters and tell    7
them the truth: that the postwar Golden Era is gone forever, and the
great middle class has gone with it. This is nobody's fault: it is just how
capitalism has developed.

*The New Yorker*

## Getting Ready to Write

### ■ Examining the Reading: Using Idea Maps to Understand a Reading

In this reading, the author presents his observations on how the average American family has been affected by economic changes since the
1970s. He illustrates the results of some of these changes with examples
and statistics. He uses this evidence to support his thesis about the middle
class.

The technique shown earlier in the chapter for drawing maps to evaluate and revise your writing can also be used to check the content and
organization of what you read. Drawing idea maps can enhance your
understanding of the material and improve your recall. By extracting key
points from an essay and recording them on an idea map, you will be better able to follow and evaluate the evidence the author uses to support his
thesis. You can use the format shown on page 207 to draw an idea map
for an article or essay.

**EXERCISE**  Construct an idea map of "The End of the Golden Era" using the format
shown on page 207.

### ■ Thinking Critically: Making Inferences

An inference is a decision about something unknown based on what is
known: available facts and information. Suppose you are driving on an
expressway when, looking in your rear-view mirror, you notice a police
car coming up behind you with its red lights flashing. You glance at your
speedometer and it reads 15 mph over the posted speed limit. What do
you think is going to happen next? By predicting that you are going to be
pulled over for speeding, you are making an inference.

Writers sometimes leave ideas and relationships unstated but expect their readers to make the necessary inferences. You can think of making inferences as a process of reading between the lines. For instance in "The End of the Golden Era," you can make the inference that the author distrusts politicians. He does not say so outright. Instead, he provides hints so that you can infer it. Specifically, Cassidy says that "both parties will have to level with the voters and tell them the truth" about declining prosperity. Cassidy implies, but does not directly state, that political parties have not been leveling with voters and have not been telling them the truth. Earlier in the reading, Cassidy mentions a "truth that the politicians dare not utter: that economic stability is becoming harder for many families to achieve." This statement again suggests that he believes politicians do not tell the truth, if the truth is not welcome.

**EXERCISE**  **11-11** Answer each of the following questions about the reading. You will need to make inferences in order to answer them. Look for evidence in the article to support your answer.

1. In the past, who has had higher aspirations, Americans or English men and women?
2. Is a college degree still valuable in the job market?
3. Do you think the author is a regular television viewer?
4. Why was the period between 1945 and 1973 called the "Golden Era"?
5. Are Hollywood producers attuned to changes in the American standard of living?

■ **Reacting to Ideas: Discussion and Journal Writing**

1. Does your standard of living differ from that of your parents or grandparents? If so, how?

2. What effect does the increasing number of women in the workforce have on families?

3. Should government intervene to close the widening economic gap between the "haves" and the "have-nots" in the United States? Explain your answer.

4. In this excerpt, Cassidy describes how the economic situation in the United States has changed, but he does not explain why the changes have occurred. Why do you think they have occurred?

# Writing Assignments

## Writing About the Reading

1. The author writes that the home economics of tens of millions of Americans have changed, that wages have plummeted, and that there has been a change in spending patterns. He also states that the great middle class no longer exists. Write an essay explaining whether you agree or disagree with these statements. Support your ideas using examples from your experience and that of your family.

## Writing About Your Ideas

2. Write an essay describing a television show that you feel presents a realistic (or unrealistic) picture of American life. Be sure to explain why you feel it is or is not realistic.

3. Cassidy expresses distrust of politicians. Is he justified? Write an essay expressing your degree of trust in political figures and supporting your position with evidence.

4. Cassidy describes what was once the American dream: buying a house in the suburbs, sending one's children to college, and so forth. Is this your dream? If not, what is your dream? That is, what are you striving toward and what do you hope to achieve? Have you been forced to revise your dream over the years? If so, why? Write an essay responding to these questions.

## REVISION CHECKLIST

1. Is your essay appropriate for your audience? Does it give them the background information they need? Will it interest them?

2. Will your essay accomplish your purpose?

3. Have you narrowed your topic so that you can cover your subject thoroughly in your essay?

4. Is your main point clearly expressed in a thesis statement in the introductory paragraph? Does your introductory paragraph capture the reader's interest and lead into the body of the essay?

5. Does each paragraph of your essay have a topic sentence that supports your main point?

6. Is each paragraph's topic sentence supported by relevant and sufficient detail?

7. Are your paragraphs arranged in a logical sequence and connected by transitional words and phrases?

8. Is the tone of your essay appropriate for your purpose and audience?

9. Does your conclusion reemphasize your thesis statement and draw the essay to a close?

10. Does your title identify the topic and interest the reader?

11. Have you proofread your paper and corrected any mechanical errors (grammar, spelling, punctuation, and so on)? (See the inside back cover of this book for a proofreading checklist.)

# SKILL REFRESHER

## Subordinate Clauses

Subordination is a way of showing that one idea is less important than another. When an idea is related to another idea, but less important, the less important idea can be expressed as a dependent clause. Dependent clauses contain a subject and a verb but do not express a complete thought and cannot stand alone as grammatically complete sentences. They are always used in combination with a complete sentence or independent clause.

## One Way to Combine Ideas of Unequal Importance

When a less important idea is combined with one of greater importance, it is helpful to show how the ideas relate to one another. Use a word such as *after, although, before, while, when,* and *because* to begin the dependent clause and show its relationship to the more important idea. In the examples below, the subordinating conjunctions are underlined.

After I finished the exam, I went to the coffee shop. [The word *after* indicates that the two ideas are related in time.]

Because I missed the bus, I was late for my math class. [The word *because* indicates that missing the bus was the reason for being late.]

I won't be able to make my tuition payment unless my student loan comes in soon. [The word *unless* indicates that the tuition payment depends on the student loan.]

## SKILL REFRESHER CONTINUED

The two clauses can appear in either order. When the dependent clause appears first, a comma follows it. (Refer to the first and second examples above.) When the independent clause comes first, a comma is usually not needed. (See the third example above.)

### Rate Your Ability to Use Subordinate Clauses

Combine each of the following pairs of sentences to form a sentence in which one idea is more important than the other. Add or delete words as necessary.

1. Mushrooms are a type of fungus. Some types are safe to eat.

2. Grape juice is fermented. Grape juice becomes wine.

3. It is important for children to be immunized. Children who are not immunized are vulnerable to many dangerous diseases.

4. A poem should be read carefully. Next, it should be analyzed.

5. The Vikings were probably the first Europeans to set foot in North America. Columbus "discovered" America much later.

6. I was giving a speech in my communications class. At the same time, Carl Sagan was giving a speech on campus.

7. I started my assignment for French class. I was relieved that it was a very easy assignment.

8. Infants may seem unaware and oblivious to their surroundings. They are able to recognize their mother's voice and smell from birth.

9. Neo-Freudians disagreed with Freud's focus on biological instincts and sexual drive. They formed new theories.

10. The hypothalamus is a tiny part of the brain. It has many very important functions, including the regulation of hormones, body temperature, and hunger.

Score_____

Check your answers using the Answer Key on page 486. If you missed more than two, you need additional review and practice in working with subordinate clauses. Refer to Part VI, "Reviewing the Basics," p. 438.

# CHAPTER SUMMARY

**Writing Skills**

1. Your thesis statement should clearly and specifically state the main point of your essay.

2. The body of your essay provides information to support your thesis statement. Focus on
   - developing each paragraph effectively.
   - arranging your paragraphs in a logical sequence.
   - connecting your paragraphs using transitional words and sentences or by repeating key words.

3. Your introductory paragraph should
   - present your thesis statement and suggest the organization of your essay.
   - interest your reader and provide background information.

4. Several types of hooks can be used to capture your reader's interest: a question, startling fact, story, quotation, or misunderstood fact.

5. Your conclusion should reemphasize your thesis statement and draw your essay to a close. You might
   - restate your thesis.
   - suggest a new direction for further thought.
   - summarize key points.
   - look ahead.

6. The title of your essay should identify your topic and interest your reader.

7. Revision involves examining and evaluating ideas. Evaluate
   - the overall effectiveness of your essay.
   - the effectiveness of each individual paragraph.

**Reading and Critical Thinking Skills**

1. Idea maps are a useful way to follow the content and organization of an essay, to improve your recall, and to evaluate evidence the author provides.

2. An inference is a decision about something unknown based on what is known, available facts, and information.

# 12

# Summarizing and Synthesizing Sources

## CHAPTER OBJECTIVES

*In this chapter you will learn to*

1. work with reference sources.

2. write annotations, paraphrases, and summaries.

3. use sources to support your ideas.

4. synthesize sources.

In completing some of the writing assignments in this book, you may have found yourself wishing you had more detailed facts or information to support your ideas. Suppose, for example, you are writing a paper about why you think radio talk shows are popular. As you write, you realize that it would be helpful to have some statistics about which talk shows draw the largest audiences and what kinds of people, in general, make up those audiences. By consulting the right books or magazine and newspaper articles, you can often find the needed information. You can then integrate this information into your paper (noting where you got it, of course) and use the facts from the books or articles to support the points you are making. Many assignments that you will be given in college will require you to locate and read several sources of information on a topic like this, and then use them to support and "flesh out" your ideas.

Other times, you may be asked to examine certain printed sources and come up with a new idea or thesis about them. For example, you may be asked to consult several essays or speeches by a member of Congress and develop a thesis about her outlook on a particular environmental issue. You may be asked to examine several sources about today's space program and come up with an idea about why it should or should not be continued. You may be asked to find several different newspaper or magazine accounts of an event and to write about how coverage varied depending on where the account was printed. This chapter will provide some tips and practice in two ways to use written sources in your writing: (1) to support your ideas, and (2) as the subject matter about which to develop your own ideas.

## Working with Reference Sources

A library is filled with sources. It houses thousands of books, journals, videos, CD-ROMs, pamphlets, tapes, and newspapers that can help you complete an assignment. One of the hardest parts of using sources is locating those that can be the most help to you.

Many books have been written on how to do library research and use and document various kinds of sources. This section gives a brief overview of the research process and offers you some advice on how to get started.

### Finding and Using Appropriate Sources

Say you are writing an essay about the effects of the computer on the quality of life today. Although the library may have many sources that deal with your topic, not all will be appropriate for your particular assignment. Some sources may be too technical; others may be too sketchy. Some may be outdated, others too opinionated. Your task is to find sources that will give you good, solid, current information or points of view. Use the following tips:

**1. Keep track of all sources you use.** There are several good reasons for doing this:

- When you use sources in a paper, you must list them all at the end of your paper in a bibliography or "Works Cited." Providing your reader with information on your sources is called *documentation*.
- You may want to refer to the source again.
- You are more likely to avoid plagiarism if you keep accurate records of your sources. Plagiarism is using an author's words or ideas without acknowledging that you have done so. It is a serious ethical error and legal violation. In some colleges, plagiarism is sufficient cause for failing a course or even being dismissed from the college. You can easily avoid plagiarism by properly acknowledging your sources within your paper.

Record all publication information about each source: title, author(s), volume, edition, place and date of publication, publisher, and page numbers. You may want to use index cards or a small bound notebook to record source information, using a separate card or page for each source. For additional information on documentation, consult Part VI, "Reviewing the Basics," p. 470.

**2. Consult the reference librarian.** If you are unsure of where to begin, ask the reference librarian for advice. It is the reference librarian's job to suggest useful sources. He or she can be very helpful to you.

**3. Use a systematic approach.** Start using general sources, such as general reference books, and, as needed, move to more specific sources such as periodicals and journals (scholarly magazines written for people focused on a particular area of study).

**4. Use current sources.** For many topics, such as controversial issues or scientific or medical advances, only the most up-to-date sources are useful. For other topics, such as moral issues involved in abortion or euthanasia, older sources can be used. Before you begin, decide on a cut-off date—a date before which you feel information will be outdated and therefore not useful to you.

**5. Sample a variety of viewpoints.** Try to find sources that present differing viewpoints on the same subject rather than counting on one source to contain everything you need. Various authors take different approaches and have different opinions on the same topic, all of which can increase your understanding of the topic.

**6. Preview articles by reading abstracts or summaries.** Many sources begin with an abstract or end with a summary. Before using the source, check the abstract or summary to determine if the source is going to be helpful.

**7. Reading sources selectively.** Many students spend time needlessly reading entire books and articles thoroughly when they should be reading selectively—skimming to avoid parts that are not on the subject and to locate portions that relate directly to their topic. To read selectively

- use indexes and tables of contents to locate the portions of books that are useful and appropriate. In articles, use abstracts or summaries as a guide to the material's organization: the order in which ideas appear in the summary or abstract is the order in which they appear in the source itself.
- after you have identified useful sections, preview (see p. 45) to get an overview of the material.
- use headings to select sections to read thoroughly.

**8. Look for sources that lead to other sources.** Some sources include a bibliography, which provides leads to other works related to your topic.

**EXERCISE 12-1**   Choose one of the broad topics below. Use a prewriting strategy to narrow the topic and develop a working thesis statement. Locate at least three reference sources that are useful and appropriate for writing a paper of two to three pages on the topic you have developed. Make a photocopy of each source. Be sure to record all the bibliographic information for each source.

1. use of alcohol by teenagers
2. drug testing in the workplace
3. date rape
4. teenage parents

5. establishing smoke-free public places
6. a patient's right to assisted suicide
7. the spread, control, or treatment of HIV
8. violence in the media
9. controversy over college athletic scholarships
10. legalized gambling (or lotteries)

# Annotating a Source

In her mass-media course, Marcie was assigned to write on how the media, such as TV, radio, and magazines, can shape how people think. In a textbook she found a report of a study that researched how the media portray men differently from women. It was the first information she had found on the different treatment of the sexes in the media, and the subject caught her interest. Deciding to narrow her paper to that topic, she read the discussion carefully, highlighter in hand, thinking about ways she could develop the topic. All kinds of questions and thoughts came to mind. By highlighting, however, she was not able to record her ideas and reactions. Putting ideas on a separate sheet of paper and copying quotations from the article would not work because she was running out of time. A friend suggested that she annotate instead.

## Why Write Annotations?

Marcie photocopied the article and recorded her reactions to the article in the margins. Both the excerpt of the article and Marcie's annotations are shown below. First, read the excerpt; then study the marginal notes, called *annotations*. Then read the following sections to discover why and how to annotate.

*Excerpt*

which media?
all media?

Media images of men and women also differ in other subtle ways. In any visual representation of a person—such as a photograph, drawing, or painting—you can measure the relative prominence of the face by calculating the percentage of the vertical dimension occupied by the model's head. When Dane Archer and his colleagues (1983) inspected 1,750 photographs from *Time*, *Newsweek*, and other magazines, they found what they called

aren't men's
faces larger?

"face-ism," a bias toward greater facial prominence in pictures of men than of women. This phenomenon is so prevalent that it appeared in analyses of

who selects them?
were they selected
randomly?

3,500 photographs from different countries, classic portraits painted in the seventeenth century, and the amateur drawings of college students.

Why is the face more prominent in pictures of men than of women? One possible interpretation is that face-ism reflects historical conceptions of the

were only portraits
and drawings
analyzed?

why?
are these
stereotypes?

sexes. The face and head symbolize the mind and *intellect*—which are tradi-tionally associated with men. With respect to women, more importance is attached to the heart, emotions, or perhaps just the body. Indeed, when peo-ple evaluate models from photographs, those pictured with high facial prominence are seen as smarter and more assertive, active, and ambitious—regardless of their gender (Schwarz & Kurz, 1989). Another interpretation is that facial prominence signals power and *dominance*.

Brehm and Kassin, *Social Psychology*

Annotating gave Marcie a way of jotting down her ideas, reactions, opinions, and comments as she read. Think of annotation as scribbling your ideas about what you are reading. It is a personal way to brainstorm and "talk back" to the author—to question, challenge, agree, disagree, or comment. Annotations are particularly useful when you are working with a source in great detail. You can use annotations to clarify meaning as well as to record your responses. To clarify meaning, you might

- underline or highlight key ideas
- place a star by key terms or definitions
- number key supporting information
- define unfamiliar words
- paraphrase a complicated idea
- bracket ([ ]) a useful example
- mark with an asterisk (*) useful summary statements
- draw arrows connecting ideas
- highlight statements that reveal the author's feelings or attitudes.

In recording your responses, you might include

| | |
|---|---|
| questions | Why would . . . ? |
| challenges to the author's ideas | If this is true, wouldn't . . . ? |
| inconsistencies | But the author has already said that . . . |
| examples | For instance . . . |
| exceptions | This wouldn't be true if . . . |
| disagreements | How could . . . ? |
| associations with other sources | This is similar to . . . |
| judgments | Good point . . . |

Overall, you will find annotating to be a useful way to make meaning clear and to interact with the author's words and ideas. When you use the source in your own paper, you will know much better what it says and thus be able to go right to the part that you need.

**EXERCISE 12-2** ▶ Reread one of the sources you located in Exercise 12-1 and write annotations for it.

## Writing a Paraphrase

Yolanda was writing a paper on animal communication for her biology class. She found one passage in a reference source that contained exactly the information she needed. She began to take notes from the passage, but realized that since she needed to remember both the author's main points and details, a paraphrase would be better. A *paraphrase* is a restatement, in your own words, of a passage. In a paraphrase you fully acknowledge who wrote the original and where you found it, but you condense it and recast it. It is a rewording of each sentence in the order in which each appears in the passage.

Here is an excerpt from the source Yolanda was using, followed by her paraphrase.

*Excerpt from Source*

Communication in the Animal Kingdom

Animal species have complex forms of communication. *Ants* send chemical signals secreted from glands to share information about food and enemies with other members of the colony. When *honeybees* discover a source of nectar, they return to the hive and communicate its location to the other worker bees through an intricate dance that signals both direction and distance. Male *songbirds* of various species sing in the spring to attract a female mate and also to warn other males to stay away from his territory to avoid a fight. *Dolphins* talk to each other at great depths of the ocean by making a combination of clicking, whistling, and barking sounds.

Kassin, *Psychology*

*Yolanda's Paraphrase of "Communication in the Animal Kingdom"*

Animals have complicated ways of communicating. Ants can tell each other about food and enemies by secreting chemicals from their glands. Honeybees tell others in their hive that they have found a source of nectar by a detailed dance that indicates both where the nectar is located and how far away it is. In the spring, male songbirds sing to draw females and to warn other males to stay away so as to avoid a dispute. Using clicks, whistles, and barking sounds, dolphins communicate with each other.

## Why Write a Paraphrase?

Paraphrasing is a useful skill for many college courses. First, in combination with careful documentation of source information, it is a way to record ideas from a source for later use in a paper. It gives you complete information in a form that is easy to understand. Sometimes your paraphrase can be incorporated directly into your paper (see p. 231). Remember, however, that though you have changed the wording, you are still working with someone else's ideas and not your own; therefore, it is still necessary to document the source in your paper. (Refer to Part VI, "Reviewing the Basics," p. 470.) Second, you can also use paraphrasing as a way of making an author's ideas clearer and more understandable, regardless of whether you plan to use them or not. When you paraphrase, you are forced to understand each idea fully and to see how ideas relate to one another. Finally, paraphrasing is a useful study and notetaking strategy. It allows the convenient review of difficult or complicated material.

### How to Paraphrase

A paraphrase involves two skills: (1) substituting synonyms and (2) rearranging the order of ideas within each sentence.

## Substituting Synonyms

A synonym is a word that has the same general meaning as another word. Take another look at Yolanda's paraphrase and the original source, noticing how Yolanda substituted synonyms. For example, in the first sentence she substituted *complicated* for *complex,* *types* for *forms,* and so forth. When selecting synonyms, use the following guidelines:

1. **Make sure the synonym you choose fits the context (overall meaning) of the sentence.** Suppose the sentence you are paraphrasing is, "The physician attempted to *neutralize* the effects of the drug overdose." All of the following words are synonyms for the word *neutralize: negate, nullify, counteract.* However, *counteract* fits the context, while *negate* and *nullify* do not. *Negate* and *nullify* suggest the ability to cancel, and a drug overdose, once taken, cannot be canceled. It can, however, be counteracted.

2. **Keep a dictionary right at hand.** Use your dictionary to check the exact meanings of words, and use your thesaurus (dictionary of synonyms) to get ideas for alternative or equivalent words.

3. **Do not try to replace every word in a sentence with a synonym.** Sometimes a substitute does not exist. In the sentence, "Archeologists study fossils of extinct species," the term *fossils* clearly and accurately describes what archeologists study. Therefore, it does not need to be replaced.

4. **Be sure to paraphrase and that you do not change *only* a few words.** Changing only a few words is plagiarizing, not paraphrasing.

### Rearranging Sentence Parts

Return to Yolanda's paraphrase on page 223. Reread her paraphrase again, noticing how the ideas within each sentence were rearranged. When rearranging sentence parts, use the following guidelines:

**1. Split lengthy, complicated sentences into two or more shorter sentences.**

**2. Be sure you understand the author's key ideas as well as related ideas.** Include both in your paraphrase. For example,

ORIGINAL: Many judges hold that television cameras should not be permitted in a court of law because the defendant's right to a fair trial may be jeopardized.

CORRECT PARAPHRASE: Since cameras may prevent a defendant from being treated fairly, many judges feel television cameras should not be allowed in the courtroom.

INCORRECT PARAPHRASE: Many judges feel television cameras should not be allowed in the courtroom.

The incorrect paraphrase does not include the reason *why* (a related idea) judges feel cameras should not be allowed.

EXERCISE  Working sentence by sentence, write a paraphrase of paragraphs 3 and 4 of "Who Has the Right to Name?" at the end of this chapter. Compare your work with that of a classmate; combine both of your paraphrases to produce a revised paraphrase.

EXERCISE  Write a paraphrase of two or three consecutive paragraphs of one of the sources you located in Exercise 12-1.

## Writing Summaries

The instructor of a speech class placed a copy of *You Just Don't Understand: Women and Men in Conversation* by Deborah Tannen on reserve in the library, then directed his students to read the excerpt below, among other sections. After a class discussion of differences in the way men and women communicate, each student was told to write a one-page paper on the subject.

One student, James, decided to write a summary of the selection from Tannen because it would provide a brief review of the ideas she presented. He did not need details and specifics; he wanted a record of the concept of anchoring gaze and its implications. In other situations, summarizing is useful in condensing lengthy sources.

Another student in the class, Carlos, also decided to write a summary of the excerpt. After you have read the excerpt from Tannen, compare the two student summaries and decide which is more effective.

### Original Selection

Differences in physical alignment, or body language among friends talking to each other, leap out at anyone who looks at segments of videotapes one after another. At every age, the girls and women sit closer to each other and look at each other directly. At every age, the boys and men sit at angles to each other—in one case, almost parallel—and never look directly into each other's faces. I developed the term *anchoring gaze* to describe this visual home base. The girls and women anchor their gaze on each other's faces, occasionally glancing away, while the boys and men anchor their gaze elsewhere in the room, occasionally glancing at each other.

The boys' and men's avoidance of looking directly at each other is especially important because researchers, and conventional wisdom, have emphasized that girls and women tend to be more indirect than boys and men in their speech. Actually, women and men tend to be indirect about different things. In physical alignment, and in verbally expressing personal problems, the men tend to be more indirect.

Tannen, *You Just Don't Understand: Women and Men in Conversation*

### Carlos's Summary

Although researchers and others have traditionally believed men to be more direct than women, the truth is that men and women tend to be indirect about different things. Specifically, men tend to be less direct than women in body language and when verbally expressing personal problems. Researchers now know this from having studied segments of videotapes that depict friends interacting. In each of these tapes, women sit closer to each other than men, and women look more directly at each other than men do. This discovery is particularly important since it has generally been widely accepted that men are more direct than women in both areas.

### James's Summary

There are many differences in physical alignment as seen on videotapes of men and women. During each tape, women and girls align themselves closer (sit closer) than men and boys. Men and boys sit at angular positions—not facing each other. In fact, they never even look at each other's faces. The word *anchoring* is used to describe their visual gaze. It is said that girls and women anchor their gaze on each other's faces, but boys and men anchor their gaze everywhere else in the room except on each other's faces. They only glance at each other sometimes.

Researchers find the fact that boys and men avoid looking into each other's faces interesting because the idea that girls and women are usually more indirect than boys and men has always been universally accepted. Also researchers have advocated the idea that girls and women have a tendency to be less direct in their speech than boys and men. In reality, men and women are both indirect about different things. In the verbal expression of problems and in physical alignment, men tend to be less direct.

Did you decide that Carlos's summary was more effective? Did you notice that James repeated each idea that appeared in the original? He did not eliminate detail or focus only on the main points. Carlos, however, identified the main point of the selection and explained it using information from Tannen.

## What Is a Summary and How Is It Used?

A *summary* is a brief statement that reviews the major points of a source. Its purpose is to give an overview of a source by presenting the key ideas in a condensed form. Usually a summary is about one-fifth of the original, or less, depending on the amount of detail needed. Summaries are useful in three key ways:

1. They will help you assess and improve your grasp of a writer's ideas. If you cannot summarize an article, it is a signal that you do not understand it. Writing a summary also clarifies your thinking. To write a summary you are forced to sort ideas and see how they relate.

2. They will help you condense information when using sources in your writing. A summary is a means of recording another writer's ideas, but in shortened form. Summaries enable you to keep track of a writer's important ideas and eliminate less important information.

3. They may be required by college instructors. You may be asked to submit a plot summary of a short story, a summary of a news article for economics, or a summary of your findings for a laboratory experiment in the sciences.

## How to Write a Summary

To write more effective summaries, follow these guidelines.

**1. Read the entire source first before writing anything.**

**2. Review the source.** Underline or highlight the main points, and make annotations in the margins.

3. **Write an opening sentence that states the author's thesis.**

4. **Explain or paraphrase the author's most important supporting ideas.** (Refer to text you have underlined or highlighted.) Be sure to express the author's main ideas in your own words. Don't copy phrases or sentences. If you can't express an idea in your own words, you probably don't yet understand it. Look up words, reread, talk to someone about the passage, and think about the passage to clarify meaning.

5. **Include restated definitions of key terms, important concepts, procedures, or principles.** Do not include examples, descriptive details, quotations, or anything incidental to the main point. Do not include your opinion, even to say it was a good article.

6. **Present the ideas in the order in which they appear in the original source.**

7. **Reread your summary to determine if it contains sufficient information.** Use this test: would your summary be understandable to someone who had not read the article? If not, revise your summary to include additional information.

Be sure to note in full the bibliographic reference for each source you summarize. When you write your paper, you will need to give credit to the writer if you use information from the summary in your paper. If you don't cite your original source, you may be guilty of plagiarism, whether you intend to "copy" it or not.

EXERCISE  12-5 | Write a summary of "What's in a Label: Black or 'African American'?" at the end of this chapter, pp. 237–238. Use the steps listed above.

EXERCISE  12-6 | Write a summary of one of the sources you located for Exercise 12-1 (a different source from the one you paraphrased).

## Using Sources to Support Your Ideas

Often when writing an essay you will find that you need additional information to support or explain your ideas. Suppose you are writing an essay on one aspect of the homeless situation in America. Your thesis states that more social programs should be funded to help homeless people regain control of their lives. In order to present a well-explained and convincing paper, you need facts, statistics, and evidence to support your opinions. For example, you might need

- statistics on the numbers of homeless
- statistics on the increase in homelessness in the past three years
- statistics on the amount of money spent on programs for the homeless
- facts on the types of social programs currently in operation
- facts on which programs work and which do not
- statistics on the costs of existing programs.

In these situations, you need to consult one or more reference sources to locate supporting information. The following guidelines will help you use sources properly.

**1. Write a first draft of your paper.** Before consulting sources to support your ideas, work through the first three steps of the writing process: prewriting, organizing, and drafting. Get your ideas down on paper. Once you have drafted your paper, you will be able to see what types of supporting information are necessary. If you research first, you might get flooded with facts and with other writers' voices and viewpoints, and lose your own.

**2. Analyze your draft to identify needed information.** Study your draft and look for statements that require supporting information in order to be believable. For example, suppose you have written

> The number of homeless people is increasing in Chicago each year, and nothing is being done about the increase.

To support the first part of this statement, you need statistics on the increase in homelessness in Chicago. To support the second part, you need evidence that there has not been an increase in federal, state, or local funding for the homeless in Chicago. The following types of statements benefit from supporting information:

- opinions

  EXAMPLE: Homeless people are (or are not) trustworthy.

  NEEDED INFORMATION: Why? What evidence supports that opinion?

- broad, general ideas

  EXAMPLE: Social programs for the homeless don't work as well as they should.

  NEEDED INFORMATION: What programs are available? What evidence suggests they don't work?

- cause-and-effect statements

  EXAMPLE: Most homeless people are on the street because they lost their jobs.

  NEEDED INFORMATION: How many are homeless because they lost their jobs? How many are homeless for other reasons?

- statements that assert what should be done

  EXAMPLE: The homeless should be given more assistance in locating jobs.

  NEEDED INFORMATION: How much are they given now? How many are helped? For how many is it not available?

**3. Write questions.** Read your draft looking for unsupported statements, underlining them as you find them. Then make a list of needed information, and form questions that need to be answered. Some students find it effective to write each question on a separate index card.

**4. Record information and note sources.** As you locate needed information, make a decision about the best way to record it. Should you photocopy the source and annotate it? Should you paraphrase? Should you write a summary? Your answer will depend on the type of information you are using, as well as the requirements of your assignment. Always include complete bibliographic information for each source (see p. 470).

As you consult sources, you will probably discover new ideas and perhaps even a new approach to your topic. For example, you may learn that the homeless are not all the same: some are well educated and employable, some down on their luck, and others burdened with problems that would make holding a job difficult. Record each of these new ideas on a separate index card, along with its source.

**5. Revise your paper.** Begin by adding or incorporating new supporting information. (The next section of this chapter, "Adding Information From Sources," will discuss how to add and document information you borrow from other sources.) Then reevaluate your draft, eliminating statements for which you could not locate supporting information, statements that you found to be inaccurate, and statements for which you found contradictory evidence.

**EXERCISE** 12-7 ▶ | Write a first draft of a paper on the topic you chose in Exercise 12-1. To support your ideas, use the three sources you located. If any of these sources prove to be too dated or not focused enough on your thesis, you may need to locate additional ones.

## Adding Information From Sources

When you locate information to support or explain your ideas, you can incorporate it into your paper in one of two ways: (1) summarize or paraphrase the information or (2) quote directly from it. In both cases, you must give credit to the authors from whom you borrowed the material. This is called *citing* a source.

## Summarized or Paraphrased Information

When you paraphrase information from a source, you need to give the author credit. Do this by using an in-text citation: a brief note that refers to a source fully described in what is called the List of Works Cited. This list appears at the end of your paper and provides all your sources in alphabetical order. Here are samples of in-text citations and a sample entry from a List of Works Cited.

### Sample In-text Citations

Masson and McCarthy argue that animals do have emotions and feelings, though humans may not know what those feelings are (1).

Researchers often disregard evidence of emotion if the animal is captive or treated as a pet (Masson and McCarthy 5).

### Sample Entry from List of Works Cited

Masson, Jeffrey Moussaieff, and Susan McCarthy. *When Elephants Weep.* New York: Delacourt, 1995.

The following guidelines will help you write in-text citations:

1. If the source is introduced by a phrase that names the author, the citation need only include the page number.
2. If the author is not named in the sentence, then include both the author's name and the page number in the citation.

Entries in the List of Works Cited must follow a specific format. That is, titles, authors, publishers, places of publication, and dates must be in a specific order and punctuated in a specific way. There are numerous systems used by various academic disciplines to cite information. One of the most common is the Modern Language Association (MLA) documentation system. Because the MLA style of documentation is used in the field of English, it is used in this text. An overview of the MLA style is presented in section G of Part VI, "Reviewing the Basics," p. 470.

## Direct Quotations

At times, you may want to use an author's exact words to explain or support one of your ideas. Be sure to limit your use of direct quotations to times when the author's wording is necessary; too many quotations make your paper seem choppy and may suggest that you rely too heavily on the wording and thinking of others. To use a direct quotation, copy the author's words exactly and place them within quotation marks. If the quotation is lengthy, set it apart from the rest of your paper by indenting it, and do not use quotation marks. You do not always have to quote full sentences; you can borrow phrases or clauses as long as they fit into your sentence, both logically and grammatically.

*Direct Quotation*

Masson and McCarthy observe that "social animals who live in groups often behave in a friendly way toward other members of the group, even when they are not relatives" (78).

*Lengthy Quotation*

In discussing how to judge animal emotions, Masson and McCarthy note

> Knowing what we feel is one way to judge whether an animal feels something similar, but may not be the only, or even the best way. Are animals' similarities [to] and differences from humans the only, or even the most important, issue? (xxi).

*Partial Sentence Quotation*

Masson and McCarthy observe that we all have seen "gorillas sitting motionless, seemingly in despair, or perhaps having abandoned all hope of ever being free" (xvii).

When you include a quotation in your paper, you should signal your reader that one is to follow. For example, use such introductory phrases as the following:

According to Masson and McCarthy, "[quotation]"
As Masson and McCarthy have noted, "[quotation]"
In the words of Masson and McCarthy, "[quotation]"

**EXERCISE**  12-8 | For the paper you drafted in Exercise 12-7, write in-text citations and entries for your List of Works Cited. Then add two direct quotations to your paper, writing entries for your List of Works Cited if the source for either is not included in the list.

## Synthesizing Sources

In many situations of daily life, we consult several sources before drawing a conclusion or making a decision. For example, you might talk with several students who have taken the course American labor history before deciding if you want to register for it. You might talk to several friends who own pick-up trucks before buying one. Suppose you're debating about whether to see a particular film. You talk with three friends who have seen it. Each liked the movie and described different scenes. However, from their various descriptions, you may conclude that the film contains too much violence and that you don't want to see it. In deciding, you drew together several sources of information and came to your own conclusion: the film is too violent for you. In these and similar situations you are synthesizing information. *Synthesis* is a process of using information from two or more sources in order to develop new ideas about a topic or to draw conclusions about it.

Many assignments that you will be given in college require you to synthesize material—that is, to locate and read several sources on a topic and use them to produce a paper. Synthesizing in the college setting, then, is a process of putting ideas together to create new ideas or insights based on what you have learned from the sources you consulted. You will be expected to know how to pull together these sources and come up with ideas about them. Some assignments may ask you to integrate the sources—that is, blend the ideas into your discussion—and write an overview of the topic. For example, in a sociology course you may be asked to consult several sources on the topic of organized crime and then write a paper describing the relationship between organized crime and illegal drug sales. In a marketing class, your instructor may direct you to consult several sources on common advertising strategies and on the persuasibility of young children and then write a paper weighing the effects of television commercials on young children. Both of these assignments involve synthesizing ideas from sources.

Let's look at several other academic situations in which synthesis is required.

- You may be required to read three excerpts from different biographies of former president Kennedy and then form an opinion about what factors contributed to his popularity.
- You may be assigned to read three articles on rap music and write a paper taking a position on censorship of lyrics.
- You may be asked to read three reviews of a newly opened art exhibit and report what features may be of particular interest to students on your campus.

Did you notice that in each of the above examples, you were asked to come up with a new idea, one that did not appear in any of the sources but was *based* on all three sources? Creating something new from things that you read is one of the most basic, important, and satisfying skills you will learn in college.

## How to Compare Sources to Synthesize

Comparing sources is part of synthesizing. Comparing involves placing them side-by-side and examining how they are the same and how they are different. However, before you begin to compare two or more sources, be sure you understand each fully. Depending on how detailed and difficult each source is, use one or more of the techniques in this chapter (annotating, paraphrasing, and summarizing) or underline, outline or draw idea maps to make sure that you have a good grasp of all your source material.

Let's assume you are taking a speech course in which you are studying nonverbal communication, or body language. You have chosen to study one aspect of body language: eye contact. Among the sources you have located are the following excerpts:

### Source A

Eye contact, or *gaze,* is also a common form of nonverbal communication. Eyes have been called the "windows of the soul." In many cultures, people tend to assume that someone who avoids eye contact is evasive, cold, fearful, shy, or indifferent; that frequent gazing signals intimacy, sincerity, self-confidence, and respect; and that the person who stares is tense, angry, and unfriendly. Typically, however, eye contact is interpreted in light of a preexisting relationship. If a relationship is friendly, frequent eye contact elicits a positive impression. If a relationship is not friendly, eye contact is seen in negative terms. It has been said that if two people lock eyes for more than a few seconds, they are either going to make love or kill each other (Kleinke, 1986; Patterson, 1983).

Brehm and Kassin, *Social Psychology*

### Source B

Eye contact often indicates the nature of the relationship between two people. One research study showed that eye contact is moderate when one is addressing a very high-status person, maximized when addressing a moderately high-status person, and only minimal when talking to a low-status person.[23] There are also predictable differences in eye contact when one person likes another or when there may be rewards involved.

Increased eye contact is also associated with increased liking between the people who are communicating. In an interview, for example, you are likely to make judgments about the interviewer's friendliness according to the amount of eye contact shown. The less eye contact, the less friendliness.[24] In a courtship relationship, more eye contact can be observed among those seeking to develop a more intimate relationship.[25] One research study suggests that the intimacy is a function of the amount of eye gazing, physical proximity, intimacy of topic, and amount of smiling.[26] This model best relates to established relationships.

Weaver, *Understanding Interpersonal Communication*

To compare these sources, ask the following questions:

**1. On what do the sources agree?** Sources A and B recognize eye contact as an important communication tool. Both agree that there is a connection between eye contact and the relationship between the people involved. Both also agree that more frequent eye contact occurs among people who are friendly or intimate.

**2. On what do the sources disagree?** Sources A and B do not disagree, though they do present different information about eye contact (see next paragraph).

**3. How do they differ?** Sources A and B differ on the information they present. Source A states that in some cultures the frequency of eye contact suggests certain personality traits (someone who avoids eye contact is considered to be cold, for example), but Source B does not discuss cultural interpretations. Source B discusses how eye contact is related to status—the level of importance of the person being addressed—while Source A does not.

**4. Are the viewpoints toward the subject similar or different?** Both Sources A and B take a serious approach to the subject of eye contact.

**5. Does each source provide supporting evidence for major points?** Source A cites two references. Source B cites a research study and provides footnotes.

After comparing your sources, the next step is to form your own ideas based on what you have discovered.

### How to Develop Ideas About Sources: The Thesis Statement

Developing your own ideas is a process of drawing conclusions. Your goal is to decide what ideas both sources taken together suggest or point toward. Together, Sources A and B recognize that eye contact is an important part of body language. However, they focus on different aspects of how eye contact can be interpreted. You can conclude that studying eye contact can be useful in understanding the relationship between two individuals: you can judge the relative status, the degree of friendship, and the level of intimacy between the people.

Once you have decided what major idea to work with, you are ready to develop a paper. Use your newly discovered idea as your thesis statement. Then use details, documented properly, from each source to develop and support your thesis statement.

**EXERCISE** 12-9 Read each of the following excerpts from sources on the topic of talk shows. Synthesize these two sources using the steps listed above, and develop a thesis statement about the functions of television talk shows.

*Source 1*

The plot [of talk shows] is always the same. People with problems—"husband says she looks like a cow," "pressured to lose her virginity or else," "mate wants more sex than I do"—are introduced to rational methods of problem solving. People with moral failings—"boy crazy," "dresses like a tramp," "a hundred sex partners"—are introduced to external standards of morality. The preaching—delivered alternately by the studio audience, the host and the ever present guest therapist—is relentless. "This is wrong to do this," Sally Jessy tells a cheating husband. "Feel bad?" Geraldo asks the girl who stole her best friend's boyfriend, "Any sense of remorse?" The expectation is that the sinner, so hectored, will see her way to reform. And indeed, a Sally Jessy update found "boy crazy," who'd been a guest only weeks ago, now dressed in schoolgirlish plaid and claiming her "attitude [had] changed"—thanks to the rough-and-ready therapy dispensed on the show.

Ehrenreich, *Time*

*Source 2*

The truth is that the fringy, emotional matters brought up by Oprah, Donahue, Sally, and the others are almost always related in some way to deep cultural and structural problems in our society. Most of us, obviously, wouldn't go on these shows and spill our guts or open ourselves to others' judgments. But the people who do are an emotional vanguard, blowing the lid off the idea that America is anything like the place Ronald Reagan pretended to live in.

But, finally, these shows are a dead end, and they're meant to be. They lead nowhere but to the drug store for more Excedrin. In fact, what's most infuriating about them is not that they are sleazy or in bad taste. It is that they work to co-opt and contain real political change. They are all talk and no action. Unless someone yells something from the floor (as a feminist did during the eating discussion), there will be no hint that there is a world of political action, or of politics at all.

We are allowed to voice our woes. We are allowed to argue, cry, shout, whatever. But we are not allowed to rock the political or economic boat of television by suggesting that things could be different.

Rapping, *The Progressive*

## Thinking Before Reading

The two readings in this section discuss the same issue: the naming of racial and ethnic groups. The readings were taken from sociology and psychology textbooks. The first reading, "What's in a Label: 'Black' or 'African American?'" is concerned with only one racial group; the second, "Who

Has the Right to Name?" takes a broader view and discusses several groups. Each could serve as a reference source for a paper on the topic of naming racial and ethnic groups. NOTE: The authors of these readings use the APA documentation system, which is common in the social sciences.

1. Preview each reading using the steps listed on page 45.
2. Activate your thinking by answering the following questions:
   a. Do you think names of racial and ethnic groups are important? Why?
   b. Why do the members of ethnic or racial groups sometimes change their names?

**READINGS**

## What's in a Label: "Black" or "African American"?
### Zick Rubin, Anne Peplar, and Peter Salovey

Today, many African Americans believe that the term "black" has outlived its usefulness and have urged adoption of "African American." Psychologist Kenneth L. Ghee (1990) is one of those African Americans who advocates this change in terminology, for several reasons:

*"Black" has negative connotations.*[1] In most languages, the term "black" is associated with dirt, wickedness (a "black soul"), and darkness. In Ghee's view, "thirty years of redefinition for political change [cannot] undo perhaps over 3,000 years of negative conceptual thinking associated with the concept of Blackness."

*Racial groups should not be defined as opposites.* The colors black and white are mutually exclusive opposites. Ghee believes that constant linguistic emphasis on the "oppositeness" of races cannot help race relations.

*African Americans should celebrate their African heritage.* Most racial and ethnic groups in America label themselves in ways that acknowledge their origins—Mexican Americans, Japanese Americans, Italian Americans, and so on. Only blacks describe themselves without reference to their geographical and cultural origins. Ghee believes that the label "black" conveys an unfortunate message: "Forget your ancestry; remember your skin color. Forget you are African; remember you are black."

1. associations

Not all black Americans agree with Ghee's call for a new label. 5
Many believe that the term "black" remains a powerful way to foster
pride and positive self-definition, especially among black children.

Does the term we use to refer to a racial or ethnic group really make 6
a difference? Psychological research suggests that it does. The words
we use to refer to ourselves can have important effects on our self-
concepts—our views of who we are and who we are striving to be.

*Psychology.* Boston: Houghton, 1993.

## Who Has the Right to Name?
### Richard Appelbaum

Before Europeans came to America, one of the largest Indian 1
nations were the *Dineh,* which, translated into English, means
"the People of the Earth." No one knows exactly when or how,
but the Spaniards renamed them "Navajo," the name by which they
have been known for centuries.

Joann Toralita is a *Dineh* (Navajo). At a tribal meeting she argued 2
that "if we change to our rightful name, we will be using the name we
have always called ourselves, not the name other people imposed on us.
Perhaps it will be a new beginning for our children and our grandchil-
dren." Others disagreed. One man countered, "we know who we are.
We are all 'the People of the Earth.' It doesn't matter if you are Navajo
or African American or Cheyenne" (cited in Pressley, 1993).

Deciding what to be called is a particularly vexing problem for minor- 3
ity groups. For example, is "American Indian" preferable to "Native
Americans"? Two prominent organizations—the National Congress of
American Indians and the American Indian Movement—use "American
Indian" to describe themselves. Yet others object to the term since, like
the word "Navajo," it was given to them by Europeans. For those who
object to "American Indian," the alternative "Native American" is seen
as capturing the fact that they alone among ethnic groups are truly native
to this continent. Yet others argue that nothing short of using the correct
name for each tribe (such as Sioux, Pawnee, or Cherokee) is acceptable.
Most Indian groups continue to use "American Indian" and "Native
American" interchangeably, a convention we will follow in this textbook
(Smithsonian, 1994).

African Americans, Latinos, Asian Americans, and many other minor- 4
ity groups have experienced similar controversies. African Americans were
referred to as "Negroes" for many years, a name many associated with

excessive dependence on white individuals and organizations. During the period of resurgence of black identity in the 1960s and 1970s, "Afro-American" came to be the preferred term, since it proudly pointed to their African heritage. Today, "black" and "African American" are used interchangeably. When "black" became common, however, some African American leaders opposed the term, partly because it emphasized skin color rather than ethnic origins (it also ignored significant variations in skin pigmentation; see Janken, 1993). Yet according to a recent national poll of approximately 1,500 black adults, 37 percent preferred to be called "black," 28 percent preferred "African American," while 24 percent claimed it made "no difference" (Roper, 1993b).

Latinos are still sometimes referred to as "Hispanics," but there     5
seems to be growing consensus among them that the term "Latino" is preferable, since "Hispanic" suggests that Spain is the source of their cultural heritage, rather than a mixture of Spanish and native Indian cultures (Moore and Pinderhughos, 1993). Yet even the term "Latino" obscures important ethnic differences between Spanish-speaking peoples from different regions of Mexico, different Central American countries, and elsewhere in Latin America.

By the same token, the term "Asian American" is commonly used to     6
characterize immigrants from Asia, but obviously enormous cultural, linguistic, and other ethnic differences exist between people from Japan, China, the Philippines, Indonesia, Vietnam, India, and dozens of other Asian countries that together comprise more than half of the world's population.

The name for a particular racial or ethnic group can be highly con-     7
tested, since it carries with it a great deal of information about the group's social history. The effort by many groups to "name themselves" reflects their belief that passive acceptance of the name bestowed by society's dominant group is to accept being silenced.

*Sociology.* New York: HarperCollins, 1995.

# Getting Ready to Write

## ■ Examining the Readings: **Using Idea Maps to Compare Sources**

Drawing idea maps is a useful way to grasp and organize ideas in an article, essay, or chapter (see Chapter 11, "Sharpening Your Essay-Writing Skills," p. 211). Idea mapping is also helpful in comparing sources.

The following map will allow you to assemble ideas from two or more sources. Use the text you've underlined, highlighted, and annotated to fill in the second and third columns. Depending on your sources, you will not always be able to fill in all the blanks. You may also want to add points of comparison, depending on your topic and the approaches taken by your sources. For example, you might want to compare statistics found in each source to support an idea. Other times, you might add a column so you can compare references to experimental studies or results of surveys.

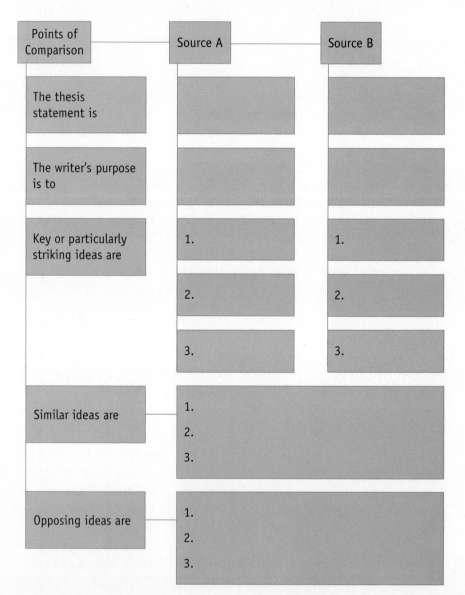

| Points of Comparison | Source A | Source B |
|---|---|---|
| The thesis statement is | | |
| The writer's purpose is to | | |
| Key or particularly striking ideas are | 1. | 1. |
| | 2. | 2. |
| | 3. | 3. |
| Similar ideas are | 1.<br>2.<br>3. | |
| Opposing ideas are | 1.<br>2.<br>3. | |

**EXERCISE** ▶ 12-10 Complete the above map for the two readings in this chapter, and add points of comparison if needed.

■ **Thinking Critically: Examining Your Sources**

When you have found a source that deals with your topic, be certain that it is reliable. That is, be sure it is a source you can trust to be accurate and complete. Here are some questions to ask when choosing sources.

**1. Is the source objective or biased?** Objective sources present an impartial view of the topic. Biased sources are those that present a particular view or opinion. Suppose you were researching how computers affect the quality of our lives. If you consulted *Wired* or *Computer Macworld*—popular periodicals written for people who use and are involved with computers on a daily basis—you would expect to find a positive viewpoint—a computer magazine being unlikely to report that computers negatively affect our lives. Be sure to recognize such bias and search for sources that provide alternative viewpoints.

**2. Is the source reputable?** To be sure that information you cite in your papers is accurate, use sources that are well known and established among scholars in the field. For example, an article in *Good Housekeeping* on acupuncture would not be considered a sound, scholarly source. However, an article from the *Journal of the American Medical Association* would be very reliable. To find out which sources are reputable, check the bibliography or reference section of your textbook, consult a research manual, or check with your reference librarian.

**3. Is the source sufficiently detailed?** Some sources, such as introductory textbooks, provide brief introductions to many topics within a general subject. Other sources research and report on a single topic in great depth. Be sure to choose a source that contains enough detail to meet your needs, but does not burden you with excess detail. For example, if you were reading about the rights of the physically disabled, an encyclopedia entry would provide a general overview, but would not explore in detail specific issues, such as laws. On the other hand, if you consulted the periodical *Mouth: The Voice of Disability Rights,* you might find particular subjects explored in great detail, but you probably would not find a discussion of the broad or major issues. You can assess the level of detail a source uses by going to its index, finding the listing for your topic, turning to one of the references, and quickly scanning a page or two.

**EXERCISE** **12-11** ❘ Answer each of the above questions for one of the readings in this chapter.

■ **Reacting to Ideas: Discussion and Journal Writing**

1. "Who Has the Right to Name?" reports that in a poll of 1500 black adults, almost one-fourth said it made no difference whether they were

called black or African American. Why do you think this term does not matter to those people?

2. At a Navajo tribal meeting, one man said, "We are all 'the People of the Earth.' It doesn't matter if you are Navajo or African American or Cheyenne." Explain what you think he meant by this statement.

3. Shakespeare wrote: "What's in a Name? That which we call a rose by any other name would smell as sweet." How do these lines relate to the readings?

## Writing Assignments

### Writing About the Readings

**Rubin Appelbaum**

1. Using information and examples from both of the readings, write an essay explaining why racial or ethnic names are important. Be sure to give credit for the ideas and information you use. (For more help with documenting sources, see Part VI, "Reviewing the Basics," p. 470.)

### Writing About Your Ideas

2. How important are names to you? Think about your given name and the nicknames family and friends may have for you—if you like them and think they fit you. If they don't fit, what would your ideal, preferred name be? Also think about when you like to be called by your first name and when you prefer a title (Mr., Ms., or Mrs.). Write an essay explaining if names you are called are important to you and if you think they affect or reflect how people think of and respond to you.

3. "What's in a Label" states that names we call ourselves can affect our self-concept—the person we think we are. Select three to five words that describe you, and write an essay explaining why each is an accurate "name" for you.

4. When a *New Yorker* reporter, John Heilemann, recently asked several prominent blacks why "black" seemed to be used more often than "African American" these days, he got these responses:

| | |
|---|---|
| Roger Wilkins, a civil-rights veteran: | "Normally, I have something to say about everything, but this leaves me speechless." |
| Glenn Loury, an author and an academic at Boston University: | "The debate between 'black' and 'African American' is over—people use both." |

| | |
|---|---|
| Alvin Poussaint, a well-known Harvard psychiatrist: | "If you use 'African American,' it sounds like you're excluding West Indian blacks. At some colleges, they're drifting back to the term 'black' for exactly that reason." |
| Maulana Karenga, the chairman of the Department of Black Studies at California State University at Long Beach: | "It's important to point to a pan-African consciousness, and 'black' is the most inclusive, universal way to do that . . . [plus,] 'black' is just more accessible." |

Heilemann, *The New Yorker*

Write an essay in which you summarize recent trends in the black/African American debate, drawing on the readings and the quotations above to support your points.

## REVISION CHECKLIST

1. Is your essay appropriate for your audience? Does it give them the background information they need? Will it interest them?

2. Will your essay accomplish your purpose?

3. Have you narrowed your topic so that you can cover your subject thoroughly in your essay?

4. Is your main point clearly expressed in a thesis statement in the introductory paragraph? Does your introductory paragraph capture the reader's interest and lead into the body of the essay?

5. Does each paragraph of your essay have a topic sentence that supports your main point?

6. Is each paragraph's topic sentence supported by relevant and sufficient detail?

7. Are your paragraphs arranged in a logical sequence and connected by transitional words and phrases?

8. Is the tone of your essay appropriate for your purpose and audience?

9. Does your conclusion reemphasize your thesis statement and draw the essay to a close?

10. Does your title identify the topic and interest the reader?

11. Have you proofread your paper and corrected any errors in grammar, mechanics, and spelling? (See the inside back cover of this book for a proofreading checklist.)

### Parallelism

Parallelism means that words, phrases, or clauses in a series should have similar grammatical form. Keeping corresponding parts of a sentence parallel in structure and length will make your writing clearer and easier to read.

### What Should Be Parallel?

**1. Words in series.** When two or more nouns, verbs, or adjectives appear together in a sentence, they should be parallel in grammatical form. Verbs should be in the same tense.

> INCORRECT:    All night long the music from the next apartment was banging, thumping, and pounded so loudly I couldn't sleep.

> CORRECT:    All night long, the music from the next apartment banged, thumped, and pounded so loudly that I couldn't sleep.

**2. Phrases.**

> INCORRECT:    My sister likes wearing crazy hats, dressing in funky clothes, and to go to classic movies.

> CORRECT:    My sister likes wearing crazy hats, dressing in funky clothes, and going to classic movies.

**3. Clauses.**

> INCORRECT:    While Yolanda studied math and worked on psychology, her husband was watching the baby.

> CORRECT:    While Yolanda studied math and worked on psychology, her husband watched the baby.

### Rate Your Ability to Use Parallel Structure

Identify the sentences that lack parallelism and correct them.

1. Melinda's professor drew an organizational chart of the human nervous system on the board, passing out a handout of it, and lectured about the way the nervous system is divided into subcategories.

2. Down's syndrome is caused by the presence of an extra chromosome, a microscopic deviation from the norm that has important consequences.

## SKILL REFRESHER CONTINUED

3. Ski jumping, speed skating, and hang glide are sports that require consideration and manipulation of velocity and wind resistance.

4. Professor Bargo's poetry class read famous poets, analyzed their poetry, and researches their lives.

5. The clam, oysters, and the mussel are examples of mollusks.

6. There are many alternative sources of energy available including solar, wind, and atomic energies.

7. The United Nations was formed in 1945 to renounce war, uphold personal freedoms, and bringing about worldwide peace and well-being.

8. In the 1980s, Sandra Day O'Connor was appointed the first female Supreme Court Justice, Geraldine Ferraro became the first female presidential candidate, and the Equal Rights Amendment is defeated.

9. The Eighteenth Amendment to the Constitution implemented Prohibition, but the Twenty-first Amendment, ratified fourteen years later, repeals it.

10. Black holes, pulsars, and quasars are studied by astronomers and physicists.

Score _____

Check your answers using the Answer Key on page 486. If you missed more than two, you need additional review and practice in using parallel structure. Refer to Part VI, "Reviewing the Basics," p. 440.

## CHAPTER SUMMARY

**Writing Skills**

1. Sources can be used in two ways: as evidence to support your ideas and as subject matter about which to develop your own ideas.

2. Be sure to locate useful, appropriate sources and keep precise information (documentation) of all the ones you use.

3. Annotating is a way of recording your ideas and to "talk back" to an author.

4. Paraphrasing is a way of recording ideas from a source for later use. It is also a way of clarifying ideas. Paraphrasing involves substituting synonyms and rearranging the order of ideas within each sentence.

5. Summarizing is a way of condensing the ideas presented in sources. A summary abbreviates the major points of a source.

6. Sources are useful in supporting or explaining your ideas. When you use information from a source, be sure to use in-text citation and prepare a List of Works Cited to give credit to the sources.

7. Synthesizing sources is a process of using information from two or more sources to develop new ideas or draw conclusions about a topic.

**Reading and Critical Thinking Skills**

1. Idea mapping is a useful way to compare two or more sources.

2. Be sure to evaluate reference sources by determining if they are impartial, reputable, and sufficiently detailed.

# Writing Expository Essays

**13**

## What Is an Expository Essay?

An expository essay presents information on a specific topic; its purpose is to explain. For example, you might want to explain your qualifications for a job, describe how to operate a microscope, or trace your family tree. For all of these topics, you want to focus clearly on facts and objective detail. Expository writing usually does not include opinions, judgments, or arguments. Expository essays follow the basic organization you learned in Chapter 11, "Sharpening Your Essay-Writing Skills." They contain an introductory paragraph with a thesis statement, supporting paragraphs, and a concluding paragraph. You generate ideas and organize them as you do for other types of essays.

Much of the writing you do in college and at work will be expository. In college, essay exams, class assignments, and term papers all demand expository-writing skills. The reports, memos, and summaries at work should present information clearly and effectively.

Depending on your topic, you may need to obtain additional information about your topic through reading or research. Although you may have general information about your topic, you may need to locate specifics—facts, statistics, or examples to support your main points. Here is a brief expository essay that a student wrote for an assignment for her interpersonal communication class. Her essay is based on her own observations and information found in *Manwatching*, a book by Desmond Morris.

### How to Spot a Liar

If you suspected a friend were lying to you, what would you do to confirm your suspicions? Most of us would listen more carefully to what the person says, and try to "catch" him or her saying a slip or something contradictory. Most liars are experienced—they've been practicing for a long time. They are very careful about what they say; therefore, they seldom

*In this chapter you will learn to*

1. plan expository essays.
2. analyze your audience and purpose.
3. organize and develop expository essays.

make a slip. To spot a liar stop paying attention to *what* is said. Instead, pay attention to the person's voice, face, and body.

How a person speaks reveals more than what he or she says. While choice of words is easy to control, the voice often betrays one's emotions. Because areas of the brain involved with emotion control the voice, the voice tends to reveal emotion. When a person lies, the voice tends to be higher pitched and the rate of speech tends to slow down.

Even more revealing than voice is a person's face. The face is the primary place we display emotions. We use different facial expressions to convey fear, anger, happiness, or guilt. Facial expressions are harder to fake than words because you can rehearse or practice what you will say, but you cannot practice how you will feel. Liars tend to make exaggerated expressions— a smile that is drawn out too long or a frown that is too severe. Eyes are especially revealing. Liars' eyes lack the genuine, warm twinkle when they smile, and they make less eye contact with the other person.

The body is the most revealing of all. While many liars try to control their voice and face, many do not know that their body has its own language. Posture and gestures reveal a person's feelings. Liars tend to make less enthusiastic gestures. At times, the gesture may not fit with what is being said. Liars tend to hold themselves at a greater distance from other people. They also have a less relaxed body position. You may notice, too, nervous behaviors such as twisting a ring or toying with a button.

Spotting a liar is never easy, but you will have the most success if you watch rather than listen. As we all know, actions are more important than words.

Notice that this essay is factual. The author does not include opinions about or personal experience with liars. The introductory sentence interests the reader by posing a hypothetical question. The next sentence tells us that our assumptions are frequently wrong and explains why. The last sentence in the paragraph states the author's thesis. The next three paragraphs explain how the voice, face, and body can be interpreted to spot liars. The concluding paragraph restates the thesis in more general terms and ends with a widely accepted expression.

## Planning Your Essay

Since the purpose of an expository essay always is to provide information that your audience can understand and use, be certain that all of your information is clear and correct. This involves selecting an appropriate level of detail, choosing a logical method of development, obtaining complete and correct information, and deciding on an appropriate tone.

## Selecting an Appropriate Level of Detail

A student wrote the following paragraph as part of an expository essay for a class assignment. His audience was his classmates.

> When the small long-iron clubhead is behind the ball, it's hard to stop tension from creeping into your arms. When this happens, your takeaway becomes fast and jerky. Your backswing becomes shorter and you lose your rhythm. Even worse, this tension causes your right hand to uncock too early. One result is that the clubhead reaches its peak speed before it hits the ball. Another result is the clubhead goes outside the line of play and cuts across the ball steeply from outside to in. A slice or pull results.

Did you find the paragraph clear and easy to understand? Unless you know a lot about golf, you probably found it difficult, confusing, and not understandable. This writer made a very serious error: he failed to analyze his audience. He assumed they knew as much about golf as he did. Readers who do not play golf would need more background information. Terms would also have to be defined.

Analyzing your audience is always the first step for any expository essay. It will help you assess how much and what type of detail to include. Here are some key questions to begin your analysis:

- Is my reader familiar with the topic?
- How much background or history does my reader need to understand the information?
- Do I need to define any unfamiliar terms?
- Do I need to explain any unfamiliar people, places, events, parts, or processes?

Suppose you are writing an expository essay on how to locate an apartment to rent. As you plan your essay, you need to decide how much information to present. This decision involves analyzing both your audience and your purpose.

First, consider how much your audience already knows about the topic. If you think your readers know a lot about renting apartments, review briefly what they already know and then move to a more detailed explanation of new information. On the other hand, if your topic is probably brand new to your readers, then capture their interest without intimidating them.

Try to relate the topic to their own experience. Show them how renting an apartment resembles something they already know. For example, you might compare renting an apartment to other types of shopping for something with certain desired features and an established price range. If you are uncertain about your audience's background, it is safer to include information they may already know rather than to assume that they know it. Readers can skim or skip over information they know, but they cannot fill in gaps in their understanding without your help.

The author of the sample essay on liars on page 247 did not assume any knowledge by the reader about nonverbal communication. Each idea was explained completely.

Once you have made these decisions about your audience, you will want to specify your purpose. Is your purpose to give your readers an overview or do you want to give your readers specific, practical information? You would need much more detail for the second purpose than you would for the first. The author's purpose in writing the sample essay on liars on page 247 was very practical. She intended to tell you exactly what to look for in identifying when someone is lying.

**EXERCISE** ▶ 13-1 For two of the following topics, define your audience and purpose and generate a list of ideas to include in an expository essay.

1. the lack of privacy in our society
2. the value of sports
3. the functions of billboards
4. attitudes toward senior citizens
5. how to make new friends

## Obtaining Complete and Correct Information

At times, you know enough about your topic to explain it clearly and completely. Other times, however, you will need additional information. For ideas on how to locate, use, and document sources, consult Chapter 12, "Summarizing and Synthesizing Sources."

## Choosing a Logical Method of Development

Analyzing your audience and purpose will also help you choose which method or methods of development to use. Expository essays use the same methods of development that you learned in Chapters 6 through 10—narration, process, description, example, classification, definition, comparison and contrast, and cause and effect. You can select the one to suit your audience and purpose best. The sample essay on liars was based on the process method of development. However, the supporting paragraphs were arranged from least to most important. Suppose you are writing an expository essay on stages of child language development. If your audience is unfamiliar with the topic, practical, realistic examples of a child's speech at each stage may be the most effective method for helping your readers understand the topic. If your audience is more knowledgeable, examples or definitions may be unnecessary. A more direct, straightforward process explanation would be appropriate.

Your method of development depends on your purpose. Here are a few examples.

| If your purpose is to | Use |
| --- | --- |
| trace events over time | Narration (see Chapter 6) |
| explain how something works or perform a specific task | Process (see Chapter 6) |
| present a visual or sensory image | Description (see Chapter 7) |
| explain a topic using specific situations | Example (see Chapter 8) |
| explain a topic by showing the parts into which it can be divided or the group to which it belongs | Classification (see Chapter 8) |
| explain what something is | Definition (see Chapter 8) |
| emphasize similarities or differences between two topics or explain something by comparing it to something already familiar | Comparison and Contrast (see Chapter 9) |
| explain why something happened | Cause and Effect (see Chapter 10) |

Suppose you are majoring in accounting and must write an expository essay about why you chose accounting as a major. You could explain your choice in several different ways. If your purpose is to show others that you made the right choice, you would probably trace the history of your decision. If your purpose is to encourage other students to choose accounting, you would probably describe the job of an accountant, giving vivid details about its opportunities and rewards. If your purpose is to get a job with an accounting firm, you might give examples of problems accountants solve and challenges they face. If you choose the first approach, narrative or cause and effect would be the best method for developing your essay. Description would be best for the second approach, and example would be best for the third. The chart below demonstrates how audience and purpose work together in your choice of method.

| Audience | Purpose | Method of Development |
|---|---|---|
| family, friends, interested others | show that you made the right choice | narrative, cause and effect |
| students | encourage them to major in accounting | description |
| potential employers | demonstrate your understanding of the job and its challenges | example |

Although your essay should have logical overall development, you can use more than one method of development within the essay. Assume you are writing an essay on family responsibility. You might choose definition for your first paragraph and define how you will use the term *responsibility*. The next three paragraphs could classify family responsibility by types, such as financial responsibility, physical-care responsibility, emotional-support responsibility, and so forth. In your last three paragraphs, a well-developed example of each type could be included. Although you chose several different methods of development, the essay followed a logical overall development. You progressed from general to specific, beginning with the broad concept of family responsibility and ending with examples of specific types. The essay might also progress from less to more personal, concluding with examples from your own family life.

**EXERCISE**  **13-2** For each of the following thesis statements, suggest at least one possible method of development. If it is appropriate, suggest several methods. Then select one thesis statement and draft an outline that demonstrates your method(s) of development.

1. Thesis Statement: The story of Saddam Hussein's rise to power reveals an exciting, yet terrifying, lesson in history.

   Method of Development: _____

2. Thesis Statement: Soap operas allow viewers to escape into a fantasy world in which they can share the characters' problems and joys.

Method of Development: _____

3. Thesis Statement: A listener reveals his or her attitude toward a speaker through nonverbal signals.

Method of Development: _____

4. Thesis Statement: Children inherit much from their parents, including good or bad financial habits.

Method of Development: _____

5. Thesis Statement: Many schools are revising their history courses to include contributions of African Americans, Native Americans, Asian Americans, and Hispanic Americans.

Method of Development: _____

## Deciding on an Appropriate Tone

Since the purpose of an expository essay is to present information, your tone should reflect your seriousness about the topic. A humorous, sarcastic, flip, or very informal tone will detract from your essay and suggest that what you say should not be taken seriously.

As a general rule, your tone should reflect your relationship to your audience. The less familiar you are with your audience, the more formal your tone should be.

A few examples of sentences in which the tone is inappropriate for most academic and career expository writing follow.

INAPPROPRIATE: Making jump shots is a mean task, but I'm gonna keep tossing 'em till I'm the best there is.

REVISED: Learning to make jump shots is difficult, but I'm going to practice until I'm the best on the team.

INAPPROPRIATE: I just couldn't believe that my best friend was a druggie.

REVISED: I was shocked to learn that my best friend uses drugs.

INAPPROPRIATE: The math exam was a real bust, and I'm sure I bombed it.

REVISED: The math exam was difficult, and I think I failed it.

Following these suggestions will help keep your tone appropriate:

1. Avoid slang expressions.

2. Use few, if any, contractions (don't, we'll).

3. Use first-person pronouns (I, me) sparingly.

4. Make your writing sound more formal than casual conversation or than a letter to a close friend.

5. To achieve a more formal tone, avoid informal or everyday words. For example:

use "met" instead of "ran into"

use "children" instead of "kids"

use "annoying" instead of "bugging"

EXERCISE  13-3 Revise each of the following statements to give it a more formal tone.

1. I used to be a goof-off when I was in high school, but now I am trying to get with education.
2. Sam is the kind of guy every woman would like to sink her claws into.
3. Because Marco is one of those easy-going types, people think they can walk all over him.
4. Ronald Reagan was a big hit as president and his staff made sure we knew it.
5. Emily Dickinson is a fabulous poet; some of her poems really hit me.

## Drafting Your Essay

Because expository writing is often highly factual and detailed, readers, especially those who are not familiar with your topic, can easily become lost or confused. There are several things you can do to help them grasp your ideas more easily.

### Begin with an Informative Introduction

Factual essays can be just as lively and interesting as personal ones. To make your introduction interesting, you might

- relate the topic to the reader's personal experience
- emphasize the value or importance of the information you are presenting
- present a little-known or surprising fact
- relate your topic to a current event or concern (for example, connect an essay on homeless people to a recent fund-raising event held for them in your community)

Your introduction should also present your thesis statement. For expository essays, your thesis statement should announce your topic clearly and directly and state your approach to it. (See Chapter 11, "Sharpening Your Essay-Writing Skills," pp. 198–199.) If possible, try to suggest, in advance, the organization your essay will follow. This technique is known as *foreshadowing*. Here are a few examples of thesis statements that foreshadow the organization of the essay:

1. There are five types of schizophrenia: residual, disorganized, catatonic, paranoid, and undifferentiated.
2. The id, the ego, and the superego are key aspects of Freud's theory of personality.
3. Psychologists who have made significant contributions to the field include Wundt, Watson, and Skinner.

These thesis statements indicate the order in which topics will be discussed.

## Maintain a Balance Between Technical and Nontechnical Information

If your essay contains a great deal of highly factual or technical explanation, it is helpful to break it up with examples, illustrations, or practical advice. For example, in the following excerpt from an essay on human communication, notice that the writer makes comparisons and offers examples.

> Human communication does not occur in a vacuum. It always takes place in a series of interacting contexts, which influence the communication that occurs. The context for communication is similar to the environment or setting in which a party occurs. Where it's held, who attends, and what is occurring affect whether you will have a good time.
>
> The first context is the temporal context. The time of day during which the communication occurs influences its effectiveness. For example, some of us are "day people"; others are "night people." When a day and a night person talk at midnight, the day person is not fully alert or receptive to conversation.

## Use Clear Transitions

In earlier chapters, you learned to use transitional words and phrases to link ideas. Transitions are particularly important in expository essays. They keep your readers on track by showing how previous ideas connect with those that follow. Transitions also reveal your train of thought. A summary chart of transitional words is shown in Chapter 11, p. 203.

### Repeat Key Words

Repeating key words also enables your reader to stay on track. Key words often appear in your thesis statement and by repeating some of them, you can remind your reader of your thesis and how each new idea is connected to it.

You need not repeat the word or phrase exactly as long as the meaning stays the same. You could substitute "keep your audience on target" for "enables your reader to stay on track," for example. The following excerpt from an essay on clothing illustrates the use of key word repetition.

#### The Real Functions of Clothing

Just as a product's packaging tells us a lot about the product, so does a person's clothing reveal a lot about the person. Clothing reflects the way we choose to present ourselves and reveals how we feel about ourselves.

Clothing reveals our emotions. We tend to dress according to how we feel. If we feel relaxed and comfortable, we tend to dress in comfortable, relaxed clothing. For instance, some people wear sweatshirts and sweatpants for a relaxed evening at home. If we feel happy and carefree, our clothing often reflects it. Think of how fans dress at a football game, for example. Their dress reflects casual comfort, and their team-supporting hats, T-shirts, etc., reveal their emotional support for the team.

Clothing also reveals our expectations and perceptions.

### Make Your Conclusion Strong

The conclusion of an expository essay should remind your reader of your thesis statement. Do not simply restate it. Summarize your main points and what your essay says about your thesis. Finally, your conclusion should draw the essay to a close. Ask questions that still need to be answered, or make a final statement about the topic.

**EXERCISE**  **13-4** | For the topic you selected in Exercise 13-1, draft an essay. Then revise the essay, using the Revision Checklist at the end of this chapter. Pay particular attention to your introduction, transitions, repetition of key words, technical-nontechnical balance, and conclusion.

## Thinking Before Reading

The two readings in this section, "A High Cost for a Small Hope" by Ellen Goodman and "Living Longer with HIV" by Geoffrey Cowley, are good illustrations of two approaches to writing expository essays. Goodman uses a narrative approach in describing a particular attempt to treat AIDS. Cowley, on the other hand, presents his information about new developments in AIDS treatment in a more straightforward, factual way.

1. Preview the reading using the steps outlined on page 45.
2. Discover what you already know about AIDS treatment by answering the following:
   a. What do you know about AIDS, the course of the disease, and how it affects the health of its victims?
   b. What is the difference between the terms HIV and AIDS?
   c. What is your sense of the progress of AIDS research and treatment? What benefits and dangers do you think are associated with this research?

**R E A D I N G S**

## A High Cost for a Small Hope
### Ellen Goodman

It is after hours, and the AIDS clinic at San Francisco General Hospital is almost empty. Just one patient remains, confused and emaciated, waiting for a ride home.     1

Dr. Steven Deeks, who works here, stops to help the man he calls "Dallas" with one of the smaller indignities of this disease. The doctor calls again for a cab to come to an address the drivers may know too well and avoid too often.     2

For three years Deeks has kept a name and address book of 100 AIDS patients. Sixty have died, and half the remaining 40 have moved on to late-stage disease. Just today, the 33-year-old doctor tells me, a patient his own age, a man just beginning his professional career, came in exhibiting the terrible, unmistakable first symptoms of AIDS-related dementia.     3

Working as he does, among patients with advanced disease, Deeks is not ashamed to describe himself as frustrated or even "a little" desperate. "In an epidemic," he says calmly, "things can't always be done in a conservative manner."     4

So it is no wonder that the doctor took a risk. Last month he became part of the most highly publicized—indeed sensationalized—AIDS research in memory. He performed a baboon bone-marrow     5 transplant to see if cells from an animal that does not get HIV could boost the deteriorating immune system of a human with the disease. And, he said, "I had no qualms."

If Deeks' desire to try something was understandable, so surely was Jeff Getty's desire. Getty advocated for this experiment, pushed for FDA approval and volunteered to be the subject.

6

After all, Dr. Christiaan Barnard might have been writing about Getty when he described the state of mind of his first heart transplant patient this way: "If a lion chases you to the bank of a river filled with crocodiles, you will leap into the water convinced you have a chance to swim to the other side when you would never accept such odds if there were no lion."

7

With the lion of AIDS chasing Getty, the 38-year-old, who told me to call him an AIDS "activist" and not a victim, was determined "not to just lie down and die." If nothing else, he would devote his body to search for a cure.

8

Now, little more than a month and innumerable banana jokes since the transplant, Deeks doesn't yet know whether the baboon cells have had any effect. But Getty has become a star of print and video in a controversy that labels him either a hero or a threat to humanity.

9

Getty has become as well the poster boy in an ethical debate about front-line medicine. What risks should medicine take for what chance of cure? What are the costs and benefits of research in a disease that has seen so many hopes raised and dashed?

10

Getty's claim to heroism comes from his role in the quest for the cure. But the threat in this xeno-transplant from baboon to man is that another devastating disease could "jump" from one species to another—as AIDS itself did. It's the fear that a transplant recipient's body could be the perfect halfway house.

11

The likelihood that Jeff Getty would provide such a halfway house is virtually nil. The FDA approved this procedure for one man, one baboon. It's easy to monitor a study of one. But you do not have to be a screenwriter to script the next scene with 50 clinics, 20 baboons, 1,000 patients—an impossible tracking job and a public health danger that, in a worst-case scenario, could outrank AIDS.

12

As ethicist Art Caplan at the University of Pennsylvania says, the baboon transplant "would be bad if it failed. It would be worse if it worked."

13

Optimistic researchers talk about a temporary boost to the immune system, not a cure for AIDS. It may be unpopular to put price tags on health care—or on life—but are we ready to pay some $200,000 or more for a "boost" when the Centers for Disease Control estimate there are between 750,000 and 1.2 million Americans with AIDS or HIV?

14

Where would the hundreds of billions come from? And at the cost of
pursuing what other avenues of AIDS research?

Every researcher holds some candle of promise, if only the elusive    15
hope that "we will learn something." But the social risks and costs of
baboon bone-marrow transplants are far too great for too small a
promise, too vague a hope.

Here, in the busiest AIDS clinic in America, keenly aware of the dev-    16
astation of this disease, it is possible to admire the bravery of an AIDS
activist and the humanity of his doctor and still believe they are going
down the wrong path.

Even a society being chased by the lion of AIDS may have more to    17
fear from the crocodiles in the river.

*The Boston Globe* 25 Jan. 1996.

## Living Longer with HIV
### Geoffrey Cowley

HIV is a wily foe. Armed with special enzymes, it splices its own    1
genes into the immune cells it infects, turning them into facto-
ries for producing more HIV. Few AIDS researchers expect any
drug to reverse the infection once it occurs; the goal is simply to make
the virus less noxious, by foiling its efforts to reproduce within the body.
The first signs of progress came in the mid-1980s, when researchers discovered that a failed cancer drug called AZT helped to keep HIV from
integrating itself into host cells. In clinical studies, the drug reduced
death rates among people with AIDS and delayed the onset of symptoms
in those who were still healthy. But the benefits proved temporary.
Because the virus mutates so rapidly within the body, it simply evades
AZT after a year or two.

That's where the new protease inhibitors come in. Unlike AZT and    2
its cousins, which help keep HIV out of the host cell's chromosomes,
these drugs help to keep successfully integrated HIV from reproducing
at the cell's expense. Experts say no other drugs have shown such striking ability to hold the virus in check, although, in studies, patients' viral
levels climbed steadily after a sharp initial decline, suggesting that drug
resistance was already setting in.

Even if their effects prove transient,[1] the new drugs should improve    3
patients' prospects simply by creating more obstacles for the virus. "The

1. lasting for only a short time

medical tool kit is growing by leaps and bounds," says Annette
Ramirez, executive director of New York's Hispanic AIDS Forum. If
patients who exhausted one combination of drugs could always turn to
another one, HIV infection might become a chronic but manageable
condition, much like diabetes or kidney failure. The catch, of course, is
that combination therapy can be breathtakingly expensive. The three-
drug regimens now coming into vogue can cost $18,000 a year—and
neither government programs nor private insurers are eager to absorb
that shock. "We may have all these drugs approved," says Moises
Agosto of the National Minority AIDS Council in Washington. "But if
the programs can't afford them, who's going to have access?" Not the
impoverished minority communities that are now at the center of the
epidemic. "The new drugs are wonderful in terms of individual medicine," says virologist June Osborne, who chaired the now defunct
National Commission on AIDS. "But they have nothing to do with public health."

Whatever their role, the new protease inhibitors aren't the only signs      4
that AIDS research is coming of age. The past few months have brought
a spate[2] of significant discoveries and innovations. In November
Australian researchers identified the critical features of a naturally
benign strain of HIV—a discovery that suggests new strategies for dis-
abling the more aggressive strains now in wide circulation. In December
German and American researchers identified several chemicals, produced by the body's own cells, that can paralyze HIV in a culture dish.
Dr. Robert Gallo, who led the U.S. team, predicts that combining such
agents with other drugs will soon make AIDS "clinically curable." Just
weeks later, a 38-year-old AIDS patient named Jeff Getty checked into
San Francisco General Hospital to have a baboon's bone marrow
pumped into his blood (baboons don't get AIDS). In principle, the procedure could leave him with an immune system impervious to HIV.

No one pretends that the baboon procedure is anything but a gam-      5
ble. But no one would deny that, like Magic Johnson, Getty embodies a
new attitude toward HIV. Infected in 1980, he fell ill in '87 and says he
has "almost bought it four or five times." But he has aggressively sought
out every new treatment in the book, from egg lipids to a three-drug
combination including indinavir. He has managed to stay alive. "If you
never do anything bold," he says, "you never get any important
answers." We may not have them all yet, but the case for boldness gets
stronger every day.

*Newsweek* 12 Feb. 1996.

2. sudden rush

## Getting Ready to Write

■ **Examining the Readings: Using Idea Maps to Examine Expository Essays**

In Chapter 12, "Summarizing and Synthesizing Sources," p. 239, you saw that idea mapping was a useful way to synthesize two or more sources. This format works particularly well for expository essays since you often need to identify similarities and differences between sources.

**EXERCISE** **13-5** ▶ Use the idea-map format shown on page 240 to help you to compare the two readings in this chapter.

■ **Thinking Critically: Evaluating Alternative Viewpoints**

Often when using two or more sources you will encounter alternative viewpoints on the same topic or issue. At times, two authors may disagree completely, holding opposite viewpoints—as is often the case, for example, when authors take pro or con positions on abortion or gun control. More often, however, the authors will agree on some points and disagree on others. The idea-map format will help you identify those similarities and differences.

Once you have identified the viewpoint on which two authors differ, your next step is to evaluate *how* the viewpoints differ. Goodman and Cowley agree on some points and disagree on others. For example, both agree that AIDS is a serious crisis and that the baboon-marrow transplant was risky. They disagree, however, on whether such measures are worth the risk. To evaluate differing viewpoints, study and weigh the evidence each provides. Ask questions such as the following:

1. Which author provides more evidence? (See no. 4 below.)

2. What types of evidence are offered? Statistical evidence, for example, may carry more weight than personal examples, depending on the issue.

3. Which evidence is most directly relevant to the issue?

4. Which author provides the stronger, more convincing evidence? In answering this question, you may need to weigh amount, type, and relevance against one another to determine overall strength.

**EXERCISE** **13-6** ▶ Write a paragraph evaluating and summarizing the evidence Goodman and Cowley offer in support of their viewpoint on the benefits of highly experimental procedures.

■ **Reacting to Ideas: Discussion and Journal Writing**

1. What public-health dangers could result from developing new cures for AIDS?
2. How effective have AIDS treatments been so far?
3. Do you believe that medical science will eventually wipe out all disease?
4. Do you think Jeff Getty is "a hero" or "a threat to humanity"?

## Writing Assignments

### Writing About the Readings

Cowley
1. Cowley quotes Getty as saying, "If you never do anything bold, you never get any important answers." Write an essay explaining the meaning of that statement.

Goodman
2. Goodman quoted Deeks as saying, "In an epidemic, things can't always be done in a conservative manner." Write a short essay explaining the meaning of that statement.

Goodman
3. Write an essay explaining what Goodman means when she writes: "Even a society being chased by the lion of AIDS may have more to fear from the crocodiles in the river."

Goodman/
Cowley
4. Write an essay summarizing the issues that recent AIDS treatments have raised. Use the two readings in this chapter as your sources.

Goodman/
Cowley
5. Write an essay comparing and contrasting Goodman's and Cowley's attitudes toward AIDS research.

### Writing About Your Ideas

6. How do you feel about sharing the expense of unusual medical treatments through government programs or by increasing health-insurance premiums for everyone? Write an essay expressing and defending your viewpoint.

7. If you had contracted AIDS or another fatal disease, would you be willing to risk an animal-organ or bone-marrow transplant? Write an essay examining the issues that you would be forced to consider.

## REVISION CHECKLIST

1. Is your essay appropriate for your audience? Does it give them the background information they need? Will it interest them?

2. Will your essay accomplish your purpose?

3. Have you narrowed your topic so that you can cover your subject thoroughly in your essay?

4. Is your main point clearly expressed in a thesis statement in the introductory paragraph? Does your introductory paragraph capture the reader's interest and lead into the body of the essay?

5. Does each paragraph of your essay have a topic sentence that supports your essay's main point?

6. Is each paragraph's topic sentence supported by relevant and sufficient detail?

7. Are your paragraphs arranged in a logical sequence and connected by transitional words and phrases?

8. Is the tone of your essay appropriate for your purpose and audience?

9. Does your conclusion reemphasize your thesis statement and draw the essay to a close?

10. Does your title identify the topic and interest the reader?

**For Expository Essays**

11. Have you obtained complete and correct information?

12. Have you documented all information sources?

13. Does your tone reflect your seriousness about your topic?

14. Does your essay maintain a balance between technical and non-technical information?

15. Have you proofread? (See the inside back cover of this book for a proofreading checklist.)

# SKILL REFRESHER

## When to Use Commas

Commas separate parts of a sentence from one another. Commas most often separate

1. items in a list or series

   I need to buy jeans, socks, T-shirts, and a new tie.

2. introductory phrases

   After a cup of coffee, I was awake enough to read the paper.

3. information that interrupts the sentence

   My biology professor, Dr. Rodriquez, has been teaching for fifteen years.

4. direct quotations

   Barbara Walters always says, "We're in touch, so you'll be in touch."

5. two independent clauses joined by a conjunction

   The cat climbed on my lap, and I remembered that I hadn't fed her today.

6. a dependent clause from an independent clause when the dependent clause comes first in the sentence

   Because I enjoy watching animals, I visit the zoo often.

Commas are also used in dates, addresses, numbers, and openings and closings of letters.

## Rate Your Ability to Use Commas Correctly

Punctuate each of the following sentences using commas.

1. Although I was late my sister was still waiting for me at the restaurant.

2. Tom invited Marie Ted Leah and Pete.

3. Following the movie we had a late lunch.

4. I bumped into a beautiful woman Lisa's mother on my way into the grocery store.

5. The phone rang but I was outside.

6. My niece began to yell "I'm Tarzan king of the jungle."

7. Bill a friend from school sent me a postcard from Florida.

## SKILL REFRESHER CONTINUED

8. When I entered the room everyone was watching television.

9. I heard her call "Wait for me."

10. Although I have visited Vancouver I have never been to Vancouver Island.

Score_____

Check your answers using the Answer Key on page 487. If you missed more than two, you need additional review and practice recognizing when to use commas. Refer to Part VI, "Reviewing the Basics," p. 452.

## CHAPTER SUMMARY

**Writing Skills**

1. An expository essay presents information on a specific topic. Its purpose is to explain.

2. To select an appropriate level of detail, analyze your audience. Assess their familiarity with your topic.

3. Consider your audience and purpose in choosing an overall logical method of development. Individual paragraphs within an essay can have their own method of development.

4. Be sure to document sources correctly using a standard documentation format.

5. Select a tone that reflects your seriousness about the topic.

6. Be sure to maintain a balance between technical and nontechnical information.

7. Use clear transitions and repeat key words to connect ideas.

**Reading and Critical Thinking Skills**

1. Use an idea map to compare two or more sources.

2. Evaluate alternative viewpoints by considering amount, type, relevance, and overall strength of evidence.

# Writing Persuasive Essays

CHAPTER
OBJECTIVES

*In this chapter you
will learn to*

1. plan a persuasive
   essay.
2. select convincing
   details.
3. present a convincing
   argument.

If you turn on the television or radio, or open a magazine or newspaper, you will encounter almost immediately one of the most common forms of persuasion—advertising. Commercials and ads are attempts to persuade you to buy a particular product or service. Here are a few examples:

1. "You've tried just about everything for your hay fever . . . Now try your doctor. Your doctor has an advanced prescription medicine called Seldane that can relieve your allergy symptoms without drowsiness."

2. "Question: How can I get luscious taste with low fat? Answer: Simplese. The all-natural ingredient that replaces fat and keeps the taste you want."

Persuasion is an attempt to convince others to agree with an idea or to take a specific action. In advertising, the specific action is purchasing a product or service.

You probably use persuasion in your daily life more than you realize. You may try to persuade your spouse or friend to see the movie of your choice, convince your child to try a new food, or persuade your employer to give you Saturday nights off.

Many academic and career situations will require you to use persuasion. In college you will be asked to write persuasive essays in which you put forth an idea and defend it. Here are a few examples:

*Academic*

1. a sociology paper defending or rejecting a new theory

*Career*

1. a memo defending a budget request

2. a position paper for environmental science on pollution controls for industry

3. an essay on your college goals for a scholarship application

2. a letter to support an employee's promotion

3. a proposal to secure a contract with a prospective client

## What Is a Persuasive Essay?

A persuasive essay presents reasons and arguments for accepting a belief or position or for taking a specific action. For instance, a persuasive essay might try to convince readers that our current welfare system is unjust, that parking regulations are unfair, or that a plus-and-minus grading system for colleges is desirable. Or a persuasive essay might urge readers to take a specific action, such as voting against a political candidate, contacting their congressional representative to support the creation of a new park, or preventing their children from viewing violent television programs.

A persuasive essay has the same basic parts as other essays: introduction, thesis statement, supporting information, and conclusion. It requires that you follow the same steps in the writing process: prewriting, planning, drafting, and revising. You are, therefore, already well equipped to learn how to write a persuasive essay. However, the most important feature of a persuasive essay may be new to you: the presentation of convincing reasons and explanations. In this chapter you will learn how to plan a persuasive strategy, select convincing evidence, and present that evidence effectively.

Here is a sample persuasive essay written by one student. Note how she presents reasons and arguments for taking a specific action.

### Buckle Up

As a paramedic, I am the first to arrive at the scene of many grim and tragic accidents. One horrid accident last month involved four women in one car. The front-seat passenger died instantly, another died during a mercy flight to the nearest hospital, one lost both legs, and one walked away from the accident without serious injury. Only one woman was wearing a seat belt. Guess which one? Though many people protest and offer excuses, seat belts do save lives.

Many people avoid wearing seat belts and say they'd rather be thrown free from an accident. Yet they seldom realize that the rate at which they will be thrown is the same rate at which the car is moving. Others fear being trapped inside by their seat belt in case of a fire. However, if not ejected, those without a belt are likely to be stunned or knocked unconscious on impact and will not be alert enough to escape uninjured.

Seat belts save lives by protecting a passenger from impact. During a crash, a body slams against the windshield or steering wheel with tremendous force if unbelted. The seat belt secures the passenger in place and protects vital organs from injury.

Recent statistics demonstrate that a passenger is five times more likely to survive a crash if a seat belt is worn. Life is a gamble, but those are good odds. Buckle up!

Notice that the author introduces the topic using a startling example from her personal experience. The thesis statement occurs at the end of the first paragraph. The second and third paragraphs offer evidence that supports the writer's thesis. The last paragraph concludes the essay by offering a convincing statistic and reminding the reader of the thesis: "Buckle up."

## First Steps in Planning a Persuasive Essay

The first step in planning a persuasive essay is to identify your subject. What issue or problem are you going to write about, and what position will you take or solution will you offer? Suppose you have an assignment to write about the issue of mandatory testing for drug use. You need to decide whether you support mandatory testing or oppose it. Begin by using freewriting, brainstorming, questioning, or branching to generate ideas. Your goal is to identify reasons, explanations, examples, and situations that will convince readers to accept your position.

If you choose your own topic, be sure to choose an issue about which you have definite feelings. It is difficult to write convincingly about a position in which you don't believe. On the other hand, if you feel you are so emotionally involved with an issue that it upsets you to think about it, consider selecting a different issue. You may find it difficult to separate your emotions from the facts and present a reasoned appeal.

### Analyzing Your Audience

Analyzing your audience is a crucial second step in planning a convincing essay. You must decide whether your audience is in agreement, is neutral, or is in disagreement with your position. In addition, decide how familiar your readers are with the issue and how reasoned or well thought out this position is.

*Audiences who agree* with your position are the easiest to write for because they already accept most of what you will say. In-agreement audiences will also be likely to feel positively about you because you think the way they do about the issue. For this audience, your essay can be structured very much like an expository essay. State your position and explain why you think it is correct.

*Neutral audiences* have not made up their minds or have not given much thought to the issue. They have questions or misunderstandings, and they may have heard arguments supporting the opposing viewpoint. An essay written for a neutral audience should be direct and straightforward, like those written for an in-agreement audience. However, a fuller explanation of the issue is necessary to answer questions, clear up misunderstandings, and respond to opposing arguments.

*Disagreeing audiences* are the most difficult to address. Some have thought about the issue and have chosen a position that opposes yours. Others who disagree may not have examined the issue at all and are making superficial judgments or are relying on misinformation. Both types think their position is correct, so they will not be eager to change. They may also distrust you, because you think differently from them. For such an audience, your biggest challenge is to build trust and confidence. Before writing, carefully analyze this audience and try to answer these questions:

1. Why does your audience disagree with your position?

2. Is their position based on real facts and sound evidence, or on personal opinion? If it is based on evidence, what type? Supply strong evidence to support your position.

3. What type of arguments or reasons are likely to appeal to your audience? For example, will they be persuaded by facts and statistics, or by statements made by authorities? Would personal anecdotes and examples work well?

Once you have a grasp of their thinking you could include sentences in your introduction that openly recognize their opposing viewpoint and that state you will address this viewpoint in the body of the essay. Here is an example:

> Advertising, like other expenditures, should be taxed. What better way to generate income and, at the same time, reduce the flood of advertising that bombards us daily on radio and television. Major corporations and radio and television stations will, of course, oppose such tax legislation, arguing that taxing advertising will reduce the amount of advertising, which in turn will reduce the public-service programming that is aired. Such opposition, however, is flawed.

For a disagreeing audience, include more preliminary discussion of the issue than you would for other audiences. For example, you might establish your authority on the issue, relate an amusing or convincing anecdote to engage your audience, or present surprising statistics or a shocking example to startle your audience. You might also offer reasons for your position before you directly state it.

## Researching Your Topic

A persuasive essay must provide specific and convincing evidence that supports the thesis statement. Often it is necessary to go beyond your own knowledge and experience. You may need to research your topic in the library. For example, if you were writing an essay urging the creation of an environmentally protected wetland area, you would need to find out what types of wildlife live there, which are endangered, and how successful other wetlands have been in protecting wildlife.

At other times you may need to interview people who are experts on your topic or directly involved with it. Suppose you are writing a persuasive essay urging other students to volunteer their time at a local shelter for homeless men and women. The director of the shelter or one of his employees could offer useful statistics, share personal experiences, and provide vivid details that would make your essay effective and convincing.

Here are a few tips for researching your topic.

*When consulting written sources*

1. Use current, up-to-date sources.
2. Sample a variety of sources to get different viewpoints.
3. Move from general to more specific sources.
4. Take careful notes as you read, and use quotation marks for all material you copy directly.
5. Keep track of all sources used so that you may include them in your bibliography.

*When interviewing*

1. Prepare a list of questions ahead of time.
2. Consult individuals who are experts or are directly involved.
3. If possible, talk with more than one person. For instance, get different viewpoints by interviewing the director of the homeless shelter, one of his employees, and one of the shelter's clients.
4. Be sure your sources understand your purpose for interviewing them. Ask permission to use their names and to quote them in your paper.
5. Take detailed notes during the interview. Immediately after the interview, fill in ideas you didn't have time to write down.

# Structuring Your Essay

After you have chosen your position, generated ideas, and analyzed your audience, you need to devise an approach that will both support your position and appeal to your audience. There are three major decisions to make:

- What will you include in your thesis statement, and where will you place it? Earlier in this book, you were told to place your thesis statement at the beginning. Now you can refine your strategy and place it where you think it will be most effective.
- What evidence will you include?
- In what order will you present your evidence?

There are no rules to follow in making these decisions. You must consider your topic, your purpose, and your audience in making them. The next sections discuss each of these decisions in detail.

**EXERCISE** ▶14-1▶ For three of the following issues, take a position and generate ideas to support it.

1. racial quotas in the workplace
2. the right of insurance companies to deny medical coverage to certain individuals
3. banning smoking in public places
4. outlawing sports hunting of wild animals
5. mandatory counseling for drunken drivers
6. buying American-made products
7. gays in the military
8. women in military combat
9. a current news issue of your choice

**EXERCISE** ▶14-2▶ For one of the issues you chose in Exercise 14-1, identify an audience that you would like to convince of your position. Think of a specific person or group. Then analyze your audience and summarize your findings.

Position: _____

Audience: _____

Analysis: _____

_____

_____

## Developing Your Thesis Statement

Your thesis statement should identify the issue, state your position on it, and, if possible, foreshadow your supporting points. The following thesis statement makes it clear that the writer will argue against the use of animals for medical research.

> The use of animals in medical research should be outlawed because it is cruel, unnecessary, and disrespectful of animals' place in the chain of life.

Notice that this thesis identifies the issue, makes it clear that the writer opposes animal research, and suggests the three major arguments she will make: (1) it is cruel, (2) it is unnecessary, and (3) it is disrespectful. You do not always have to include the major points of your argument in your thesis statement, but this foreshadowing does help the reader know what to expect. This thesis statement also makes clear what action the author thinks is appropriate: using animals in medical research should be outlawed.

Here are a few more thesis statements. Notice that they use the verbs *must, would, should,* and *ought.*

> If we expect industries to dispose of their wastes properly, then we should provide tax breaks to cover the extra expense.
>
> It would be a mistake to assume racial discrimination has been eliminated or even reduced significantly over the past twenty years.
>
> The proportion of tenured women and minority faculty on our campus should be increased.

Place your thesis statement where it will be most effective. There are three common choices:

1. in the beginning
2. after you respond to objections to your position, but before you provide reasons for accepting it
3. at the end, after you state reasons for accepting your position

You can visualize these three organizations as follows:

1. thesis statement in the beginning
   Paragraph 1 } Introduction
                } Thesis Statement
   2 ⎫
   3 ⎬ Supporting Evidence
   4 ⎭
   5 ⎭
   6   Conclusion

2. thesis statement after responding to objections
Paragraph 1    Introduction
       2    Response to Objections
       3 ⎫
       4 ⎬ Thesis Statement
           Supporting Evidence
       5 ⎭
       6    Conclusion

3. thesis statement at the end
Paragraph 1    Introduction
       2 ⎫
       3 ⎬ Supporting Evidence
       4 ⎭
       5    Concluding Paragraph with Thesis Statement

In general, placing the thesis in the beginning is best for in-agreement or neutral audiences. For disagreeing audiences, a later placement gives you the opportunity to respond to the audience's objections before you present your thesis.

**EXERCISE**  **14-3** Write a thesis statement for a persuasive essay on each of three of the following topics:

1. recycling garbage
2. crime prevention
3. television sitcoms
4. volunteer work
5. athletics and the use of steroids

**EXERCISE** **14-4** | Write a thesis statement for the issue you selected in Exercise 14-2.

## Selecting Convincing Evidence

When you write a persuasive essay, your goal is to provide readers with evidence that they cannot easily refute (disagree with or prove wrong). It is important to evaluate each piece of evidence you include. Ask yourself questions such as: What does this prove? Are there other ways it could be interpreted? How might a disagreeing reader reject this information? The evidence you choose to include will depend on your topic and your analysis of the audience.

The most commonly used types of evidence are

1. facts and statistics
2. quotes from authorities
3. examples
4. personal experience

## Facts and Statistics

Facts are statements that can be verified as correct. As in writing any other type of paragraph or essay, you must choose facts that directly support the position you express in your thesis statement. Here is an excerpt from a persuasive essay that uses facts as evidence to argue that more funds should be devoted to researching a particular form of cancer.

> Cancer research funds should be directed toward early identification of stomach cancer. While the exact cause is unknown, it is a particularly deadly form of cancer since the five-year survival rate is only eight percent. Further, little progress has been made in the past twenty-five years. The death rate per 100,000 people is 4.4, only a slight decrease from 1971 statistics (Watson 66).
>
> Traci Watson, Rita Rubin, and Corinna Wu, "The Most Deadly Cancers"

Facts expressed as numbers are called statistics. It is usually more effective to present more than one statistic. Suppose you are writing to persuade taxpayers that state lotteries have become profitable businesses. You might state that more than 60 percent of the adult population now buy lottery tickets regularly. This statistic would have little meaning by itself. However, if you were to state that 60 percent of adults now purchase lottery tickets, whereas five years ago only 30 percent purchased them, then the first statistic becomes more meaningful.

In selecting statistics to support your position, be sure to

1. Obtain statistics from reliable sources such as almanacs, encyclopedias, articles in reputable journals and magazines, or other trustworthy reference material from your library.

2. Use up-to-date information, preferably from the past year or two. Dated statistics may be incorrect or misleading.

3. Make sure you define terms and units of measurement. For example, if you say that 60 percent of adults regularly play the lottery, you should define what "regularly" means. Does it mean daily, weekly, monthly?

4. Verify that the statistics you obtain from more than one source are comparable. For example, if you compare the crime rate in New York City with that of Los Angeles, be sure that each crime rate was computed the same way, that each represented the same types of crimes, and that report sources were similar.

## Quotations from Authorities

You can also support your position by using expert or authoritative statements of opinion or conclusions. Experts or authorities are those who have studied your subject extensively, conducted research on it, or written widely about it. For example, if you are writing an essay calling for stricter preschool-monitoring requirements to prevent child abuse, the opinion of a psychiatrist who works extensively with abused children would provide convincing support.

## Examples

Examples are specific situations that illustrate a point. Refer to Chapter 8, "Example, Classification, and Definition," pp. 130–133, for a review of how to use them as supporting details. In a persuasive essay, your examples must represent your position and should illustrate as many aspects of your position as possible. Suppose your position is that a particular movie should have been X-rated because it contains excessive violence. The evidence you choose to support this position should be clear, vivid examples of violent scenes.

The examples you choose should, if possible, relate to your audience's experience. Familiar examples will be more appealing, convincing, and easily understandable than those your audience has not experienced. Suppose you are writing a persuasive essay advocating a pro-choice position on abortion. Your audience consists of career women between 30 and 40 years old. It would be most effective to use as examples women of the same age and occupational status.

## Personal Experience

If you are knowledgeable about a subject, your personal experiences can be convincing evidence. For example, if you were writing an essay supporting the position that physical separation from parents encourages a teenager or young adult to mature, you could discuss your own experiences leaving home and assuming new responsibilities.

EXERCISE  14-5 | Generate evidence to support one of the thesis statements you wrote for Exercise 14-3. Evaluate your evidence, and research your topic further if needed. Write the first draft of an essay.

## The Introduction and Conclusion

The introduction of a persuasive essay should interest the reader in the issue and suggest why it is important. It may include your thesis statement, a definition of a key term, or other explanatory information.

If you delay stating your thesis until the end of your essay, make sure your conclusion contains a clear, direct statement. If you state your thesis earlier, then your conclusion should summarize key points and make a final call for action. You may request that your reader take specific action, such as writing a letter to a congressional leader or joining a local environmental concern group.

**EXERCISE 14-6**  For the essay you drafted in Exercise 14-5, add to or revise your introduction and conclusion to be more clear, effective, or powerful. Then revise your essay using the checklist at the end of this chapter.

## Thinking Before Reading

These two persuasive essays examine the question of whether or not we should eat meat. Michael Castleman's "Flesh Wounds," first published in *Sierra* magazine, is a good example of an essay that persuades by presenting facts and statistics. Castleman tries to convince his readers to stop eating meat by relying on their acceptance of the evidence he presents on health and environmental issues. In "Growing Up Game," Brenda Peterson, a woman who grew up with wildlife as part of her Native American heritage, examines not only the question of whether or not we should eat meat, but also the question of whether we should eat wild game. By presenting her personal experiences, and her own mixed feelings on this matter, she invites the reader to think these questions through with her.

1. Preview the reading using the steps listed on page 45.
2. Activate your thinking by answering the following questions:
   a. Do you know any vegetarians? Are you or could you become one?
   b. Do you think animals should be killed for food?
   c. Is eating wild game different from eating hamburger made from beef?

**READINGS**

## Flesh Wounds
**Michael Castleman**

There are two excellent reasons to stop eating meat: your own well-being, and that of the planet.

Many studies show that a diet high in flesh, especially beef, pork, and lamb, increases the risk of heart disease and several cancers,

1

2

especially those of the breast, prostate gland, and colon. A study published last July in the *British Medical Journal* compared the health of 6,000 vegetarians and a similar number of their omnivorous[1] friends and relatives. The vegetarians' death rate from heart disease was 28 percent lower, and they had 39 percent fewer deaths from cancer.

The most troublesome fat for your health is the saturated variety. Saturated fats lurk in whole-milk dairy foods—cheeses, butter, ice cream—but red meats are still the nation's major source. Even lean red meats can contain more fat than many nutrition authorities advise eating. 3

Meat's fat content and the downside of a high-fat diet may seem like yesterday's news. But meat does more than clog our arteries. It takes such a tremendous toll on our land and water that even if you're not counting milligrams of cholesterol, you might want to pass up that burger in favor of a fresh salad and a hearty bowl of lentil soup. 4

About 50 percent of the land in the United States is devoted to agriculture; approximately 80 percent of that is used for grazing or growing feed. The situation is similar in the tropical rainforests, where more than a third of the 150 acres of jungle cleared each day is used for large-scale cattle ranching. For every burger produced from Central American rainforest, 55 square feet of forest life are sacrificed. 5

Cattle also use an extraordinary amount of water. About 50 percent of the water consumed in the U.S. goes to livestock. In some regions, the proportion is even higher; 75 percent of the water drawn from the Ogallala Aquifer, main water source for the High Plains, is for beef production. 6

Our dietary choices can make a dramatic difference: it takes about 300 gallons of water a day to provide all the food for the average vegan, a person who consumes no animal products whatsoever. For those who eschew flesh foods but eat eggs and dairy products, the figure is 1,200 gallons a day. For the typical meat-eating American, it's 4,200 gallons. 7

While livestock raising soaks up half the water supply, it pollutes a significant amount of the other half. The typical cow produces 2,000 pounds of manure each year; less than half is recycled into fertilizer. The remainder, along with other livestock-industry wastes, accounts for more than half of the water pollution in the United States. 8

According to the American Dietetic Association, a balanced vegetarian diet can provide all essential vitamins, minerals, proteins, carbohydrates, and fatty acids. But a survey commissioned by *Vegetarian Times* magazine shows that while 76 percent of Americans call themselves environmentalists, only 2.8 percent are vegetarians. Maybe it's time to eat our words. 9

*Sierra* 80 (1995): 26.

1. eating both animal and vegetable foods

## Growing Up Game
**Brenda Peterson**

When I went off to college my father gave me, as part of my tuition, 50 pounds of moose meat. In 1969, eating moose meat at the University of California was a contradiction in terms. Hippies didn't hunt. I lived in a rambling Victorian house which boasted sweeping circular staircases, built-in lofts, and a landlady who dreamed of opening her own health food restaurant. I told my house-mates that my moose meat in its nondescript white butcher paper was from a side of beef my father had bought. The carnivores in the house helped me finish off such suppers as sweet and sour moose meatballs, mooseburgers (garnished with the obligatory avocado and sprouts), and mooseghetti. The same dinner guests who remarked upon the lean sweetness of the meat would have recoiled if I'd told them the not-so-simple truth: that I grew up on game, and the moose they were eating had been brought down, with one shot through his magnificent heart, by my father—a man who had hunted all his life and all of mine.

One of my earliest memories is of crawling across the vast conti-nent of crinkled linoleum in our Forest Service cabin kitchen, down splintered back steps, through wildflowers growing wheat-high. I was eye-level with grasshoppers who scolded me on my first solo trip out-side. I made it to the shed, a cool and comfortingly square shelter that held phantasmagoric metal parts; they smelled good, like dirt and grease. I had played a long time in this shed before some maternal shriek made me lift up on my haunches to listen to those urgent, possessive sounds that were my name. Rearing up, my head bumped into something hang-ing in the dark; gleaming white, it felt sleek and cold against my cheek. Its smell was dense and musty and not unlike the slabs of my grand-mother's great arms after her cool, evening sponge baths. In that shed I looked up and saw the flensed[1] body of a doe; it swung gently, slapping my face. I felt then as I do even now when eating game: horror and awe and hunger.

Growing up those first years on a forest station high in the Sierra was somewhat like belonging to a white tribe. The men hiked off every day into their forest and the women stayed behind in the circle of official cabins, breeding. So far away from a store, we ate venison and squirrel, rattlesnake and duck. My brother's first rattle, in fact, was from a King

1

2

3

1. stripped of skin

Rattler my father killed as we watched, by snatching it up with a stick and winding it, whip-like, around a redwood sapling. Rattlesnake tastes just like chicken, but has many fragile bones to slither one's way through; we also ate salmon, rabbit, and geese galore. The game was accompanied by such daily garden dainties as fried okra, mustard greens, corn fritters, wilted lettuce (our favorite because of that rare, blackened bacon), new potatoes and peas, stewed tomatoes, barbecued butter beans.

I was 4 before I ever had a beef hamburger and I remember being disappointed by its fatty, nothing taste and the way it fell apart at the seams whenever my teeth sank into it. Smoked pork shoulder came much later in the South; and I was 21, living in New York City, before I ever tasted leg of lamb. I approached that glazed rack of meat with a certain guilty self-consciousness, as if I unfairly stalked those sweet-tempered white creatures myself. But how would I explain my squeamishness to those urban sophisticates? How explain that I was shy with mutton when I had been bred on wild things?

Part of it, I suspect, had to do with the belief I'd also been bred on—we become the spirit and body of animals we eat. As a child eating venison I liked to think of myself as lean and lovely just like the deer. I would never be caught dead just grazing while some man who wasn't even a skillful hunter crept up and konked me over the head. If someone wanted to hunt me, he must be wily and outwitting. He must earn me.

My father had also taught us as children that animals were our brothers and sisters under their skin. They died so that we might live. And of this sacrifice we must be mindful. "God make us grateful for what we are about to receive" took on a new meaning when one knew the animal's struggle pitted against our own appetite. We also used *all* the animal so that an elk became elk steaks, stew, salami, and sausage. His head and horns went on the wall to watch us more earnestly than any babysitter, and every Christmas Eve we had a ceremony of making our own moccasins for the new year out of whatever Father had tanned. "Nothing wasted," my father would always say, or, as we munched on sausage cookies made from moosemeat or venison, "Think about who you're eating." We thought of ourselves as intricately linked to the food chain. We knew, for example, that a forest fire meant, at the end of the line, we'd suffer too. We'd have buck stew instead of venison steak and the meat would be stringy, withered-tasting because in the animal kingdom, as it seemed with humans, only the meanest and leanest and orneriest survived.

Once when I was in my early teens, I went along on a hunting trip as the "main cook and bottle-washer," though I don't remember any bottles; none of these hunters drank alcohol. There was something else coursing through their veins as they rose long before dawn and disappeared, returning to my little camp most often dragging a doe or pheasant or rabbit. We ate innumerable cornmeal-fried catfish, had rabbit stew seasoned only with blood and black pepper.

This hunting trip was the first time I remember eating game as a conscious act. My father and Buddy Earl shot a big doe and she lay with me in the back of the tarp-draped station wagon all the way home. It was not the smell I minded, it was the glazed great, dark eyes and the way that head flopped around crazily on what I knew was once a graceful neck. I found myself petting this doe, murmuring all those graces we'd been taught long ago as children. *Thank you for the sacrifice, thank you for letting us be like you so that we can grow up strong as game.* But there was an uneasiness in me that night as I bounced along in the back of the car with the deer.

8

What was uneasy is still uneasy—perhaps it always will be. It's not easy when one really starts thinking about all this: the eating game, the food chain, the sacrifice of one for the other. It's never easy when one begins to think about one's most basic actions, like eating. Like becoming what one eats: lean and lovely and mortal.

9

Why should it be that the purchase of meat at a butcher shop is somehow more righteous than eating something wild? Perhaps it has to do with our collective unconscious that sees the animal bred for slaughter as doomed. But that wild doe or moose might make it without the hunter. Perhaps on this primitive level of archetype and unconscious knowing we even believe that what's wild lives forever.

10

My father once told this story around a hunting campfire. His own father, who raised cattle during the Depression on a dirt farm in the Ozarks, once fell on such hard times that he had to butcher the pet lamb for supper. My father, bred on game or their own hogs all his life, took one look at the family pet on that meat platter and pushed his plate away from him. His siblings followed suit. To hear my grandfather tell it, it was the funniest thing he'd ever seen. "They just couldn't eat Bo-Peep," Grandfather said. And to hear my father tell it years later around that campfire, it was funny, but I saw for the first time his sadness. And I realized that eating had become a conscious act for him that day at the dinner table when Bo-Peep offered herself up.

11

Now when someone offers me game I will eat it with all the qualms and memories and reverence with which I grew up eating it. And I think it will always be this feeling of horror and awe and hunger. And something else—full knowledge of what I do, what I become.

12

*Living by Water* Seattle: Alaska Northwest, 1990.

# Getting Ready to Write

■ **Examining the Readings:** **Using Idea Maps to Examine Persuasive Essays**

One of the best ways to understand persuasive writing is to reduce the ideas to a simple map or outline. Many authors of persuasive essays use highly charged language and emotional appeals to influence their audience. Separately, examining the major pieces of evidence in the essays will allow you to analyze the relationship among the ideas objectively. Use the following format to map the major steps of an argument.

**POSITION:**

    **EVIDENCE (REASONS TO ACCEPT)**

    **RESPONSES TO OPPOSING VIEWPOINTS (IF INCLUDED)**

    **SPECIFIC ACTION(S) CALLED FOR (IF INCLUDED)**

In "Thinking Critically: Evaluating Persuasive Writing," on this page, you will learn how to use this mapping format to evaluate an essay.

Here is a sample map for "Buckle Up," the persuasive essay at the beginning of this chapter.

**POSITION: BECAUSE SEAT BELTS SAVE LIVES, EVERYONE SHOULD WEAR THEM**

> **EVIDENCE**
>
> > 1. protects from impact by holding you in place
> >
> > 2. protects vital organs
>
> **RESPONSES TO OPPOSING VIEWPOINTS**
>
> > 1. rather be thrown free—thrown at rate car is moving
> >
> > 2. fear being trapped inside—would not be alert enough to escape
>
> **SPECIFIC ACTION CALLED FOR**
>
> > 1. buckle up

**EXERCISE** 14-7 ▶ Make a map of the arguments presented in each of the readings in this chapter. Follow the pattern on page 281.

■ **Thinking Critically: Evaluating Persuasive Writing**

Persuasive writing is meant to be convincing. As you read a convincing piece, it is easy to be swept along by the writer's line of reasoning. Although Castleman and Peterson do not, some writers tug unfairly at your emotions, making it more difficult not to accept the author's argument.

The best way to read persuasive writing is with a critical, questioning attitude. As you read, ask yourself questions such as: Why should I believe this? How do I know this is correct? Mark and annotate as you read. Place question marks next to ideas you want to question or consider further. Then, when you've finished reading, list and organize the arguments in the idea map shown on page 281. Now you are ready to evaluate the writer's evidence. Work through your list, item by item. For the first piece of evidence, ask the appropriate questions from the list below.

*Facts and Statistics*

Are they relevant?

Are they up to date?

Do they logically connect with the issue in question?

*Examples*

Is each example relevant to the issue?

Does each example illustrate something that is typical or exceptional?

Can you think of other examples that would confirm or disprove the writer's position?

*Quotation from an Authority*

Is the person an expert?

Would other experts agree?

What does the quotation contribute to the writer's ideas?

*Personal Experience*

Is the writer's personal experience relevant to the issue?

Is the writer's personal experience typical of most people's?

Can you think of other personal experiences that would confirm or disprove the writer's position?

Each of the readings deals with the consequences of eating meat. Though one is more direct and the other more gentle and subtle, both present arguments effectively.

**EXERCISE**   | Refer to Exercise 14-7 and your maps of the supporting evidence each author uses. Evaluate the strength of each major piece of evidence presented, and write a paragraph on each argument explaining why you accept or reject it.

■ **Reacting to Ideas: Discussion and Journal Writing**

1. Which author is more persuasive? Why?

2. Can someone who eats meat call himself or herself an environmentalist? Explain your response.

3. If you had to slaughter a cow in order to eat beef, could you? How about a chicken? How about a fish? If your answer to each of these questions is not the same, explain why.

## Writing Assignments

### Writing About the Reading

Castleman/
Peterson

1. From a purely environmental standpoint, would Castleman accept Peterson's decision to continue eating game? Write a brief essay explaining your answer.

Castleman

2. Explain what Castleman means when he says "while 76 percent of Americans call themselves environmentalists, only 2.8 percent are vegetarians. Maybe it's time to eat our words."

Peterson

3. Explain what Peterson means by "becoming what one eats."

4. Write a persuasive essay stating your position on the issue of whether or not we should eat meat.

Castleman/
Peterson

5. Write a brief essay explaining how you think Peterson would respond to Castleman's statement that you can't be an environmentalist and a meat eater.

### Writing About Your Ideas

6. Castleman expresses a clear, definite position on the issue of eating meat. Write a persuasive essay on an issue on which you have a definite and clear opinion.

7. Peterson's essay does not express a strong and definite position on eating meat and game. Write a persuasive essay on an issue on which you lean in a certain direction but are uncommitted.

## REVISION CHECKLIST

1. Is your essay appropriate for your audience? Does it give them the background information they need? Will it interest them?

2. Will your essay accomplish your purpose?

3. Have you narrowed your topic so that you can cover your subject thoroughly in your essay?

4. Is your main point clearly expressed in a thesis statement in the introductory paragraph? Does your introductory paragraph capture the reader's interest and lead into the body of the essay?

5. Does each paragraph of your essay have a topic sentence that supports your essay's main point?

6. Is each paragraph's topic sentence supported by relevant and sufficient detail?

7. Are your paragraphs arranged in a logical sequence and connected by transitional words and phrases?

8. Is the tone of your essay appropriate for your purpose and audience?

9. Does your conclusion reemphasize your thesis statement and draw the essay to a close?

10. Does your title identify the topic and interest the reader?

| For Persuasive Essays | 11. Have you analyzed the position of your audience on the issue about which you are writing? |
|---|---|
| | 12. Have you researched your topic to obtain adequate and convincing evidence? |
| | 13. Does your thesis statement identify the issue and state your position on it? |
| | 14. Does your thesis statement foreshadow your supporting points? |
| | 15. Have you provided convincing evidence? |
| | 16. Have you proofread? (See the inside back cover of this book for a proofreading checklist.) |

# SKILL REFRESHER

## Using Colons and Semicolons

### When to Use Colons
Colons are most commonly used

1. after an independent clause to introduce a concluding explanation

   Fashion is fickle: what looks stylish one year looks dated the next.

2. after an independent clause to introduce a list or series

   The American poetry class surveyed a wide range of poets: Whitman, Dickinson, Ashbery, and Pound.

3. after an independent clause to introduce a long or formal quotation

### When to Use Semicolons
Semicolons are most commonly used

1. between two independent clauses not connected by a coordinating conjunction (*and, but, for, nor, or, so, yet*)

   Each state has equal representation in the Senate; representation in the House of Representatives is based on population.

2. to separate items in a list when they themselves contain commas

   The library bulletin board has a display of "Pioneers in Thought," which includes Freud, the creator of psychoanalysis; Marx, the famous communist writer; Copernicus, the father of modern astronomy; and Watson and Crick, the alleged discoverers of DNA.

### Rate Your Ability to Use Colons and Semicolons Correctly
Place colons and semicolons where needed in the following sentences.

1. Anthropologists believe human life began in the Middle East skeletons that have been found provide evidence for this.

2. The natural sciences include botany, the study of plants chemistry, the study of elements that compose matter and biology, the study of all living things.

3. The courses I am taking cover a wide range of subjects linguistics, racquetball, calculus, anatomy, and political science.

## SKILL REFRESHER CONTINUED

4. Introductory courses tend to be broad in scope they do give a good overview of the subject matter.

5. The poet, John Milton, tells how Eve must have felt when she was created "That day I remember, when from sleep / I first awaked, and found myself reposed / under a shade on flowers, much wond'ring where / and what I was, whence thither brought, and how."

6. Trigonometry incorporates many other math skills geometry, algebra, and logic.

7. I enjoy a variety of sports tennis, which is my favorite golf, because it is relaxing basketball, because it is a team sport and racquetball, because it is a good workout.

8. When a skull is dug up by a gravedigger, Hamlet begins what is now a famous meditation on mortality, "Alas, poor Yorick!—I knew him, Horatio."

9. Spanish is important to learn because many Americans speak it exclusively it is also useful to understand another culture.

10. My botany text has a section about coniferous trees pines, firs, cedars, and spruces.

Score _____

Check your answers using the Answer Key on page 487. If you missed more than two, you need additional review and practice recognizing when to use colons and semicolons. Refer to Part VI, "Reviewing the Basics," p. 456.

## CHAPTER SUMMARY

**Writing Skills**

1. A persuasive essay presents reasons and arguments for accepting a belief or position or for taking a specific action.

2. To plan a persuasive essay
   - identify your topic and what position you will take.
   - analyze your audience, then decide if your audience will agree with you, be neutral, or disagree with you.

3.  Conduct necessary research to obtain adequate and convincing evidence to support your position.

4.  In your thesis statement, identify the issue, state your position toward it, and, if possible, foreshadow your supporting points.

5.  Three common placements for the thesis statement are (1) at the beginning, (2) after responding to objections, and (3) at the end.

6.  Use convincing evidence: facts and statistics, quotations, examples, and personal experience.

**Reading and Critical Thinking Skills**

1.  One of the best ways to closely follow arguments is to draw a map of them.

2.  To evaluate the evidence a writer uses to support an argument, look closely at the facts and statistics, quotations, examples, and personal experience included.

# Writing Essay Exams and Competency Tests

## 15

This chapter will discuss how to prepare for and take essay exams and competency or placement essay exams. Many instructors give essay exams because they reveal students' ability to think about the test material, whereas multiple-choice and true/false tests require only that you *recognize* correct answers. Writing an essay exam involves the same steps as other kinds of writing: generating, organizing, and writing down ideas. But because exams are usually timed, there is little opportunity for revising or proofreading.

## Preparing for Essay Exams

The best way to prepare for an essay exam involves a thorough study and review of assigned textbook and lecture material. Simply rereading this material is seldom enough. Instead, work actively with it, identifying what is important, organizing and relating ideas and concepts, and expressing ideas in your own words. If you have been applying the getting-ready-to-write techniques suggested throughout this book to your textbooks, you'll have a head start. Reviewing these techniques, which are listed in Table 15-1 on page 290, will enable you to identify key points and express the author's ideas in your own words.

In addition to reviewing your textbooks, you will want to review the following:

- class notes (underline and annotate these, too)
- in-class handouts (underline and mark)
- assignments and papers (note key topics)
- previous exams and quizzes (look for patterns of error and emphasized topics)
- additional assigned readings (summarize these)

| TABLE 15-1 | Getting-Ready-to-Write Strategies |
|---|---|
| Strategy | Chapter and Page Reference |
| underlining | Ch. 3, p. 49 |
| immediate review | Ch. 3, p. 49 |
| recognizing supporting details | Ch. 4, p. 68 |
| marking actions, descriptions, and statements | Ch. 7, p. 125 |
| annotating | Ch. 12, p. 221 |
| paraphrasing | Ch. 12, p. 223 |
| summarizing | Ch. 12, p. 225 |
| idea mapping | Chs. 5, 6, 8–14, pp. 88, 106, 147, 167, 186, 211, 239, 261, 281 |

Using these materials as well as your textbook, make a study sheet listing key definitions, dates, facts, principles, or events that you must commit to memory. An excerpt from a study sheet for a psychology unit on consciousness is shown below. It illustrates how information can be concisely organized for easy review.

### Study Sheet Excerpt

Sleeping and Dreaming

Stages  1. quiet sleep - 4 stages          move back
        2. REM sleep                        ＆ forth in
                                            these stages
                                            frequently

Purpose — not completely understood
        — part of circadian rhythm
        — rest and bodily repair
        — brain - check its circuits

Dreams — storylike sequences of images
          and events
        — may be meaningless brain activity,
          but how a person recalls and
          organizes them is revealing
        — lucid dreaming — control own dreams

Disorders  1. insomnia - can't sleep
           2. hypersomnia - too much sleep

## Predicting Exam Questions

Once you have assembled and reviewed all of your course materials, a good way to prepare for an essay exam is to predict questions that might be asked on the test. Essay-exam questions are based on broad, general topics or themes that are important to the course. To predict these questions, then, you must identify the "big ideas"—important issues or concepts your instructor has emphasized. To identify these

**1. Reread your course syllabus or objectives.** These are often distributed on the first day of class, and the major headings or objectives refer to the important issues. For example, a sociology-course objective may be "Students will understand the concept of socialization and the roles of the family, peer, and reference groups." This objective identifies the key topic and suggests what you need to learn about it.

**2. Study your textbook's table of contents and the organization of individual chapters.** Identify important topics that run through several chapters. For example, in a marketing textbook, you may discover that chapters on the impact of technology, federal regulations, and consumer-protection legislation all relate to the market environment.

**3. Study your notes.** Identify lecture topics and group them into larger subjects or themes. For example, in a psychology course, individual lectures on retardation, creativity, and IQ can be grouped together under mental abilities.

**4. Evaluate previous exams to see what key ideas were emphasized.** For example, in a history course you may find questions on the historical significance of events appearing on each exam.

**5. Listen carefully when your instructor announces, discusses, or reviews for the exam.** He or she is likely to reveal important information. Make detailed notes and study them later. For example, a biology instructor may say, "Be sure to review the structure of plants, as well as their reproduction, development, and growth cycles." This remark indicates that these topics will be on the exam.

As you'll see from Table 15-2 on page 295, the way that essay exam questions are worded often suggests a method of development: narration, process, definition, classification, description, comparison and contrast, or cause and effect. For example, the following question, "Trace the events that resulted in the dissolution of the Soviet Union," suggests a chronological order of development. The question "Discuss similarities in the poetic works of Frost and Sandburg" suggests a comparison-and-contrast method of development.

**EXERCISE  15-1** Predict and write an essay question for each of the following. Be sure to write the questions in complete sentences, using one of the key words shown in Table 15-2.

1. A mass-communications textbook chapter titled "Newspapers" with the following headings:

   The Colonial Press

   Press of the New Republic

   The People's Publishers: Pulitzer, Hearst, and Scripps

   Twentieth-Century Trends

   The Black Press

   New Latino and Native American Media

   Current Popular Journalists

   The Future of Journalism

2. "The Ways We Lie," p. 144
3. "Are There Sex Differences in Emotion?" p. 165

## Preparation of Rough-Draft Answers

Once you have predicted possible exam questions, the next step is to draft answers. Generate ideas by locating information in your textbook and class notes that relate to the question. Organize the information, using the method of development suggested in the question, and write a rough-draft answer. This draft will be helpful in several ways:

• It will force you to think about and analyze ideas. This is a better way to review than just rereading your notes and underlining passages in your textbook.
• You will get practice expressing important ideas in your own words.
• Your ability to retain the information will increase.
• You will save time on the exam because you will already have thought about the ideas and how to organize and express them.

To be sure that you can recall important ideas at the time of the exam, you can take one more step: reduce your draft to a brief outline or list of key topics and details.

You probably won't be able to predict all of your essay-exam questions. Some may have a different focus or require a different method of development than you predicted. However, this does *not* mean you have wasted your time. Whatever form a question may take, you will be well prepared to answer it if you've already thought about and organized your ideas on the topic.

## Taking Essay Exams

Here are a few general tips on taking essay exams. Many of these suggestions are useful for other types of exams as well.

**1. Arrive a few minutes early.** This will give you time to get organized and collect your thoughts.

**2. Sit in the front of the room.** You'll be able to hear directions and read changes or corrections written on the chalkboard. Also, you won't be easily distracted by other students in the exam room.

**3. Read the directions carefully.** They may, for example, tell you to answer only two out of four questions.

**4. If given a choice of questions, take time to make a careful choice.** Otherwise, you may realize midway through the exam that you've picked a question you're not fully prepared to answer.

**5. Plan your time.** For example, if you have to answer two essay questions in a 50-minute class session, give yourself 20 to 25 minutes for each one. There is always a strong tendency to spend the most time on the first question, but you should guard against this. Keep track of time so that enough time remains to finish both questions. Allow a few minutes at the end of an in-class exam to check and proofread your answer. Allow more time for a final exam.

**6. Know how many points each question is worth.** If that information is not written on the exam, ask the instructor. Use the information to budget your time and to decide how much to write for each question. Suppose you are taking an exam that has three questions with the following values:

Question 1: 20 points
Question 2: 30 points
Question 3: 50 points

Since Question 3 is worth the most points (half the total), you should spend approximately half of your time on it. Roughly divide the remaining time equally on Questions 1 and 2. Point distribution can suggest how many ideas to include in your answer. For a 20-point question, your instructor probably expects four or five main points (4 × 5 = 20), and most instructors don't work with fractions of points. If you can think of additional ideas to include and time permits it, include them because point distribution is only an indicator, not a rule.

**7. Answer the easiest question first.** It may take you less time than you budgeted, and consequently, you can spend additional time on harder questions. Also, you'll get off to a positive and confident start.

**EXERCISE**  **15-2** For each of the following sets of exam-question values, decide how you would budget your time.

1. *Exam 1* (50-minute class)

    Question 1        20 points        Time: _____

    Question 2        20 points        Time: _____

    Question 3        60 points        Time: _____

2. *Exam 2* (75-minute class)

    Question 1        15 points        Time: _____

    Question 2        30 points        Time: _____

    Question 3        20 points        Time: _____

    Question 4        35 points        Time: _____

3. *Exam 3* (two-hour final exam)

    Question 1        10 points        Time: _____

    Question 2        30 points        Time: _____

    Question 3        20 points        Time: _____

    Question 4        40 points        Time: _____

## Analyzing Exam Questions

Exam questions often follow a recognizable format that tells you not only *what* to write but also *how* to organize it. Here is a sample exam question.

> Trace the history of advertising in the United States.

This question identifies the topic—the history of advertising—and limits or narrows the topic to U.S. advertising. Notice the word *trace*. This verb suggests the method of development to use in writing the essay. *Trace* means to track something through time. Therefore, this word indicates that you should use time order for the method of development. Your answer should begin with the earliest example of advertising you know about and end with the latest. Here is another example.

Justify the United Nations' decision to authorize military action against Iraq.

This question focuses on military action against Iraq, but limits the topic to the United Nations' decision to authorize it. The verb *justify* means to explain *why* something is correct or reasonable. *Justify*, then, suggests a cause-and-effect organization, and your answer should illustrate what caused the UN to make the decision.

Table 15-2 lists verbs commonly used in essay questions, gives examples of their use, and indicates the methods of organization they suggest.

**TABLE 15-2**   **Verbs Commonly Used in Essay Questions**

| Verb | Example | Information to Include and Method of Development |
| --- | --- | --- |
| Trace | Trace changes in water-pollution-control methods over the past 20 years. | Describe the development or progress of a particular trend, event, or process in chronological order. |
| Describe | Describe the two types of chromosomal abnormalities that can cause Down's syndrome. | Tell how something looks or happened, including the answers to *who, where, why.* |
| List | List the different types of family structures and marriage relationships. | List or discuss one-by-one. Use most-to-least or least-to-most organization. |
| Illustrate | Illustrate with examples from your experience how religion shapes values. | Explain using examples that demonstrate a point or clarify an idea. |
| Define | Define an institution and list three primary characteristics. | Give an accurate definition of the term with enough detail to demonstrate you understand it. |
| Discuss | Discuss the antigen-antibody response in the immune system. | Consider important characteristics and main points. |
| Compare | Compare the poetry of Langston Hughes with that of one of his contemporaries. | Show how items are similar as well as different; use details or examples. |
| Contrast | Contrast Marx's and Weber's theories of social stratification. | Show how the items are different; use details or examples. |

| TABLE 15-2 | Verbs Commonly Used in Essay Questions   continued | |
|---|---|---|
| Verb | Example | Information to Include and Method of Development |
| Explain | Explain the functions of peptide and steroid hormones. | Use facts and details to make the idea or concept clear and understandable. |
| Evaluate | Evaluate the accomplishments of the civil-rights movement over the past fifty years. | Assess the merits, strengths, weaknesses, advantages, or limitations of the topic. |
| Summarize | Summarize Parson's theory of social evolution. | Cover the major points in brief form; use a sentence and paragraph form. |
| Justify | Justify the use of racial quotas in police-department hiring policies. | Give reasons that support an action, decision, or policy. |

Words other than verbs can also provide clues about how to organize essay answers. In a question that begins "Explain three common types," the key word is *types*. The word *types* suggests classification. A question that directs you to explain effects requires you to use cause-and-effect organization.

### Answering Two-Part Questions

Some essay questions have two verbs that ask you to do two different things. Here is an example:

> Describe the characteristics of psychotic behavior, and explain how it can be treated.

This question asks you to *describe* characteristics and *explain* treatment methods. If you get a question like this, it is especially important to plan your time carefully. It is easy to get so involved in writing the first part that you don't leave enough time for the second.

Other two-part questions have only one verb, but they still require two separate discussions. Here is an example:

> Explain the effects of U.S. trade agreements on Canada and Mexico.

You would have to first discuss the effects on Canada and then discuss those on Mexico.

To make sure you respond to such questions accurately, underline and mark parts of the exam questions as you read them. Underline the topic and any limitations, then draw a box around the verbs that suggest which method of development you should use. Number each part of two-part questions clearly:

Explain the effects of U.S. trade agreements on Canada and Mexico.

**EXERCISE 15-3** For the following essay questions, underline the topics and box the verbs that suggest the method of development (narration, process, description, definition, example, classification, comparison and contrast, or cause and effect). In the space provided, indicate the method(s) you would use to answer each question.

1. Define and illustrate the three approaches to collective behavior.

   Method of Development: _____

2. Explain the function of memory cells in the human immune system and indicate how they differ from plasma cells.

   Method of Development: _____

3. Discuss the advantages and disadvantages of the three basic market-survey methods.

   Method of Development: _____

4. Explain the stages involved in the process of establishing prices.

   Method of Development: _____

5. Trace the increasing prominence of gender-discrimination issues over the past three decades.

   Method of Development: _____

## Considering Audience and Purpose

The essay-exam answer has a special audience and purpose. The audience consists of your instructor, and you know that he or she is knowledgeable about the topic. Your purpose in writing an essay answer is to demonstrate that *you* are knowledgeable about the topic. Consequently, your answer should explain the topic thoroughly and completely. It is best to write as if your audience were *not* knowledgeable about the topic.

## Planning Your Answer

Because you are working within a time limit, you won't be able to revise your answer. Consequently, it is even more important than usual to plan your essay carefully before you begin.

After you have read and marked each question, jot down ideas you'll include in your essay on the back of the exam, or on a separate sheet of paper that you won't turn in. If the question is one that you predicted, jot down the outline of your draft essay, making adjustments and additions to fit the actual question. Arrange your ideas to follow the method of development suggested in the question. Number them to indicate the order in which you'll present them in your essay. Keep in mind, too, the point value of the essay, and be sure to include sufficient ideas and explanations.

In response to the following question,

Identify the stages of sleep and describe four sleep disorders.

one student made these notes:

| Stages | Disorders |
|---|---|
| 1 wakefulness | 4 hypersomnia |
| 2 quiet sleep | 1 insomnia |
| 3 REM sleep (active) | 2 sleepwalking |
| | 3 night terrors |

As you write your essay, other ideas may occur to you; add them to your list so they won't slip your mind.

**EXERCISE    15-4**    Make a list of ideas to use in answering one of the following questions. Then number them to reflect how you plan to organize your essay.

1. The U.S. national debt has become an increasingly serious problem. One economist has suggested that each American take a 10-percent pay cut for one year. He presented statistics that demonstrated how this would drastically reduce the debt. Explain and justify your personal response to this proposal.

2. Describe the effects of the computerization of business and society on our daily lives.

3. Recently television cameras have been allowed at several public-interest trials. Discuss the pros and cons of this practice.

## Writing Your Answer

Because you will have little time to revise, it is important to write in complete sentences, supplying sufficient detail and following a logical organization. (Your instructor will not be put off by minor changes, additions, and corrections.)

Organize your essay answers as you would the other types of essays you've learned to write: begin with a thesis statement, then explain and support it.

## Writing Your Thesis Statement

Thesis statements in essay-answer tests should be simple and straightforward. In fact, you often can simply rephrase the essay question. Here are a few examples:

| *Essay Question* | *Thesis Statement* |
|---|---|
| 1. Describe the psychological factors that may affect the consumer buying process. | There are five psychological factors that may affect the consumer buying process. |
| 2. Identify and give an example of the principal forms of price discrimination. | Retailers use numerous forms of price discrimination. |
| 3. Coastal areas have more moderate temperatures than inland areas at the same latitude. Explain this phenomenon. | The high specific heat of water accounts for variations between coastal and inland areas at the same latitude. |

At times you may decide to add more information, as in the following examples:

| *Essay Question* | *Thesis Statement* |
|---|---|
| 1. Describe the strategies individuals use to reinterpret a stressful event. | Individuals cope with stressful events by using reappraisal, social comparison, avoidance, or humor to reinterpret them. |
| 2. Explain the differences between primary and secondary groups. | Primary groups differ from secondary groups in their membership, purpose, level of interaction, and level of intimacy. |

In the above examples, the essay question provided a structure to which the writer added more information.

Make your thesis statement as concise and specific as possible. It should announce to your instructor that you know the answer and how you will organize it.

**EXERCISE** ▶ **15-5** | Write a thesis statement for three of the following essay questions.

1. How does advertising differ from publicity?

   Thesis Statement: _____

2. Explain the common types of magazines and identify the intended audience of each.

   Thesis Statement: _____

3. Describe the rise of the women's movement over the past decade.

   Thesis Statement: _____

4. Discuss the major ways in which a group ensures that its members conform to its cultural rules.

   Thesis Statement: _____

5. Discuss several ways to test the effectiveness of an advertising campaign.

   Thesis Statement: _____

## Presenting Supporting Details

Write a separate paragraph for each major supporting detail. Begin each one with a topic sentence that introduces the new point. Suppose your thesis statement is

> There are four social factors that may affect the consumer buying process.

Your topic sentences might read as follows:

Paragraph 1    First, social role and family influence are factors that affect consumer decisions.

Paragraph 2    Reference groups are a second social factor.

Paragraph 3    Social class also affects the consumer's purchase decisions.

Paragraph 4    Finally, cultures and subcultures affect buying decisions.

The remainder of each paragraph should include supporting details about each factor.

## Developing Your Answers with Supporting Details

Each paragraph should provide relevant and sufficient explanation of the topic sentence. For the above sample question on consumer buying, explain or define each psychological factor and discuss how it affects the buying decision. Here is an example of how one student developed an essay in response to the above question. Notice that he added a general explanation after his thesis statement.

> There are four social factors that may affect the consumer buying process. Social factors are those forces that other people exert on a buyer. First, social role and family influence affect who buys what. Everyone holds a position within a group. How you are expected to act in that position is your role. Your role, especially within your family, determines which types of purchases you are in charge of. For example, women are responsible for food and household supplies, while men buy home-repair and auto supplies.
>
> Reference groups are a second social factor influencing buying decisions. A reference group is the group a person connects himself or herself with. The person accepts the attitudes and behaviors of the reference group. As a result, a person buys the same things as others in the reference group. For example, teenagers in a particular high-school class may all purchase one expensive brand of sneakers.
>
> Social class also affects purchasing decisions. Social class is a group of people who have similar social rank, which is determined by such things as money, education, and property. People in the same social class have common attitudes and value the same things. Because they value the same things, they purchase similar items. For example, upper-middle-class business men and women buy luxury cars, like BMWs.
>
> Finally, cultures and subcultures influence buying decisions. Culture means everything in our surroundings made by human beings and includes values and behavior. We tend to do things the way everyone else in our culture does. Because we imitate others, we buy the same things. For example, because many women in American culture work full-time, many of them buy convenience foods. Subcultures are subdivisions within a culture—they are often created on the basis of age, geography, or ethnic background. There are even more similarities in subcultures, so the buying influence is even stronger. Thus, since consumer buying decisions are determined by numerous social forces, retailers and advertisers find predicting consumer purchases challenging and complex.

## Proofreading Your Answer

Be sure to leave enough time to proofread your answer. Check for errors in spelling, punctuation, and grammar. If time permits, make minor revisions. If you think of an important fact to add, do so. Pay attention to sentences that do not make sense, and make your changes as neatly as possible.

### If You Run Out of Time

If you run out of time before you have finished answering the last question, don't panic. Take the last minute or two to make a list or outline of the remaining points you planned to cover. Some instructors will give you partial credit for this.

## Competency Tests and Exit Exams

Some colleges require students to pass competency tests for such skills as reading, writing, and mathematics. These tests assess skills required in more advanced college courses, so think of them as readiness tests. Competency tests are designed so that you will not be placed into courses that you are inadequately prepared for or that are too difficult. Try your best, but don't be upset if you don't score at the required level. It is best to be certain you've got the skills you need before tackling more difficult courses.

This section focuses on competency tests, but many suggestions here apply to other tests.

### Finding Out About the Test

To feel confident and prepared for the test, find out as much about it as possible ahead of time. You'll want to know

- what kinds of questions are included (do you write an essay or correct errors in paragraphs, for example)
- how many questions there are
- if there is a time limit and, if so, what it is
- what skills the test measures
- how the test is scored (do some skills count more than others)
- if it is an essay, if you are expected to revise or recopy it

Your instructor may be able to answer many of these questions. Also, talk with other students who have taken the test. They may be able to offer useful tips and advice.

## Preparing for Competency Tests

If you are taking the test right after you have finished a writing course, you will be well prepared. Only a few last-minute things remain.

## Essay Tests

If your test requires that you write an essay, the following suggestion will help:

1. Study your error log (see Chapter 5, "Strategies for Revising," pp. 82–83). If you haven't kept one, review papers your instructor has marked to identify and make a list of your most common errors. As you revise and proofread your competency-test answers, check for each of these errors.

2. Construct a mental revision checklist before you go into the exam. Use revision checklists in this book as a guide. If time permits, jot your list down on scrap paper during the exam; use it to revise your essay.

3. Reread sections of your learning journal in which you have written about skills you are learning and how well they work. If you have discovered, for example, that branching usually works well for generating ideas, use it during the test.

4. If your test is timed, plan how to divide your time. Estimate how much you will need for each step in the writing process. Gauge your time on a practice test (see next paragraph). Wear a watch to the exam, and check periodically to see that you're on schedule.

5. Take a practice test. Ask a classmate to make up a topic or question for you to write about. It should be the same type of question as those that will be on the test. Give yourself the time limit that will be used on the test. Then ask your classmate to evaluate your essay.

## Error-Correction Tests

If your test requires you to edit or correct another writer's sentences or paragraphs, do the following:

1. Review your error log or graded papers. The errors you make when you write are likely to be those you'll have difficulty spotting on the test.

2. If time permits, read each sentence or paragraph several times, looking for different types of errors each time. For example, read it once looking for spelling errors, another time to evaluate sentence structure, and so forth.

3. Practice with a friend. Write sample test items for each other. Pay attention to the kinds of errors you are failing to spot; you're likely to miss them on the test as well.

4. If you are taking a state exam, practice manuals or review books may be available. Check with your college bookstore. Take the sample tests and work through the practice exercises. Note your pattern of errors and, if necessary, get additional help from your instructor or your college's academic skills center.

## Thinking Before Reading

This reading was taken from a college textbook, *Human Anatomy and Physiology,* by Elaine Marieb. "Sunlight and the Clock Within" represents the type of textbook material you might review for an essay exam.

1. Preview the reading using the steps listed on page 45.
2. Activate your thinking by answering the following questions:
    a. Is your mood different on dark dreary days than it is on bright sunny days?
    b. Have you ever worked night schedules, or do you know someone who has? If so, what effects on behavior and mood did you observe?
    c. Does the change from standard to daylight-savings time affect you? How? Why?
    d. Do you know people who are "sun worshipers," who enjoy spending time in the sun? Why do they enjoy it, knowing the risk of skin cancer?

**R E A D I N G**

## Sunlight and the Clock Within
### Elaine Marieb

It has been known for a long time that many body rhythms move in step with one another. Body temperature, pulse, and the sleep-wake cycles seem to follow the same "beat" over approximate 24-hour cycles, while other processes follow a different "drummer." What can throw these rhythms out of whack? Illness, drugs, jet travel, and changing to the night shift are all candidates. So is sunlight.

1

Light exerts its internal biochemical effects through the eye. Light hit-    2
ting the retina generates nerve impulses along the optic nerve, tract, and
radiation to the visual cortex (where "seeing" occurs) and via the retino-
hypothalamic tracts to the superchiasmatic nucleus (SCN), the so-called
biological clock of the hypothalamus. The SCN regulates multiple-drive
rhythms, including the rhythmic melatonin output of the pineal gland
and the output of various anterior pituitary hormones. Generally speaking, release of melatonin is inhibited by light and enhanced during darkness, and historically, the pineal gland has been called the "third eye."

Light produces melatonin-mediated effects on reproductive, eating,    3
and sleeping patterns of other animals, but until very recently, humans
were believed to have evolved free of such effects. Thanks to the
research of many scientists, however, we now know that people are
influenced by three major variables of light: its intensity, its spectrum
(color mixture), and its timing (day/night and seasonal changes).

A number of human processes are known to be influenced by light:    4

**1.** *Behavior and Mood.* Many people have seasonal mood rhythms,    5
particularly those of us who live far from the equator, where the day/night
cycle changes dramatically during the course of a year. We seem to feel
better during the summer and become cranky and depressed in the long,

gray days of winter. Is this just our imagination? Apparently not. Researchers have found a relatively rare emotional disorder called seasonal affective disorder, or SAD, in which these mood swings are grossly exaggerated. As the days grow shorter each fall, people with SAD become irritable, anxious, sleepy, and socially withdrawn. Their appetite becomes insatiable; they crave carbohydrates and gain weight. Phototherapy, the use of very bright lights for 6 hours daily, reversed these symptoms in nearly 90% of patients studied in two to four days (considerably faster than any antidepressant drug could do it). When patients stopped receiving therapy or were given melatonin, their symptoms returned as quickly as they had lifted, indicating that melatonin may be the key to seasonal mood changes.

Symptoms of SAD are virtually identical to those of individuals with *carbohydrate-craving obesity (CCO)* and *premenstrual syndrome (PMS)*, except that CCO sufferers are affected daily and PMS sufferers are affected monthly (2 weeks prior to menses onset). Photoperiodism appears to be the basis of these cyclic behavioral disorders as well, and phototherapy relieves PMS symptoms in some women.    6

2. *Night work schedules and jet lag.* People who work at night (the graveyard shift) exhibit reversed melatonin secretion patterns, with no hormone released during the night (when they are exposed to light) and high levels secreted during daytime sleeping hours. Waking such people and exposing them to bright light causes their melatonin levels to drop. The same sort of melatonin inversion (but much more precipitous) occurs in those who fly from coast to coast.    7

3. *Immunity.* Ultraviolet light activates white blood cells called suppressor T cells, which partially block the immune response. UV therapy has been found to stop rejection of tissue transplants from unrelated donors in animals. This technique offers the hope that diabetics who have become immune to their own pancreas islet tissue may be treated with pancreas transplants in the future.    8

People have worshipped sunlight since the earliest times. Scientists are just now beginning to understand the reasons for this, and as they do, they are increasingly distressed about windowless offices, restricted and artificial illumination of work areas, and the growing numbers of institutionalized elderly who rarely feel the sun's warm rays. Artificial lights do not provide the full spectrum of sunlight: Incandescent bulbs used in homes provide primarily the red wavelengths, and fluorescent bulbs of institutions provide yellow-green; neither provides the invisible UV or infrared wavelengths that are also components of sunlight. Animals exposed for prolonged periods to artificial lighting exhibit reproductive abnormalities and an enhanced susceptibility to cancer. Could it be that some of us are unknowingly expressing the same effects?    9

*Human Anatomy and Physiology*

## Getting Ready to Write

■ **Examining the Reading: Underlining and Reviewing**

Reread and underline passages in the reading, as if you were preparing for an exam that includes this material. Use any other getting-ready-to-write strategy that will help you organize and recall the material. (Refer to Table 15-1, p. 290, for a list of strategies.)

■ **Thinking Critically: Predicting Exam Questions**

Think of at least one essay-exam question that could be based on this reading.

■ **Reacting to Ideas: Discussion and Journal Writing**

Compare your essay-question prediction with those of other students. Discuss ways you might respond to their questions as well as your own.

## Writing Assignments

### Writing About the Reading

1. Answer the following essay question without quoting directly from the reading.

   Explain the effects of sunlight on humans, both biologically and psychologically.

### Writing About Your Ideas

2. Assume you are taking an exit exam for your writing course. Select one of the following assignments, and approach it as you would a competency exam.
   a. Write an essay describing how seasonal and/or time changes affect you.
   b. Write an essay explaining factors that affect your mood.
   c. Write an essay describing how it feels when your biological clock is out of whack.

## REVISION CHECKLIST—ESSAY EXAMS

1. Is your essay written as if for an audience unfamiliar with the topic?
2. Does your essay demonstrate your purpose—that you are knowledgeable about the topic?
3. Is your thesis statement concise and straightforward?
4. Is each main point developed in a separate paragraph?
5. Does each paragraph provide relevant and sufficient detail?
6. Have you made minor revisions, and have you proofread the essay?

## REVISION CHECKLIST—COMPETENCY TESTS

1. Is your essay appropriate for your audience? Does it give them the background information they need? Will it interest them?
2. Will your essay accomplish your purpose?
3. Have you narrowed your topic so that you can cover your subject thoroughly in your essay?
4. Is your main point clearly expressed in a thesis statement in the introductory paragraph? Does your introductory paragraph capture the reader's interest and lead into the body of the essay?
5. Does each paragraph of your essay have a topic sentence that supports your essay's main point?
6. Is each paragraph's topic sentence supported by relevant and sufficient detail?
7. Are your paragraphs arranged in a logical sequence and connected by transitional words and phrases?
8. Is the tone of your essay appropriate for your purpose and audience?
9. Does your conclusion reemphasize your thesis statement and draw the essay to a close?
10. Have you proofread your paper and corrected any mechanical errors (grammar, spelling, punctuation, and so on)? (See the inside back cover of this book for a proofreading checklist.)

# SKILL REFRESHER

## When to Use Capital Letters
Capital letters are commonly used to

1. mark the beginning of a sentence
2. identify names of specific people, places, organizations, companies, products, titles, days, months, weeks, religions, and holidays
3. mark the beginning of a direct quotation

## Rate Your Ability to Use Capitalization Correctly
In each of the following sentences, capitalize wherever necessary by crossing out the letter and replacing it with a capital. If any letters are incorrectly capitalized, change them to lowercase.

1. because I spent last sunday in pittsburgh, I missed my favorite television show—*60 minutes.*
2. This summer I plan to visit the Baltic states—estonia, latvia, lithuania—former Republics of the soviet union.
3. this may, professor gilbert will give us our final exam.
4. Last week I rented my favorite movie from the video rental store on elmwood avenue.
5. One of shakespeare's most famous plays is *hamlet.*
6. I live next door to joe's mobile gas station.
7. my brother will eat only rice krispies for breakfast.
8. Jean Griffith is a senator who lives in washington county.
9. I love to vacation in california because the pacific ocean is so beautiful.
10. My neighbors, mr. and mrs. wilson, have a checking account at the lincoln bank.

Score _____

Check your answers using the Answer Key on page 488. If you got more than two wrong, you need additional review and practice recognizing when to use capital letters. Refer to Part VI, "Reviewing the Basics," p. 456.

## CHAPTER SUMMARY

**Writing Skills**

1. Preparing for an essay exam involves identifying important ideas, organizing related ideas and concepts, and expressing these in your own words. Useful strategies include underlining, immediate review, recognizing supporting details, annotating, paraphrasing, summarizing, and idea mapping.

   • Use study sheets to organize material concisely for review.

   • Predict possible exam questions by identifying important issues or concepts that your instructor has emphasized. Practice answering the questions you predicted by writing rough-draft answers.

   • When taking essay exams, read directions carefully, plan your time, and notice the point value of each question.

   • Analyze each question by identifying the topic, its limitations, and the method of development suggested.

   • Plan your answer by jotting down a brief outline.

   • Be sure your thesis statement is clear and direct.

   • Include sufficient supporting detail. Write a separate paragraph on each major detail.

2. To prepare for competency tests and exit exams

   • find out about the test (content, time, scoring)

   • using your error log, discover common errors you make

   • create a mental revision checklist

   • take a practice test

**Reading and Critical Thinking Skills**

1. Underlining and reviewing important passages are essential skills for preparing for an essay exam.

2. Predicting essay-exam questions is an effective way to prepare for essay exams.

Part

V

# ADDITIONAL READINGS

## Narrative

## Taken for a Stranger
### Armin A. Brott

I was pushing my daughter on a swing at our favorite park when I heard   1
the screams. Just a few feet away, a panicked little girl was teetering on
the small platform at the top of a long, steep slide. As I watched,
she lost her grip on the handrail and began to fall. Without thinking, I
leaped over to the slide, caught the girl and set her down on the sand.

I knelt down and was about to ask her if she was all right when a   2
woman picked the girl up, gave me a withering look and hustled the
child away.

"Didn't I tell you not to talk to strange men in the park?" the woman   3
asked her daughter, glaring over her shoulder at me. "Did he hurt you?"

I stood there for a few seconds, stunned, as the woman bundled her   4
child into a car and drove off. I wondered what she had been thinking.
Hadn't she seen me playing with a happy girl who called me "Daddy"?
It was a cloudless summer day, and as I looked around the park I realized I was the only man there. That was when it hit me: I—the father—
was invisible. What had come to that woman's mind was what was
most ingrained and automatic: the stereotyped image of a man in the
park, menacing and solitary.

I often notice that the day after I've gone to the dictionary to look   5
up an unfamiliar word I'll hear the same word used four or five times—
in perfectly ordinary conversation. Just a few days after I made my
"discovery" about fathers, I began hearing similar stories from other
men. A cousin told me about an incident that had happened in a playground near his house. His son had fallen and cut his knee and my
cousin ran to pick him up. The park supervisor, a woman, saw a man
with a beard holding a screaming child and without asking a single
question called the police. A few days later, I read about a man who had
gone to pick up his daughter at day care. There was a new teacher, and
the man went over to introduce himself. But before he could get a word
out, the teacher demanded a picture ID. "As a father, I appreciated the
security," he said, "but as a man, I took offense at having to prove that
I was not a pervert." These days, the contemporary rhetoric[1] that depicts
every man as a potential rapist or child molester seems to have combined
with ordinary fear of strangers to form a very dangerous mixture.

I remember another article in which the author, a young black man,   6
describes the pain, anger and frustration he feels when he walks through

1. verbal communication

his own neighborhood and white people routinely cross the street to avoid him. The author, and many others like him, is rightfully outraged that people who know nothing about him make all sorts of assumptions about him—based simply on his race. As I read the article, I wondered whether I'd ever done the same thing and tried to imagine how helpless he must have felt. At the time, I was sympathetic, but ultimately couldn't empathize—the author's experience was too foreign from anything I'd ever known. But now, as the victim of a purely sexist attitude, I know exactly what he was talking about.

One of the most paradoxical—and perhaps the most horrifying—aspects 7 of this type of antimale sexism is that men themselves are just as likely to be the perpetrators as women. And, if I'm honest, I have to admit that I'm probably no more immune from prejudice against men than that woman in the park. If I'd turned around and seen a strange man kneeling near my daughter, I might have jumped to the worst possible conclusions, too. When my wife and I have interviewed baby sitters for our daughter, *I'm* the one who has had the most serious objections to hiring a man for the job.

Ashamed of my irrational reservations, but wondering if (maybe 8 even hoping) they were reasonable, I decided to do a little research. The truth only made me more disgusted with myself *and* that woman in the park. The fact is that, according to the National Child Abuse and Neglect Data System and the National Resource Center on Child Sexual Abuse, about 90 percent of children who are physically abused (and over 80 percent of those who are abused sexually) are hurt by someone they know—more often than not a relative. And although men are the offenders in most sexual abuse cases (which account for less than a quarter of total child abuse cases), *overall* the child abuser is more often a woman than a man, contrary to popular belief and media hype. What this means is that a child is more likely to be harmed by Aunt Sophia who baby-sits Tuesday nights than by a strange man in the park in broad daylight, especially one who's pushing a kid on a swing.

I began to wonder exactly where I—and so many other people, for 9 that matter—get this strange fear of seeing men and children together. Almost every time I take my daughter to the park, I'm the only man there and in a way it seems perfectly natural to fear the unknown. But that isn't the only answer.

For me, it may have started with the "safety" movies I saw in the 10 third or fourth grade. I still remember the scary images of the sinister, mustachioed men—and they were always *men*—lurking behind trees in the park or trying to entice us into their cars. Now, 25 years later, I know that estranged parents, including mothers, are responsible for the vast majority of abductions, and I wonder why most of the suspects the media choose to tell us about are the same safety movie guys—spiced up with speculation about possible sexual abuse.

As a parent, I'm faced with the rather daunting task of having to      11
teach my child to strike a balance between a healthy wariness of
strangers and an equally healthy politeness toward new neighbors. But
as a man, I want society to re-examine the factual basis for its prejudices
and try to understand how the victims of this prejudice feel. When we
are finally able to look at a man holding hands with a child and see a
father, not a child molester, we'll know we've made some progress.

A few months ago, my daughter and I went back to our favorite      12
park. As soon as we got through the gate, she dashed off to play with
some of the other kids. I'd been reading that letting children play by
themselves helps build their independence, so I sat down on a nearby
bench, keeping one eye on her, the other on my newspaper. Not five
minutes later, I heard her distinctive yelp and looked up to see a young
woman snatch my daughter out of the path of an oncoming swing. I
rushed over, comforted my startled 3-year-old and thanked the woman.
"Don't worry about it," she said. "Someday you'll do the same thing for
me." The day I do, I hope she thinks to thank me.

Brott, *New York Times Magazine*

## Reacting to Ideas: Discussion and Journal Writing

1. If you saw a man you didn't know speaking to your child, how would
   you react?

2. Do you agree with the author that people are more suspicious of
   male—as opposed to female—strangers? Why or why not?

3. When you were growing up, were you allowed to speak with
   strangers? With your own children how would you or do you teach
   them to "strike a balance between a healthy wariness of strangers and
   an equally healthy politeness toward new neighbors"?

4. In what other situations have you observed someone misjudging the
   intent or actions of another?

## Writing Assignments

### Writing About the Reading

1. Write a paragraph in response to this reading. Do you agree or disagree with the author that people often misjudge the intentions of

males, especially in relation to children? Support your ideas with examples from your own experience.

2. At the beginning of this reading, the author described how, when a woman hurried her child away from him, he said nothing. Rewrite this portion of the reading (paragraph 4) describing what you think would have happened if he had tried to explain his good intentions.

### Writing About Your Ideas

3. The author was able to understand the young black man's experience as a result of his own experience in the park. Has this reading helped you understand stereotyping or prejudice? Think of an example of prejudice or stereotyping that you have observed or experienced, and write an essay explaining it.

4. Write a paragraph about a person whom you later realized you had misjudged. Explain how and why you misjudged the person.

5. The woman in the park assumed the author had planned to harm her daughter. Write a paragraph describing a situation in which someone made an incorrect assumption about you or your behavior.

6. The stereotype of men as child molesters is explored in this essay. What other antimale stereotypes exist? What antifemale stereotypes exist? Choose one, and write an essay explaining the stereotype and giving examples (some stereotypes: men as bad cooks, women as bad drivers).

## Narrative/Process

## Stuck with Strangers
### Castle Freeman Jr.

On a bright January morning a couple of years ago I was coming home up the hill, driving carelessly along trying to remember what, exactly, happened in the Defenestration[1] of Prague, when suddenly I felt the hindquarters of my wagon begin to describe a counterclockwise arc—speedily, irresistibly, in a classic rear-end skid.   1

In this situation the advice of the experts is unanimous. You remain calm. You don't brake. You steer deftly in the direction of the skid, so that the momentum of the car can straighten it out. That is good   2

1. act of throwing something or someone out a window

advice—but I seldom follow it. I find that what works for me in a skid is to hit the brakes as hard as I can, shut my eyes, and repeat certain words at increasing volume until I land wherever I'm going to land.

So it happened that morning in January: the rear went east, the front went west, and the whole show, with me in it, wound up half on the road, half in the ditch, pointing back down the hill, and stuck, stuck, stuck.

At this point in any such debacle my procedure is always the same. I turn off the motor and get out of the car. I then walk around the car, examining it closely but dispassionately, as though it were no car of mine but one I have discovered inexplicably abandoned by persons unknown. Doing this introduces an element of disassociation into the episode which prepares me to receive help when it arrives.

Help arrived this morning in the form of two fellows in a truck. They stopped, got out, and joined me in surveying the problem. We agreed that the road was slick, the car was mine, the car was stuck. (Here and in the next several paragraphs I reduce a fairly prolonged and complex exchange to its essentials.)

"Not bad stuck," one of the men said to his partner. "He's headed downhill. He ought to start up, straighten his wheels, and just tickle the accelerator. Just ease it out."

"He doesn't want to ease it," the other said. "He wants to punch it. 7
Get in. Start up. Straighten out. Then punch it. Punch it."

"He doesn't want to punch it," said the first. "He punches it, he'll 8
dig in. He'll never get off. We'll have to pull him."

*Pull him?* I thought. *Yes.* 9

Another car came up the road and stopped. A young woman got 10
out. She wore a red woolen hat with a pompon. She came over to the
car, got down on her knees and looked underneath, brushed snow away
from the ditched rear wheel, and looked some more. She stood.

"He ought to ease it," the first man said. 11

"He ought to punch it," the second man said. 12

"He's only spinning one tire," the young woman said. "He ought to 13
throw the wheel hard left, put it in reverse, and back it up. That will
make him roll off the patch he's spinning on. Then he gets into forward
and drives right out. Easy."

"He doesn't want to reverse," the first man said. "He reverses, he'll 14
get so far down in there he'll never get out. We'll have to pull him."

*Pull him?* I thought. *Why not?* 15

"Nobody's going to pull anybody," the young woman said. "Just do 16
it," she said to me.

I did it. It didn't work. We had a storm of flying snow and dirt, and 17
we had considerable screaming of tires, but I ended up a couple of feet
farther down in the ditch than I had been, with my front end tilted now
at a jaunty angle to the horizon. I got out of the car.

"It was worth a shot," the young woman said. 18

"I guess now we'll have to pull it?" I said. 19

"We can't pull it," the second man said. "We've got no chain." 20

"I've got a chain," the young woman said. 21

So the two fellows got her chain and hooked me up to their truck, 22
and with them in the truck pulling, the young woman beside the car
pushing, and me driving, we got me back in business easily enough.
There followed the unhooking, the stowing of the chain, the thanks,
the offer of payment, the offer's refusal, the return to vehicles, the beep,
the wave, the parting. Time elapsed since help arrived: twenty minutes.
Time required for effective help to be applied: two minutes. Time
required for advice: eighteen minutes. Exactly 90 percent of the
transaction, therefore, was occupied not with practical assistance
but with . . . what?

What was served? I'm not sure, but I suspect that these unhurried 23
rural negotiations of suggestion and advice, assertion and doubt,
amount to a kind of ceremony affirming a principle that many people—
including, I'm afraid, me—prefer to neglect: Nobody does anything
alone. Even those people who think they do—those people especially—
need help, get help, take help gratefully, but never quite on their own

terms. When your helpers arrive, they give what they have, in their own way, in their own time. Your part is to receive, to accept, and to learn, so that when you come to the same ceremony in the opposite role, you'll know what offering to bring. Someday the adviser will be you. What will you say?

I always tell them to punch it. "Punch it," I say. "Just punch it."    24

Freeman, *The Atlantic Monthly*

## Reacting to Ideas: Discussion and Journal Writing

1. Although the essay describes how a car was pulled from a ditch, what more important process is this essay really about?

2. What do you think motivates people who stop to offer assistance to stranded motorists?

3. In what sense does advice giving amount to a ceremony? What is being recognized or celebrated by the ceremony?

## Writing Assignments

### Writing About the Reading

1. Write an essay agreeing or disagreeing with this statement: "Nobody does anything alone. Even those people who think they do—those people especially—need help, get help, take help gratefully, but never quite on their own terms."

### Writing About Your Ideas

2. The author notes that two minutes of action required eighteen minutes of discussion and advice giving. Have you observed "much talk, little action" to be the case in accomplishing things that involve other people? Write an essay describing an example from your experience, how it was accomplished, and whether it involved mostly talk or action.

3. The writer humorously describes a predictable human behavior: volunteers disagreeing about how to help. Write an essay describing another predictable human behavior you have observed or have experienced firsthand.

## Paired Readings Assignment: "Taken for a Stranger"
## "Stuck with Strangers"

Both "Taken for a Stranger" and "Stuck with Strangers" discuss how people interact with strangers. Using these two readings as sources, write an essay discussing what things determine how we react to strangers and how they react to us.

## Narrative

## A Brother's Death
### Barbara Lazear Ascher

I t could have been a parade of Civil War soldiers, wounded and near defeat, marching toward another battle. They stared ahead with eyes from which all joy had been banished.

They had marched in too many funeral processions, they had watched as disease dismissed courage and defiantly claimed their friends. This day, three months ago, they marched in a New Orleans jazz funeral for my brother, Bobby, dead of AIDS at 31.

I rode with my sister, mother and father, and my brother's companion, George, in a mule-drawn wagon, ahead of the parade of friends, and behind the musicians, old black men who knew the route and the music by heart.

The street was closed for the occasion. The citizens were shuttered inside cool interiors away from the fireball that is New Orleans' August sun. The day was ours, the streets were ours. The sun beat down on us alone. We, in the cart, sat as still as stones.

George cradled a carved wooden box that looked like an ornate bird house—the house of ashes that had been my brother's bones.

Still as stone we rode through the streets of New Orleans as jazz rose up around us and the old men played "The Old Rugged Cross" to lead us to the church. If we moved, if we cried, we might never stop moving, never stop crying. It was better to be still.

My brother was a wild thing. The confines of our New England home could not contain him. He kept flying into windows. Released, he flew south to warmth, to a landscape large enough to absorb his exuberance. To sympathetic souls who held him when exuberance failed.

A friend who volunteers at the Gay Men's Health Crisis Center tells me, "You would be surprised how many families first learn that their son or brother is gay at the same time they learn he has AIDS. They get a phone call that says, 'I've got two things to tell you.'" My family was more fortunate. We knew that my brother was gay, and his openness had enabled my parents to share the happiness he and George were finding together, to know and accept that in a careless world, love is precious whatever the pairing. But there is no accepting that one's child is doomed.

We are not alone in our anger, grief and disbelief. The horizon is filling up with parents burying young sons. Fewer and fewer of us are allowed the smug certainty that AIDS has nothing to do with our lives. Soon, each of us will have a child, brother, friend, friend of a friend, a distant relative who is doomed. 9

Until recently, the statistics have insulated many of us. We've read that the risk group comprises homosexuals, bisexuals and intravenous drug users. If we didn't fit in the categories, we said, "Well, I'm safe," and turned the page. To number fatalities is to depersonalize them. The body count in Vietnam. The deaths from drunk driving. Numbers don't touch our hearts. 10

My parents, well known in their community, broke through those barriers of denial by making it clear, in their son's prominent obituary, that the cause of Bobby's death was AIDS. Not "pneumonia" or "heart attack" or "respiratory failure," or other causes of death we now see in obituary columns when we read about single men dying in their prime. 11

The letters of sympathy began to come in immediately. 12

"Thank you for being honest about Bobby's illness. My best friend's son has AIDS." 13

"When my cousin died of AIDS, it was a family secret. That robbed us of the opportunity to mourn and be supported in our grief." 14

"My best friend in college, captain of the football team, a Rhodes scholar, just died of AIDS." 15

It became clear from the letters that AIDS was coming home. AIDS had come to Donna Reed America, to Father Knows Best America. AIDS was killing kids who once wore Mickey Mouse Club caps and wrote mash notes to Annette Funicello. 16

When we first learned of Bobby's illness it seemed incomprehensible that this could be happening to our baby brother. My sister and I began a journey into paralysis. There were days when it seemed we had to concentrate on putting one foot in front of the other if we were to walk at all. If we traveled more than a couple of blocks, we were exhausted for the rest of the day. 17

We were hungry, we weren't hungry. We made chocolate chip cookies and chocolate brownies and didn't eat them. We opened and closed the refrigerator door, looking for something that might cushion the pain, fill the chasm that was opening from within. 18

Now I realize that this was the beginning of grief which starts in the stomach, yawning like the gaping mouth in Munch's painting, "The Scream." But what did we know of grief? We were young, our beloveds had not yet died. I began to understand that grieving is like walking. The urge is there, but you need a guiding hand, you need someone to teach you how.

I went to speak with a wise and trusted minister at my church who warned that there were bad times ahead. The death of a sibling, he said, grievous in itself, is also a startling reminder of our own mortality. I suppose it's not dissimilar to the time in youth when we first learned of our origins and began to understand, if they made me, then they can make another. After that we became the nervous sentinels[1] of our territory. When a sibling dies, the absolute certainty of death replaces the cherished illusion that maybe we'll be the exceptions. When a sibling dies, death tugs at our own shirt tails. There's no unclasping its persistent grip. "You too," it says. "Yes, even you."

When you are new to grief, you learn that there's no second-guessing it. It will have its way with you. Don't be fooled by the statistics you read: Widows have one bad year; orphans three. Grief doesn't read schedules.

One morning, three weeks after Bobby died, I arose feeling happy and energetic. Well, now, I thought, I guess we've taken care of that. Wrong. The next morning I was awakened by a wail I thought was coming from the storm outside until I realized it was coming from me.

Grief will fool you with its disguises. Some days you insist that you're fine, you're just angry at a friend who said the wrong thing. One day I wept into the lettuce and peaches at our local market when an acquaintance approached to scold me for my stand in an old battle. Of course, we both assumed that she was responsible for my tears.

You learn that you can cry and stop and laugh and even follow a taxi driver's commands to "Have a nice day," and then cry again. You learn that there is no such thing as crying forever. Three months ago I was certain that I would never be happy again. I was wrong.

Grief is like the wind. When it's blowing hard, you adjust your sails and run before it. If it blows too hard, you stay in the harbor, close the hatches and don't take calls. When it's gentle, you go sailing, have a picnic, take a swim.

You go wherever it takes you. There are no bulwarks[2] to withstand it. Should you erect one, it will eventually tire of the game and blow the walls in.

1. guardians
2. barricades

We cannot know another's grief, as deeply personal as love and     27
pain. I cannot measure my own against the sorrow of my brother's
friends who must wonder every day which among them will be next.
Who must have wondered, as they marched through the streets of New
Orleans, which of their families would sit one day in the mule-drawn
cart. I shy away from the magnitude of my brother's own grief when,
upon being diagnosed, he heard the final click of a door as it closed on
possibility.

A friend of mine said of her son when he died at 30, "He was just     28
beginning to look out at the world and make maps." So was my
brother. And then there was no place to go.

Ascher, *New York Times Magazine*

## Reacting to Ideas: Discussion and Journal Writing

1. What is the author's attitude toward Bobby's homosexuality?

2. How does the author describe the homosexual community in New Orleans?

3. Do you think the death of a sibling would be a startling reminder of one's own mortality? Why? How is it different from the death of a close friend who is close in age?

4. What types of "maps" (paragraph 28) was Bobby just beginning to make?

5. Evaluate the effectiveness of Ascher's introduction and conclusion.

## Writing Assignments

### Writing About the Reading

1. Write a paragraph explaining the statement "AIDS had come to Donna Reed America, to Father Knows Best America."

2. Write a three- or four-paragraph essay that answers this question: do you think the article is primarily about AIDS or about death and grief? (This question asks you to identify the author's purpose in writing. Refer to "Discovering the Author's Purpose," on p. 50.) Support your answer with specific examples from the reading.

### Writing About Your Ideas

3. Write a paragraph explaining whether you think our society has become more accepting of AIDS victims than it was in 1989, when this article was published.

4. Write a paragraph describing an experience you have had with grief (the loss of a friend, family member, or loving pet).

5. The author states that "fewer and fewer of us are allowed the smug certainty that AIDS has nothing to do with our lives" (paragraph 9) and that "until recently, the statistics have insulated many of us" (paragraph 10). What other problems or social issues do you feel many of us are ignoring? Select one issue or problem, and write an essay explaining why or how we are ignoring it.

## Example

### Toddler Terrorism
#### Gerri Hirshey

Baby crime. You've seen it. You've probably been a victim. Baby crime is on the rise, all but unchecked by the current crop of enthusiastic new parents. It's hard to blame the Infant Offender. Yet when he strikes, his power is awesome. Take Teddy, a.k.a. Ninja Tot, a wee terrorist in OshKosh B'Gosh and perpetrator[1] of a grisly summer's day crime spree. It took place a few years ago at a baby shower, the first in a monsoon of showers and birthings now blessing my 30-and-counting friends. NT was with us because his parents had declared themselves morally opposed to "adult occasions." A half hour into the proceedings, it was clear that his mother—a witty, savvy career woman, and the only experienced parent among us—had turned into a simp, rendered stupid with mother love. "Oooh, Teddy," she chirped, as NT upended a glass of wine. He howled for the fuzzy bunnies and *Goodnight Moon*'s intended for the unborn. He screeched, he whined, he climbed us and he slimed us. Mother beamed. We bore it until he did the unspeakable and hijacked one woman's purse, tore open the makeup

1

1. person who commits a crime

case, and held a dozen women at bay with an unsheathed mascara
wand. He cackled, lurched toward a pale yellow armchair. Down came
the mascara wand. The purse owner dove and caught him by the wrist.
She retrieved her makeup and hissed to Mother:

"Don't you ever tell him NO?"

At the time, I chalked Ninja Tot and his goony mom up as an aberration,[2] but the intervening years have yielded a growing tribe of fine
young savages. Wild things. Spoiled things, loved beyond measure and
indulged to alarming excess. The resultant baby tyranny has a swelling
legion of silent victims, in public spaces and in private homes. Baby
tyranny's not cute. And it sure ain't pretty.

I have seen a two-year-old order his father out of an easy chair—
successfully. I have had a three-year-old hand back a bagel I spread with
cream cheese and snort, "I want *Montrachet*."[3] At her parents' request, I
have held dinner for six adults two and a half hours while a toddler was
being "settled down" for the night. Oh, it wasn't that she was staying in
a strange bed. They went through this *every* night. Had eaten cold suppers with the 11 o'clock news for the past three years. Yes, their wise
65-year-old pediatrician had counseled, "Let her cry," but that's
so . . . '50s. So barbaric.

2. something departing from the normal
3. goat cheese

Standing over a withered chicken, I waved a wooden spoon and   5
howled at the other hungry adults: "Who is this kid, the MESSIAH?"

Maybe. Boomer offspring are doubtless the most *awaited* children   6
in the history of our species. Having babies at ages unprecedented in
biological annals, we dare to dote in ways unimagined by millennia
of loving parents. News magazines, TV features, even comic strips
have chronicled the mania for boutique parenting—the teach-them-
logarithms-in-the-womb school, the upscale kiddie health clubs. What
the media hasn't addressed is the behavioral fallout of this delayed
parenthood.

Which brings us to a compendium of common Baby Crimes. Honk   7
if you've been there.

**Restaurant hell:** Here they come, knapsack full o'baby, heads full of   8
Attitude: We are the world, we are the PARENTS. Let Junior eat rice
cake. And if he wants to, let him lob it into the next booth. Do not
fetter the wee one, but let him roam the aisles like a free-range pullet,
drooling on pant legs and grabbing tablecloths. Titter as he makes a
beeline for the couple currently spending $8 an hour to leave their
own little criminals with a sitter.

Recently, I dined with a fractious infant and his parents at a Chinese   9
restaurant that discreetly reserves a back room for the little ones. The
walls are stippled with the greasy skidmarks of airborne egg rolls. I
asked the maitre d' about his savvy segregation and he said that such
measures had only been necessary for the last half-decade—that of the
boomer ninjas. He said the waiters had a Chinese name for the room
and volunteered a translation: "Cage for baby pork."

**Baby grandstanding:** When I was growing up in *Leave It to Beaver-*   10
Land, there was a crime more heinous than all: Showing Off for company. It was unspeakable.

These days, some children are *encouraged* to do this, like the young   11
Sun King (not his real name). In a roomful of visitors, the Sun King has
license to play earsplitting drums, records, videos. Try and eat dinner
and he starts the floor show—he's a LITTLE TEAPOT. Put down that
fork, he's Tubby the Tuba now. HEY, YOU'RE NOT WATCHING . . .
HEY. Mom and Dad giggle and beam. There is no uninterrupted conversation involving anything but THE CHILD—unless the Sun King is
in bed, unconscious.

Such an imbalance of power is avoidable even in New York City's   12
cramped apartments. Kids can and should join the party—they just
needn't run it.

**Baby wars:** Baby-to-baby crime is also ancient and natural, but the   13
latest methods for dealing with sandbox scuffles are not. There are few

things more terrifying than a face-off of righteous and aggrieved begetters with conflicting parenting styles. It goes like this:

Young Dante is whacking petite Amber with the business end of his Ghostbusters Proton Pack. Dante's mom is laissez-faire.[4] Amber's is a committed interventionist; thus she yells at Dante's mom by speaking oh-so-adult-like to him, a clever bit of displaced aggression. 14

"DAN-TAYYY. I don't think our Amber is rilly enjoying what you are doing, which is rilly unacceptable, don't you think, DAN-TAYYY. . . ." 15

Dante's mom: "Amber, you can tell Dante yourself just EXACTLY HOW YOU FEEL, can't you, honey? Mommy's taught you how to express your feelings, HASN'T SHE?" 16

Whoa. Mommy's about to express *her* feelings. Neutral adults yap feverishly to change the subject, fast. Do we miss Davey Johnson? Can the Simpsons really put a half Nielsen on Cosby this season? Never mind, it's the end of civility. Soon, the air is rent with the *zizzzz, zizzzz* of snowsuits being zipped in anger. 17

You've probably noticed that all these baby crimes are really born of the sins of adults. Men and women who love too much. Of course, there is no malice at the heart of baby crime, only love. And a hefty dollop of guilt, given the maddening strains of '90s family life. But baby love, untempered, does breed baby tyranny. 18

What I'm pleading for here is a bilateral balance of power, at the very least. Nobody can tell any other body how to raise their kids. But as a hitherto silent victim of many baby crimes, I will undertake to counsel others similarly oppressed. The next time you see a baby crime in progress, say it loud, be firm and be proud: 19

"NO." 20

And if you must: 21

"Pretty please? With Gummi Bears on top?" 22

Hirshey, *New York Woman*

4. does not get involved

## Reacting to Ideas: Discussion and Journal Writing

1. Discuss the author's use of humor in the essay. What parts were particularly effective?

2. Did the examples of baby crime ring true? That is, have you seen or experienced them yourself?

3. Why do parents allow "toddler terrorism"?

4. What should you do (or have you done) if you are (or have been) the victim of a "baby crime"?

## Writing Assignments

### Writing About the Reading

1. Although the essay is intended to be humorous, a serious message exists behind the humor. Write an essay explaining the author's serious message about child rearing.

### Writing About Your Ideas

2. Write a paragraph describing a "baby crime" that you have observed. Try to invent your own "crime," if possible, and give your "criminal" a descriptive fictitious name, too.

3. Write an expository essay explaining your philosophy of child rearing.

## Definition

## What Is Stress?
### Douglas A. Bernstein et al.

Stress is the process of adjusting to or dealing with circumstances that disrupt, or threaten to disrupt, a person's physical or psychological functioning. Here are two examples.

*Marlene has spent ten hours of a sweltering August day on a crowded bus from Cleveland, Ohio, to Muncie, Indiana. The air conditioner is not working, and she discovers that the person next to her has apparently not had a bath since the beginning of the decade. By the time she reaches Muncie, Marlene is hot, dizzy, depressed, tired, and irritable.*

*Jack is waiting in a room full of other college seniors to interview for a job with a large accounting firm. His grades are not outstanding, but he hopes to get by on his personality. He feels that his parents and his fiancée expect him to land a high-prestige, high-paying position. He*

1

2

3

# The Process of Stress

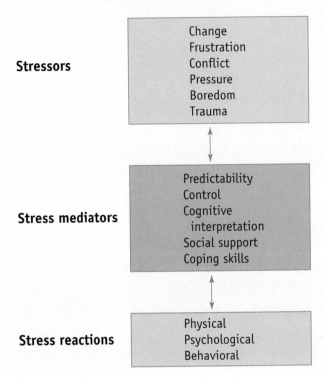

**Stressors**

> Change
> Frustration
> Conflict
> Pressure
> Boredom
> Trauma

**Stress mediators**

> Predictability
> Control
> Cognitive
>   interpretation
> Social support
> Coping skills

**Stress reactions**

> Physical
> Psychological
> Behavioral

*is very nervous. His mouth is dry, his stomach feels tight, his heart is pounding, and perspiration has begun to soak through his new suit.*

These sketches illustrate that stress involves a relationship between people and their environments—more specifically, between stressors and stress reactions. **Stressors** are events and situations (such as bus rides or interviews) to which people must react. **Stress reactions** are the physical, psychological, and behavioral responses (such as nausea, nervousness, and fatigue) people display in the face of stressors. *Mediating factors,* such as the circumstances in which stressors occur and each person's characteristics, make people more or less sensitive to stressors and to stress responses. Thus, stress is not a specific event but a process. We consider stressors and stress responses first and then examine some of the factors that influence the relationship between them.

4

## Stressors

Many stressors involve physical demands such as invading viruses, extreme temperatures, or strenuous work. For humans, however, many of the most significant stressors are psychological. The person who must give

5

a speech to impress a potential employer is facing stressors that can be just as demanding as a day of hard physical labor. Many, perhaps most, human stressors include both physical and psychological components. Athletes, for example, are challenged by the demands of physical exertion, as well as by the pressure of competition. In this section, we focus on the psychological stressors that, combined with the physical demands of life, contribute most significantly to the stress process.

## Major Psychological Stressors

Even very pleasant events can be stressors. For example, the increased salary and status associated with a promotion may be desirable, but the upgrade also requires finding ways of handling new responsibilities and increased pressures. Similarly, it is not uncommon for people to feel exhausted after the travel and intense fun-seeking of a vacation and somewhat depressed by the "real world" when the excitement of a wedding is over. Still, the events and situations most likely to be associated with stress are unpleasant ones—those involving frustration, pressure, boredom, trauma, conflict, or change.

*Frustrating* situations contain some obstacle that stands between a person and his or her goals. Waiting in a long line at the bank or being unable to find a phone to make an important call are simple examples of frustrating situations. More substantial illustrations include being unable to earn a decent living because of adverse economic conditions or job discrimination or failing in repeated attempts to find a love relationship.

*Pressure* situations require a person to do too much in too short a time. If you are trying to fix Thanksgiving dinner for twenty people on a day's notice, or if you are struggling to finish the last two questions on an essay test in ten minutes, you are under pressure. Many air-traffic controllers, physicians, nurses, and police officers face constant or long-lasting pressure. They must make many difficult decisions, sometimes involving life and death, under heavy time pressure. People under such pressure day after day sometimes begin to perform poorly and develop physical illness, alcoholism, anxiety, and many of the other stress-related problems.

*Boredom,* or understimulation, is the opposite of pressure, but it, too, can be a stressor, especially if it continues for a long time. The agony of solitary confinement in prison or the tedium of a remote military post are probably the most extreme examples.

*Trauma* is a shocking physical or emotional experience. Catastrophes such as rape, military combat, fire, tornadoes, or torture are only a few examples. More common disasters, such as a divorce or the sudden death of someone close, can be equally devastating.

6

7

8

9

10

*Conflict* is almost always stressful. The most obvious examples are    11
disputes in which friends, family members, or coworkers fight with,
insult, or otherwise get nasty with each other. If you can recall the last
time you experienced one of these interpersonal conflicts (even if you
were just a spectator), you can probably also remember the discomfort
you felt. Internal conflicts can be equally, if not more, distressing than
those with other people. Imagine, for example, the stress that might
result when a woman stays with a man she does not love only because
she fears he will commit suicide if she leaves.

*Change* can also be a major stressor. Divorce, illness in the family,    12
unemployment, and moving to a new city are just a few examples of
change that create social, psychological, financial, and physical demands
to which people must adapt and adjust.

Bernstein et al., *Psychology*

## Reacting to Ideas: Discussion and Journal Writing

1. If this material were to be tested on an essay exam in a psychology
class, what would you predict one question to be?

2. Why do different people react to stress differently?

3. Stress is usually thought of as caused by unpleasant events. Do you
agree with the authors that pleasant events also can cause stress?

## Writing Assignments

### Writing About the Reading

1. The reading identifies six sources of psychological stress. Evaluate
your life over the past several months. Which sources of stress have
you experienced? Write an essay describing these sources.

### Writing About Your Ideas

2. Think of a high-pressure or conflict situation. Write a paragraph
describing it.

3. College students face numerous frustrations. Write an essay agreeing
or disagreeing with this statement.

## Comparison and Contrast

## The Environment: What We Say Versus What We Do
### Joe Schwartz and Thomas Miller

Saving the environment is a high priority for most American citizens. 1
But as consumers, most of us are not willing to act on our beliefs.
Over three-quarters (78 percent) of adults say that our nation
must "make a major effort to improve the quality of our environment,"
according to a recent study commissioned by S. C. Johnson and Son
and conducted by the Roper Organization. But at the same time,
most say that individuals can do little, if anything, to help improve
the environment.

Public concern about the environment is growing faster than con- 2
cerns about any other issue monitored by Roper—at least before the
Persian Gulf crisis and the softening of the economy. Businesses are tun-
ing into this trend by producing "green" products, services, and advertising campaigns. But banking on environmental awareness can backfire,
because the majority of Americans are already convinced that businesses
are not environmentally responsible.

Americans tend to blame businesses for the environmental problems 3
they see at global, national, and local levels. More than eight in 10
Americans say that industrial pollution is the main reason for our environmental problems, and nearly three-quarters of the public say that the
products businesses use in manufacturing also harm the environment.
Six in 10 Americans blame businesses for not developing environmentally sound consumer products, and an equal share believes that some
technological advancements made by businesses eventually produce
unanticipated environmental problems.

Consumer behavior usually affects the environment at two points. 4
First, consumers can either buy or reject environmentally unsound products. After the purchase, they affect the environment by either recycling
products or sending them to the dump.

At the moment, recycling appears to be the most rapidly growing 5
pro-environmental behavior. Between March 1989 and February 1990,
the share of Americans who say they regularly recycle bottles and cans
rose from 41 percent to 46 percent, and the share who regularly recycle
newspapers rose from 20 percent to 26 percent. Those who sort their
trash on a regular basis rose from 14 percent to 24 percent of all
adults.

Altruism[1] isn't the only force behind the recycling boom. Many                    6
states and municipalities have passed "bottle bills" and other mandatory
recycling laws. People may be complying with the new rules and may
even be doing more than is required. But in many cases, legislation stim-
ulated their behavioral changes.

More than half of all adults (52 percent) never recycle newspapers.              7
Only 16 percent say they avoid products that come from environmentally irresponsible companies, and just seven percent regularly avoid
restaurants that use foam containers. Only eight percent of Americans
say they regularly cut down on their driving to protect the environment.
More than three-quarters (76 percent) say they just motor on as usual,
even though most acknowledge that emissions from private automobiles
are a leading cause of air pollution. . . .

The first stage—deep public concern about environmental prob-               8
lems—has certainly been reached. So far, voters have been largely
unwilling to take the next step and approve sweeping changes. But the
important attitudinal shifts of the 1980s should gradually change environmental behavior in the 1990s.

Vast majorities of Americans are worried about our environmental            9
future. So far, only a minority have adopted more environmentally
responsible lifestyles. But attitudinal changes generally precede behavioral ones. The stage is finally set for the "greening of America."

Schwartz and Miller, *American Demographics*

1. concern for the welfare of others

## Reacting to Ideas: Discussion and Journal Writing

1. What method of organization did the author use?

2. Why do you think there is a discrepancy between belief and action
   regarding environmental problems?

3. What can or should be done to encourage Americans to *act* responsi-
   bly toward the environment?

4. For what other issues do you think a discrepancy between belief and
   action exists?

5. Describe what you consider an environmentally responsible lifestyle
   includes.

# Writing Assignments

### Writing About the Reading

1. The author states that "voters have been largely unwilling to take the next step and approve sweeping changes." Write a paragraph explaining why you think this is so.

2. Drawing from the information contained in the reading, write an essay that compares an environmentally responsible lifestyle with an environmentally irresponsible one. Develop your paragraph using subject-by-subject organization.

3. Using point-by-point organization, rewrite the essay you wrote for number 2.

### Writing About Your Ideas

4. Write an essay discussing the discrepancy you have observed between someone's beliefs and his or her subsequent actions regarding one of the following topics:
   a. telling lies
   b. nutritional or eating habits
   c. job responsibility
   d. punctuality
   e. loyalty to friends or family

5. If you had two job offers, one from an environmentally responsible company and one from an environmentally irresponsible company, would the companies' degree of environmental responsibility be a factor in your choice? If so, how important would it be? What factors would be more important, if any? Explain your position in a short essay.

## Cause and Effect

## Why Some Families Succeed Against the Odds
### Jeff Iseminger

Families form the core concern for a teacher-cum-researcher at UW-Madison, Hamilton McCubbin, dean of the School of Family Resources and Consumer Sciences. McCubbin has spent years

1

trying to answer a question that burns at the heart of his work: Why
do some families succeed and endure when they should have failed?
What gives families being battered by stress the resiliency they need
to survive?

Early in his career, McCubbin served as a member of a special     2
Department of Defense team asked to design programs to help the families of prisoners of war or hostages. Those families experience stress in
the extreme during the post-release period, when the divorce rate for
them hits 60 to 90 percent.

As Family Resources dean, McCubbin has helped make the school     3
a hotbed of research on the family. It's the home of the Institute for
the Study of Resiliency in Families, as well as the Center for Excellence
in Family Studies, which recently received a gift of $116,000 from
Aid Association for Lutherans. McCubbin holds thirty-two copyrights
for research instruments used by counselors and other researchers
throughout the world; he plows back the royalties into Family
Resources.

In his own research, McCubbin has found five common qualities     4
among families that show resiliency under stress. Here is a distillation of
what he's learned and witnessed through focus groups, one-on-one interviews and fieldwork involving hundreds of families:

"A sense of culture and ethnicity—*any* ethnicity—often has a signifi-     5
cant positive value for families," says McCubbin. Traditions, celebrations, and routines all can nurture a sense of self that helps you bend
instead of break. Too often, he says, people treat ethnicity as a social
variable that classifies people, but doesn't reveal our values that guide
our behavior.

"We have seen in our studies the importance of spiritual beliefs in     6
surviving stress," says McCubbin. "A spiritual underpinning not only
explains the unexplainable, such as death, but it also gives you a frame
of reference for the world, a lens for viewing life."

Communication can be a lifeline to survival—or a greased chute to     7
disaster. "We can distinguish between what I call incendiary[1] versus
affirming communication, which are found in differing balances in all
families," he says. The incendiary style includes blaming—everything
that goes wrong *has* to be somebody's fault—and recalling past injus-
tices, effectively preventing others from ever starting anew. The affirming style means you value people for what they are and take the time to
notice—and esteem—people close to you.

---

1. causing fire or explosion; provoking anger

A family that copes with stress is pro-active, attacking a problem and breaking it down into more manageable parts. "That kind of family either changes its environment or changes themselves," says McCubbin. Passive coping, in contrast, is watching TV and strewing blame over the social landscape. It's a brittle response that lacks the flexibility McCubbin says is essential for effective coping. 8

Resilient families look at a crisis as both a danger and an opportunity. They see the brighter side while not ignoring the danger. 9

"A mother, even living in a slum, may single out one or two things about her kids she wants to nurture," says McCubbin. Optimism like that can help you transcend[2]—and sometimes transform—the circumstances you face. 10

Often suffusing[3] all these facets of resiliency is something as mysterious as it is powerful: love. Whatever its source, love can move mountains. Listen to a story told by McCubbin, an aboriginal Hawaiian, about his own family: "My father had two brothers who had Hanson's Disease, more commonly known as leprosy, and lived in a leper colony on Molokai," he recalls. "On weekends my mother and father would sneak over to the island—leprosy was socially stigmatized—to work as volunteers doing odd jobs. They could see and talk to my uncles, but they could never touch. Family life was maintained." 11

Picture McCubbin's parents working weekends in the leper colony, just to be near his uncles. That touchless expression of love, says McCubbin, was rooted in a native Hawaiian philosophy called aina, a "we" concept of family and nature antithetical[4] to the "I" philosophy of modern American culture. 12

That spirit animates the investment of McCubbin's professional life . . . in teasing out the intricacies of society's core institution, the family. 13

He believes that the family and children are research subjects of surpassing importance. Through his work he is telling us that when families and neighborhoods crumble, the very ground beneath our children's feet is wracked by social ruptures. But when the family thrives—when children receive the economic and social resources a healthy life requires, when "I" enlarges into "we"—our culture gets ignition and liftoff from a rock-solid launching pad. 14

Iseminger, from *On Wisconsin*

2. to go beyond
3. spreading through
4. opposite

## Reacting to Ideas: Discussion and Journal Writing

1. Do you agree that traditions and celebrations hold families together? If so, why do you think they do?

2. Which form of communication—incendiary or affirming—holds families together? Why do you think so?

3. Give some examples of incendiary communication you have heard of or experienced yourself.

4. Do you know a person or family that is "strewing blame over the social landscape"? Describe how this person or family handles problems.

## Writing Assignments

### Writing About the Reading

1. The author quotes Hamilton McCubbin as saying that spiritual beliefs give you "a frame of reference for the world, a lens for viewing life." Explain the meaning of that statement, indicating whether you agree or disagree.

2. The author describes "aina," the "we" concept of family and nature. Write an essay explaining whether you think our society is moving from a "we" culture to an "I" culture. Give examples from your experience.

### Writing About Your Ideas

3. Write an essay describing a situation in which you used an active coping strategy: one in which you identified the problem, broke it down, and made changes. Be sure to explain whether or not your strategy was effective.

4. The author identifies five characteristics of family strength. Analyze a family, either your own or another with which you are familiar. Identify which of these five characteristics the family shares and which it lacks, if any. Then decide whether or not you agree that the five characteristics do contribute to family strength. Write an essay describing your findings.

## Expository

## Fathers, Sons, and Sports
**Scott Russell Sanders**

The lore[1] of sports may be all that some fathers have to pass           1
down to their sons in place of lore about hunting animals, planting seeds, killing enemies, or placating[2] the gods. Instead of telling him how to shoot a buffalo, the father whispers in the son's ear how
to shoot a lay-up. Instead of consulting the stars or the entrails of birds,
father and son consult the smudged newspapers to see how their chosen
spirits are faring. They fiddle with the dials of radios, hoping to catch
the oracular murmur of a distant game. The father recounts heroic deeds,
not from the field of battle but from the field of play. The seasons about
which he speaks lead not to harvests but to championships. No longer
intimate with the wilderness, no longer familiar even with the tamed
land of farms, we create artificial landscapes bounded by lines of paint
or lime. Within those boundaries, as within the frame of a chessboard
or painting, life achieves a memorable, seductive clarity. The lore of
sports is a step down from that of nature, perhaps even a tragic step,
but it is lore nonetheless, with its own demigods and demons, magic
and myths.

The sporting legends I carry from my father are private rather than       2
public. I am haunted by scenes that no journalist recorded, no camera
filmed. Father is playing a solo round of golf, for example, early one
morning in April. The fairways glisten with dew. Crows rasp and fluster
in the pines that border the course. Father lofts a shot toward a par-
three hole, and the white ball arcs over the pond, over the sand trap,
over the shaggy apron of grass, onto the green, where it bounces, settles
down, then rolls toward the flag, rolls unerringly, inevitably, until it falls
with a scarcely audible click into the hole. The only eyes within sight
besides his own are the crows'. For once, the ball has obeyed him perfectly, harmonizing wind and gravity and the revolution of the spheres;
one shot has gone where all are meant to go, and there is nobody else to
watch. He stands on the tee, gazing at the distant hole, knowing what
he has done and that he will never do it again.

Here is another story I live by: The man who will become my father     3
is twenty-two, a catcher for a bush-league baseball team in Tennessee.

1. traditional knowledge
2. quiet the anger of

He will never make it to the majors, but on weekends he earns a few
dollars for squatting behind the plate and nailing runners foolish enough
to try stealing second base. From all those bus rides, all those red-dirt
diamonds, the event he will describe for his son with deepest emotion is
an exhibition game. Father's team of whites, most of them fresh from
two-mule farms, is playing a touring black team, a rare event for that
day and place. To make it even rarer, and the sides fairer, the managers
agree to mix the teams. And so my father, son of a Mississippi cotton
farmer, bruised with racial notions that will take a lifetime to heal,
crouches behind the plate and for nine innings catches fastballs and
curves, change-ups and screwballs from a whirling muttering wizard
of the Negro Baseball League, one Leroy Robert Paige, known to the
world as Satchel. Afterward, Satchel Paige tells the farm boy, "You
catch a good game," and the farm boy answers, "You've got the stuff,
mister." And for the rest of my father's life, this man's pitching serves as
a measure of mastery.

I am conscious of my father's example whenever I teach a game to      4
my son. Demonstrating a stroke in tennis or golf, I amplify my gestures,
like a ham actor playing to the balcony. My pleasure in the part is
increased by the knowledge that others, and especially my father, have
played it before me. What I know about hitting a curve or shooting a
hook shot or throwing a left jab, I know less by words than by feel.
When I take Jesse's hand and curl his fingers over the baseball's red
stitches, explaining how to make it deviously spin, I feel my father's
hands slip over mine like gloves. Move like so, like so. I feel the same
ghostly guidance when I hammer nails or fix a faucet or pluck a banjo.
Working on the house or garden or car, I find myself wearing more than
my father's hands, find myself clad entirely in his skin.

As Jesse nears thirteen, his estimate of my knowledge and my pow-      5
ers declines rapidly. If I were a potter, say, or a carpenter, my skill would
outreach his for decades to come. But where speed and stamina are the
essence, a father in his forties will be overtaken by a son in his teens.
Training for soccer, Jesse carries a stopwatch as he jogs around the park.
I am not training for anything, only knocking rust from joints and
beguiling my heart, but I run along with him, puffing to keep up. I
know that his times will keep going down, while I will never run faster
than I do now. This is as it should be, for his turn has come. Slow as I
am, and doomed to be slower, I relish his company.

I mean to live the present year before rushing off to any future ones.      6
I mean to keep playing games with my son, so long as flesh will permit,
as my father played games with me well past his own physical prime.
Now that sports have begun to give me lessons in mortality, I realize

they have also been giving me, all the while, lessons in immortality. These games, these contests, these grunting conversations of body to body, father to son, are not substitutes for some other way of being alive. They are the sweet and sweaty thing itself.

Sanders, *Secrets of the Universe*

## Reacting to Ideas: Discussion and Journal Writing

1. What is the author's main point? Explain the connection among fathers, sons, and sports.

2. Have you observed or experienced the relationship the author describes among fathers, sons, and sports?

3. If sports link fathers and sons, what activities or experiences link mothers and daughters?

4. Have you experienced knowing how to do something by feel rather than by words?

## Writing Assignments

### Writing About the Reading

1. Write a paragraph explaining what you think Sanders meant when he said, "Now that sports have begun to give me lessons in mortality, I realize they have also been giving me, all the while, lessons in immortality."

### Writing About Your Ideas

2. Write a paragraph describing an experience in which you have felt as if you were wearing your father's or mother's hands.

3. Write an essay describing an experience you shared with your mother or father that provided a bond or permanent link between you.

## Expository

## Five Things You Can Do to Make a Difference
**Michael Powell**

Slowdog's hanging out upstairs at the @ Cafe, in New York's East           1
Village, sipping cup after cup of coffee and tap-tap-tapping into the
Internet on one of the computer terminals that looms over every
table like a television set. Slowdog is 25 years old, with black pants,
black T-shirt, black baseball cap, black sneakers, long black eyelashes
and a face that sees very little sun.

Born Christopher Frankonis, Slowdog used to work in the New           2
York Public Library and log on, stop at the @ Cafe and log on, traipse
back to his basement flat in Brooklyn, N.Y., and log on, surfing the
Internet that runs like a vast river through wired America.

No real point, no particular politics, just another college dropout           3
hooked on the Net. A kid from upstate New York with a mouse and a
quick wit.

Then came Sen. J. James Exon, D.-Neb., and his Communications           4
Decency Act. Exon introduced a bill this March that proposes to tame
the Internet. This senator wanted to pasteurize Slowdog's wild river of
words and symbols, criminalize the transmission of lewd and lascivious
language, make the computer world safe for June Cleaver.

An activist was born.           5

"Instead of understanding a new medium, they want to extend an           6
old law from television," Slowdog says. "It's going to chill speech, make
users liable for content. I knew I had to go beyond my insular little
world on the Net. Here is my shot."

Slowdog and a half-dozen young activists worked with the Center           7
for Democracy and Technology, in Washington, D.C., and started a
computer petition. They hoped for 10,000 signatures in three weeks.
They got that many in three days. Two and a half months later the tally
stood at 121,284, with support ranging from the libertarian Cato
Institute to First Amendment absolutists. "Man, we were getting 1,000
signatures an hour," Slowdog says.

In late April a messenger walked into the office of Sen. Larry           8
Pressler, R-S.D., whose committee was holding hearings on the bill, with
a 1,000-sheet printout containing the names of the petition's signers.
"To a politician, that's like carrying a political loaded gun," one staffer
recalls. The petition came on top of the e-mail messages and faxes that
Pressler's office had been getting for weeks.

Slowdog takes a hit of latte[1] and smiles. "I don't know that I was         9
ever political before," he says. "But this was so severe and showed so
little understanding of something new. All of a sudden I had to put up
or shut up."

You could dismiss Slowdog as an aberration,[2] one inspired young         10
man in a sea of generational self-absorption and cynicism, of angry-
white-male backlash and careerism. But a closer look confounds that
view. From the college environmental activist who blocked a road in
Arizona's Pinaleno mountains to the journalist who returned to his
college town to start an alternative newspaper to the student who
helped raise children in the housing projects of Hartford, Conn.,
hundreds of thousands of young people display a desire to make a
difference. . . .

The statistics are startling: The number of youth activists and         11
volunteers has increased steadily in the past decade. The Independent
Sector, a coalition of volunteer groups, reports that nearly 50 percent
of 18- to 24-year-olds are involved in what might loosely be called
good works.

"There is an overwhelming climate of blame toward young people—         12
that we are without values or are nihilistic,[3]" says Miya Yoshitani, 25,
who works for a grass-roots environmental network. "But we've dis-
proved that time and again."

Still, while the number of volunteers is up, voter participation         13
among those 30 and under stands at less than 45 percent, suggesting
that political parties have yet to connect with the considerable activist
impulses of the young. "It's less left-right, because those separations
don't always make sense," says Craig Bowman, 27, who counsels gay
and lesbian youth in Washington, D.C.

Today's volunteer work is often intensely local, even personal. The         14
focus is on feeding a few people or protecting a small patch of trees.
This could be read as retreat, or as understandable reticence in the face
of economic uncertainty, corporate downsizing and the collapse of Great
Society liberalism.

Finally, the technological revolution has transformed today's volun-         15
teer. The Internet, video and satellites reach into homes and cast webs
over vast distances. So, then, five ideas for making a difference, a list
provocative rather than comprehensive.

1. coffee with milk
2. exception
3. skeptical, rejecting religious and moral values

## 1. Free a Condemned Man

Princeton undergraduate Marc Ricks, 20, began with a girlfriend who
pushed him to "get involved" and a vague sense that he was "coddled
on this cushy campus and self-centered."    16

Ricks wound up working to free men from death row.    17

Founded by James McCloskey, a successful businessman turned sem-
inarian, Centurion Ministries devotes itself to ferreting out and freeing
the imprisoned innocent. McCloskey and his small band do painstaking
work, reading trial transcripts, filing petitions, and reinterviewing wit-
nesses and finding new ones.    18

Ricks spent three months reading transcripts of the cases of three
men whom McCloskey is strongly considering representing. "You want
to declare everyone innocent, and, of course, some aren't," Ricks says.
"But I also don't believe in 100 percent guilty any more."    19

Since 1983, Centurion Ministries has helped free 16 men. It relies on
volunteers who offer 10 hours a week and long-term commitment.    20

## 2. The Joy of Cooking

After leaving Brown University, Chef Duskie Estes, 27, worked at a
string of the best restaurants, cooking food she loved for "great chefs."    21

But when Estes landed at the four-star Kinkead's, in Washington,
D.C., she offered to teach a daytime cooking class to poor Hispanic
women. They wrote up menus, chatted about shopping, pawed over
fruit, talked nutrition. "We became like family," Estes says. A couple
years later, Estes is now directing Operation Frontline, in Seattle, a
chapter of Share Our Strength, a national food, cooking and nutrition
organization for the poor. Estes convinced 48 Seattle chefs to teach
nutrition and cooking to more than 300 families a year—from teen
mothers to elderly widowers—experiencing their first taste of tight budgeting. "We go into the housing authority, we teach homeless who've
scavenged and never worked with a pot or pan," Estes says. And in
Estes' spare time? She shops for 45 to 50 families a week.    22

Operation Frontline and SOS rely on volunteers to cook, teach,
shop, handle freebies and work the phones.    23

## 3. Organize Something

Elizabeth Wolff, 35, looks at a hundred wide-brim hats and pairs of
cowboy boots and sees the raw material of community organizing.
"Rush Limbaugh is a jerk, but I keep telling people he's tapping into
real anger; these are *our* people," the experienced community organizer
in Dallas says with a chuckle.    24

Wolff signed on with the Association of Community Organizations     25
for Reform Now (ACORN) 13 years ago, figuring that she would
leaven her physics degree with a year of community work before diving
into public policy. Instead she spent the 1980s and '90s organizing
public-housing tenants, fighting toxic waste and building schools. "I
keep my eye on the long-term," she says.

ACORN works in thousands of neighborhoods across the nation,     26
building schools in New York, fighting a polluting meat-processing
plant in Denver, pushing down utility rates in Arkansas.

## 4. Save a Mountain

Stretched across the twisting road going up Mount Graham lay 150     27
environmental activists from the University of Arizona at Tucson. Some
had chained themselves to the gates guarding a half-built astronomy station planned by the university and its partner, the Vatican. Student
Environmental Action Coalition had struck, tackling construction on
one of the nation's most remote mountain ranges. The university fought
back, of course. Students were arrested, roads cleared. But in the
months that followed, SEAC, which has 2,200 chapters at high schools
and colleges, never gave up.

When the university sought to put up more telescopes, the students     28
blocked them in federal court. When the university sought partners at
Michigan State University and the University of Pittsburgh, SEAC con-
tacted its chapters. Within a year, the MSU board of trustees voted
down the plan, and hundreds of demonstrating students convinced the
Pittsburgh City Council to oppose the telescopes.

"They keep throwing everything at us," says Shane Jimerfield, 32, a     29
Tucson resident who grew up camping in those mountains. "But we're
turning them into pariahs.[4]"

SEAC relies on volunteers and interns and runs several scholarship     30
programs. . . .

## 5. Raise a Child

Berzet May hears the voices first, high pitched and crackling with     31
early morning enthusiasm, then the sound of feet in the hall and a
dozen hands knocking on her door in Hartford's Charter Oak public
houses. The door opens, and she finds "her girls," a throng of 8- and
9-year-olds.

The girls start to sing: "I feel *good*, oh, I feel so good."     32

4. social outcasts

May, 21, a Trinity College undergraduate, spends the summer living    33
in the projects with 12 other counselors. Members of the New Haven,
Conn., Leadership Education and Athletics in Partnership (LEAP), they
counsel, teach, play, talk and travel with the kids from early morning
until 8 each night. "I grew up in the Bronx, and I want to give something back," she says.

Run by 30 staffers—at 27, executive director Henry Fernandez is    34
one of the oldest—LEAP trains and places high school and college students in public housing. "Our work can be dangerous, but this is organizing that makes a difference," says Fernandez, who, with the help of
others, founded LEAP while attending Yale Law School.

LEAP draws hundreds of volunteers, 70 percent minorities, from    35
campuses and schools. . . .

Powell, *Rolling Stone*

## Reacting to Ideas: Discussion and Journal Writing

1. Why do you think the author begins with the story of Slowdog? That
   is, what does the story of Slowdog contribute to the essay?

2. Is the author correct in saying there is a negative attitude toward
   young people?

3. Is it important to "make a difference"? If so, in response to what issues?

4. What is the connection between the technological revolution and
   volunteerism?

5. Why do people volunteer? Do most of them volunteer to make themselves feel good or to help others?

## Writing Assignments

### Writing About the Reading

1. The author states that his list is intended to be "provocative rather
   than comprehensive." Write a paragraph explaining what this statement reveals about the author's purpose for writing the essay.

2. Write an essay in which you evaluate the five ways to make a difference described by the author. Which, if any, are important to you?
   Which are less important? Explain your choices.

### Writing About Your Ideas

3. Write an essay creating your own list of things you can do or have done to make a difference. You could write about causes you would like to get involved with, people whom you would like to help, and so forth.

4. Write an essay explaining whether or not you feel a need to "get involved," as Marc Ricks's girlfriend felt he should.

## Persuasive

## Crack and the Box

### Pete Hamill

One sad rainy morning last winter, I talked to a woman who was addicted to crack cocaine. She was twenty-two, stiletto-thin, with eyes as old as tombs. She was living in two rooms in a welfare hotel with her children, who were two, three, and five years of age. Her story was the usual tangle of human woe: early pregnancy, dropping out of school, vanished men, smack and then crack, tricks with johns in parked cars to pay for dope. I asked her why she did drugs. She shrugged in an empty way and couldn't really answer beyond "makes me feel good." While we talked and she told her tale of squalor, the children ignored us. They were watching television.

Walking back to my office in the rain, I brooded about the woman, her zombielike children, and my own callous indifference. I'd heard so many versions of the same story that I almost never wrote them anymore; the sons of similar women, glimpsed a dozen years ago, are now in Dannemora or Soledad or Joliet; in a hundred cities, their daughters are moving into the same loveless rooms. As I walked, a series of homeless men approached me for change, most of them junkies. Others sat in doorways, staring at nothing. They were additional casualties of our time of plague, demoralized reminders that although this country holds only 2 percent of the world's population, it consumes 65 percent of the world's supply of hard drugs.

*Why,* for God's sake? Why do so many millions of Americans of all ages, races, and classes choose to spend all or part of their lives stupefied? I've talked to hundreds of addicts over the years; some were my friends. But none could give sensible answers. They stutter about the pain of the world, about despair or boredom, the urgent need for magic or pleasure in a society empty of both. But then they just shrug. Americans have the money to buy drugs; the supply is plentiful. But almost nobody in power asks, *Why?* Least of all, George Bush and his drug warriors.

William Bennett talks vaguely about the heritage of sixties permissiveness, the collapse of Traditional Values, and all that. But he and Bush offer the traditional American excuse: It Is Somebody Else's Fault. This posture set the stage for the self-righteous invasion of Panama, the bloodiest drug arrest in world history. Bush even accused Manuel Noriega of "poisoning our children." But he never asked *why* so many Americans demand the poison.

And then, on that rainy morning in New York, I saw another one of those ragged men staring out at the rain from a doorway. I suddenly remembered the inert postures of the children in that welfare hotel, and I thought: *television.*

Ah, no, I muttered to myself: too simple. Something as complicated as drug addiction can't be blamed on television. Come on . . . . but I remembered all those desperate places I'd visited as a reporter, where there were no books and a TV set was always playing and the older kids had gone off somewhere to shoot smack, except for the kid who was at the mortuary in a coffin. I also remembered when I was a boy in the forties and early fifties, and drugs were a minor sideshow, a kind of dark little rumor. And there was one major difference between that time and this: television.

We had unemployment then; illiteracy, poor living conditions, racism, governmental stupidity, a gap between rich and poor. We didn't have the all-consuming presence of television in our lives. Now two generations of Americans have grown up with television from their earliest moments of consciousness. Those same American generations are afflicted by the pox of drug addiction.

Only thirty-five years ago, drug addiction was not a major problem in this country. There were drug addicts. We had some at the end of the nineteenth century, hooked on the cocaine in patent medicines. During the placid fifties, Commissioner Harry Anslinger pumped up the budget of the old Bureau of Narcotics with fantasies of reefer madness. Heroin was sold and used in most major American cities, while the bebop generation of jazz musicians got jammed up with horse.

But until the early sixties, narcotics were still marginal to American life; they weren't the $120-billion market they make up today. If anything, those years have an eerie innocence. In 1955 there were 31,700,000 TV sets in use in the country (the number is now past 184 million). But the majority of the audience had grown up without the dazzling new medium. They embraced it, were diverted by it, perhaps even loved it, but they weren't *formed* by it. That year, the New York police made a mere 1,234 felony drug arrests; in 1988 it was 43,901. They confiscated ninety-seven *ounces* of cocaine for the entire year; last year it was hundreds of pounds. During each year of the fifties in New York, there were only about a hundred narcotics-related deaths. But by the end of the sixties, when the first generation of children *formed* by television had come to maturity (and thus to the marketplace), the number of such deaths had risen to 1,200. The same phenomenon was true in every major American city.

In the last Nielsen survey of American viewers, the average family was watching television seven hours a day. This has never happened before in history. No people has ever been entertained for seven hours a *day*. The Elizabethans didn't go to the theater seven hours a day. The pre-TV generation did not go to the movies seven hours a day. Common sense tells us that this all-pervasive diet of instant imagery, sustained now for forty years, must have changed us in profound ways.    10

Television, like drugs, dominates the lives of its addicts. And though some lonely Americans leave their sets on without watching them, using them as electronic companions, television usually absorbs its viewers the way drugs absorb their users. Viewers can't work or play while watching television; they can't read; they can't be out on the streets, falling in love with the wrong people, learning how to quarrel and compromise with other human beings. In short they are asocial. So are drug addicts.    11

One Michigan State University study in the early eighties offered a group of four- and five-year-olds the choice of giving up television or giving up their fathers. Fully one third said they would give up Daddy. Given a similar choice (between cocaine or heroin and father, mother, brother, sister, wife, husband, children, job), almost every stoned junkie would do the same.    12

There are other disturbing similarities. Television itself is a consciousness-altering instrument. With the touch of a button, it takes you out of the "real" world in which you reside and can place you at a basketball game, the back alleys of Miami, the streets of Bucharest, or the cartoony living rooms of Sitcom Land. Each move from channel to channel alters moods, usually with music or a laugh track. On any given evening, you can laugh, be frightened, feel tension, thump with excitement. You can even tune in *MacNeil/Lehrer* and feel sober.    13

But none of these abrupt shifts in mood is *earned*. They are attained as easily as popping a pill. Getting news from television, for example, is simply not the same experience as reading it in a newspaper. Reading is *active*. The reader must decode little symbols called words, then create images or ideas and make them connect; at its most basic level, reading is an act of the imagination. But the television viewer doesn't go through    14

that process. The words are spoken to him by Dan Rather or Tom
Brokaw or Peter Jennings. There isn't much decoding to do when
watching television, no time to think or ponder before the next set of
images and spoken words appears to displace the present one. The
reader, being active, works at his or her own pace; the viewer, being passive, proceeds at a pace determined by the show. Except at the highest
levels, television never demands that its audience take part in an act of
imagination. Reading always does.

In short, television works on the same imaginative and intellectual          15
level as psychoactive drugs. If prolonged television viewing makes the
young passive (dozens of studies indicate that it does), then moving to
drugs has a certain coherence. Drugs provide an unearned high (in contrast to the earned rush that comes from a feat accomplished, a human
breakthrough earned by sweat or thought or love).

And because the television addict and the drug addict are alienated         16
from the hard and scary world, they also feel they make no difference in
its complicated events. For the junkie, the world is reduced to him and
the needle, pipe, or vial; the self is absolutely isolated, with no desire for
choice. The television addict lives the same way. Many Americans who
fail to vote in presidential elections must believe they have no more control over such a choice than they do over the casting of *L.A. Law.*

The drug plague also coincides with the unspoken assumption of            17
most television shows: Life should be *easy.* The most complicated events
are summarized on TV news in a minute or less. Cops confront murder,
chase the criminals, and bring them to justice (usually violently) within
an hour. In commercials, you drink the right beer and you get the girl.
*Easy!* So why should real life be a grind? Why should any American
have to spend years mastering a skill or a craft, or work eight hours a
day at an unpleasant job, or endure the compromises and crises of a
marriage? Nobody *works* on television (except cops, doctors, and
lawyers). Love stories on television are about falling in love or breaking
up; the long, steady growth of a marriage—its essential *dailiness*—is seldom explored, except as comedy. Life on television is almost always
simple: good guys and bad, nice girls and whores, smart guys and
dumb. And if life in the real world isn't that simple, well, hey, man,
have some dope, man, be happy, feel good.

The doper always whines about how he *feels;* drugs are used to           18
enhance his feelings or obliterate them, and in this the doper is very
American. No other people on earth spend so much time talking about
their feelings; hundreds of thousands go to shrinks, they buy self-help
books by the millions, they pour out intimate confessions to virtual
strangers in bars or discos. Our political campaigns are about emotional
issues now, stated in the simplicities of adolescence. Even alleged statesmen

can start a sentence, "I feel that the Sandinistas should . . . " when they once might have said, "I *think* . . . " I'm convinced that this exaltation of cheap emotions over logic and reason is one by-product of hundreds of thousands of hours of television.

Most Americans under the age of fifty have now spent their lives        19
absorbing television; that is, they've had the structures of drama pounded into them. Drama is always about conflict. So news shows, politics, and advertising are now all shaped by those structures. Nobody will pay attention to anything as complicated as the part played by Third World debt in the expanding production of cocaine; it's much easier to focus on Manuel Noriega, a character right out of *Miami Vice,* and believe that even in real life there's a Mister Big.

What is to be done? Television is certainly not going away, but its        20
addictive qualities can be controlled. It's a lot easier to "just say no" to television than to heroin or crack. As a beginning, parents must take immediate control of the sets, teaching children to watch specific television *programs,* not "television," to get out of the house and play with other kids. Elementary and high schools must begin teaching television as a subject, the way literature is taught, showing children how shows are made, how to distinguish between the true and the false, how to recognize cheap emotional manipulation. All Americans should spend more time reading. And thinking.

For years, the defenders of television have argued that the networks        21
are only giving the people what they want. That might be true. But so is the Medellín cartel.

Hamill, *Esquire*

## Reacting to Ideas: Discussion and Journal Writing

1. Hamill states that, unlike television, reading is active. It requires the reader to "take part in an act of imagination." Do you agree?

2. Do you agree that television viewing alienates viewers from the real world?

3. Does television give a realistic view of life? Why do or don't you think so?

4. What factors, other than television, could account for the dramatic increase in drug use in America?

5. Does Hamill recognize and respond to the viewpoint a disagreeing audience might have? Why do you think he chose to respond or not respond?

6. Discuss the types of evidence Hamill offers in support of his thesis.

## Writing Assignments

### Writing About the Reading

1. Write a persuasive essay on the issue of whether a course on television-watching skills should be taught in elementary and high schools.

2. Write a persuasive essay on the issue of whether parents should control their children's television viewing.

### Writing About Your Ideas

3. Is television addictive? Write a persuasive essay explaining your position.

4. Should Americans read and think more, as Hamill recommends? Write a persuasive essay explaining your position.

## Persuasive

## The Captive Panther
**Michael W. Fox**

Some experiences can be so painfully intense that they are soon forgotten. Amnesia protects the psyche.[1] Then again, in anticipation of vicarious suffering, we may simply tune out certain experiences altogether. Other times, perhaps for good reason, the psyche is not so protected. It is as if the soul—the observing, feeling self—is actually burned by certain experiences. The imprint is branded so indelibly that we can go back and review every detail so completely that the experience is actually relived. I had just such an experience with a panther in a zoo many years ago.

1. mind

The first time that I ever really *saw* an animal in a cage was in a    2
small zoo at the Jardin des Plantes, a natural history museum in Paris. I
entered a large, ornate Victorian rotunda that housed a few animals in
small wrought-iron cages. I now recall seeing only one animal there. At
first it appeared not to see me even though I stood beside its cage for a
long time.

Time did end that day as a part of me separated and was incorpo-    3
rated as part of the creature in the cage.

In retrospect, I was probably mesmerized by what at first appeared    4
to be a shiny black serpent in constant motion. Its liquid form brushed
across the front of the cage. After insinuating itself around some artificial rocks and a body-polished tree stump toward the back of the enclo-
sure, it ricocheted off a ceramic-tiled wall to again caress the front of
the cage. Form and motion were so unified and the pattern of movement within the confines of the cage so repetitive that at first encounter
the creature was barely recognizable as a panther, or black leopard. Her
movements were executed with such precision—even to the point of
always touching the tree trunk with her left hip and the same ceramic
tile with her right front paw—that she was more like a perpetual motion
machine than a sentient[2] being.

And then I saw the blood—a streak of blood down her left thigh,    5
draining from an open sore that would never heal until the cat was freed
from the hypnotic lines she traced and was so inexorably bound to exe-
cute. Each scraping turn around the tree trunk kept the sore open, like a
broken heart bleeding for the loss of all that was wild and free.

I wondered if she felt any pain. Her yellow-green eyes were like cold    6
glass, with neither fire nor luster. Perhaps this was a slow ritual form of
suicide, gradually grinding and rubbing and shredding the body to pieces
to free the wild spirit within. I saw the glint of white bone—or was it
tendon—through the cat's thigh muscles winking as she turned and paced
before me. And there was no pad left on the right front paw that struck
the tile wall polished ocher with the patina of dried blood and serum. Yet
still the crippled creature continued her measured minuet.[3]

The panther body, denied freedom of expression and fulfillment of    7
purpose, had become a prison for the creature spirit within. Following
and anticipating every movement she made, I began to breathe in
rhythm with the cat. I felt part of myself entering her cage while the
rotunda started to revolve faster and faster around that part of my consciousness that remained in my body outside of the cage. Then when I
entered the prison of her body the other visitors strolling around the

2. conscious
3. dance

rotunda became ephemeral[4] shadow-beings, as if they were part of a dream and the only thing that was real was the measured universe of the tortured panther.

Confined in such limited space, how else could this boundless spirit of the jungle respond? Her rhythmic, trancelike actions were more than thwarted attempts to escape. Was her compulsive animation designed simply to help her cope with the emptiness of existing in body without any purpose for the spirit, a kind of living death?

The cage may be the last refuge for many endangered species, but such "protective custody" is a sad reflection indeed of how far we have desecrated[5] nature's creation. Zoos have been as slow to address the psychological needs of the animals they keep as they have to question their own purpose. But times are changing; more and more people have begun to feel and see the world through the eyes of the animals. The cage bars are disappearing as we begin to empathize and come to realize that the fate of the animal kingdom is inextricably linked with the fate of humanity. The black panther in the cage is a mirror reflecting our own condition. And we are not helpless to do something about both.

But when we reach into the cage with our hearts, we may feel very differently about keeping animals in zoos or ever visiting a zoo again.

Do zoos educate the public adequately to political action and compassionate concern for the plight of wildlife and nature? Are they not too tame, sanitized, and beautiful? They are becoming facsimiles of how animals once were in the wild. Some zoo safari parks are run for profit and secondarily for entertainment. And zoos are also an illusion, a false assurance to the public that lions and cheetahs and tigers and elephants are plentiful and lead free and easy lives. Some amusement parks even have safari zoos purely for public entertainment. This is surely an unethical exploitation of wildlife.

Even the best of zoos cannot justify their existence if they do not sufficiently inform and even shock the public into compassionate concern and political action. I know of no zoo that exhibits crippled but otherwise healthy animals that have been maimed by trappers and hunters.

Regarding the claim that the best zoos are helping save species from extinction by breeding them in captivity, it may be best to let them become extinct if there is no place for them in the wild. Life in captivity can never fulfill any species or individual, because the animal *is* its natural environment, and no species lives in isolation from others. Certainly the better zoos have seminatural environments—miniswamps, artificial rivers, climatrons, and mixed-species exhibits. But to what end? For exhibition. They

4. short-lived
5. treat as if not sacred

are not conserving nature by creating high-tech facsimiles thereof. And even if such artificial environments enhance the overall welfare and reproductivity of endangered species, where are their offspring to go? To other zoo collections.

I believe that even the best zoos and aquaria in the world are not doing an adequate job of nature conservation. They have taken more species from the wild than they have ever put back, and until this situation is dramatically reversed, zoos cannot make any claim to effective nature conservation. Breeding endangered species in captivity is animal preservation, not conservation, and animals preserved forever in a cage or synthetic habitat are at best unreal.

As for zoos' often high-blown research into exotic animal diseases, nutrition, and reproduction, all of this would be unnecessary if we had just left wildlife alone and respected their rights and protected their habitats.

Are zoos a necessary evil? Wildlife's last refuge? Sometimes I think so. Sometimes I think not. I respect the many people who are dedicated to good zoo management, research, species preservation, and veterinary medicine. But all this dedication may be seriously misplaced if we lose sight of the fact that the problems of zoo animals and the crisis of wildlife's threatened annihilation[6] are primarily man-made.

Building better zoos at the expense of efforts to conserve nature is wrong. We should need no zoos and we are misguided if we do not work toward this end, however far into the future it might be. Zoos are not so much a necessary evil as they are a tragic mirror of an evil for which we may yet atone.

As it is estimated that at the current rate of habitat destruction, some 500,000 to 2 million plant and animal (including insect) species will be extinct by the year 2000, obviously captive breeding in zoos is not the answer. Habitat protection is the only solution, and all nations and peoples must be prepared to make the necessary adjustments and sacrifices if the health and vitality of the Earth is to be preserved.

One of the best exhibits in any zoo that I have ever visited was a large mirror behind bars. The caption read: *Homo sapiens*, a dangerous, predatorial tool- and weapon-making primate. Status: endangered by its own doing.

There can be no communion with our animal kin when they are held captive, no matter what the justifications may be for their "protective custody." The zoo is a trick mirror that can delude us into believing that we love and respect animals and are helping to preserve them. And like the animal circus, the zoo can have a pernicious influence on children's

6. destruction, elimination

attitudes toward wild creatures. We cannot recognize or celebrate the sanctity and dignity of nonhuman life under such conditions. There can be no communion: only amusement, curiosity, amazement, and perhaps sympathy. The deprivation of these creatures and the loss of wildness and wilderness are ours also. When we fail collectively to feel these things, and in the process come to accept and patronize the zoo as some cultural norm, we lose something of our own humanity—that intuitive wisdom and a sense of reverence for all life that are the hallmarks of a truly civilized society.

Fox, *Inhumane Society: The American Way of Exploiting Animals*

## Reacting to Ideas: Discussion and Journal Writing

1. What is Fox's thesis?

2. Analyze the audience for whom the essay is written. Does Fox perceive his audience as agreeing, disagreeing, or neutral?

3. What is the most and least convincing evidence Fox offers?

4. Why did Fox begin the essay with the description of the panther?

5. What is the difference between animal preservation and animal conservation?

6. Do you agree that the zoo is "a trick mirror," which deludes us into believing that we love and respect animals?

## Writing Assignments

### Writing About the Reading

1. Write a persuasive essay to your state or local officials (a) urging the closing of a nearby zoo, (b) the building of a more humane zoo, or (c) the expansion of the existing zoo.

### Writing About Your Ideas

2. Write a paragraph describing an animal you have observed. Reflect your attitude toward the animal through your description.

3. Write a persuasive essay arguing for or against using animals in a circus.

4. Write an essay for or against people wearing coats made of animal fur.

## Expository

## Predators on the Prowl
**Marc Peyser**

For Iris Kenna, Cuyamaca Rancho State Park near San Diego was like a second home. By day, she strolled its fields in search of exotic birds. At night, the 56-year-old high-school counselor sometimes slept under the stars. But one morning almost exactly a year ago, Kenna encountered something unfamiliar, and it saw her first. Without warning, a 140-pound male mountain lion pounced on her from behind. The struggle was brief. The animal dragged the dying, 5-foot-4 Kenna into dense brush to hide her from competing predators. Rangers found her only after two hikers spotted a pair of glasses, a backpack and a human tooth by the path she had been on. The rangers followed a trail of her clothes for 30 yards until they came to Kenna's body. The back of her scalp was ripped off; the rest of her was riddled with bites. No one had heard a scream, or even a roar.

1

Kenna is the most vivid symbol of an angry, shifting debate over    2
how people and predators can coexist. In the high-growth Western
states, many residents love living near the wild, and they are inclined to
preserve it no matter what the risks. But violent deaths like Kenna's—
and a string of other mountain-lion attacks—are making a powerful
case for fighting back. Californians will vote in March on opening the
way to mountain-lion hunting, which has been prohibited there for
more than 20 years. But Oregon, Arizona and Colorado recently
changed their hunting laws to ensure that predatory animals—including
bears, wolves and coyotes—would be protected. "It's overwhelmingly
popular to have these animals in our ecosystems," says Tom Dougherty
of the National Wildlife Federation. "But if they're in your backyard,
some people aren't loving it."

The most acute mountain-lion problem is in California. That's    3
partly because the state's human population has doubled every 25 years
this century. As more people built more houses, they usurped territory
once largely inhabited by wild animals. But the mountain lion (alternately called cougar, puma and panther) has also been questionably
served by environmentalists. In 1972, preservation-minded Californians
banned hunting the majestic animals (except when they pose an immi-
nent danger to people or livestock). The cougar population ballooned,
from an estimated 2,400 lions to 6,000 today. Without hunters to thin
the ranks, increased competition for food has sent hungry mountain
lions to suburban backyards, shopping centers and elementary schools
in search of nourishment—a deer or, lacking that, a collie. Even children have been mauled. "People are afraid to go on a picnic without
taking a firearm," says state Sen. Tim Leslie, a prominent anti-cougar
advocate. In the wake of Kenna's death, Gov. Pete Wilson authorized
the March ballot initiative—one that could lead to controlling the
cougar population.

But in other places, sentiment favors animals at least as much as    4
people. A survey of Coloradans living near the Rockies found that 80
percent believe that development in mountain-lion territory should be
restricted. What's more, when wildlife authorities killed the cougar that
killed a woman named Barbara Schoener in California in 1994, donors
raised $21,000 to care for the cougar's cub—but only $9,000 for
Schoener's two children. Arizona recently outlawed trapping cougars
(though hunting is legal), while Colorado and Oregon don't allow
mountain-lion hunters to use bait or dogs. "There's a value shift about
how people view wildlife, a high willingness to accept mountain lions
on the urban fringe—even if they kill people," says Michael Manfredo,
who conducted the survey at Colorado State University. That

open-mindedness will certainly be tested as Westerners reintroduce predators—grizzly bears in Idaho, wolves in New Mexico and in Yellowstone National Park. It's a jungle out there—and it's getting more junglelike every day.

Glick, *Newsweek*

## Reacting to Ideas: Discussion and Journal Writing

1. Why do you think the public contributed more money to caring for the cougar's cub than to caring for Barbara Schoener's children? To which fund would you prefer to contribute?

2. What do you think those in favor of protecting predators would say to Kenna's family if it urged tighter restrictions on predators? What arguments might those in favor of protection raise?

3. Who do you think should have first rights to an area of land—the people who own it or the animals who live there?

## Writing Assignments

### Writing About the Reading

1. Write an essay discussing whether the author is for or against restricting wildlife predators. Refer to sections of the reading to support your points.

### Writing About Your Ideas

2. What is your position on the issue of restricting wildlife predators? If you are for it, write an essay describing what laws should be enacted, restrictions imposed, or guarantees offered. If you oppose restriction, what actions should be taken to protect wildlife predators?

3. Write an essay describing what you think Iris Kenna's family would say to those who want to protect predators. Summarize the arguments they might use.

## Paired Readings Assignment: "The Captive Panther" "Predators on the Prowl"

Both "The Captive Panther" and "Predators on the Prowl" deal with wild animals and their relationship to humans. Using these two readings as sources, write an essay discussing the dilemma of wild animals when faced with the necessity of human interaction. What issues are involved? What problems arise?

# REVIEWING THE BASICS

# GUIDE TO REVIEWING THE BASICS

Most of us know how to communicate in our language. When we talk or write, we put our thoughts into words, and, by and large, we make ourselves understood. But many of us do not know the specific terms and rules of grammar. Grammar is a system that describes how language is put together. Grammar must be learned, almost as if it is a foreign language.

Why is it important to study grammar, to understand grammatical terms like *verb*, *participle*, and *gerund* and concepts like *agreement* and *subordination*? There are several good reasons. Knowing grammar will allow you to

- **recognize an error in your writing and correct it.** Your papers will read more smoothly and communicate more effectively when they are error free.
- **understand the comments of your teachers and peers.** People who read and critique your writing may point out a "fragment" or a "dangling modifier." You will be able to revise and correct the problems.
- **write with more impact.** Grammatically correct sentences are signs of clear thinking. Your readers will get your message without distraction or confusion.

As you will see in this section, "Reviewing the Basics," the different areas of grammatical study are highly interconnected. The sections on parts of speech, sentences, punctuation, and mechanics and spelling fit together into a logical whole. To recognize and correct a run-on sentence, for example, you need to know both sentence structure *and* punctuation. To avoid errors in capitalization, you need to know parts of speech *and* mechanics. In other words, grammar cannot be studied piecemeal, nor can it be studied superficially. If grammar is to do you any good, your knowledge of it must be thorough. As you review the following "basics," be alert to the interconnections that make language study so interesting.

Grammatical terms and rules demand your serious attention. Mastering them will pay handsome dividends: error-free papers, clear thinking, and effective writing.

# Understanding the Parts of Speech

The eight parts of speech are **nouns, pronouns, verbs, adjectives, adverbs, conjunctions, prepositions,** and **interjections.** Each word in a sentence functions as one of these parts of speech. Being able to identify the parts of speech in sentences allows you to analyze and improve your writing and to understand grammatical principles discussed later in this section.

It is important to keep in mind that *how* a word functions in a sentence determines *what* part of speech it is. Thus, the same word can be a noun, a verb, or an adjective, depending on how it is used.

He needed some blue <u>wallpaper</u>. ⌐noun⌐

He will <u>wallpaper</u> the hall. ⌐verb⌐

He went to a <u>wallpaper</u> store. ⌐adjective⌐

## A.1 Nouns

A **noun** names a person, place, thing, or idea.

| | |
|---|---|
| People | *woman, winner, Maria Alvarez* |
| Places | *mall, hill, Indiana* |
| Things | *lamp, ship, air* |
| Ideas | *goodness, perfection, harmony* |

The form of many nouns changes to express **number** (**singular** for one, **plural** for more than one): *one bird, two birds; one child, five children.* Most nouns can also be made **possessive** to show ownership by the addition of *-'s: city's, Norma's.*

Sometimes a noun is used to modify another noun:

noun modifying diploma

Her goal had always been to earn a college diploma.

Nouns are classified as **proper, common, collective, concrete, abstract, count,** and **noncount.**

1. **Proper nouns** name specific people, places, or things and are always capitalized: *Martin Luther King Jr., East Lansing, Ford Taurus.* Days of the week and months are considered proper nouns and are capitalized.

proper noun  proper noun          proper noun

In September Allen will attend Loyola University.

2. **Common nouns** name one or more of a general class or type of person, place, thing, or idea and are not capitalized: *president, city, car, wisdom.*

common noun    common noun      common noun          common noun

Next fall the students will enter college to receive an education.

3. **Collective nouns** name a whole group or collection of people, places, or things: *committee, team, jury.* They are usually singular in form.

collective noun                    collective noun

The flock of mallards flew over the herd of bison.

4. **Concrete nouns** name tangible things that can be tasted, seen, touched, smelled, or heard: *sandwich, radio, pen.*

concrete noun              concrete noun

The frozen pizza was stuck in the freezer.

5. **Abstract nouns** name ideas, qualities, beliefs, and conditions: *honesty, goodness, poverty.*

abstract nouns    abstract noun

Their marriage was based on love, honor, and trust.

6. **Count nouns** name items that can be counted. Count nouns can be made plural, usually by adding *-s* or *-es: one river, three rivers; one box, ten boxes.* Some count nouns form their plural in an irregular way: *man, men; goose, geese.*

count noun      count noun      count noun

The children put the eggs in their baskets.

7. **Noncount nouns** name ideas or qualities that cannot be counted. Noncount nouns almost always have no plural form: *air, knowledge, unhappiness.*

noncount noun                                        noncount noun

As the rain pounded on the windows, she tried to find the courage to walk home.

## A.2 Pronouns

A **pronoun** is a word that substitutes for or refers to a noun or another pronoun. The noun or pronoun to which a pronoun refers is called the pronoun's **antecedent.** A pronoun must agree with its antecedent in person, number, and gender (these terms are discussed later in this section).

> After the <u>campers</u> discovered the <u>cave</u>, <u>they</u> mapped <u>it</u> for the next <u>group</u>, which was arriving next week. [The pronoun *they* refers to its antecedent, *campers*; the pronoun *it* refers to its antecedent, *cave*; the pronoun *which* refers to its antecedent, *group*.]

The eight kinds of pronouns are **personal, demonstrative, reflexive, intensive, interrogative, relative, indefinite,** and **reciprocal.**

1. **Personal pronouns** take the place of nouns or pronouns that name people or things. A personal pronoun changes form to indicate **person, gender, number,** and **case.**

   **Person** is the grammatical term used to distinguish the speaker (**first person:** *I, we*); the person spoken to (**second person:** *you*); and the person or thing spoken about (**third person:** *he, she, it, they*). **Gender** is the term used to classify pronouns as **masculine** *(he, him)*; **feminine** *(she, her)*; or **neuter** *(it)*. **Number** classifies pronouns as **singular** (one) or **plural** (more than one). Some personal pronouns also function as adjectives modifying nouns (<u>our</u> house).

|  | *Singular* | *Plural* |
|---|---|---|
| First person | I, me, my, mine | we, us, our, ours |
| Second person | you, your, yours | you, your, yours |
| Third person | | |
| Masculine | he, him, his | |
| Feminine | she, her, hers | they, them, their, theirs |
| Neuter | it, its | |

I called my mother about the twins. She wanted to know as soon as they took their first steps. "Your babies are talented," she said.

[1st person singular (pronoun/adjective); 1st person singular; 3rd person singular; 3rd person plural; 3rd person plural (pronoun/adjective); 2nd person singular (pronoun/adjective); 3rd person singular]

A pronoun's **case** is determined by its function as a subject (**subjective** or **nominative case**) or an object (**objective case**) in a sentence. A pronoun that shows ownership is in the **possessive case.** (See p. 426 for a discussion of pronoun case.)

2. **Demonstrative pronouns** refer to particular people or things. The demonstrative pronouns are *this* and *that* (singular) and *these* and *those* (plural). (*This, that, these,* and *those* can also be demonstrative adjectives when they modify a noun. See p. 374.)

<u>This</u> is more thorough than <u>that</u>.

The red shuttle buses stop here. <u>These</u> go to the airport every hour.

3. **Reflexive pronouns** indicate that the subject performs actions to, for, or upon itself. Reflexive pronouns end in *-self* or *-selves*.

|  | *Singular* | *Plural* |
|---|---|---|
| First person | myself | ourselves |
| Second person | yourself | yourselves |
| Third person | himself | |
| | herself | themselves |
| | itself | |

We excused <u>ourselves</u> from the table and left.

4. An **intensive pronoun** emphasizes the word that comes before it in a sentence. Like reflexive pronouns, intensive pronouns end in *-self* or *-selves*.

The filmmaker <u>herself</u> could not explain the ending.

They <u>themselves</u> washed the floor.

NOTE: A reflexive or intensive pronoun should not be used as a subject of a sentence. An antecedent for the reflexive pronoun must appear in the same sentence.

INCORRECT: <u>Myself</u> create colorful sculpture.
CORRECT:   I <u>myself</u> create colorful sculpture.

5. **Interrogative pronouns** are used to introduce questions: *who, whom, whoever, whomever, what, which, whose.* The correct use of *who* and *whom* depends on the role the interrogative pronoun plays in a sentence or clause. When the pronoun functions as the subject of the sentence or clause, use *who*. When the pronoun functions as an object in the sentence or clause, use *whom*. (See p. 426.)

<u>What</u> happened?

<u>Which</u> is your street?

<u>Who</u> wrote *Ragtime*? [*Who* is the subject of the sentence.]

<u>Whom</u> should I notify? [*Whom* is the object of the verb *notify: I should notify whom*?]

6. **Relative pronouns** relate groups of words to nouns or other pronouns and often introduce adjective clauses or noun clauses (see p. 396). The relative pronouns are *who, whom, whoever, whomever,* and *whose* (referring to people) and *that, what, whatever,* and *which* (referring to things).

In 1836 Charles Dickens met John Forster, <u>who</u> became his friend and biographer.

Don did not understand <u>what</u> the child said.

We read some articles <u>that</u> were written by former astronauts.

7. **Indefinite pronouns** are pronouns without specific antecedents. They refer to people, places, or things in general.

<u>Someone</u> has been rearranging my papers.

<u>Many</u> knew the woman, but <u>few</u> could say they knew her well.

Here are some frequently used indefinite pronouns:

| *Singular* | | *Plural* |
|---|---|---|
| another | nobody | all |
| anybody | none | both |
| anyone | no one | few |
| anything | nothing | many |
| each | one | more |
| either | other | most |
| everybody | somebody | others |
| everyone | someone | several |
| everything | something | some |
| neither | | |

8. The **reciprocal pronouns** *each other* and *one another* indicate a mutual relationship between two or more parts of a plural antecedent.

Bernie and Sharon congratulated <u>each other</u> on their high grades.

**EXERCISE** **1**

In each of the following sentences (a) circle each noun and (b) underline each pronoun.

EXAMPLE:  (Mark) parked his (car) in the (lot) that is reserved for (commuters) like <u>him</u>.

1. Shakespeare wrote many plays that have become famous and important.
2. Everyone who has visited Disneyland wishes to return.
3. Jonathan himself prepared the delicious dinner that the guests enjoyed.

4. That hat used to belong to my great-grandmother.
5. Aretha's integrity was never questioned by her coworkers.
6. The class always laughed at Professor Wayne's jokes even though they were usually corny.
7. When will humankind be able to live in outer space for long periods?
8. Whoever wins this week's lottery will become quite wealthy.
9. As the plane landed in the Atlanta airport, many of the passengers began gathering their carry-on luggage.
10. This week in physics class we are studying gravity.

## A.3 Verbs

Verbs express action or state of being. A grammatically complete sentence has at least one verb in it.

There are three kinds of verbs: **action verbs, linking verbs,** and **helping verbs** (also known as **auxiliary verbs**).

1. **Action verbs** express physical and mental activities.

Mr. Royce <u>dashed</u> for the bus.

The incinerator <u>burns</u> garbage at high temperatures.

I <u>think</u> that seat is taken.

The baby <u>slept</u> until 3:00 A.M.

Action verbs are either **transitive** or **intransitive.** The action of a **transitive verb** is directed toward someone or something, called the **direct object** of the verb. Direct objects receive the action of the verb. Transitive verbs require direct objects to complete the meaning of the sentence.

subject / transitive verb / direct object
Amalia made clocks.

An **intransitive verb** does not need a direct object to complete the meaning of the sentence.

subject / intransitive verb
The traffic stopped.

Some verbs can be both transitive and intransitive, depending on their meaning and use in a sentence.

INTRANSITIVE: The traffic <u>stopped</u>. [No direct object.]

direct object
TRANSITIVE: The driver <u>stopped</u> the <u>bus</u> at the corner.

2. A **linking verb** expresses a state of being or a condition. A linking verb connects a noun or pronoun to words that describe the noun or pronoun. Common linking verbs are forms of the verb *be* (*is, are, was, were, being, been*), *become, feel, grow, look, remain, seem, smell, sound, stay,* and *taste.*

> Their child <u>grew</u> tall.

> The boat <u>smells</u> fishy.

> Mr. Davenport <u>is</u> our accountant.

3. A **helping (auxiliary) verb** helps another verb, called the **main verb,** to convey when the action occurred (through verb tense) and to form questions. One or more helping verbs and the main verb together form a **verb phrase.** Some helping verbs, called **modals,** are always helping verbs:

| | |
|---|---|
| can, could | shall, should |
| may, might | will, would |
| must, ought to | |

The other helping verbs can sometimes function as main verbs as well:

am, are, be, been, being, did, do, does
had, has, have
is, was, were

The verb *be* is a very irregular verb, with eight forms instead of the usual five: *am, are, be, being, been, is, was, were.*

helping main<br>verb  verb

The cat <u>will</u> <u>nap</u> on that windowsill for hours.

helping          main<br>verb            verb

<u>Will</u> the cat <u>nap</u> through the noise of the vacuum cleaner?

## Forms of the Verb

All verbs except *be* have five forms: the **base form** (or dictionary form), the **past tense,** the **past participle,** the **present participle,** and the **-s form.** The first three forms are called the verb's **principal parts.** The infinitive consists of "to" plus a base form: *to go, to study, to talk.* For **regular verbs,** the past tense and past participle are formed by adding *-d* or *-ed* to the base form. **Irregular verbs** follow no set pattern to form their past tense and past participle.

|  | *Regular* | *Irregular* |
|---|---|---|
| Infinitive | work | eat |
| Past tense | worked | ate |
| Past participle | worked | eaten |
| Present participle | working | eating |
| -*s* form | works | eats |

Verbs change form to agree with their subjects in person and number (see p. 417); to express the time of their action (**tense**); to express whether the action is a fact, command, or wish (**mood**); and to indicate whether the subject is the doer or the receiver of the action (**voice**).

## Principal Parts of Irregular Verbs

Consult the following list and your dictionary for the principal parts of irregular verbs.

| *Base Form* | *Past Tense* | *Past Participle* |
|---|---|---|
| be | was | been |
| become | became | become |
| begin | began | begun |
| bite | bit | bitten |
| blow | blew | blown |
| burst | burst | burst |
| catch | caught | caught |
| choose | chose | chosen |
| come | came | come |
| dive | dived, dove | dived |
| do | did | done |
| draw | drew | drawn |
| drive | drove | driven |
| eat | ate | eaten |
| fall | fell | fallen |
| find | found | found |
| fling | flung | flung |
| fly | flew | flown |
| get | got | gotten |
| give | gave | given |
| go | went | gone |
| grow | grew | grown |
| have | had | had |
| know | knew | known |
| lay | laid | laid |

| Base Form | Past Tense | Past Participle |
|-----------|------------|-----------------|
| lead | led | led |
| leave | left | left |
| lie | lay | lain |
| lose | lost | lost |
| ride | rode | ridden |
| ring | rang | rung |
| rise | rose | risen |
| say | said | said |
| set | set | set |
| sit | sat | sat |
| speak | spoke | spoken |
| swear | swore | sworn |
| swim | swam | swum |
| tear | tore | torn |
| tell | told | told |
| throw | threw | thrown |
| wear | wore | worn |
| write | wrote | written |

### Tense

The **tenses** of a verb express time. They convey whether an action, process, or event takes place in the present, past, or future.

The three **simple tenses** are **present, past,** and **future.** The **simple present** tense is the base form of the verb (and the *-s* form of third-person singular subjects; see p. 409); the **simple past** tense is the past-tense form; and the **simple future** tense consists of the helping verb *will* plus the base form.

The **perfect tenses,** which indicate completed action, are **present perfect, past perfect,** and **future perfect.** They are formed by adding the helping verbs *have* (or *has*), *had,* and *will have* to the past participle.

In addition to the simple and perfect tenses, there are six progressive tenses. The **simple progressive tenses** are the **present progressive,** the **past progressive,** and the **future progressive.** The progressive terms are used for continuing actions or actions in progress. These progressive tenses are formed by adding the present, past, and future forms of the verb *be* to the present participle. The **perfect progressive tenses** are the **present perfect progressive,** the **past perfect progressive,** and the **future perfect progressive.** They are formed by adding the present perfect, past perfect, and future perfect forms of the verb *be* to the present participle.

The following chart shows all the tenses for a regular verb and an irregular verb in the first person. (For more on tenses, see p. 409.)

| | Regular | Irregular |
|---|---|---|
| Simple present | I talk | I go |
| Simple past | I talked | I went |
| Simple future | I will talk | I will go |
| Present perfect | I have talked | I have gone |
| Past perfect | I had talked | I had gone |
| Future perfect | I will have talked | I will have gone |
| Present progressive | I am talking | I am going |
| Past progressive | I was talking | I was going |
| Future progressive | I will be talking | I will be going |
| Present perfect progressive | I have been talking | I have been going |
| Past perfect progressive | I had been talking | I had been going |
| Future perfect progressive | I will have been talking | I will have been going |

## Mood

The mood of a verb indicates the writer's attitude toward the action. There are three moods in English: **indicative, imperative,** and **subjunctive.**

The **indicative mood** is used for ordinary statements of fact or questions.

The light flashed on and off all night.

Did you check the batteries?

The **imperative mood** is used for commands, suggestions, or directions. The subject of a verb in the imperative mood is *you,* though it is not always included.

Stop shouting!

Come to New York for a visit.

Turn right at the next corner.

The **subjunctive mood** is used for wishes, requirements, recommendations, and statements contrary to fact. For statements contrary to fact or for wishes, the past tense of the verb is used. For the verb *be,* only the past-tense form *were* is used.

If I had a million dollars, I'd take a trip around the world.

If my grandmother were younger, she could live by herself.

To express suggestions, recommendations, or requirements, the infinitive form is used for all verbs.

> I recommend that the houses <u>be</u> sold after the landscaping is done.

> The registrar required that Maureen <u>pay</u> her bill before attending class.

## Voice

Transitive verbs (those that take objects) may be in either the active voice or the passive voice. (See p. 414.) In an **active-voice** sentence, the subject performs the action described by the verb; that is, the subject is the actor. In a **passive-voice** sentence, the subject is the receiver of the action. The passive voice of a verb is formed by using an appropriate form of the helping verb *be* and the past participle of the main verb.

subject            active
is actor            voice

Dr. Hillel <u>delivered</u> the report on global warming.

subject is receiver                           passive voice

The report on global warming <u>was delivered</u> by Dr. Hillel.

**EXERCISE** 2 ▶  Revise the following sentences, changing each verb from the present tense to the tense indicated.

EXAMPLE:    I <u>know</u> the right answer.

PAST TENSE:  *I knew the right answer.* _____

1. The boy <u>loses</u> the ball in the water.

   SIMPLE PAST: _____

2. Malcolm <u>begins</u> classes at the community college.

   PAST PERFECT: _____

3. The microscope <u>enlarges</u> the cell.

   PRESENT PERFECT: _____

4. Sunflowers <u>follow</u> the sun's path.

   SIMPLE FUTURE: _____

5. Meg Ryan <u>receives</u> excellent reviews.

   FUTURE PERFECT: _____

6. Juanita <u>writes</u> a computer program.

   PRESENT PERFECT: _____

7. The movie <u>stars</u> Whoopi Goldberg.

    SIMPLE FUTURE: _____

8. Dave <u>wins</u> a medal at the Special Olympics.

    SIMPLE PAST: _____

9. Many celebrities <u>donate</u> money to AIDS research.

    PRESENT PERFECT: _____

10. My nephew <u>vacations</u> in Michigan's Upper Peninsula.

    PAST PERFECT: _____

## A.4 Adjectives

**Adjectives** modify nouns and pronouns. That is, they describe, identify, qualify, or limit the meaning of nouns and pronouns. An adjective answers the question *Which one? What kind?* or *How many?* about the word it modifies.

    WHICH ONE? The <u>twisted</u>, <u>torn</u> umbrella was of no use to its owner.

    WHAT KIND? The <u>spotted</u> owl has caused <u>heated</u> arguments in the Northwest.

    HOW MANY? <u>Many</u> people waited in line for <u>four</u> hours before the ticket office opened.

In form, adjectives can be **positive** (implying no comparison), **comparative** (comparing two items), or **superlative** (comparing three or more items). (See p. 428 for more on the forms of adjectives.)

               positive

The scissors are <u>sharp</u>.

               comparative

Your scissors are <u>sharper</u> than mine.

         superlative

These are the <u>sharpest</u> scissors I have ever used.

There are two general categories of adjectives. **Descriptive adjectives** name a quality of the person, place, thing, or idea they describe: *mysterious man, green pond, healthy complexion.* **Limiting adjectives** narrow the scope of the person, place, or thing they describe: *my hat, this tool, second try.*

## Descriptive Adjectives

A **regular** (or **attributive**) adjective appears next to (usually before) the word it modifies. Several adjectives can modify the same word.

The enthusiastic new barber gave short, lopsided haircuts.

The wealthy dealer bought an immense blue vase.

Sometimes nouns function as adjectives modifying other nouns: *tree house*, *hamburger bun*.

A **predicate adjective** follows a linking verb and modifies or describes the subject of the sentence or clause (see p. 386). (See p. 394 on clauses.)

predicate adjective
The meeting was long. [Modifies the subject, *meeting*.]

## Limiting Adjectives

The **definite article**, *the*, and the **indefinite articles**, *a* and *an*, are classified as adjectives. *A* and *an* are used when it is not important to specify a particular noun or when the object named is not known to the reader (*A radish adds color to a salad*). *The* is used when it is important to specify one or more of a particular noun or when the object named is known to the reader or has already been mentioned (*The radishes from the garden are on the table*).

A squirrel visited the feeder that I just built. The squirrel tried to eat some bird food.

When the possessive pronouns *my, your, his, her, its, our,* and *their* are used as modifiers before nouns, they are considered **possessive adjectives**. (See p. 427.)

Your friend borrowed my jacket for his wife.

When the demonstrative pronouns *this, that, these,* and *those* are used as modifiers before nouns, they are called **demonstrative adjectives**. (See p. 365.) *This* and *these* modify nouns close to the writer; *that* and *those* modify nouns more distant from the writer.

Eat these sandwiches, not those sardines.

This freshman course is a prerequisite for those advanced courses.

**Cardinal adjectives** are words used in counting: *one, two, twenty,* and so on.

I read four biographies of Jack Kerouac and seven articles about his work.

**Ordinal adjectives** note position in a series.

The <u>first</u> biography was too sketchy, whereas the <u>second</u> one was too detailed.

**Indefinite adjectives** provide nonspecific, general information about the quantities and amounts of the nouns they modify. Some common indefinite adjectives are *another, any, enough, few, less, little, many, more, much, several,* and *some.*

<u>Several</u> people asked me if I had <u>enough</u> blankets or if I wanted the thermostat turned up a <u>few</u> degrees.

The **interrogative adjectives** *what, which,* and *whose* modify nouns and pronouns used in questions.

<u>Which</u> radio station do you like? <u>Whose</u> music do you prefer?

The words *which* and *what,* along with *whichever* and *whatever,* are **relative adjectives** when they modify nouns and introduce subordinate clauses.

She couldn't decide <u>which</u> dessert she wanted to eat.

**Proper adjectives** are adjectives derived from proper nouns: *Spain* (noun), *Spanish* (adjective); *Freud* (noun), *Freudian* (adjective). (See p. 363.) Most proper adjectives are capitalized.

Shakespeare lived in <u>Elizabethan</u> England.

The parrot knows many <u>French</u> expressions.

**EXERCISE 3**

Review each of the following sentences by adding at least three adjectives.

EXAMPLE: The cat slept on the pillow.

REVISED: <u>The old yellow cat slept on the expensive pillow.</u>

1. Before leaving on a trip, the couple packed their suitcases.

   _____

   _____

2. The tree dropped leaves all over the lawn. _____

   _____

3. While riding the train, the passengers read newspapers.

   _____

   _____

4. The antiques dealer said that the desk was more valuable than the chair. _____

_____

5. As the play was ending, the audience clapped their hands and tossed roses onstage. _____

_____

6. Stew is served nightly at the shelter. _____

_____

7. The engine roared as the car stubbornly jerked into gear. _____

_____

8. The tourists tossed pennies into the fountain. _____

_____

9. Computer disks were stacked on the desk next to the monitor.

_____

_____

10. Marina's belt and shoes were made of the same material and complemented her dress. _____

_____

## A.5 Adverbs

**Adverbs** modify verbs, adjectives, other adverbs, or entire sentences or clauses (see p. 394 on clauses). Like adjectives, adverbs describe, qualify, or limit the meaning of the words they modify.

An adverb answers the question *How? When? Where? How often?* or *To what extent?* about the word it modifies.

| | |
|---|---|
| HOW? | Cheryl moved <u>awkwardly</u> because of her stiff neck. |
| WHEN? | I arrived <u>yesterday</u>. |
| WHERE? | They searched <u>everywhere</u>. |
| HOW OFTEN? | He telephoned <u>repeatedly</u>. |
| TO WHAT EXTENT? | Simon was <u>rather</u> slow to answer his doorbell. |

Many adverbs end in *-ly (lazily, happily)*, but some adverbs do not *(fast, here, much, well, rather, everywhere, never, so)*, and some words that end in *-ly* are not adverbs *(lively, friendly, lonely)*. Like all parts of speech, an adverb may be best identified by examining its function within a sentence.

I quickly skimmed the book. [Modifies the verb *skimmed*.]

Very cold water came from the shower. [Modifies the adjective *cold*.]

He was injured quite seriously. [Modifies the adverb *seriously*.]

Apparently, the job was bungled. [Modifies the whole sentence.]

Like adjectives, adverbs have three forms: **positive** (does not suggest any comparison), **comparative** (compares two actions or conditions), and **superlative** (compares three or more actions or conditions). (See also p. 428.)

positive               positive
Andy rose early and crept downstairs quietly.

comparative            comparative
Jim rose earlier than Andy and crept downstairs more quietly.

superlative            superlative
Bill rose earliest of anyone in the house and crept downstairs most quietly.

Some adverbs, called **conjunctive adverbs** (or **adverbial conjunctions**)—such as *however, therefore,* and *besides*—connect the ideas of one sentence or clause to those of a previous sentence or clause. They can appear anywhere in a sentence. (See p. 407 for how to punctuate sentences containing conjunctive adverbs.)

conjunctive adverb
James did not want to go to the library on Saturday; however, he knew he needed to write his paper.

conjunctive adverb
The sporting-goods store was crowded because of the sale. Leila, therefore, decided to come back another day.

Some common conjunctive adverbs are listed here, including several phrases that function as conjunctive adverbs.

| | | | |
|---|---|---|---|
| accordingly | for example | meanwhile | otherwise |
| also | further | moreover | similarly |
| anyway | furthermore | namely | still |
| as a result | hence | nevertheless | then |
| at the same time | however | next | thereafter |
| besides | incidentally | nonetheless | therefore |
| certainly | indeed | now | thus |
| consequently | instead | on the contrary | undoubtedly |
| finally | likewise | on the other hand | |

**EXERCISE 4**    Write a sentence using each of the following comparative or superlative adverbs.

EXAMPLE:    better: <u>My car runs better now than ever before.</u>

1. farther: _____

2. most: _____

3. more: _____

4. best: _____

5. least neatly: _____

6. more loudly: _____

7. worse: _____

8. less angrily: _____

9. later: _____

10. earliest: _____

## A.6 Conjunctions

**Conjunctions** connect words, phrases, and clauses. There are three kinds of conjunctions: **coordinating, correlative,** and **subordinating. Coordinating** and **correlative conjunctions** connect words, phrases, or clauses of equal grammatical rank. (A **phrase** is a group of related words lacking a subject, a predicate, or both. A **clause** is a group of words containing a subject and a predicate. See pp. 383 and 384.)

The **coordinating conjunctions** are *and, but, nor, or, for, so,* and *yet.* These words must connect words or word groups of the same kind. In other words, two nouns may be connected by *and,* but a noun and a clause cannot be. *For* and *so* can connect only independent clauses.

coordinating<br>
noun    conjunction    noun<br>
We studied the novels of Toni Morrison and Alice Walker.

coordinating<br>
conjunction<br>
verb    verb<br>
The copilot successfully flew and landed the disabled plane.

coordinating independent<br>
independent clause    conjunction    clause<br>
The carpentry course sounded interesting, so Meg enrolled.

We hoped that the mail would come soon and that it would contain our bonus check.

*subordinate clause* — *coordinating conjunction* — *subordinate clause*

**Correlative conjunctions** are pairs of words that link and relate grammatically equivalent parts of a sentence. Some common correlative conjunctions are *either/or, neither/nor, both/and, not/but, not only/but also,* and *whether/or.* Correlative conjunctions are always used in pairs.

— correlative conjunctions —

Either the electricity was off, or the bulb had burned out.

**Subordinating conjunctions** connect dependent, or subordinate, clauses to independent clauses (see p. 407). Some common subordinating conjunctions are *although, because, if, since, until, when, where,* and *while.*

subordinating conjunction

Although the movie got bad reviews, it drew big crowds.

subordinating conjunction

She received a lot of mail because she was a reliable correspondent.

## A.7 Prepositions

A **preposition** links and relates its **object** (a noun or a pronoun) to the rest of the sentence. Prepositions often show relationships of time, place, direction, and manner.

preposition   object of preposition

I walked around the block.

preposition   object of preposition

She called during our vacation.

### Common Prepositions

| | | | | |
|---|---|---|---|---|
| along | besides | from | past | up |
| among | between | in | since | upon |
| around | beyond | near | through | with |
| at | by | off | till | within |
| before | despite | on | to | without |
| behind | down | onto | toward | |
| below | during | out | under | |
| beneath | except | outside | underneath | |
| beside | for | over | until | |

Some prepositions consist of more than one word; they are called **phrasal prepositions** or **compound prepositions.**

phrasal preposition   object of preposition

**According to** our **records,** you have enough credits to graduate.

phrasal preposition   object of preposition

We decided to make the trip **in spite of** the **snowstorm.**

### Common Compound Prepositions

| | | |
|---|---|---|
| according to | in addition to | on account of |
| aside from | in front of | out of |
| as of | in place of | prior to |
| as well as | in regard to | with regard to |
| because of | in spite of | with respect to |
| by means of | instead of | |

The object of the preposition often has modifiers.

obj. of                         obj. of

prep.   modifier prep.   prep.   modifier prep.

Not a sound came **from** the **child's room** except a **gentle snoring.**

Sometimes a preposition has more than one object (a **compound object**).

compound object of preposition

preposition

The laundromat was **between campus** and **home.**

Usually the preposition comes before its object. In interrogative sentences, however, the preposition sometimes follows its object.

object of preposition                         preposition

**What** did your supervisor ask you **about?**

The preposition, the object or objects of the preposition, and the object's modifiers all form a **prepositional phrase.**

prepositional phrase

The scientist conducted her experiment **throughout the afternoon and early evening.**

There may be many prepositional phrases in a sentence.

prepositional phrase                         prepositional phrase

The water **from the open hydrant** flowed **into the street.**

The noisy kennel was **underneath the beauty salon,** despite the complaints of customers.

Alongside the weedy railroad tracks, an old hotel stood **with faded grandeur near the abandoned brick station on the edge of town.**

Prepositional phrases frequently function as adjectives or adverbs. If a prepositional phrase modifies a noun or pronoun, it functions as an adjective. If it modifies a verb, adjective, or adverb, it functions as an adverb.

The auditorium <u>inside the new building</u> has a special sound system. [Adjective modifying the noun *auditorium*.]

The doctor looked cheerfully <u>at the patient</u> and handed the lab results <u>across the desk</u>. [Adverbs modifying the verbs *looked* and *handed*.]

**EXERCISE 5** ▷ Expand each of the following sentences by adding a prepositional phrase in the blank.

EXAMPLE:    A cat hid <u>under the car</u> when the garage door opened.

1. Fish nibbled ＿＿＿＿＿＿ as the fisherman waited.

2. The librarian explained that the books about Africa are located ＿＿＿＿＿＿.

3. When the bullet hit the window, shards flew ＿＿＿＿＿＿.

4. ＿＿＿＿＿＿, there is a restaurant that serves alligator meat.

5. Polar bears are able to swim ＿＿＿＿＿＿.

6. Heavy winds blowing ＿＿＿＿＿＿ caused the waves to hit the house.

7. One student completed her exam ＿＿＿＿＿＿.

8. A frog jumped ＿＿＿＿＿＿.

9. The bus was parked ＿＿＿＿＿＿.

10. Stacks of books were piled ＿＿＿＿＿＿.

## A.8 Interjections

**Interjections** are words that express emotion or surprise. They are followed by an exclamation point, comma, or period, depending on whether they stand alone or serve as part or all of a sentence. Interjections are used in speech more than in writing.

<u>Wow</u>! What a hat!

<u>So</u>, was that lost letter ever found?

<u>Well</u>, I'd better be going.

# B

# Understanding the Parts of Sentences

A sentence is a group of words that expresses a complete thought about something or someone. A sentence must contain a **subject** and a **predicate.**

| *Subject* | *Predicate* |
|-----------|-------------|
| Children | grow. |
| Cecilia | laughed. |
| Time | will tell. |

Depending on their purpose and punctuation, sentences are **declarative, interrogative, exclamatory,** or **imperative.**

A **declarative sentence** makes a statement. It ends with a period.

subject predicate
The snow fell steadily.

An **interrogative sentence** asks a question. It ends with a question mark (?).

subject predicate
Who called?

An **exclamatory sentence** conveys strong emotion. It ends with an exclamation point (!).

subject predicate
Your picture is in the paper!

An **imperative sentence** gives an order or makes a request. It ends with either a period or an exclamation point, depending on how mild or strong the command or request is. In an imperative sentence, the subject is *you,* but this often is not included.

predicate
Get me a fire extinguisher now! [The subject *you* is understood: *(You)* get me a fire extinguisher now!]

# B.1 Subjects

The subject of a sentence is who or what the sentence is about. It is who or what performs or receives the action expressed in the predicate. The subject is often a **noun,** a word that names a person, place, thing, or idea.

Paul Simon released a new video.

The rose bushes must be watered.

Honesty is the best policy.

The subject of a sentence can also be a **pronoun,** a word that refers to or substitutes for a noun.

They saw the movie three times.

I will attend the rally.

Although the ink spilled, it did not go on my shirt.

The subject of a sentence can also be a group of words used as a noun.

Lying on a beach is my idea of a good time.

## Simple Versus Complete Subjects

The **simple subject** is the noun or pronoun that names what the sentence is about. It does not include any **modifiers**—that is, words that describe, identify, qualify, or limit the meaning of the noun or pronoun.

simple subject
The bright red concert poster caught everyone's eye.

simple subject
High-speed computers have revolutionized the banking industry.

When the subject of a sentence is a proper noun (the name of a particular person, place, or thing), the entire name is considered the simple subject.

——— simple subject ———
Martin Luther King Jr. was a famous leader.

The simple subject of an imperative sentence is you.

simple subject
[You] Remember to bring the cooler.

The **complete subject** is the simple subject plus its modifiers.

——— complete subject ———
simple subject
The sleek, black limousine waited outside the church.

———————————————— complete subject ————————————

Fondly remembered as a gifted songwriter, fiddle player, and storyteller, <u>Quintin Lotus Dickey</u> lived in a cabin in Paoli, Indiana.

simple subject

## Compound Subjects

Some sentences contain two or more subjects joined with a coordinating conjunction (*and, but, nor, or, for, so, yet*). Those subjects together form a **compound subject**.

compound subject

Neither <u>Maria</u> nor <u>I</u> completed the marathon.

————— compound subject —————

The microwave <u>oven</u>, the <u>dishwasher</u>, and the <u>refrigerator</u> were not usable during the blackout.

# B.2 Predicates

The **predicate** indicates what the subject does, what happened to the subject, or what is being said about the subject. The predicate must include a **verb,** a word or group of words that expresses an action or a state of being (for example, *run, invent, build, know, become*).

Joy <u>swam</u> sixty laps.

The thunderstorm <u>replenished</u> the reservoir.

Sometimes the verb consists of only one word, as in the previous examples. Often, however, the main verb is accompanied by a **helping verb** (see p. 368).

helping   main
verb     verb

By the end of the week, I <u>will have</u> <u>worked</u> twenty-five hours.

helping main
verb  verb

The play <u>had</u> <u>begun.</u>

helping main
verb   verb

The professor <u>did</u> <u>return</u> the journal assignments.

## Simple Versus Complete Predicates

The **simple predicate** is the main verb plus its helping verbs (together known as the **verb phrase**). The simple predicate does not include any modifiers.

simple predicate
The proctor hastily collected the blue books.

┌ simple predicate ┐
The moderator had introduced the next speaker.

The **complete predicate** consists of the simple predicate, its modifiers, and any complements (words that complete the meaning of the verb; see p. 386). In general, the complete predicate includes everything in the sentence except the complete subject.

┌──────────── complete predicate ───────────┐
simple predicate
The music sounds better from the back of the room.

┌───────────── complete predicate ──────────
simple predicate
Bill decided to change the name of his band to something less controversial and confusing.

## Compound Predicates

Some sentences have two or more predicates joined by a coordinating conjunction (*and, but, or,* or *nor*). These predicates together form a **compound predicate.**

┌──── compound predicate ───┐
Marcia unlocked her bicycle and rode away.

┌──── compound predicate ───┐
The supermarket owner will survey his customers and order the specialized foods they desire.

**EXERCISE 6** ▶ Underline the simple subject(s) and circle the simple predicate(s) in each of the following sentences.

EXAMPLE: Pamela Wong (photographed) a hummingbird.

1. A flock of geese flew over the park on its way south for the winter.
2. The campground for physically challenged children is funded and supported by the Rotary Club.
3. Forty doctors and lawyers had attended the seminar on malpractice insurance.
4. Sullivan Beach will not reopen because of pollution.
5. The boys ran to the store and rushed home with ice cream.
6. Greenpeace is an environmentalist organization.
7. Talented dancers and experienced musicians performed and received much applause at the open-air show.

8. Some undergraduate students have been using empty classrooms for group study.
9. A police officer, with the shoplifter in handcuffs, entered the police station.
10. The newly elected senator walked up to the podium and began her first speech to her constituents.

## B.3 Complements

A **complement** is a word or group of words used to complete the meaning of a subject or object. There are four kinds of complements: **subject complements,** which follow linking verbs; **direct objects** and **indirect objects,** which follow transitive verbs (verbs that take an object); and **object complements,** which follow direct objects.

### Linking Verbs and Subject Complements

A linking verb (such as *be, become, seem, feel, taste*) links the subject to a **subject complement,** a noun or adjective that renames or describes the subject. (See p. 368 for more about linking verbs.) Nouns that function as complements are called **predicate nominatives** or **predicate nouns.** Adjectives that function as complements are called **predicate adjectives.**

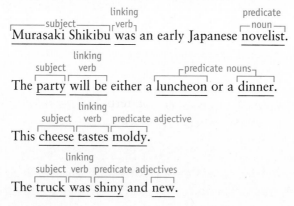

### Direct Objects

A **direct object** is a noun or pronoun that receives the action of a transitive verb (see p. 367). A direct object answers the question *What?* or *Whom?*

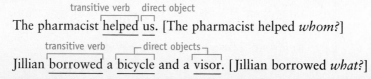

## Indirect Objects

An **indirect object** is a noun or pronoun that receives the action of the verb indirectly. Indirect objects name the person or thing *to whom* or *for whom* something is done.

transitive verb⎯ indirect object  direct object

The oil-delivery man gave me the bill. [He gave the bill *to whom?*]

transitive verb      indirect objects                    direct objects

Eric bought his wife and son some sandwiches and milk. [He bought food *for whom?*]

## Object Complements

An **object complement** is a noun or adjective that modifies (describes) or renames the direct object. Object complements appear with verbs like *name, find, think, elect, appoint, choose,* and *consider.*

direct object      noun as object complement

We appointed Dean our representative. [*Representative* renames the direct object, *Dean.*]

direct object  adjective as object complement

The judge found the defendant innocent of the charges. [*Innocent* modifies the direct object, *defendant.*]

# B.4 Basic Sentence Patterns

There are five basic sentence patterns in English. They are built with combinations of subjects, predicates, and complements. The order of these elements within a sentence may change, or a sentence may become long and complicated when modifiers, phrases, or clauses are added. Nonetheless, one of five basic patterns stands at the heart of every sentence.

**Pattern 1**

### Subject + Predicate

| | |
|---|---|
| I | shivered. |
| Cynthia | swam. |

**Pattern 2**

### Subject + Predicate      + Direct Object

| | | |
|---|---|---|
| Anthony | bought | a sofa. |
| We | wanted | freedom. |

## Pattern 3

| Subject + Predicate | | + Subject Complement |
|---|---|---|
| The woman | was | a welder. |
| Our course | is | interesting. |

## Pattern 4

| Subject + Predicate | | + Indirect Object | + Direct Object |
|---|---|---|---|
| My friend | loaned | me | a typewriter. |
| The company | sent | employees | a questionnaire. |

## Pattern 5

| Subject + Predicate | | + Direct Object | + Object Complement |
|---|---|---|---|
| I | consider | her singing | exceptional. |
| Lampwick | called | Jiminy Cricket | a beetle. |

**EXERCISE  7**

Complete each sentence with a word or words that will function as the type of complement indicated.

EXAMPLE:  The scientist acted ____*proud*____ as he announced his
latest invention.  predicate adjective

1. The delivery person handed _____ the large brown package.
   indirect object

2. George Bush was an American _____.
   predicate noun

3. The chairperson appointed Judith our _____.
   object complement

4. Protesters stood on the corner and handed out _____.
   direct object

5. The secretary gave _____ the messages.
   indirect object

6. Before the storm, many clouds were _____.
   predicate adjective

7. The beer advertisement targeted _____.
   direct object

8. The Super Bowl players were _____.
   predicate noun

9. The diplomat declared the Olympics _____.
   object complement

10. Shopping malls are _____ before Christmas.
    predicate adjective

# B.5 Expanding the Sentence with Adjectives and Adverbs

A sentence may consist of just a subject and a verb.

> Linda studied.

> Rumors circulated.

Most sentences, however, contain additional information about the subject and the verb. Information is commonly added in three ways:

- by using adjectives and adverbs;
- by using phrases (groups of words that lack either a subject or a predicate or both);
- by using clauses (groups of words that contain both a subject and a predicate).

## Using Adjectives and Adverbs to Expand Your Sentences

**Adjectives** are words used to modify or describe nouns and pronouns. (See p. 373.) Adjectives answer questions about nouns and pronouns such as *Which one? What kind? How many?* Using adjectives is one way to add detail and information to sentences.

> WITHOUT ADJECTIVES:  Dogs barked at cats.
> WITH ADJECTIVES:  Our three large brown dogs barked at the two terrified spotted cats.

NOTE: Sometimes nouns and participles are used as adjectives. (See p. 391 on participles.)

noun used as adjective

People are rediscovering the milk bottle.

present participle used as adjective       past participle used as adjective

Mrs. Simon had a swimming pool with a broken drain.

**Adverbs** add information to sentences by modifying or describing verbs, adjectives, or other adverbs (see p. 376). An adverb usually answers the question *How? When? Where? How often?* or *To what extent?*

> WITHOUT ADVERBS:  I will clean.
> The audience applauded.
> WITH ADVERBS:  I will clean very thoroughly tomorrow.
> The audience applauded loudly and enthusiastically.

## B.6 Expanding the Sentence with Phrases

A **phrase** is a group of related words that lacks a subject, a predicate, or both. A phrase cannot stand alone as a sentence. Phrases can appear at the beginning, middle, or end of a sentence.

WITHOUT PHRASES: I noticed the stain.
Sal researched the topic.
Manuela arose.

WITH PHRASES: Upon entering the room, I noticed the stain on the expensive carpet.
At the local aquarium, Sal researched the topic of shark attacks.
An amateur astronomer, Manuela arose in the middle of the night to observe the lunar eclipse but, after waiting ten minutes in the cold, gave up.

There are eight kinds of phrases: **noun; verb; prepositional;** three kinds of **verbal phrases (participial, gerund,** and **infinitive); appositive;** and **absolute.**

### Noun and Verb Phrases

A noun plus its modifiers is a **noun phrase** (*red shoes, the quiet house*). A main verb plus its helping verb is a **verb phrase** (*had been exploring, is sleeping*). (See p. 368 on helping verbs.)

### Prepositional Phrases

A **prepositional phrase** consists of a preposition (for example, *in, above, with, at, behind*), an object of the preposition (a noun or pronoun), and any modifiers of the object. (See p. 379 for a list of common prepositions.) A prepositional phrase functions like an adjective (modifying a noun or pronoun) or an adverb (modifying a verb, adjective, or adverb). You can use prepositional phrases to tell more about people, places, objects, or actions. A prepositional phrase usually adds information about time, place, direction, manner, or degree.

#### As Adjectives

The woman with the briefcase is giving a presentation on meditation techniques.

Both of the telephones behind the partition were ringing.

## As Adverbs

The fire drill occurred <u>in the morning</u>.

I was curious <u>about the new coffee shop</u>.

My niece came <u>from Australia</u>.

<u>With horror</u>, the crowd watched the rhinoceros's tether stretch <u>to the breaking point</u>.

A prepositional phrase can function as part of the complete subject or as part of the complete predicate but should not be confused with the simple subject or simple predicate.

The red leather-bound <u>volumes</u> on the dusty shelf <u>were filled</u> with obscure facts.
(complete subject: simple subject = *volumes*, prepositional phrase = *on the dusty shelf*; complete predicate: simple predicate = *were filled*, prepositional phrase = *with obscure facts*)

Pat <u>ducked</u> quickly behind the potted fern.
(complete predicate: simple predicate = *ducked*, prepositional phrase = *behind the potted fern*)

## Verbal Phrases

A **verbal** is a verb form that cannot function as the main verb of a sentence. The three kinds of verbals are **participles, gerunds,** and **infinitives.** A **verbal phrase** consists of a verbal and its modifiers.

## Participles and Participial Phrases

All verbs have two participles: present and past. The **present participle** is formed by adding *-ing* to the infinitive form (*walking, riding, being*). The **past participle** of regular verbs is formed by adding *-d* or *-ed* to the infinitive form (*walked, baked*). The past participle of irregular verbs has no set pattern (*ridden, been*). (See p. 369 for a list of common irregular verbs and their past participles.) Both the present participle and the past participle can function as adjectives modifying nouns and pronouns.

<u>Irritated</u>, Martha circled the <u>confusing</u> traffic rotary once again.
(*Irritated* = past participle as adjective; *confusing* = present participle as adjective)

A **participial phrase** consists of a participle and any of its modifiers.

We listened for Isabella <u>climbing</u> the rickety stairs.
(participial phrase; *climbing* = participle)

┌──────── participial phrase ────────┐
│ participle │
**Disillusioned** with the whole system, Kay sat down to think.

┌──────── participial phrase ────────┐
│ participle │
The singer, **having caught** a bad cold, canceled his performance.

## Gerunds and Gerund Phrases

A **gerund** is the present participle (the *-ing* form) of the verb used as a noun.

> **Shoveling** is good exercise.

> Rex enjoyed **gardening**.

A **gerund phrase** consists of a gerund and its modifiers. A gerund phrase, like a gerund, is used as a noun and can therefore function in sentence as a subject, a direct or indirect object, an object of a preposition, a subject complement, or an appositive.

┌──── gerund phrase ────┐
**Knitting** the sweater took longer than Alice anticipated. [Subject.]

┌──────── gerund phrase ────────┐
The director considered **making** another monster movie. [Direct object.]

┌──── gerund phrase ────┐
She gave **running** three miles daily credit for her health. [Indirect object.]

┌─ gerund phrase ─┐
Before **learning** Greek, Omar spoke only English. [Object of the preposition.]

┌──────── gerund phrase ────────┐
Her business is **designing** collapsible furniture. [Subject complement.]

┌──────── gerund phrase ────────┐
Wayne's trick, **memorizing** license plates, has come in handy. [Appositive.]

## Infinitives and Infinitive Phrases

The **infinitive** is the base form of the verb as it appears in the dictionary preceded by the word "to." An **infinitive phrase** consists of the word *to* plus the infinitive and any modifiers. An infinitive phrase can function as a noun, an adjective, or an adverb. When it is used as a noun, an infinitive phrase can be a subject, object, complement, or appositive.

┌──── infinitive phrase ────┐
**To love** one's enemies is a noble goal. [Noun used as subject.]

┌infinitive phrase┐
The season to plant bulbs is the fall. [Adjective modifying *season*.]

┌──────── infinitive phrase ────────┐
The chess club met to practice for the state championship. [Adverb modifying *met*.]

Sometimes the *to* in an infinitive phrase is not written.

Frank helped us learn the dance. [The *to* before *learn* is understood.]

NOTE: Do not confuse infinitive phrases with prepositional phrases beginning with the preposition *to*. In an infinitive phrase, *to* is followed by a verb; in a prepositional phrase, *to* is followed by a noun or pronoun.

## Appositive Phrases

An **appositive** is a noun that explains, restates, or adds new information about another noun. An **appositive phrase** consists of an appositive and its modifiers. (See p. 455 for punctuation of appositive phrases.)

┌─ appositive ─┐
Claude Monet completed the painting *Water Lilies* around 1903. [Adds information about the noun *painting*.]

┌──────── appositive phrase ────────┐
┌─ appositive ─┐
Francis, my neighbor with a large workshop, lent me a wrench. [Adds information about the noun *Francis*.]

## Absolute Phrases

An **absolute phrase** consists of a noun or pronoun and any modifiers followed by a participle or a participial phrase (see p. 391). An absolute phrase modifies an entire sentence, not any particular word within the sentence. It can appear anywhere in a sentence and is set off from the rest of the sentence with a comma or commas. There may be more than one absolute phrase in a sentence.

┌── absolute phrase ──┐
The winter being over, the geese returned.

┌──────── absolute phrase ────────┐
Senator Arden began his speech, his voice rising to be heard over the loud applause.

┌──── absolute phrase ────┐
A vacancy having occurred, the cottage owner called the first name on the rental waiting list.

Expand each of the following sentences by adding adjectives, adverbs, and/or phrases (prepositional, verbal, appositive, or absolute).

EXAMPLE:   The professor lectured.

EXPANDED:   *Being an expert on animal behavior, the professor lectured about animal-intelligence studies.*

1. Randall will graduate. _____

   _____

2. The race began. _____

   _____

3. The Smiths are remodeling. _____

   _____

4. Hillary walked alone. _____

   _____

5. Manuel repairs appliances. _____

   _____

6. The motorcycle was loud. _____

   _____

7. My term paper is due Tuesday. _____

   _____

8. I opened my umbrella. _____

   _____

9. Austin built a garage. _____

   _____

10. Lucas climbs mountains. _____

   _____

## B.7 Expanding the Sentence with Clauses

A **clause** is a group of words that contains a subject and a predicate. A clause is either **independent** (also called **main**) or **dependent** (also called **subordinate**).

An **independent clause** can stand alone as a grammatically complete sentence.

```
      independent clause        independent clause
       subject   predicate     subject   predicate
The rooster crowed, and I awoke.
```

```
      independent clause              independent clause
        subject   predicate            subject      predicate
The scientist worried. The experiment might fail.
```

```
       independent clause              independent clause
     subject predicate               subject      predicate
He bandaged his ankle. It had been sprained.
```

A **dependent clause** has a subject and a predicate, but it cannot stand alone as a grammatically complete sentence because it does not express a complete thought. Most dependent clauses begin with either a **subordinating conjunction** or a **relative pronoun**. These words connect the dependent clause to an independent clause.

### *Common Subordinating Conjunctions*

| | | |
|---|---|---|
| after | inasmuch as | that |
| although | in case that | though |
| as | in order that | unless |
| as if | insofar as | until |
| as far as | in that | when |
| as soon as | now that | whenever |
| as though | once | where |
| because | provided that | wherever |
| before | rather than | whether |
| even if | since | while |
| even though | so that | why |
| how | supposing that | |
| if | than | |

### *Relative Pronouns*

| | |
|---|---|
| that | which |
| what | who (whose, whom) |
| whatever | whoever (whomever) |

```
subordinating
conjunction   subject     predicate
because the rooster crowed
```

```
subordinating
conjunction   subject     predicate
that the experiment might fail
```

relative pronoun
(subject)       predicate

which had been sprained

These clauses do not express complete thoughts and therefore cannot stand alone as sentences. When joined to independent clauses, however, dependent clauses function as adjectives, adverbs, and nouns and are known as **adjective** (or **relative**) **clauses, adverb clauses,** and **noun clauses.** Noun clauses can function as subjects, objects, or complements.

### Adjective Clause

—— dependent clause ——

He bandaged his ankle, which had been sprained. [Modifies *ankle*.]

### Adverb Clause

—— dependent clause ——

Because the rooster crowed, I awoke. [Modifies *awoke*.]

### Noun Clause

—— dependent clause ——

The scientist worried that the experiment might fail. [Direct object of *worried*.]

Sometimes the relative pronoun or subordinating conjunction is implied or understood rather than stated. Also, a dependent clause may contain an implied predicate. When a dependent clause is missing an element that can clearly be supplied from the context of the sentence, it is called an **elliptical clause.**

—— elliptical clause ——

The circus is more entertaining than television [is]. [*Is* is the understood predicate in the elliptical dependent clause.]

—— elliptical clause ——

Canadian history is among the subjects [that] the book discusses. [*That* is the understood relative pronoun in the elliptical dependent clause.]

Relative pronouns are generally the subject or object in their clauses. *Who* and *whoever* change to *whom* and *whomever* when they function as objects. (See p. 428.)

## B.8 Basic Sentence Classifications

Depending on its structure, a sentence can be classified as one of four basic types: **simple, compound, complex,** or **compound-complex.**

## Simple Sentences

A **simple sentence** has one independent (main) clause and no dependent (subordinate) clauses. (See p. 394.) A simple sentence contains at least one subject and one predicate. It may have a compound subject, a compound predicate, and various phrases, but it has only one clause.

subject   predicate
Sap rises.

subject   ———— compound predicate ————
In the spring the sap rises in the maple trees and is boiled to make a thick, delicious syrup.

## Compound Sentences

A **compound sentence** has at least two independent clauses and no dependent clauses. (See p. 395.) The two independent clauses are usually joined with a comma and a coordinating conjunction (*and, but, nor, or, for, so,* or *yet*). Sometimes the two clauses are joined with a semicolon and no coordinating conjunction or with a semicolon and a conjunctive adverb like *nonetheless* or *still* followed by a comma. (See p. 377 on conjunctive adverbs and p. 407 on punctuation.)

———————————— independent clause ————————————
Reading a novel by Henry James is not like reading a thriller, but with patience the rewards are greater.

independent clause

———— independent clause ————    —— independent clause ——
I set out to explore the North River near home; I ended up at Charlie's Clam Bar.

## Complex Sentences

A **complex sentence** has one independent clause and one or more dependent clauses. (See p. 394.) The clauses are joined by subordinating conjunctions or relative pronouns. (See p. 395.)

———— independent clause ————    —— dependent clause ——
We tried to find topics to talk about while we waited for the bus.

———— independent clause ————   — dependent clause —   — dependent clause —
The butcher greeted me warmly as I entered the shop because I hadn't seen him in a long time.

## Compound-Complex Sentences

A **compound-complex sentence** contains two or more independent clauses and one or more dependent clauses. (See p. 394.)

┌─────── dependent clause ───────┐┌─────── independent clause ───────┐  ┌──

If students work part-time, they must plan their studies carefully and they

must limit their social lives.
└─────── independent clause ───────┘

┌─ independent clause ─┐  ┌─────── independent clause ───────┐┌─ independent clause ─

It was mid-March and the pond had begun to melt; I walked toward it

expectantly as I wondered if I could go skating one last time.
└─────────┴─────────┘└─────────┴─────────┘
        dependent clause          dependent clause

**EXERCISE** ▶ 9

Combine each of the following pairs of sentences into a single sentence by forming independent and/or dependent clauses. You may need to add, change, or delete words.

EXAMPLE:  a. The levy broke.
b. The flood waters rose rapidly.

COMBINED:  *After the levy broke, the flood waters rose rapidly.*

1. a. Margot is a picky eater.
b. Ivan, Margot's cousin, will eat anything.

_____

_____

2. a. Joe broke his wrist rollerblading.
b. Joe started to wear protective gear.

_____

_____

3. a. Rick waited in line at the Department of Motor Vehicles.
b. At the same time, Jean waited in line at the bank.

_____

_____

4. a. Beer is high in calories.
b. Some beer companies now make low-calorie beer.

_____

_____

5. a. Keith says he is politically active.
b. Keith is not registered to vote.

_____

_____

6. a. Miguel sprained his ankle.
   b. His friends drove him to the hospital.

   _____

   _____


7. a. The boat sped by.
   b. The Coast Guard was in hot pursuit.

   _____

   _____


8. a. The weather report predicted rain.
   b. I brought my umbrella.

   _____

   _____


9. a. Graffiti had been spray-painted on the subway wall.
   b. Maintenance workers were scrubbing it off.

   _____

   _____


10. a. Shoppers were crowding around a display table.
    b. Everything on the table was reduced by 50 percent.

    _____

    _____

# Avoiding Sentence Errors

## C.1 Sentence Fragments

A complete sentence contains at least one subject and one verb and expresses a complete thought. It begins with a capital letter and ends with a period, question mark, or exclamation point. (See p. 451.) A **sentence fragment** is an incomplete sentence because either it lacks a subject, a verb, or both or it is a dependent (subordinate) clause unattached to a complete sentence. In either case, it does not express a complete thought. Occasionally, a writer may knowingly use a fragment for effect or emphasis. This is known as an **intentional fragment.** However, it is best to avoid fragments in your writing; instead, use complete sentences.

| | |
|---|---|
| FRAGMENT: | Walked across campus this afternoon. [This group of words lacks a subject.] |
| COMPLETE SENTENCE: | Pete walked across campus this afternoon. |
| FRAGMENT: | The car next to the fence. [This group of words lacks a verb.] |
| COMPLETE SENTENCE: | The car next to the fence stalled. |
| FRAGMENT: | Alert and ready. [This group of words lacks a subject and a verb.] |
| COMPLETE SENTENCE: | Juan appeared alert and ready. |
| FRAGMENT: | While I was waiting in line. [This group of words is a subordinate clause unattached to a complete sentence.] |
| COMPLETE SENTENCE: | While I was waiting in line, I studied the faces of people walking by. |

### How to Spot Fragments

To find sentence fragments in your writing, use the following questions to evaluate each group of words.

**1. Does the group of words have a verb?** Be sure that the verb is a complete sentence verb and not a verbal or part of a verbal phrase (see p. 391).

```
        ┌────── complete sentence ──────┐  ┌──── fragment ────┐
           sentence verb                       verbal
Doug swam laps every night. To win the prize.
```

```
        ┌── complete sentence ──┐  ┌──────── fragment ────────┐
           sentence verb                    verbal
She felt very sleepy. Wanting him to leave now.
```

```
        ┌── complete sentence ──┐  ┌────────── fragment ──────────┐
          sentence verb              verbal
My son is excited. Going to the fair tomorrow.
```

```
        ┌────── complete sentence ──────┐  ┌──── fragment ────┐
           sentence verb                       verbal
I am starting banjo lessons. Beginning next week.
```

Each of the underlined phrases needs to be either (1) rewritten as a complete sentence or (2) combined with a complete sentence.

REWRITTEN: Doug swam laps every night. He practiced to win the prize.

REWRITTEN: She felt very sleepy. She wanted him to leave now.

COMBINED: My son is excited because he is going to the fair tomorrow.

COMBINED: Beginning next week, I am starting banjo lessons.

To distinguish between a complete sentence verb and a verbal, keep in mind the following rule: a sentence verb can change tense to show differences in time—past, present, and future. A verbal cannot demonstrate these shifts in time. You can change the sentence *I have a lot of homework* to *I had a lot of homework* or *I will have a lot of homework,* but the verbal phrase *riding a horse* cannot be changed to show differences in time.

**2. Does the group of words have a subject?** After you have found the verb, look for the subject. The subject is a noun or pronoun that performs or receives the action of the sentence. (See p. 383.) To find the subject, ask *who* or *what* performs or receives the action of the verb.

```
           ┌ subject ┐┌ verb ┐
The corner bookstore opens at noon. [What opens? The bookstore opens.]
```

Notice, however, what happens when you ask *who* or *what* about the following fragments.

Will study math with a tutor. [*Who* will study? The question cannot be answered; no subject exists.]

And walked away quickly. [*Who* walked away? Again, the question cannot be answered because there is no subject.]

Every sentence must have a subject. Even if one sentence has a clear subject, the sentence that follows it must also have a subject, or else it is a fragment.

——————sentence——————    ——————fragment——————
subject    verb        verb

Peter slammed the door. And stormed out into the hall.

You know from the first sentence that it was Peter who stormed out, but the second group of words is nonetheless a fragment because it lacks a subject. Combining it with the first sentence would eliminate the problem.

COMBINED:   Peter slammed the door and stormed out into the hall.

Imperative sentences (sentences that command or suggest) have a subject that is usually not explicitly stated. They are not fragments.

Follow me. [The subject *you* is understood: (*You*) Follow me.]

## 3. Does the group of words begin with a subordinating conjunction (such as *after, although, as, because, however, since,* or *that*)? A group of words beginning with a subordinating conjunction is a fragment unless that group of words is attached to an independent clause. (See p. 394.)

FRAGMENT:           *subordinating conjunction*
                      While I was waiting for the train.

COMPLETE SENTENCE:   While I was waiting for the train, I saw Robert DeNiro.   *independent clause*

FRAGMENT:           *subordinating conjunction*
                      Although the politician campaigned feverishly.

COMPLETE SENTENCE:   Although the politician campaigned feverishly, the public supported her opponent.   *independent clause*

You can also correct a fragment that is a dependent clause by omitting the subordinating conjunction and making the clause into an independent clause, a complete sentence.

COMPLETE SENTENCE:   I was waiting for the train.
COMPLETE SENTENCE:   The politician campaigned feverishly.

## 4. Does the group of words begin with a relative pronoun (*that, what, whatever, which, who, whoever, whom, whomever, whose*)? A group of words beginning with a relative pronoun is a fragment unless it forms a question with a subject and a verb or is attached to an independent clause.

FRAGMENT:           *relative pronoun*
                      Who lost these keys.

COMPLETE SENTENCE:   *relative pronoun (subject) verb     question mark*
                      Who lost these keys? [Question with subject and verb.]

COMPLETE SENTENCE: *independent clause* — *relative pronoun* — *dependent clause*
I am looking for the person who lost these keys.
[Attached to independent clause.]

FRAGMENT: *relative pronoun*
That we discussed after class.

COMPLETE SENTENCE: *independent clause* — *relative pronoun* — *dependent clause*
This assignment is the one that we discussed after class.
[Attached to independent clause.]

Also check groups of words beginning with *how, when, where,* and *why.* If a clause beginning with one of these words neither asks a question nor is attached to an independent clause, then the word group is a fragment.

FRAGMENT: *subordinating word*
Where the party will be held.

COMPLETE SENTENCE: *verb* *subject* *question mark*
Where will the party be held? [Question with subject and verb.]

COMPLETE SENTENCE: *independent clause* — *dependent clause*
We peeked into the room where the party will be held.
[Attached to independent clause.]

## How to Correct Fragments

**1. Attach the fragment to a complete sentence or an independent clause.** (See p. 394.)

FRAGMENT: *dependent clause*
While my toddler was bathing. She began to eat the soap.

COMPLETE SENTENCE: *dependent clause* — *independent clause*
While my toddler was bathing, she began to eat the soap.

FRAGMENT: *no sentence verb*
Students who missed five classes. They are ineligible for the final exam.

COMPLETE SENTENCE: *subject* *sentence verb*
Students who missed five classes are ineligible for the final exam.

FRAGMENT: *no subject*
Marge sketched portraits all morning. And read art history all afternoon.

subject ⌐————compound sentence verb————⌐

COMPLETE SENTENCE: Marge sketched portraits all morning and read art history all afternoon.

## 2. Remove the subordinating conjunction or relative pronoun and make sure that the remaining group of words has a subject and a sentence verb—that is, that it can stand alone as a complete sentence.

FRAGMENT: I did not finish the book. Because its tedious style bored me.

⌐————independent clause————⌐
subject   sentence verb

COMPLETE SENTENCE: I did not finish the book. Its tedious style bored me.

## 3. Add the missing subject or verb or both.

FRAGMENT: The baby knocked over her glass of milk. And then started wailing.

subject added

COMPLETE SENTENCE: The baby knocked over her glass of milk. Then she started wailing.

FRAGMENT: The Winter Olympics were held in Norway. Snowing every day.

subject sentence verb
added        added

COMPLETE SENTENCE: The Winter Olympics were held in Norway. It snowed every day.

FRAGMENT: I had to leave the car in the driveway. The snow against the garage door.

COMPLETE SENTENCE: I had to leave the car in the driveway. The snow had drifted against the garage door.

sentence verb added

---

**EXERCISE 10**

Make each of the following sentence fragments a complete sentence by combining it with an independent clause, removing the subordinating conjunction or relative pronoun, or adding the missing subject or verb.

EXAMPLE: Many environmentalists are concerned about the spotted owl. Which is almost extinct.

COMPLETE SENTENCE: Many environmentalists are concerned about the spotted owl, which is almost extinct.

1. Renting a tape of the movie *Citizen Kane*. _____

_____

2. Spices that had been imported from India. _____

_____

3. The police officer walked to Jerome's van. To give him a ticket.

_____

4. My English professor, with the cup of tea he brought to each class.

_____

_____

5. After the table was refinished. _____

_____

6. Roberto memorized his lines. For the performance tomorrow night.

_____

7. A tricycle with big wheels, painted red. _____

_____

8. On the shelf, an antique crock used for storing lard. _____

_____

9. Because I always wanted to learn to speak Spanish. _____

_____

10. Looking for the lost keys. I was late for class. _____

_____

## C.2 Run-on Sentences and Comma Splices

Independent clauses contain both a subject and a predicate. When two independent clauses are joined in one sentence, they must be separated by a comma and a coordinating conjunction or by a semicolon. Failure to properly separate independent clauses creates the errors known as **run-on sentences** and **comma splices**.

A **run-on sentence** (or **fused sentence**) contains two independent clauses that are not separated by any punctuation or a coordinating conjunction (*and, but, nor, or, for, so, yet*).

A **comma splice** (or comma fault) contains two independent clauses joined only by a comma (the coordinating conjunction is missing). A comma by itself cannot join two independent clauses. (See p. 394.)

### How to Spot Run-on Sentences and Comma Splices

**1. You can often spot run-on sentences by reading them aloud.** Listen for a pause or a change in your voice. That may signal that you are moving from the first clause to the second. Read the following run-on sentences aloud, and see if you can hear where the two clauses in each should be separated.

RUN-ON:   We watched the football game then we ordered pizza.

CORRECT:   We watched the football game. Then we ordered pizza.

RUN-ON:   My throat feels sore I hope I am not catching a cold.

CORRECT:   My throat feels sore; I hope I am not catching a cold.

**2. You can spot a comma splice by looking carefully at your use and placement of commas.** If you see a comma between two independent clauses but no coordinating conjunction after the comma, then you have probably spotted a comma splice.

COMMA SPLICE:   The average person watches fifteen hours of television a week, my parents allow my brother only two hours a week.

CORRECT:   The average person watches fifteen hours of television a

coordinating conjunction

week, but my parents allow my brother only two hours a week.

### How to Correct Run-on Sentences and Comma Splices

There are four ways to correct a run-on sentence or a comma splice. Not every run-on sentence or comma splice can be corrected in the same way. The method you choose will depend on the meaning of the clauses.

**1. Create two separate sentences.** End the first independent clause with a period. Begin the next with a capital letter.

RUN-ON:   We went for a walk in the woods we saw the leaves turning red and orange.

CORRECT:   We went for a walk in the woods. We saw the leaves turning red and orange.

**2. Use a semicolon.** Use a semicolon when the thoughts expressed in the independent clauses are closely related and you want to emphasize that relationship. (The word immediately following the semicolon does not begin with a capital letter unless it is a proper noun.)

RUN-ON:  It is unlikely that school taxes will increase this year citizens have expressed their opposition.

CORRECT:  It is unlikely that school taxes will increase this year; citizens have expressed their opposition.

NOTE: An independent clause containing a conjunctive adverb (such as *finally, however, meanwhile, otherwise,* or *therefore*) must be separated from another independent clause with a period or a semicolon. (See p. 377 for a list of conjunctive adverbs.) In most cases, the conjunctive adverb itself is set off with a comma or pair of commas.

COMMA SPLICE:  The road crew was repairing potholes, therefore traffic was snarled.

CORRECT:  The road crew was repairing potholes; therefore, traffic was snarled.

**3. Insert a comma and a coordinating conjunction** (*and, but, for, nor, or, so, yet*).

RUN-ON:  Americans are changing their eating habits they still eat too much red meat.

                                coordinating conjunction

CORRECT:  Americans are changing their eating habits, but they still eat too much red meat.

**4. Make one clause subordinate to the other.** This method is especially effective when the idea expressed in one of the clauses is more important than the idea in the other clause. By adding a subordinating conjunction (such as *after, although, because,* or *until*), you can link a dependent clause to an independent clause. (See p. 408 for a list of subordinating conjunctions.) Be sure to use a subordinating conjunction that explains the relationship between the dependent clause and the independent clause to which it is joined.

COMMA SPLICE:  I left the house, I shut off all the lights.

          —— dependent clause ——
          subordinating conjunction       independent clause

CORRECT:  Before I left the house, I shut off all the lights.

The subordinating conjunction *before* in the above sentence indicates the sequence in which the two actions were performed. In addition to time, subordinating conjunctions can indicate place, time, cause or effect, condition or circumstance, contrast, or manner.

| Meaning | Subordinating Conjunction | Example |
|---|---|---|
| place | where, wherever | I will go <u>wherever</u> you go. |
| time | after, before, when, until, once, while | <u>After</u> I left work, I went to the mall. |
| cause or effect | because, since, so that, that, as | I missed the bus <u>because</u> I overslept. |
| condition or circumstance | if, unless, as long as, in case, whenever, once, provided that | <u>If</u> I get an A on the paper, I'll be happy. |
| contrast | although, even though, even if, whereas, while | <u>Even though</u> I lost my job, I have to make my car payment. |
| manner | as, as if, as though | Marge acted <u>as if</u> she were angry. |

The dependent clause can be placed *before* or *after* the independent clause. If it is placed before the independent clause, put a comma at the end of it. Usually no comma is needed when the independent clause comes first.

COMMA SPLICE: I studied psychology, I was thinking about some of Freud's findings.

CORRECT:     ┌───── dependent clause ─────┐┌───── independent clause ─────┐
When I studied psychology, I was thinking about some of Freud's findings.

CORRECT:     ┌───────── independent clause ─────────┐┌
I was thinking about some of Freud's findings when I studied psychology.
    └── dependent clause ──┘

You may add a dependent clause to a sentence that has more than one independent clause. (See p. 397.)

RUN-ON: We toured the hospital we met with its chief administrator she invited us to lunch.

CORRECT: ┌──── dependent clause ────┐┌──── independent clause ────┐
After we toured the hospital, we met with its chief administrator and she invited us to lunch.
                   └── independent clause ──┘

EXERCISE ▶ 11  In the blank before each of the following word groups, identify if it is a run-on sentence (RO), a comma splice (CS), or a correct sentence (C). Revise the word groups that contain errors.

EXAMPLE:  _____CS_____ ~~T~~ When t The children chased the ball into the street, cars screeched to a halt.

_____ 1. Inez packed for the camping trip she remembered everything except insect repellent.

_____ 2. A limousine drove through our neighborhood, everybody wondered who was in it.

_____ 3. The defendant pleaded not guilty the judge ordered him to pay the parking ticket.

_____ 4. Before a big game, Louis, who is a quarterback, eats a lot of pasta and bread he says it gives him energy.

_____ 5. Four of my best friends from high school have decided to go to law school, I have decided to become a legal secretary.

_____ 6. Felicia did not know what to buy her parents for their anniversary, so she went to a lot of stores she finally decided to buy them a camera.

_____ 7. After living in a dorm room for three years, Jason found an apartment the rent was very high, so he had to get a job to pay for it.

_____ 8. The cherry tree had to be cut down, it stood right where the new addition was going to be built.

_____ 9. Amanda worked every night for a month on the needlepoint pillow that she was making for her grandmother.

_____ 10. Driving around in the dark, we finally realized we were lost, Dwight went into a convenience store to ask for directions.

## C.3 Uses of Verb Tenses

The **tense** of a verb expresses the time. It conveys whether an action, process, or occurrence takes place in the present, past, or future. There are twelve tenses in English, and each is used to express a particular time. (See p. 370 for information about how to form each tense.)

The **simple present tense** expresses actions that are occurring at the time of the writing or that occur regularly. The **simple past tense** is used for actions that have already occurred. The **simple future tense** is used for actions that will occur in the future.

SIMPLE PRESENT: The chef <u>cooks</u> a huge meal.

SIMPLE PAST: The chef <u>cooked</u> a huge meal.

SIMPLE FUTURE: The chef <u>will cook</u> a huge meal.

The **present perfect tense** is used for actions that began in the past and are still occurring in the present or are finished by the time of the writing. The **past perfect tense** expresses actions that were completed before other past actions. The **future perfect tense** is used for actions that will be completed in the future.

PRESENT PERFECT: The chef <u>has cooked</u> a huge meal every night this week.

PAST PERFECT: The chef <u>had cooked</u> a huge meal before the guests canceled their reservation.

FUTURE PERFECT: The chef <u>will have cooked</u> a huge meal by the time we arrive.

The six progressive tenses are used for continuing actions or actions in progress. The **present progressive tense** is used for actions that are in progress in the present. The **past progressive tense** expresses past continuing actions. The **future progressive tense** is used for continuing actions that will occur in the future. The **present perfect progressive, past perfect progressive,** and **future perfect progressive tenses** are used for continuing actions that are, were, or will be completed by a certain time.

PRESENT PROGRESSIVE: The chef <u>is cooking</u> a huge meal this evening.

PAST PROGRESSIVE: The chef <u>was cooking</u> a huge meal when she ran out of butter.

FUTURE PROGRESSIVE: The chef <u>will be cooking</u> a huge meal all day tomorrow.

PRESENT PERFECT PROGRESSIVE: The chef <u>has been cooking</u> a huge meal since this morning.

PAST PERFECT PROGRESSIVE: The chef <u>had been cooking</u> a huge meal before the electricity went out.

FUTURE PERFECT PROGRESSIVE: The chef <u>will have been cooking</u> a huge meal for eight hours when the guests arrive.

Writing all forms of a verb for all tenses and all persons (first, second, and third, singular and plural) is called **conjugating** the verb. Irregular verbs have an irregularly formed past tense and past participle (used in the past tense and the perfect tenses). (See p. 369 for a list of the forms of common irregular verbs.) Here is the complete conjugation for the regular verb *walk*.

## Conjugation of the Regular Verb *Walk*

|  | *Singular* | *Plural* |
|---|---|---|
| Simple present tense | I walk<br>you walk<br>he/she/it walks | we walk<br>you walk<br>they walk |
| Simple past tense | I walked<br>you walked<br>he/she/it walked | we walked<br>you walked<br>they walked |
| Simple future tense | I will (shall) walk<br>you will walk<br>he/she/it will walk | we will (shall) walk<br>you will walk<br>they will walk |
| Present perfect tense | I have walked<br>you have walked<br>he/she/it has walked | we have walked<br>you have walked<br>they have walked |
| Past perfect tense | I had walked<br>you had walked<br>he/she/it had walked | we had walked<br>you had walked<br>they had walked |
| Future perfect tense | I will (shall) have walked<br>you will have walked<br>he/she/it will have walked | we will (shall) have walked<br>you will have walked<br>they will have walked |
| Present progressive tense | I am walking<br>you are walking<br>he/she/it is walking | we are walking<br>you are walking<br>they are walking |
| Past progressive tense | I was walking<br>you were walking<br>he/she/it was walking | we were walking<br>you were walking<br>they were walking |
| Future progressive tense | I will be walking<br>you will be walking<br>he/she/it will be walking | we will be walking<br>you will be walking<br>they will be walking |

| | *Singular* | *Plural* |
|---|---|---|
| Present perfect progressive tense | I have been walking<br>you have been walking<br>he/she/it has been walking | we have been walking<br>you have been walking<br>they have been walking |
| Past perfect progressive tense | I had been walking<br>you had been walking<br>he/she/it had been walking | we had been walking<br>you had been walking<br>they had been walking |
| Future perfect progressive tense | I will have been walking<br>you will have been walking<br>he/she/it will have been walking | we will have been walking<br>you will have been walking<br>they will have been walking |

Following are the simple present and simple past tenses for the irregular verbs *have*, *be*, and *do*, which are commonly used as helping verbs. (See p. 368.)

## Irregular Verbs *Have, Be,* and *Do*

| | *Have* | *Be* | *Do* |
|---|---|---|---|
| Simple present tense | I have<br>you have<br>he/she/it has<br>we/you/they have | I am<br>you are<br>he/she/it is<br>we/you/they are | I do<br>you do<br>he/she/it does<br>we/you/they do |
| Simple past tense | I had<br>you had<br>he/she/it had<br>we/you/they had | I was<br>you were<br>he/she/it was<br>we/you/they were | I did<br>you did<br>he/she/it did<br>we/you/they did |

## Special Uses of the Simple Present Tense

Besides expressing actions that are occurring at the time of the writing, the simple present tense has several special uses.

HABITUAL OR RECURRING ACTION:  She <u>works</u> at the store every day.

GENERAL TRUTH:  The sun <u>rises</u> in the east.

| DISCUSSION OF LITERATURE: | Gatsby <u>stands</u> on the dock and <u>gazes</u> in Daisy's direction. |
|---|---|
| THE FUTURE: | He <u>leaves</u> for Rome on the 7:30 plane. |

## Emphasis, Negatives, and Questions

The simple present and the simple past tenses of the verb *do* are used with main verbs to provide emphasis, to form negative constructions with the adverb *not,* and to ask questions.

| SIMPLE PRESENT: | Malcolm <u>does</u> <u>want</u> to go to the movies. |
|---|---|
| SIMPLE PRESENT: | He <u>does</u> <u>not</u> <u>want</u> to stay home alone. |
| SIMPLE PRESENT: | <u>Do</u> you <u>want</u> to go with him? |
| SIMPLE PAST: | Judy <u>did</u> <u>paint</u> the house herself. |
| SIMPLE PAST: | She <u>did</u> <u>not</u> <u>have</u> the money to pay professionals. |
| SIMPLE PAST: | <u>Did</u> she <u>do</u> a good job? |

The modal verbs *can, could, may, might, must, shall, should, will,* and *would* are also used to add emphasis and shades of meaning to verbs. Modals are used only as helping verbs, never alone, and do not change form to indicate tense. Added to a main verb, they are used in the following situations, among others.

| CONDITION: | We <u>can</u> play tennis if she gets here on time. |
|---|---|
| PERMISSION: | You <u>may</u> have one more piece of candy. |
| POSSIBILITY: | They <u>might</u> call us from the airport. |
| OBLIGATION: | I <u>must</u> visit my mother tomorrow. |

## Common Mistakes to Avoid with Verb Tense

Check your writing carefully to make sure you have avoided these common mistakes with verb tenses.

**1. Make sure the endings *-d* and *-ed* (for past tenses) and *-s* and *-es* (for third-person singular, simple present tense) are on all verbs that require them.**

| INCORRECT: | I have <u>walk</u> three miles since I left home. |
|---|---|
| CORRECT: | I <u>have walked</u> three miles since I left home. |

**2. Use irregular verbs correctly.** (See p. 369.)

| INCORRECT: | I will <u>lay</u> down for a nap. |
|---|---|
| CORRECT: | I will <u>lie</u> down for a nap. |

**3. Use helping verbs where they are necessary to express the correct time.**

> INCORRECT: I go to class tomorrow.
> CORRECT: I will go to class tomorrow.

**4. Avoid colloquial language or dialect in writing.** Colloquial language is casual, everyday language often used in conversation. Dialect is the language pattern of a region or an ethnic group.

> INCORRECT: I didn't get the point of that poem.
> CORRECT: I didn't understand the point of that poem.

> INCORRECT: The train be gone.
> CORRECT: The train has gone.

Other common mistakes with verbs are failing to make the verb agree with the subject (see p. 417) and using inconsistent or shifting tenses (see p. 434).

**EXERCISE 12** ▶ Correct any of the following sentences with an error in verb form or verb tense. If a sentence contains no errors, write *Correct* beside it.

> *are*
> EXAMPLE: You ~~is~~ next in line.

1. Molly called and ask Jen if she wanted a ride to the basketball game.
2. Eric went to a party last week and meets a girl he knew in high school.
3. I cook spaghetti every Wednesday, and my family always enjoys it.
4. A package come in yesterday's mail for my roommate.
5. Louisa wears a beautiful red dress to her sister's wedding last week.
6. Marni answered a letter she receive from her boyfriend.
7. Rob waited until he was introduced, and then he run on stage.
8. The audience laughed loudly at the comedian's jokes and applauds spontaneously at the funniest ones.
9. The group had ordered buffalo-style chicken wings, and it was not disappointed when the meal arrived.
10. Julie spends the afternoon stringing beads when it rained.

## C.4 Active and Passive Voices

When a verb is in the active voice, the subject performs the action of the verb. The direct object receives the action. (See p. 386.) The active voice expresses action in a lively, vivid, energetic way.

> subject active-voice
> (actor)    verb      direct object
> Carlos   dropped   his  calculator.

subject        active-voice
(actor)          verb    direct object

The supermarket gave samples of prepared food.

When a verb is in the passive voice, the subject is the receiver of the action of the verb. The passive voice is formed by using an appropriate form of the verb *be* plus the past participle of the main verb. The actor is often expressed in a prepositional phrase introduced by the preposition *by*. Thus the passive voice tends to be wordier and to express action in a more indirect way than the active voice.

subject        passive-voice          object of preposition
(receiver)          verb                    (actor)

The calculator was dropped by Carlos.

subject                      passive-voice          object of preposition
(receiver)                        verb                    (actor)

Samples of prepared food were given by the supermarket.

Sometimes the actor is not expressed in a passive-voice sentence.

ACTIVE:  I did not remove the Halloween decorations until Christmas.
PASSIVE:  The Halloween decorations were not removed until Christmas.

As a general rule, you should use the active voice because it is more effective, simpler, and more direct than the passive. In two situations, however, the passive may be preferable: (1) if you do not know who performs the actions, and (2) if the object of the action is more important than the actor.

PASSIVE:  The handle of the dagger had been wiped clean of fingerprints. [It is not known who wiped the dagger.]

PASSIVE:  The poem "Richard Corey" by Edwin Arlington Robinson was discussed in class. [The poem is more important than who discussed the poem.]

**EXERCISE** ▶ **13**

Revise each of the following sentences by changing the verb from passive voice to active voice.

EXAMPLE:  The patient was operated on by an experienced surgeon.

REVISED:  *An experienced surgeon operated on the patient.*

1. The coin collection was inherited by Roderick from his grandfather.

_____

_____

2. A large bunch of roses was cut by my sister. _____

_____

3. The president's advisers were relied on by the president. _____

_____

4. Ice cream was served to the children at the birthday party by one of

the adults. _____

_____

5. Tools were packed in a box by Terry. _____

_____

6. Scuba-diving equipment was handed to the students by the licensed

instructor. _____

_____

7. Alaska was visited by my parents last fall. _____

_____

8. A large rock bass was caught by James. _____

_____

9. The newspaper was delivered by a twelve-year-old girl on her bike.

_____

_____

10. Trash was collected and disposed of by the picnickers before they

left for home. _____

_____

## C.5 Subjective Mood

The **mood** of a verb conveys the writer's attitude toward the expressed thought. There are three moods in English. The **indicative mood** is used to make ordinary statements of fact and to ask questions. The **imperative mood** is used to give commands or make suggestions. The **subjunctive mood** is used to express wishes, requirements, recommendations, and statements contrary to fact. (See p. 371.)

INDICATIVE: Laurel lies in the sun every afternoon.

IMPERATIVE: Lie down and rest!

SUBJUNCTIVE: It is urgent that she lie down and rest.

The subjunctive mood requires some special attention because it uses verb tenses in unusual ways. Verbs in the subjunctive mood can be in the present, past, or perfect tense.

PRESENT:  His mother recommended that he apply for the job.
          If truth be told, Jacob is luckier than he knows.

PAST:     If she walked faster, she could get there on time.
          She ran as if she were five years old again.

PERFECT:  If I had known his name, I would have said hello.

Here are several rules for using the subjunctive correctly:

**1. For requirements and recommendations, use the present subjunctive (the infinitive) for all verbs, including *be*.**

Mr. Kenefick requires that his students be drilled in safety procedures.

The dentist recommended that she brush her teeth three times a day.

**2. For present conditions contrary to fact and for present wishes, use the past subjunctive (the simple past tense) for all verbs; use *were* for the verb *be* for all subjects.**

If Andrew were not so stubborn, he would admit that Adele is right.

I wish that the workday began later.

**3. For past conditions contrary to fact and for past wishes, use the perfect subjunctive (*had* plus the past participle) for all verbs, including *be*.**

If Monty had been at home, he would have answered the phone when you called.

When Peter told me what an exciting time he had abroad last summer, I wished I had gone with him.

# C.6 Subject-Verb Agreement

A subject and its verb must agree (be consistent) in person (first, second, third) and in number (singular, plural). (See p. 426 on person of pronouns and p. 371 on verb forms in all persons and numbers.) The most common problems with subject-verb agreement occur with third-person present-tense verbs, which are formed for most verbs by adding -s or -es to the infinitive. (See pp. 369–370 for the present- and past-tense forms for certain irregular verbs.)

## Agreement Rules

**1. Singular subjects.** For a singular subject (one person, place, thing, or idea), use a singular form of the verb: *I dance, he dances, Sally dances, the dog dances; I am, you are, Sally is.*

**2. Plural subjects.** For a plural subject (two or more persons, places, things, or ideas), use the plural form of the verb: *we dance, they dance, the girls dance, the dogs dance; we are, they are, children are.*

## Common Mistakes to Avoid

**1. Third-person singular.** Do not omit the *-s* or *-es* for a present-tense verb used with the pronoun *he, she,* or *it* or any singular noun.

INCORRECT:   She watch the movie.
CORRECT:     She watches the movie.

INCORRECT:   Professor Simmons pace while he lectures.
CORRECT:     Professor Simmons paces while he lectures.

**2. Compound subjects.** Two or more subjects joined by the coordinating conjunction *and* require a plural verb, even if one or both of the subjects are singular.

INCORRECT:   Anita and Mark plays cards.
CORRECT:     Anita and Mark play cards.

When both of the subjects refer to the same person or thing, however, use a singular verb.

The President and Chairman of the Board is in favor of more aggressive marketing.

When a compound subject is joined by the conjunction *or* or *nor* or the correlative conjunctions *either/or, neither/nor, both/and, not/but,* or *not only/but also,* the verb should agree in number with the subject nearer to it.

Neither the books nor the article was helpful to my research.

Sarah or the boys are coming tomorrow.

**3. Verbs before subjects.** When a verb comes before a subject, as in sentences beginning with *here* or *there,* it is easy to make an agreement error. Because *here* and *there* are adverbs, they are never subjects of a sentence and do not determine the correct form of the verb. Look for the subject *after* the verb, and, depending on its number, choose a singular or plural verb.

singular  singular
verb     subject

There is a bone in my soup.

plural    plural
verb    subject

There are two bones in my soup.

**4. Words between subject and verb.** Words, phrases, and clauses coming between the subject and verb do not change the fact that the verb must agree with the subject. To check that the verb is correct, mentally cancel everything between the subject and its verb to see if the verb agrees in number with its subject.

singular subject          singular verb

The new list of degree requirements comes out in the spring.

plural subject           plural verb

Expenses surrounding the sale of the house were unexpectedly low.

Phrases beginning with prepositions such as *along with, as well as*, and *in addition to* are not part of the subject and should not be considered in determining if the verb is singular or plural.

singular subject

The lamp, together with some plates, glasses, and china teacups, was broken during the move.

singular verb

**5. Indefinite pronouns as subjects.** Some indefinite pronouns (such as *everyone, neither, anybody, nobody, one, something*, and *each*) take a singular verb. (See p. 366.)

Everyone likes my father.

Of the two apples, neither smells rotten.

The indefinite pronouns *both, many, several*, and *few* always take a plural verb. Some indefinite pronouns, such as *all, any, most, none*, and *some*, may take either a singular or plural verb. Treat the indefinite pronoun as singular if it refers to something that cannot be counted and as plural if it refers to more than one of something that can be counted.

Some of the ice is still on the road.

Some of the ice cubes are still in the tray.

All of the spaghetti tastes overcooked.

All of the spaghetti dishes taste too spicy.

**6. Collective nouns.** A collective noun refers to a group of people or things (*audience, class, flock, jury, team, family*). When the noun refers to the group as one unit, use a singular verb.

The <u>herd</u> <u>stampedes</u> toward us.

When the noun refers to the group members as separate individuals, use a plural verb.

The <u>herd</u> <u>scatter</u> in all directions.

**7. Nouns with plural forms but singular meaning.** Some words appear plural (that is, they end in *-s* or *-es*) but have a singular meaning. *Measles, hysterics, news,* and *mathematics* are examples. Use a singular verb with them.

<u>Mathematics</u> <u>is</u> a required course.

NOTE: Other nouns look plural and have singular meanings, but take a plural verb: *braces, glasses, trousers, slacks, jeans, jodhpurs,* and *pajamas.* Even though they refer to a single thing (to one pair of jeans, for example), these words take a plural verb.

His <u>pajamas</u> <u>were covered</u> with pictures of tumbling dice.

**8. Relative pronouns in adjective clauses.** The relative pronouns *who, which,* and *that* sometimes function as the subject of an adjective clause. When the relative pronoun refers to a singular noun, use a singular verb. When the pronoun refers to a plural noun, use a plural verb.

Anita is a person <u>who</u> never <u>forgets</u> faces. [*Who* refers to *person*, which is singular.]

**EXERCISE 14**

Circle the verb that correctly completes each sentence.

EXAMPLE: Everybody (like, (likes)) doughnuts for breakfast.

1. Physics (is, are) a required course for an engineering degree.
2. Most of my courses last semester (was, were) in the morning.
3. The orchestra members who (is, are) carrying their instruments will be able to board the plane first.
4. Suzanne (sing, sings) a touching version of "America the Beautiful."
5. Here (is, are) the performers who juggle plates.
6. Kin Lee and his parents (travel, travels) to Ohio tomorrow.
7. A box of old and valuable stamps (is, are) in the safety deposit box at the bank.

8. The family (sit, sits) on different chairs arranged throughout the living room.
9. Judith and Erin (arrive, arrives) at the train station at eleven o'clock.
10. Directions for the recipe (is, are) on the box.

## C.7 Pronoun-Antecedent Agreement

A pronoun must agree with its **antecedent,** the word it refers to or replaces, in person (first, second, or third), in number (singular or plural), and in gender (masculine, feminine, or neuter).

> <u>Ronald</u> attended the party, but I did not have a chance to talk with <u>him</u>. [The third-person, masculine, singular pronoun *him* agrees with its antecedent, *Ronald*.]

> <u>We</u> had planned to call <u>our</u> sister, but <u>her</u> line was busy. [*Our* agrees with its antecedent, *We*; *her* agrees with its antecedent, *sister*.]

### Agreement Rules

**1. Use a singular pronoun to refer to or replace a singular noun.** (A singular noun names one person, place, or thing.)

> <u>Juanita</u> washed <u>her</u> car.

**2. Use a plural pronoun to refer to or replace a plural noun.** A plural noun names two or more persons, places, or things.)

> The <u>shirts</u> are hung on <u>their</u> hangers.

**3. (a) Use singular pronouns to refer to indefinite pronouns that are singular in meaning.**

| | | | | |
|---|---|---|---|---|
| another | each | everything | no one | somebody |
| anybody | either | neither | nothing | someone |
| anyone | everybody | nobody | one | something |
| anything | everyone | none | other | |

singular antecedent   singular pronoun
> <u>Someone</u> left <u>her</u> handbag under this table.

singular antecedent      singular compound pronoun
> <u>Everyone</u> in the office must do <u>his or her</u> own photocopying.

NOTE: To avoid the awkwardness of *his or her,* consider rephrasing your sentence with a plural antecedent and plural pronoun.

plural antecedent   plural pronoun
> Office <u>workers</u> must do <u>their</u> own photocopying.

**(b) Use a plural pronoun to refer to indefinite pronouns that are plural in meaning.**

both　　few　　many　　several

Both of the journalists said that they could see no violations of the cease-fire.

**(c) The indefinite pronouns *all, any, most, none,* and *some* can be singular or plural, depending on how they are used.** If the indefinite pronoun refers to something that cannot be counted, use a singular pronoun to refer to it. If the indefinite pronoun refers to something that can be counted, use a plural pronoun to refer to it.

Most of the voters feel they can make a difference.

Most of the air on airplanes is recycled repeatedly, so it becomes stale.

**4. Use a plural pronoun to refer to a compound antecedent joined by *and*, unless both parts of the compound refer to the same person, place, or thing.**

plural antecedent　　　　plural pronoun

My girlfriend and I planned our wedding.

singular antecedent　　　　singular pronoun

My neighbor and best friend started her book bindery at the local warehouse.

**5. When antecedents are joined by *or, nor, either/or, neither/nor, both/and, not/but,* or *not only/but also,* the pronoun agrees in number with the nearer antecedent.**

Neither his brothers nor Sam has made his plane reservations.

Neither Sam or his brothers have made their plane reservations.

NOTE: Two or more singular antecedents joined by *or* or *nor* require a singular pronoun.

Neither Larry nor Richard signed his name legibly.

Eva or Anita will bring her saxophone.

**6. Collective nouns refer to a specific group *(army, class, family).*** When the group acts as a unit, use a singular pronoun to refer to the noun. When each member of the group acts individually, use a plural pronoun to refer to the noun.

The band marched its most intricate formation.

The band found their seats in the bleachers but could not see the game because the sun was in their eyes.

**EXERCISE 15** Revise the sentences below that contain agreement errors. If a sentence contains no errors, write *Correct* beside it.

EXAMPLE: Somebody dropped ~~their~~ *his or her* ring down the drain.

1. Many of the residents of the neighborhood have had their homes tested for radon.
2. Each college instructor establishes their own grading policies.
3. The apples fell from its tree.
4. Anyone may submit their painting to the contest.
5. All the engines manufactured at the plant have their vehicle-identification numbers stamped on.
6. No one requested that the clerk gift-wrap their package.
7. Either Professor Judith Marcos or her assistant, Maria, graded the exams, writing their comments in the margins.
8. James or his parents sails the boat every weekend.
9. Few classes were canceled because of the snowstorm; it met as regularly scheduled.
10. Not only Ricky but also the Carters will take his children to Disneyland this summer.

## C.8 Pronoun Reference

A pronoun refers to or replaces a noun or pronoun previously mentioned, called the pronoun's **antecedent.** As you write, you must always make sure that a reader knows to which noun or pronoun a pronoun refers. The antecedent of each pronoun must be clear. Sometimes you may need to reword a sentence to solve a problem of unclear antecedent.

INCORRECT: Lois walked with Pam because she did not know the route. [Who did not know the route? The antecedent of *she* is unclear.]

CORRECT: Lois did not know the route, so she walked with Pam.

### How to Use Pronouns Correctly

**1. A pronoun may refer to two or more nouns in a compound antecedent.**

Mark and Dennis combined their efforts to fix the leaky faucet.

**2. Avoid using a pronoun that could refer to more than one possible antecedent.**

INCORRECT: Rick told Garry that he was right.

CORRECT: Rick told Garry, "You are right."

**3. Avoid using vague pronouns like *they* and *it,* which often have no clear antecedent.**

INCORRECT:   <u>It</u> says in the paper that K-Mart is expanding the Williamsville store.

CORRECT:   <u>The article in the paper</u> says that K-Mart is expanding the Williamsville store.

INCORRECT:   <u>They</u> told me that we were required to wear surgeons' masks to view the newborns.

CORRECT:   <u>The obstetrics nurses</u> told me that we were required to wear surgeons' masks to view the newborns.

INCORRECT:   On the bulletin boards, <u>it</u> says that there is a fire drill today.

CORRECT:   <u>The notice</u> on the bulletin board says that there is a fire drill today.

**4. Avoid unnecessary or repetitious pronouns.**

INCORRECT:   My sister <u>she</u> said that she lost her diamond ring.

CORRECT:   My sister said that she lost her diamond ring.

**5. Be sure to use the relative pronouns *who, whom, which,* and *that* with the appropriate antecedent.** *Who* and *whom* refer to persons or named animals. *That* and *which* refer to unnamed animals and to things.

<u>Mary Anne</u> was the team member <u>who</u> scored the most points this year.

<u>Dublin</u>, <u>who</u> is a golden retriever, barked at everyone.

The ring <u>that</u> my sister gave me has three opals.

Highway 33, <u>which</u> has ten hairpin turns, is difficult to drive.

**6. Use *one* if you are not referring specifically to the reader.** Use the second-person pronoun *you* only to refer to the reader. In academic writing, avoid using *you.*

INCORRECT:   Last year, <u>you</u> had to watch the news every night to keep up with world events.

CORRECT:   Last year, <u>one</u> had to watch the news every night to keep up with world events.

**7. Place the pronoun close to its antecedent so that the relationship is clear.**

INCORRECT:   Margaux found a <u>shell</u> on the beach <u>that</u> her sister wanted.

CORRECT:   On the beach Margaux found a <u>shell</u> <u>that</u> her sister wanted.

**EXERCISE 16** | Revise each of the following sentences to correct problems in pronoun reference. If a sentence contains no errors, write *Correct* beside it.

> EXAMPLE: It said that the grades would be posted on Tuesday.
>
> REVISED: *The professor's note said that the grades would be posted on Tuesday.*

1. The puppy whom my sister brought home was quite cute.

   _____

2. Laverne and Louise they pooled their money to buy a new stereo system. _____

   _____

3. They said on the news that the naval base will be shut down.

   _____

4. The street that was recently widened is where I used to live.

   _____

5. Ivan sat on the couch in the living room that he had bought yesterday. _____

   _____

6. You should underline in your textbooks for higher comprehension.

   _____

7. Christina handed Maggie the plate she had bought at the flea market.

   _____

8. Bridget found the cake mix in the aisle with the baking supplies that she needed for tonight's dessert. _____

   _____

9. The answering machine who answered the phone beeped several times. _____

   _____

10. It said in the letter that my payment was late. _____

    _____

## C.9 Pronoun Case

A pronoun changes **case** depending on its grammatical function in a sentence. Pronouns may be in the **subjective case,** the **objective case,** or the **possessive case.**

### PERSONAL PRONOUNS

| *Singular* | *Subjective* | *Objective* | *Possessive* |
|---|---|---|---|
| First person | I | me | my, mine |
| Second person | you | you | your, yours |
| Third person | he, she, it | him, her, it | his, her, hers, its |

| *Plural* | *Subjective* | *Objective* | *Possessive* |
|---|---|---|---|
| First person | we | us | our, ours |
| Second person | you | you | your, yours |
| Third person | they | them | their, theirs |

### RELATIVE OR INTERROGATIVE PRONOUNS

| | *Subjective* | *Objective* | *Possessive* |
|---|---|---|---|
| Singular and plural | who whoever | whom whomever | whose |

### Pronouns in the Subjective Case

Use the **subjective case** (also known as the **nominative case**) when the pronoun functions as the subject of a sentence or clause (see p. 383) or as a subject complement (also known as a predicate nominative) (see p. 386). A predicate nominative is a noun or pronoun that follows a linking verb and identifies or renames the subject of the sentence.

subject
She has won recognition as a landscape architect.

subject complement
Cathie volunteers at the local hospital. The most faithful volunteer is she.

The subjective case is also used when a pronoun functions as an appositive to a subject or subject complement (see p. 386).

The only two seniors, she and her best friend, won the top awards.

### Pronouns in the Objective Case

Use the objective case when a pronoun functions as a direct object, indirect object, or object of a preposition. (See pp. 386, 387, and 389.)

direct object
George helped her with the assignment.

indirect object
George gave her a book.

objects of the preposition
George gave the book to him and her.

The objective case is also used when the pronoun functions as the subject of an infinitive phrase or an appositive to an object.

subject of infinitive   infinitive phrase
I wanted him to go straight home.

direct object   appositive to object
The principal chose two representatives, Marnie and me.

NOTE: When a sentence has a compound subject or compound objects, you may have trouble determining the correct pronoun case. To determine how the pronoun functions, mentally recast the sentence without the noun or other pronoun in the compound construction. Determine how the pronoun functions by itself and then decide which case is correct.

subjective case
Mary Jo and they brought the beverages. [Think: "*They* brought the beverages." *They* is the subject of the sentence, so the subjective case is correct.]

objective case
Behind you and me, the drapery rustled. [Think: "Behind *me*." *Me* is the object of the preposition *behind*, so the objective case is correct.]

## Pronouns in the Possessive Case

Possessive pronouns indicate to whom or to what something belongs. The possessive pronouns *mine, yours, his, hers, its, ours,* and *theirs* function just as nouns do.

subject
Hers is the hat with the long green feather.

direct object
I liked hers the best.

The possessive pronouns *my, your, his, her, its, our,* and *their* are used as adjectives to modify nouns and gerunds. (See p. 374.)

Our high-school reunion surprised everyone by its size.

Your attending that reunion will depend on your travel schedule.

### *Who* and *Whom* As Interrogative Pronouns

When *who, whoever, whom,* and *whomever* introduce questions, they are interrogative pronouns. How an interrogative pronoun functions in a clause determines its case. Use *who* or *whoever* (the subjective case) when the interrogative pronoun functions as a subject or subject complement. (See p. 386.) Use *whom* or *whomever* (the objective case) when the interrogative pronoun functions as a direct object or an object of a preposition.

SUBJECTIVE CASE: <u>Who</u> is there? [subject]

OBJECTIVE CASE: To <u>whom</u> did you give the letter? [object of preposition]

### *Who* and *Whom* As Relative Pronouns

When *who, whoever, whom,* and *whomever* introduce subordinate clauses, they are relative pronouns. How a relative pronoun functions in a clause determines its case. Use *who* or *whoever* (subjective case) when a relative pronoun functions as the subject of the subordinate clause. Use *whom* or *whomever* (objective case) when a relative pronoun functions as an object in the subordinate clause.

SUBJECTIVE CASE: The lecturer, <u>who</u> is a journalist from New York, speaks with great insight and wit. [*Who* is the subject of the subordinate clause.]

OBJECTIVE CASE: The journalist, <u>whom</u> I know from college days, came to give a lecture. [*Whom* is the direct object of the verb *know* in the subordinate clause.]

## C.10 Correct Adjective and Adverb Use

Adjectives and adverbs modify, describe, explain, qualify, or restrict the words they modify. (See pp. 373 and 376.) **Adjectives** modify nouns and pronouns. **Adverbs** modify verbs, adjectives, and other adverbs; adverbs can also modify phrases, clauses, or whole sentences.

ADJECTIVES: <u>red</u> car; the <u>quiet</u> one

ADVERBS: <u>quickly</u> finish; <u>only</u> four reasons; <u>very</u> angrily

### Comparison of Adjectives and Adverbs

**Positive** adjectives and adverbs modify but do not involve any comparison: *green, bright, lively.*

**Comparative** adjectives and adverbs compare two persons, things, actions, or ideas.

COMPARATIVE ADJECTIVE: Michael is <u>taller</u> than Bob.

COMPARATIVE ADVERB: Antonio reacted <u>more calmly</u> than Robert.

Here is how to form comparative adjectives and adverbs. (Consult your dictionary if you are unsure of the form of a particular word.)

**1. If the adjective or adverb has one syllable, add *-er.* For some two-syllable words, also add *-er.***

cold → colder     slow → slower     narrow → narrower

**2. For most words of two or more syllables, place the word *more* in front of the word.**

reasonable → more reasonable     interestingly → more interestingly

**3. For two-syllable adjectives ending in *-y,* change the *-y* to *-i* and add *-er.***

drowsy → drowsier     lazy → lazier

**Superlative** adjectives and adverbs compare more than two persons, things, actions, or ideas.

SUPERLATIVE ADJECTIVE: Michael is the <u>tallest</u> member of the team.

SUPERLATIVE ADVERB: She studied <u>most diligently</u> for the test.

Here is how to form superlative adjectives and adverbs.

**1. Add *-est* to one-syllable adjectives and adverbs and to some two-syllable words.**

cold → coldest     fast → fastest     narrow → narrowest

**2. For most words of two or more syllables, place the word *most* in front of the word.**

reasonable → most reasonable     interestingly → most interestingly

**3. For two-syllable adjectives ending in *-y,* change the *-y* to *-i* and add *-est.***

drowsy → drowsiest     lazy → laziest

## Irregular Adjectives and Adverbs

Some adjectives and adverbs form their comparative and superlative forms in irregular ways.

|        | Positive | Comparative | Superlative |
|--------|----------|-------------|-------------|
| **Adjectives** | | | |
|        | good     | better          | best             |
|        | bad      | worse           | worst            |
|        | little   | littler, less   | littlest, least  |
| **Adverbs** | | | |
|        | well     | better          | best             |
|        | badly    | worse           | worst            |
| **Adjectives and Adverbs** | | | |
|        | many     | more            | most             |
|        | some     | more            | most             |
|        | much     | more            | most             |

## Common Mistakes to Avoid

**1.  Do not use adjectives to modify verbs, other adjectives, or adverbs.**

INCORRECT:   Peter and Mary take each other serious.

CORRECT:      Peter and Mary take each other seriously. [Modifies the verb *take*.]

**2.  Do not use the adjectives *good* and *bad* when you should use the adverbs *well* and *badly*.**

INCORRECT:   Juan did good on the exam.

CORRECT:      Juan did well on the exam. [Modifies the verb *did*.]

**3.  Do not use the adjectives *real* and *sure* when you should use the adverbs *really* and *surely*.**

INCORRECT:   Jan scored real well on the exam.

CORRECT:      Jan scored really well on the exam. [Modifies the adverb *well*.]

INCORRECT:   I sure was surprised to win the lottery.

CORRECT:      I surely was surprised to win the lottery. [Modifies the verb *was surprised*.]

**4.  Do not use *more* or *most* with the *-er* or *-est* form of an adjective or adverb.** Use one form or the other, according to the rules above.

INCORRECT:   That was the most tastiest dinner I've ever eaten.

CORRECT:      That was the tastiest dinner I've ever eaten.

**5.  Avoid double negatives—that is, two negatives in the same clause.**

INCORRECT:   He did not want nothing in the refrigerator.

CORRECT:      He did not want anything in the refrigerator.

**6. When using the comparative and superlative forms of adverbs, do not create an incomplete comparison.**

INCORRECT:  The heater works <u>more efficiently</u>. [More efficiently than what?]

CORRECT:  The heater works <u>more efficiently than it did before we had it repaired</u>.

**7. Do not use the comparative form for adjectives and adverbs that have no degree.** It is incorrect to write, for example, *more square, most perfect, more equally,* or *most straight.* Do not use a comparative or superlative form for any of the following adjectives and adverbs.

### Adjectives

| | | | | |
|---|---|---|---|---|
| complete | equal | infinite | pregnant | unique |
| dead | eternal | invisible | square | universal |
| empty | favorite | matchless | supreme | vertical |
| endless | impossible | parallel | unanimous | whole |

### Adverbs

| | | |
|---|---|---|
| endlessly | infinitely | uniquely |
| equally | invisibly | universally |
| eternally | perpendicularly | |
| impossibly | straight | |

**EXERCISE** 17

Revise each of the following sentences so that all adjectives and adverbs are used correctly.

EXAMPLE:  I answered the question polite~~,~~ *ly*

1. Michael's apartment was more expensive.
2. When I heard the man and woman sing the duet, I decided that the woman sang best.
3. Our local movie reviewer said that the film's theme song sounded badly.
4. The roller coaster was excitinger than the merry-go-round.
5. *The Scarlet Letter* is more good than *War and Peace.*
6. Susan sure gave a rousing speech.
7. Last week's storm seemed worst than a tornado.
8. Some women thought that the Equal Rights Amendment would guarantee that women are treated more equally.
9. Taking the interstate is the most fast route to the outlet mall.
10. Professor Reed had the better lecture style of all my instructors.

# Writing Effective Sentences

## D.1 Misplaced and Dangling Modifiers

A **modifier** is a word, phrase, or clause that describes, qualifies, or limits the meaning of another word. Modifiers that are not correctly placed can make a sentence confusing.

### Misplaced Modifiers

**Misplaced modifiers** do not describe or explain the words the writer intended them to. A misplaced modifier often appears to modify the wrong word or can leave the reader confused as to which word it does modify.

MISPLACED: Max bought a chair at the used-furniture shop that was large and dark. [Was the chair or the furniture shop large and dark?]

MISPLACED: The instructor announced that the term paper was due on April 25 at the beginning of class. [Are the papers due at the beginning of class on the 25th, or did the instructor make the announcement at the beginning of class?]

You can easily avoid misplaced modifiers if you make sure that modifiers immediately precede or follow the words they modify.

CORRECT: Max bought a chair that was large and dark at the used-furniture shop.

CORRECT: Max bought a large, dark chair at the used-furniture shop.

CORRECT: At the beginning of class, the instructor announced that the term paper was due on April 25.

## Dangling Modifiers

**Dangling modifiers** do not clearly describe or explain any part of the sentence. Dangling modifiers create confusion and sometimes unintentional humor. To avoid dangling modifiers, make sure that each modifier has a clear antecedent.

DANGLING: Rounding the curve, a fire hydrant was hit by the speeding car. [The modifier suggests that the hydrant rounded the curve.]

CORRECT: Rounding the curve, the speeding car hit the fire hydrant. [Modifies *car.*]

DANGLING: Uncertain of what courses to take next semester, the academic adviser listed five options. [The modifier suggests that the adviser was uncertain of what courses to take.]

CORRECT: Uncertain of what courses to take next semester, the student spoke to an academic adviser, who listed five options.

DANGLING: Flood damage was visible crossing the river. [The modifier makes it sound as though flood damage was crossing the river.]

CORRECT: Flood damage was visible as we crossed the river.

There are two common ways to revise dangling modifiers:

1. **Add a word or words that the modifier clearly describes.** Place the new material just after the modifier, and rearrange other parts of the sentence as necessary.

   DANGLING: While watching television, the cake burned.
   CORRECT: While watching television, Sarah burned the cake.

2. **Change the dangling modifier to a subordinate clause.** (See p. 394.) You may need to change the verb form in the modifier.

   DANGLING: While watching television, the cake burned.
   CORRECT: While Sarah was watching television, the cake burned.

EXERCISE 18 | Revise each of the following sentences to correct misplaced or dangling modifiers.

EXAMPLE: Deciding which flavor of ice cream to order, another customer cut in front of Roger.

REVISED: *While Roger was deciding which flavor of ice cream to order, another customer cut in front of him.*

1. Tricia saw an animal at the zoo that had black fur and long claws.

   _____

2. Before answering the door, the phone rang. _____

   _____

3. I could see large snowflakes falling from the bedroom window.

   _____

4. Honking, Felicia walked in front of the car. _____

   _____

5. After leaving the classroom, the door automatically locked.

   _____

6. Applauding and cheering, the band returned for an encore.

   _____

7. The waiter brought a birthday cake to our table that had twenty-
   four candles. _____

   _____

8. Books lined the library shelves about every imaginable subject.

   _____

9. While sobbing, the sad movie ended and the lights came on.

   _____

10. Turning the page, the book's binding cracked. _____

    _____

# D.2 Shifts in Person, Number, and Verb Tense

The parts of a sentence should be consistent. Shifts within a sentence in person, number, or verb tense will make the sentence confusing and difficult to read.

### Shifts in Person

**Person** is the grammatical term used to distinguish the speaker or writer (**first person:** *I, we*), the person spoken to (**second person:** *you*), and the person or thing spoken about (**third person:** *he, she, it, they,* and any noun, such as *Joan* or *children*). A sentence or a paragraph should use the same person throughout.

SHIFT:   If a <u>student</u> studies effectively, <u>you</u> will get good grades.
CORRECT:   If <u>you</u> study effectively, <u>you</u> will get good grades.

## Shifts in Number

**Number** distinguishes between singular and plural. A pronoun must agree in number with its antecedent, the word to which it refers. (See p. 421.) Related nouns within a sentence also must agree in number. (Sometimes you need to change the form of the verb when you correct the inconsistent nouns or pronouns.)

SHIFT:   When a <u>homeowner</u> <u>does</u> not <u>shovel</u> the snow in front of <u>their</u> <u>house</u>, <u>they</u> risk getting fined.
CORRECT:   When <u>homeowners</u> <u>do</u> not <u>shovel</u> the snow in front of <u>their</u> <u>houses</u>, <u>they</u> risk getting fined.

## Shifts in Verb Tense

The same verb tense should be used throughout a sentence unless meaning requires a shift.

REQUIRED SHIFT:   After my cousin $\overset{\lceil \text{present} \rceil}{\underline{\text{arrives}}}$, we $\overset{\lceil \text{future} \rceil}{\underline{\text{will go}}}$ to the movies.

INCORRECT:   After Marguerite $\overset{\text{past}}{\underline{\text{joined}}}$ the food co-op, she $\overset{\text{present}}{\underline{\text{seems}}}$ healthier.

CORRECT:   After Marguerite $\overset{\lceil \text{past} \rceil}{\underline{\text{joined}}}$ the food co-op, she $\overset{\lceil \text{past} \rceil}{\underline{\text{seemed}}}$ healthier.

INCORRECT:   Pamela $\overset{\text{past}}{\underline{\text{watched}}}$ the moon rise, and then she $\overset{\text{present}}{\underline{\text{goes}}}$ for a midnight swim.

CORRECT:   Pamela $\overset{\lceil \text{past} \rceil}{\underline{\text{watched}}}$ the moon rise, and then she $\overset{\lceil \text{past} \rceil}{\underline{\text{went}}}$ for a midnight swim.

**EXERCISE 19** ▶ Revise each of the following sentences to correct errors in shift of person, number, or tense. If a sentence contains no errors, write Correct beside it.

EXAMPLE:   Boats along the river were tied to their dock̩.

1. When people receive a gift, you should be gracious and polite.
2. When we arrived at the inn, the lights are on and a fire is burning in the fireplace.

3. Before Trey drove to the cabin, he packs a picnic lunch.
4. The artist paints portraits and weaves baskets.
5. The lobsterman goes out on his boat each day and will check his lobster traps.
6. All the cars Honest Bob sells have a new transmission.
7. Rosa ran the 100-meter race and throws the discus at the track meet.
8. Public schools in Florida have an air-conditioning system.
9. Office workers sat on the benches downtown and are eating their lunches outside.
10. Before a scuba diver goes underwater, you must check and recheck your breathing equipment.

## D.3 Coordination

**Coordination** is a way to give related ideas equal emphasis within a single sentence. Your readers will better understand the flow of your thought if you connect coordinate ideas.

### How to Combine Ideas of Equal Importance

There are three ways to combine ideas of equal importance when those ideas are expressed in independent clauses. (See p. 394.)

**1. Join the two independent clauses with a comma and a coordinating conjunction (*and, but, nor, or, for, so, yet*).**

    independent clause        independent clause
    I passed the ball, but Sam failed to catch it.

You should choose a coordinating conjunction that properly expresses the relationship between the ideas in the two clauses.

| *Coordinating Conjunction* | *Meaning* | *Example* |
|---|---|---|
| and | addition; one idea added to another | I went shopping, <u>and</u> I spent too much money. |
| but, yet | contrast | I wanted to grill fish, <u>but</u> Peter was a vegetarian. |
| or | alternatives or choices | Tonight I might go to the movies, <u>or</u> I might work out. |
| nor | not either | Julie was not in class, <u>nor</u> was she in the snack bar. |
| for | cause and effect | We went walking, <u>for</u> it was a beautiful evening. |

| so | result | I was early for the appointment, so I decided to doze for a few minutes. |

## 2. Join the two independent clauses with a semicolon.

We decided to see the new Spike Lee film; it was playing at three local theaters.

Use this method when the relationship between the two ideas is clear and requires no explanation. Usually, the two clauses must be very closely related.

NOTE: If you join two independent clauses with only a comma and fail to use a coordinating conjunction or semicolon, you will produce a comma splice. If you join two independent clauses without using a punctuation mark and a coordinating conjunction, or a semicolon, you will produce a run-on sentence. (See p. 406.)

## 3. Join the two independent clauses with a semicolon and a conjunctive adverb followed by a comma. A conjunctive adverb can also be used at the beginning of a sentence to link the sentence with an earlier one.

| Conjunctive Adverb | Meaning | Example |
|---|---|---|
| therefore, consequently, thus, hence | cause and effect | I am planning to become a nurse; consequently, I'm taking a lot of science courses. |
| however, nevertheless, nonetheless, conversely | differences or contrast | We had planned to go bowling; however, we went to hear music instead. |
| furthermore, moreover, also | addition; a continuation of the same idea | To save money I am packing my lunch; also, I am walking to school instead of taking the bus. |
| similarly, likewise | similarity | I left class as soon as I finished the exam; likewise, other students also left. |
| then, subsequently, next | sequence in time | I walked home; then I massaged my aching feet. |

**EXERCISE 20** ▶ Complete each of the following sentences by adding a coordinating conjunction or a conjunctive adverb and the appropriate punctuation.

EXAMPLE: Teresa vacationed in Denver last year _; similarly,_
Jan will go to Denver this year.

1. Our professor did not complete the lecture _____ did he give an assignment for the next class.
2. A first-aid kit was in her backpack _____ the hiker was able to treat her cut knee.
3. An opening act began the concert _____ the headline band took the stage.
4. I always put a light on when I leave the house _____ I often turn on a radio to deter burglars.
5. Sue politely asked to borrow my car _____ she thanked me when she returned it.
6. My roommate went to the library _____ I had the apartment to myself.
7. Steve and Todd will go to a baseball game _____ they will go to a movie instead.
8. Cheryl looks like her father _____ her hair is darker and curlier than his.
9. Maureen took a job at a bookstore _____ she was offered a job at a museum.
10. Our neighbors bought a barbecue grill _____ we decided to buy one.

## D.4 Subordination

Subordination is a way to show that one idea is not as important as another. When two clauses are related, but one is less important, the less important one can be expressed as a dependent (subordinate) clause. (See p. 394.) Dependent clauses do contain a subject and a verb, but they do not express a complete thought. They always must be added to a complete sentence or independent clause. If a dependent clause is used alone, it is a fragment and must be corrected. (See p. 402.)

### How to Combine Ideas of Unequal Importance

**1. Introduce the less important idea with a subordinating conjunction.** Choose a subordinating conjunction that properly shows the relationship of the less important idea to the more important one. Common subordinating conjunctions are *after, although, because, before, unless, when,* and *while.* (See p. 395 for a complete list.)

```
        ┌──────── dependent clause ────────┐
 subordinating conjunction                        independent clause
┌─────┐                                  ┌─────────────────────────┐
After I finished cleaning my fish tank, I worked on my paper.
```

```
        ┌──── dependent clause ────┐
 subordinating conjunction                   independent clause
┌──────┐                          ┌──────────────────────────┐
Unless I win the lottery, I will not be able to buy a new car.
```

**2. Introduce the less important idea with a relative pronoun (such as *who, which, that,* or *what*).** A relative pronoun usually introduces a clause that functions as a noun when the clause is attached to an independent clause. (See p. 366 for more on relative pronouns.)

┌─── dependent clause ───┐
relative pronoun

The professor who won the award is on leave this semester.

┌──────── dependent clause ────────┐
relative pronoun

The courses that I am taking in night school are challenging.

**EXERCISE** 21 ▶ Combine each of the following pairs of sentences by subordinating one idea to the other with a coordinating conjunction or a relative pronoun.

EXAMPLE:    a. One kind of opossum can glide like a bird.
            b. The opossum lives in Australia.

COMBINED: *One kind of opossum, which lives in Australia, can glide like a bird.*

1. a. Trina can get discount movie tickets.
   b. Trina's husband manages a movie theater.

   _____

   _____

2. a. Rob hit the ground with his tennis racket.
   b. Rob's tennis racket broke.

   _____

   _____

3. a. The car has wire hubcaps and a sun roof.
   b. I bought the car yesterday.

   _____

   _____

4. a. Visitors to the automobile museum can learn a lot about the mechanics of cars.
   b. Visitors enjoy looking at many old cars.

   _____

   _____

5. a. The sorority will hold its fall picnic next week.
   b. The picnic will be held if it does not rain.

   _____

   _____

6. a. Vicky went to the library to work on her term paper.
   b. Then Vicky went to pick up her son from the day-care center.

   _____

   _____

7. a. Phil Donahue may run for public office someday.
   b. Phil Donahue is a talk-show host.

   _____

   _____

8. a. I will go shopping for a rain slicker tomorrow.
   b. I will not go if my roommate has one that I can borrow.

   _____

   _____

9. a. Linda and Pablo got divorced.
   b. They could not agree on anything.

   _____

   _____

10. a. The yacht sailed into the marina.
    b. The yacht is owned by the Kennedy family.

    _____

    _____

## D.5 Parallelism

Parallelism is a method of ensuring that words, phrases, and clauses in a series are in the same grammatical form.

### What Should Be Parallel?

**1. Words or phrases in a series.** When two or more nouns, verbs, adjectives, adverbs, or phrases appear together in a sentence connected by a coordinating conjunction (such as *and, or,* or *but*), the words or phrases should be parallel in grammatical form.

NOT PARALLEL: The dentist told me to stop eating so much candy and that I should floss my teeth.

*infinitive phrase* — to stop

*relative pronoun* — that I should floss

*subordinate clause*

PARALLEL: The dentist told me to stop eating so much candy and to floss my teeth.

*infinitive phrase* — to stop

*infinitive phrase* — to floss

NOT PARALLEL: A well-rounded diet, exercising, and to get enough sleep are essential to good health.

*noun* — diet; *gerund* — exercising; *infinitive phrase* — to get enough sleep

PARALLEL: A well-rounded diet, exercise, and enough sleep are essential to good health.

*noun* — diet; *noun* — exercise; *noun* — sleep

## 2. Independent clauses joined with a coordinating conjunction.
Independent clauses within a sentence should be parallel in tense and in construction.

NOT PARALLEL: The drivers waited patiently as the work crew cleaned up the wreck, but after an hour the horns were honked loudly by all the drivers.

*active voice* — waited; *passive voice* — were honked

PARALLEL: The drivers waited patiently as the work crew cleaned up the wreck, but after an hour they honked their horns loudly.

*active voice* — waited; *active voice* — honked

NOT PARALLEL: Barry wanted to go to the concert, but Julia wants to stay home and watch a video.

*past tense* — wanted; *present tense* — wants

PARALLEL: Barry wanted to go to the concert, but Julia wanted to stay home and watch a video.

*past tense* — wanted; *past tense* — wanted

## 3. Items being compared.
When elements of a sentence are compared or contrasted, use the same grammatical form for each element.

INCORRECT: Mark wanted a vacation rather than to save money to buy a house.

*noun* — vacation; *infinitive phrase* — to save

infinitive phrase      infinitive phrase

CORRECT: Mark wanted to take a vacation rather than to save money to buy a house.

**EXERCISE 22**　Revise each of the following sentences to achieve parallelism.

 EXAMPLE: Rosa has decided to study nursing instead of going into accounting.

 REVISED: *Rosa has decided to study nursing instead of accounting.*

1. The priest baptized the baby and congratulates the new parents.

2. We ordered a platter of fried clams, a platter of corn on the cob, and fried shrimp.

3. Lucy entered the dance contest, but the dance was watched by June from the side.

4. Léon purchased the ratchet set at the garage sale and buying the drill bits there too.

5. The exterminator told Brandon the house needed to be fumigated and spraying to eliminate the termites.

6. The bus swerved and hit the dump truck, which swerves and hit the station wagon, which swerved and hit the bicycle.

7. Channel 2 covered the bank robbery, but a python that had escaped from the zoo was reported by Channel 7.

   _____

   _____

8. Sal was born while Nixon was president, and Johnson was president when Rob was born.

   _____

   _____

9. The pediatrician spent the morning with sore throats, answering questions about immunizations, and treating bumps and bruises.

   _____

   _____

10. Belinda prefers to study in the library, but her brother Marcus studies at home.

    _____

    _____

## D.6 Sentence Variety

Good writers use a variety of sentence structures to avoid wordiness and monotony and to show relationships among thoughts. To achieve **sentence variety,** do not use all simple sentences or all complex or compound sentences (see pp. 396–398), and do not begin or end all sentences in the same way. Instead, vary the length, the amount of detail, and the structure of your sentences.

**1. Use sentences of varying lengths.**

**2. Avoid stringing simple sentences together with coordinating conjunctions (*and, but, or,* and so on).** Instead, use some introductory participial phrases (see p. 391).

SIMPLE:  There was a long line at the deli, so Chris decided to leave.
VARIED:  Seeing the long line at the deli, Chris decided to leave.

**3. Begin some sentences with a prepositional phrase.** A preposition shows relationships between things (*during, over, toward, before, across, within, inside, over, above*). Many prepositions suggest chronology, direction, or location. (See p. 379.)

During the concert, the fire alarm rang.

Inside the theater, the crowd waited expectantly.

4. **Begin some sentences with a present or past participle (***cooking, broken***).** (See p. 391.)

Barking and jumping, the dogs greeted their master.

Still laughing, two girls left the movie.

Tired and exhausted, the mountain climbers fell asleep quickly.

5. **Begin some sentences with adverbs.** (See p. 376.)

Angrily, the student left the room.

Patiently, the math instructor explained the assignment again.

6. **Begin some sentences with infinitive phrases (***to*** plus the infinitive form: ***to make, to go***).** (See p. 392.)

To get breakfast ready on time, I set my alarm for 7 A.M.

7. **Begin some sentences with a dependent clause introduced by a subordinating conjunction.** (See p. 395.)

Because I ate shellfish, I developed hives.

8. **Begin some sentences with a conjunctive adverb.**

Consequently, we decided to have steak for dinner.

**EXERCISE  23**  ▶  Combine each of the following pairs of simple sentences into one sentence using the technique suggested in brackets.

EXAMPLE:   a.  The dog barked and howled.
           b.  The dog warned a stranger away.
               [Use present participle (*-ing* form).]

COMBINED:   *Barking and howling, the dog warned a stranger away.*

1. a.  Professor Clark has a Civil War battlefield model.
   b.  He has it in his office.
       [Use prepositional phrase.]

   _____

2. a.  Toby went to Disneyland for the first time.
   b.  He was very excited.

[Use past participle (-*ed* form).]

_____

3. a. Teresa received a full scholarship.

   b. She does not need to worry about paying her tuition.
   [Use subordinating conjunction.]

_____

4. a. Lance answered the phone.

   b. He spoke with a gruff voice.
   [Use adverb.]

_____

5. a. The truck choked and sputtered.

   b. The truck pulled into the garage.
   [Use present participle (-*ing* form).]

_____

6. a. Rich programmed his VCR.

   b. He taped his favorite sitcom.
   [Use infinitive (*to*) phrase.]

_____

7. a. The postal carrier placed a package outside my door.

   b. The package had a foreign stamp on it.
   [Use prepositional phrase.]

_____

8. a. The instructor asked the students to take their seats.

   b. She was annoyed.
   [Use past participle (-*ed* form).]

_____

9. a. Shyla stood outside the student union.

   b. She waited for her boyfriend.
   [Use present participle (-*ing* form).]

_____

10. a. Bo walked to the bookstore.

    b. He was going to buy some new highlighters.
    [Use infinitive (*to*) phrase.]

_____

## D.7 Redundancy and Wordiness

Redundancy results when a writer says the same thing twice. Wordiness results when a writer uses more words than necessary to convey a meaning. Both redundancy and wordiness detract from clear, effective sentences by distracting and confusing the reader.

### Eliminating Redundancy

A common mistake is to repeat the same idea in slightly different words.

> The remaining chocolate-chip cookie is the only one left, so I saved it for you. [*Remaining* and *only one left* mean the same thing.]

> The vase was oval in shape. [Oval is a shape, so *in shape* is redundant.]

To revise a redundant sentence, eliminate one of the redundant elements.

### Eliminating Wordiness

**1. Eliminate wordiness by cutting out words that do not add to the meaning of your sentence.**

WORDY: In the final analysis, choosing the field of biology as my major resulted in my realizing that college is hard work.

REVISED: Choosing biology as my major made me realize that college is hard work.

WORDY: The type of imitative behavior that I notice among teenagers is a very important, helpful aspect of their learning to function in groups.

REVISED: The imitative behavior of teenagers helps them learn to function in groups.

Watch out in particular for empty words and phrases.

| *Phrase* | *Substitute* |
|---|---|
| until such time as | until |
| due to the fact that | because |
| at this point in time | now |
| in order to | to |

**2. Express your ideas simply and directly, using as few words as possible.**
Often by rearranging your wording, you can eliminate two or three words.

> the fleas that my dog has → my dog's fleas

> workers with jobs that are low in pay → workers with low-paying jobs

**3. Use strong, active verbs that convey movement and give additional information.**

WORDY: I was in charge of two other employees and needed to watch over their work and performance.

REVISED: I supervised two employees, monitored their performance, and checked their work.

**4. Avoid sentences that begin with** *"There is"* **and** *"There are."* These empty phrases add no meaning, energy, or life to sentences.

WORDY: There are many children who suffer from malnutrition.
REVISED: Many children suffer from malnutrition.

**EXERCISE 24** Revise each of the following sentences to eliminate redundancy and wordiness.

EXAMPLE: Janice, who is impatient, usually cannot wait for class to end and packs up all of her books and notebooks in her backpack before the class is over.

REVISED: *Janice is impatient and usually packs everything in her backpack before class ends.*

1. My neighbors are friendly, nice, and cooperative and always willing to help me. _____

2. Fran and Joe are returning again to the movie theater where they met. _____

3. Lynn changed from her regular clothes into her shorts and T-shirt in order that she could play basketball. _____

4. Due to the fact that Professor Reis assigned 100 pages of reading for tomorrow, I will be unable to join the group of my friends at the restaurant tonight. _____

5. In my mythology class we discussed and talked about the presence of a Noah's ark–type story in most cultures. _____

6. Darryl offered many ideas and theories as to the reason why humans exist. _____

7. There are many children who have not been immunized against dangerous childhood diseases. _____

_____

8. Scientists have been studying the disease AIDS for many years, but they have been unable to find a cure for the disease. _____

_____

9. The brown-colored chair was my father's favorite chair.

_____

10. The briefcase that Julio has carried belonged to his brother.

_____

## D.8 Diction

**Diction** is the use and choice of words. Words that you choose should be appropriate for your audience and express your meaning clearly. The following suggestions will help you improve your diction.

**1. Avoid slang expressions.** Slang refers to the informal, special expressions created and used by groups of people who want to give themselves a unique identity. Slang is an appropriate and useful way to communicate in some social situations and in some forms of creative writing. However, it is not appropriate for academic or career writing.

> SLANG:    My sister seems permanently out to lunch.
> REVISED:  My sister seems out of touch with the world.

> SLANG:    We pigged out at the ice-cream shop.
> REVISED:  We consumed enormous quantities of ice cream at the ice-cream shop.

**2. Avoid colloquial language.** Colloquial language refers to casual, everyday, spoken language. It should be avoided in formal situations. Words that fall into this category are labeled *informal* or *colloquial* in your dictionary.

> COLLOQUIAL:  I almost flunked bio last sem.
> REVISED:     I almost failed biology last semester.

COLLOQUIAL: What are you all doing later?
REVISED: What are you doing later?

**3. Avoid nonstandard language.** Nonstandard language consists of words and grammatical forms that are used in conversation but are neither correct nor acceptable standard written English.

| Nonstandard | Standard |
|---|---|
| hisself | himself |
| knowed | known, knew |
| hadn't ought to | should not |
| she want | she wants |
| he go | he goes |

**4. Avoid trite expressions.** Trite expressions are old, worn-out words and phrases that have become stale and do not convey meaning as effectively as possible. These expressions are also called *clichés*.

*Trite Expressions*

| | | |
|---|---|---|
| needle in a haystack | sadder but wiser | as old as the hills |
| hard as a rock | white as snow | pretty as a picture |
| face the music | gentle as a lamb | |

**EXERCISE 25**

Revise each of the following sentences by using correct diction.

EXAMPLE: This here building is Clemens Hall.

REVISED: <u>This building is Clemens Hall.</u>

1. Jean freaked out when I told her she won the lottery. _____

   _____

2. He go to the library. _____

   _____

3. The campus is wider than an ocean. _____

   _____

4. Marty sits next to me in chem. _____

   _____

5. Sandy's new stereo is totally cool and has an awesome sound.

   _____

6. We went nuts when our team won the game. _____

   _____

7. Them CD players sure are expensive. _____

_____

8. I think Nathan is as sharp as a tack because he got every question

on the exam right. _____

_____

9. Nino blew class off today to go rock climbing with his pals.

_____

10. Dr. Marings was beeped in the middle of the play and had to high-

tail it to a phone. _____

_____

# Using Punctuation Correctly

## E.1 End Punctuation

### When to Use Periods

Use a period in the following situations:

**1. To end a sentence unless it is a question or an exclamation.**

> We washed the car even though we knew a thunderstorm was imminent.

> NOTE: Use a period to end a sentence that states an indirect question or indirectly quotes someone's words or thoughts.

> INCORRECT:  Margaret wondered if she would be on time?
> CORRECT:    Margaret wondered if she would be on time.

**2. To punctuate many abbreviations.**

> M.D.    B.A.    P.M.    B.C.    Mr.    Ms.

Do not use periods in acronyms, such as *NATO* and *AIDS,* or in abbreviations for most organizations, such as *NBC* and *NAACP.* (See p. 463.)

> NOTE: If a sentence ends with an abbreviation, the sentence has only one period, not two.

> The train was due to arrive at 7:00 P.M.

### When to Use Question Marks

Use question marks after direct questions. Place the question mark within the closed quotation marks.

> She asked the grocer, "How old is this cheese?"

NOTE: Use a period, not a question mark, after an indirect question.

She asked the grocer how old the cheese was.

### When to Use Exclamation Points

Use an exclamation point at the end of a sentence that expresses particular emphasis, excitement, or urgency. Use exclamation points sparingly, however, especially in academic writing.

What a beautiful day it is!          Dial 911 right now!

## E.2 Commas

The comma is used to separate parts of a sentence from one another. If you omit a comma when it is needed, you risk making a clear and direct sentence confusing.

### When to Use Commas

Use a comma in the following situations:

**1. Before a coordinating conjunction that joins two independent clauses.** (See p. 436.)

Terry had planned to leave work early, but he was delayed.

**2. To separate a dependent (subordinate) clause from an independent clause when the dependent clause comes first in the sentence.** (See p. 407.)

After I left the library, I went to the computer lab.

**3. To separate introductory words and phrases from the rest of the sentence.**

<u>Unfortunately</u>, I forgot my umbrella.

<u>To pass the baton</u>, I will need to locate my teammate.

<u>Exuberant over their victory</u>, the football-team members carried the quarterback on their shoulders.

**4. To separate a nonrestrictive phrase or clause from the rest of a sentence. A nonrestrictive** phrase or clause is added to a sentence but does not change the sentence's basic meaning.

To determine whether an element is nonrestrictive, read the sentence without the element. If the meaning of the sentence does not essentially change, then the commas are *necessary*.

My sister, who is a mail carrier, is afraid of dogs. [The essential meaning of this sentence does not change if we read the sentence without the subordinate clause: *My sister is afraid of dogs.* Therefore, commas are needed.]

Mail carriers who have been bitten by dogs are afraid of them. [If we read this sentence without the subordinate clause, its meaning changes considerably: *Mail carriers are afraid of (dogs).* It seems to say that *all* mail carriers are afraid of dogs. In this case, adding commas is not correct.]

**5. To separate three or more items in a series.**

NOTE: A comma is *not* used *after* the last item in the series.

I plan to take math, psychology, and writing next semester.

**6. To separate coordinate adjectives: two or more adjectives that are not joined by a coordinating conjunction and that equally modify the same noun or pronoun.**

The thirsty, hungry children returned from a day at the beach.

To determine if a comma is needed between two adjectives, use the following test. Insert the word *and* between the two adjectives. Also try reversing the order of the two adjectives. If the phrase makes sense in either case, then a comma is needed. If the phrase does not make sense, do not use a comma.

The tired, angry child fell asleep. [*The tired and angry child* makes sense; so does *The angry, tired child.* Consequently, the comma is needed.]

Sarah is an excellent psychology student. [*Sarah is an excellent and psychology student* does not make sense, nor does *Sarah is a psychology, excellent student.* A comma is therefore not needed.]

**7. To separate parenthetical expressions from the clauses they modify.** Parenthetical expressions are added pieces of information that are not essential to the meaning of the sentence.

Most students, I imagine, can get jobs on campus.

**8. To separate a transition from the clause it modifies.**

In addition, I will rake leaves.

**9. To separate a quotation from the words that introduce or explain it.**

NOTE: The comma goes *inside* the closed quotation marks.

"Shopping," Barbara explained, "is a form of relaxation for me."

Barbara explained, "Shopping is a form of relaxation for me."

**10. To separate dates, place names, and long numbers.**

October 10, 1961, is my birthday.

Dayton, Ohio, was the first stop on the tour.

Participants numbered 1,777,716.

**11. To separate phrases expressing contrast.**

Sam's good nature, not his wealth, explains his popularity.

**EXERCISE 26** ▶ Revise each of the following sentences by adding commas where needed.

EXAMPLE:  Until the judge entered, the courtroom was noisy.

1. "Hello" said the group of friends when Joan entered the room.
2. Robert DeNiro the actor in the film was very handsome.
3. My parents frequently vacation in Miami Florida.
4. Drunk drivers I suppose may not realize they are not competent to drive.
5. Jeff purchased a television couch and dresser for his new apartment.
6. Luckily the windstorm did not do any damage to our town.
7. Frieda has an early class and she has to go to work afterward.
8. After taking a trip to the Galápagos Islands Mark Twain wrote about them.
9. The old dilapidated stadium was opened to the public on September 15 1931.
10. Afterward we will go out for ice cream.

# E.3 Unnecessary Commas

It is as important to know where *not* to place commas as it is to know where to place them. The following rules explain where it is incorrect to place them.

**1. Do not place a comma between subject and verb, between verb and complement, or between an adjective and the word it modifies.**

INCORRECT: The stunning, imaginative, and intriguing, painting, became the hit of the show.

*adjective* intriguing, *subject* painting, *verb* became

CORRECT: The stunning, imaginative, and intriguing painting became the hit of the show.

## 2. Do not place a comma between two verbs, subjects, or complements used as compounds.

INCORRECT: Sue called, and asked me to come by her office.

*compound verb* called, and asked

CORRECT: Sue called and asked me to come by her office.

## 3. Do not place a comma before a coordinating conjunction joining two dependent clauses. (See p. 395.)

INCORRECT: The city planner examined blueprints that the park designer had submitted, and that the budget officer had approved.

*dependent clause* that the park designer had submitted
*dependent clause* that the budget officer had approved

CORRECT: The city planner examined blueprints that the park designer had submitted and that the budget officer had approved.

## 4. Do not place commas around restrictive clauses, phrases, or appositives. Restrictive clauses, phrases, and appositives are modifiers that are essential to the meaning of the sentence.

INCORRECT: The girl, who grew up down the block, became my life-long friend.

CORRECT: The girl who grew up down the block became my life-long friend.

## 5. Do not place a comma before the word *than* in a comparison or after the words *like* and *such as* in an introduction to a list.

INCORRECT: Some snails, such as, the Oahu Tree Snail, have more colorful shells, than other snails.

CORRECT: Some snails, such as the Oahu Tree Snail, have more colorful shells than other snails.

## 6. Do not place a comma next to a period, a question mark, an exclamation point, a dash, or an opening parenthesis.

INCORRECT: "When will you come back?," Dillon's son asked him.

CORRECT: "When will you come back?" Dillon's son asked him.

INCORRECT: The bachelor button, (also known as the cornflower) grows well in ordinary garden soil.

CORRECT:   The bachelor button (also known as the cornflower)
grows well in ordinary garden soil.

**7. Do not place a comma between cumulative adjectives.** Cumulative
adjectives, unlike coordinate adjectives (see p. 453), cannot be joined by
*and* or rearranged.

INCORRECT:   The light, yellow, rose blossom was a pleasant birthday
surprise. [*The light and yellow and rose blossom* does
not make sense, so the commas are incorrect.]

CORRECT:   The light yellow rose blossom was a pleasant birthday
surprise.

# E.4 Colons and Semicolons

## When to Use a Colon

A colon follows an independent clause and usually signals that the clause is
to be explained or elaborated on. Use a colon in the following situations:

**1. To introduce items in a series after an independent clause.** The series
can consist of words, phrases, or clauses.

I am wearing three popular colors: magenta, black, and white.

**2. To signal a list or a statement introduced by an independent clause
ending with *the following* or *as follows*.**

The directions are as follows: take Main Street to Oak Avenue and then
turn left.

**3. To introduce a quotation that follows an introductory independent
clause.**

My brother made his point quite clear: "Never borrow my car without asking me first!"

**4. To introduce an explanation.**

Mathematics is enjoyable: it requires a high degree of accuracy and peak
concentration.

**5. To separate titles and subtitles of books.**

*Biology: A Study of Life*

NOTE: A colon must always follow an independent clause. It should not be used in the middle of a clause.

INCORRECT: My favorite colors are: red, pink, and green.
CORRECT:   My favorite colors are red, pink, and green.

## When to Use a Semicolon

Use a semicolon in the following situations:

**1. To separate two closely related independent clauses not connected by a coordinating conjunction.** (See p. 407.)

Sam had a 99 average in math; he earned an A in the course.

**2. To separate two independent clauses joined by a conjunctive adverb.** (See p. 377.)

Margaret earned an A on her term paper; consequently, she was exempt from the final exam.

**3. To separate independent clauses joined with a coordinating conjunction if the clauses are very long or if they contain numerous commas.**

By late afternoon, having tried on every pair of black checked pants in the mall, Marsha was tired and cranky; but she still had not found what she needed to complete her outfit for the play.

**4. To separate items in a series if the items are lengthy or contain commas.**

The soap opera characters include Marianne Loundsberry, the heroine; Ellen and Sarah, her children; Barry, her ex-husband; and Louise, her best friend.

**5. To correct a comma splice or run-on sentence.** (See p. 407.)

**EXERCISE 27**

Correct each of the following sentences by placing colons and semicolons where necessary. Delete any incorrect punctuation.

EXAMPLE: Samuel Clemens disliked his name; therefore, he used Mark Twain as his pen name.

1. The large, modern, and airy, gallery houses works of art by important artists, however, it has not yet earned national recognition as an important gallery.
2. Rita suggested several herbs to add to my spaghetti sauce, oregano, basil, and thyme.

3. Vic quickly typed the paper, it was due in less than an hour.
4. Furniture refinishing is a great hobby, it is satisfying to be able to make a piece of furniture look new again.
5. The bridesmaids in my sister's wedding are as follows, Judy, her best friend Kim, our sister, Franny, our cousin, and Sue, a family friend.
6. Mac got a speeding ticket, he has to go to court next Tuesday.
7. I will go for a swim when the sun comes out, it will not be so chilly then.
8. Will was hungry after his hockey game, consequently, he ordered four hamburgers.
9. Sid went to the bookstore to purchase *Physical Anthropology Man and His Makings,* it is required for one of his courses.
10. Here is an old expression, "The way to a man's heart is through his stomach."

## E.5 Dashes, Parentheses, Hyphens, Apostrophes, Quotation Marks

### Dashes (—)

The dash is used to (1) separate nonessential elements from the main part of the sentence, (2) create a stronger separation, or interruption, than commas or parentheses, and (3) emphasize an idea, create a dramatic effect, or indicate a sudden change in thought.

My sister—the friendliest person I know—will visit me this weekend.

My brother's most striking quality is his ability to make money—or so I thought until I heard of his bankruptcy.

When typing, use two hyphens (--) to indicate a dash. No space appears between the dash and the words it separates.

### Parentheses ( )

Parentheses are used in pairs to separate extra or nonessential information that often amplifies, clarifies, or acts as an aside to the main point. Unlike dashes, parentheses de-emphasize information.

Some large breeds of dogs (golden retrievers and Newfoundlands) are susceptible to hip deformities.

The prize was dinner for two (maximum value, $50.00) at a restaurant of one's choice.

## Hyphens (-)

Hyphens have the following primary uses:

**1. To split a word when dividing it between two lines of writing or typing** (see p. 464).

**2. To join two or more words that function as a unit, either as a noun or as a noun modifier.**

mother-in-law                single-parent families

twenty-year-old             school-age children

state-of-the-art sound system

## Apostrophes (')

Use apostrophes in the following situations:

**1. To show ownership or possession.** When the person, place, or thing doing the possessing is a singular noun, add -'s to the end of it, regardless of what its final letter is.

The man's CD player        John Keats's poetry

Aretha's best friend

With plural nouns that end in -s, add only an apostrophe to the end of the word.

the twins' bedroom         postal workers' hours

teachers' salaries

With plural nouns that do not end in -s, add -'s.

children's books           men's slacks

Do not use an apostrophe with the possessive adjective *its*.

INCORRECT:  It's frame is damaged.

CORRECT:    Its frame is damaged.

**2. To indicate omission of one or more letters in a word or number.** Contractions are used in informal writing, but not in academic writing.

it's [it is]                hasn't [has not]
doesn't [does not]         '57 Ford [1957 Ford]
you're [you are]           class of '89 [class of 1989]

## Quotation Marks (" ")

Quotation marks separate a direct quotation from the sentence that contains it. Here are some rules to follow in using quotation marks.

### 1. Quotation marks are always used in pairs.

> NOTE: A comma or period goes at the end of the quotation, inside the quotation marks.

> Marge declared, "I never expected Peter to give me a watch for Christmas."

> "I never expected Peter to give me a watch for Christmas," Marge declared.

### 2. Use single quotation marks for a quotation within a quotation.

> My literature professor said, "Byron's line 'She walks in beauty like the night' is one of his most sensual."

> NOTE: When quoting long prose passages of more than four typed lines, do not use quotation marks. Instead, set off the quotation from the rest of the text by indenting each line ten spaces from the left margin. This format is called a **block quotation.**

> The opening lines of the Declaration of Independence establish the purpose of the document:

> When in the Course of human events it becomes necessary for one people to dissolve the political bonds which have connected them with another, and to assume among the powers of the earth, the separate and equal station to which the Laws of Nature and of Nature's God entitle them, a decent respect to the opinions of mankind requires that they should declare the causes which impel them to the separation.

### 3. Use **quotation marks to indicate titles of songs, short stories, poems, reports, articles, and essays.** Books, movies, plays, operas, paintings, statues, and the names of television series are italicized (or underlined to indicate italics).

> "Rappaccini's Daughter" (short story)
> *60 Minutes* [or 60 Minutes] (television series)
> "The Road Not Taken" (poem)

**EXERCISE** ▶ **28** | To the following sentences, add dashes, apostrophes, parentheses, hyphens, and quotation marks where necessary.

EXAMPLE:  "You are not going out dressed that way!" said Frank's roommate.

1. My daughter in law recently entered medical school.
2. At the bar I worked in last summer, the waitresses tips were always pooled and equally divided.
3. Youre going to Paris next summer, aren't you?
4. The career counselor said, The computer field is not as open as it used to be.
5. We heard Peter, Paul, and Mary sing Puff, the Magic Dragon in concert.
6. Frank asked me if I wanted to rent a big screen television for our Super Bowl party.
7. Rachel she was the teaching assistant for my linguistics class spent last year in China.
8. Macy's is having a sale on womens boots next week.
9. Trina said, My one year old's newest word is Bzz, which she says whenever she sees a fly.
10. Some animals horses and donkeys can interbreed, but they produce infertile offspring.

# Managing Mechanics and Spelling

## F.1 Capitalization

In general, capital letters are used to mark the beginning of a sentence, to mark the beginning of a quotation, and to identify proper nouns. Here are some guidelines on capitalization.

| What to Capitalize | Example |
|---|---|
| 1. First word in every sentence | Prewriting is useful. |
| 2. First word in a direct quotation | Sarah commented, "That exam was difficult!" |
| 3. Names of people and animals, including the pronoun *I* | Aladdin<br>Janet Reno<br>Spot |
| 4. Names of specific places, cities, states, nations, geographic areas or regions | New Orleans<br>the Southwest<br>Lake Erie |
| 5. Government and public offices, departments, buildings | Williamsville Library<br>House of Representatives |
| 6. Names of social, political, business, sporting, cultural organizations | Boy Scouts<br>Buffalo Bills |
| 7. Names of months, days of the week, holidays | August<br>Tuesday<br>Halloween |
| 8. In titles of works: the first word following a colon, the first and last words, and all other words except articles, prepositions, and conjunctions | "Once More to the Lake"<br>*Biology: A Study of Life* |

9. Races, nationalities, languages — African American, Italian, English
10. Religions, religious figures, sacred books — Hindu, Hinduism, God, Allah, the Bible
11. Names of products — Tide, Buick
12. Personal titles when they come right before a name — Professor Rodriguez, Senator Hatch
13. Major historic events — World War I
14. Specific course titles — History 201, Introduction to Psychology

**EXERCISE 29**

Capitalize words as necessary in the following sentences.

EXAMPLE: Farmers in the M̲idwest were devastated by floods last summer.

1. My mother is preparing some special foods for our hanukkah meal; rabbi epstein will join us.
2. My american politics professor used to be a judge in the town of evans.
3. A restaurant in the galleria mall serves korean food.
4. A graduate student I know is writing a book about buddha entitled *the great one: ways to enlightenment.*
5. at the concert last night, cher changed into many different outfits.
6. An employee announced over the loudspeaker, "attention, customers! we have pepsi on sale in aisle ten for a very low price!"
7. Karen's father was stationed at fort bradley during the vietnam war.
8. Last tuesday the state assembly passed governor allen's budget.
9. Boston is an exciting city; be sure to visit the museum of fine arts.
10. Dan asked if i wanted to go see the bolshoi ballet at shea's theatre in november.

## F.2 Abbreviations

An abbreviation is a shortened form of a word or phrase that is used to represent the whole word or phrase. The following is a list of common acceptable abbreviations.

| *What to Abbreviate* | *Example* |
|---|---|
| 1. Some titles before or after people's names | Mr. Ling<br>Samuel Rosen, M.D.<br>*but* Professor Ashe |
| 2. Names of familiar organizations, corporations, countries | CIA, IBM, VISTA, USA |

3. Time references preceded or followed by a number

7:00 A.M.
3:00 P.M.
A.D. 1973

4. Latin terms when used in footnotes, references, or parentheses

i.e. [*id est,* "that is"]
et al. [*et alii,* "and others"]

Here is a list of things that are usually *not* abbreviated.

|  | Example | |
| --- | --- | --- |
| *What Not to Abbreviate* | *Incorrect* | *Correct* |
| 1. Units of measurement | thirty in. | thirty inches |
| 2. Geographic or other place names when used in sentences | N.Y.<br>Elm St. | New York<br>Elm Street |
| 3. Parts of written works when used in sentences | ch. 3 | chapter 3 |
| 4. Names of days, months, holidays | Tues. | Tuesday |
| 5. Names of subject areas | psych. | psychology |

**EXERCISE  30 ▶**  Correct the inappropriate use of abbreviations in the following sentences. If a sentence contains no errors, write *Correct* beside it.

EXAMPLE:  We live thirty ~~mi.~~ outside ~~NYC.~~
(handwritten: miles New York City)

1. Frank enjoys going swimming at the YMCA on Oak St.
2. Prof. Jorge asked the class to turn to pg. 8.
3. Because he is seven ft. tall, my brother was recruited for the high-school b-ball team.
4. When I asked Ron why he hadn't called me, he said it was Northeast Bell's fault—i.e., his phone hadn't been working.
5. Tara is flying TWA to KC to visit her parents next Wed.
6. At 11:30 P.M., we turned on NBC to watch *The Tonight Show.*
7. Last wk. I missed my chem. lab.
8. The exam wasn't too difficult; only ques. no. 15 and ques. no. 31 were extremely difficult.
9. Dr. Luc removed the mole from my rt. hand with lasers.
10. Mark drove out to L.A. to audition for a role in MGM's new movie.

## F.3 Hyphenation and Word Division

On occasion you must divide and hyphenate a word on one line and continue it on the next. Here are some guidelines for dividing words.

**1. Divide words only when necessary.** Frequent word divisions make a paper difficult to read.

**2. Divide words between syllables.** Consult a dictionary if you are unsure how to break a word into syllables.

    di-vi-sion          pro-tect

**3. Do not divide one-syllable words.**

**4. Do not divide a word so that a single letter is left at the end of a line.**

    INCORRECT:  a-typical
    CORRECT:     atyp-ical

**5. Do not divide a word so that fewer than three letters begin the new line.**

    INCORRECT:  visu-al
    CORRECT:     vi-sual
    INCORRECT:  caus-al [This word cannot be divided at all.]

**6. Divide compound words only between the words.**

    some-thing         any-one

**7. Divide words that are already hyphenated only at the hyphen.**

    ex-policeman

**EXERCISE 31** | Insert a diagonal (/) mark where each word should be divided. Mark "N" in the margin if the word should not be divided.

    EXAMPLE:  every/where

| | |
|---|---|
| 1. enclose | 6. disgusted |
| 2. house | 7. chandelier |
| 3. saxophone | 8. headphones |
| 4. hardly | 9. swings |
| 5. well-known | 10. abyss |

## F.4 Numbers

Numbers can be written as numerals (600) or words (six hundred). Here are some guidelines for when to use numerals and when to use words.

| *When to Use Numerals* | *Example* |
|---|---|
| 1. Numbers that are spelled with more than two words | 375 students |
| 2. Days and years | August 10, 1993 |

| | |
|---|---|
| 3. Decimals, percentages, fractions | 56.7<br>59 percent<br>1³/4 cups |
| 4. Exact times | 9:27 A.M. |
| 5. Pages, chapters, volumes; acts and lines from plays | chapter 12<br>volume 4 |
| 6. Addresses | 122 Peach Street |
| 7. Exact amounts of money | $5.60 |
| 8. Scores and statistics | 23–6<br>5 of every 12 |

| *When to Use Words* | *Example* |
|---|---|
| 1. Numbers that begin sentences | Two hundred ten students attended the lecture. |
| 2. Numbers of one or two words | sixty students, two hundred women |

**EXERCISE 32**    Correct the misuse of numbers in the following sentences. If a sentence contains no errors, write *Correct* next to it.

EXAMPLE:   The reception hall was filled with ~~500~~ *five hundred* guests.

1. At 6:52 A.M. my roommate's alarm clock went off.
2. I purchased 9 turtlenecks for one dollar and fifty-five cents each.
3. 35 floats were entered in the parade, but only 4 received prizes.
4. Act three of *Othello* is very exciting.
5. Almost fifty percent of all marriages end in divorce.
6. The Broncos won the game 21–7.
7. We were assigned volume two of *Don Quixote*, beginning on page 351.
8. The hardware store is located at three forty-four Elm Street, 2 doors down from my grandmother's house.
9. Maryanne's new car is a 2-door V-8.
10. Our anniversary is June ninth, nineteen eighty-nine.

## F.5 Suggestions for Improving Spelling

Correct spelling is important to a well-written paragraph or essay. The following suggestions will help you submit papers without misspellings.

**1. Do not worry about spelling as you write your first draft.** Checking a word in a dictionary at this point will interrupt your flow of ideas. If you do not know how a word is spelled, spell it the way it sounds. Circle or underline the word so you remember to check it later.

**2. Keep a list of words you commonly misspell.** This list can be part of your error log.

**3. Every time you catch an error or find a misspelled word on a paper returned by your instructor, add it to your list.**

**4. Study your list.** Ask a friend to quiz you on the words. Eliminate words from the list after you have passed several quizzes on them.

**5. Develop a spelling awareness.** You'll find that your spelling will improve just by being aware that spelling is important. When you encounter a new word, notice how it is spelled and practice writing it.

**6. Pronounce words you are having difficulty spelling.** Pronounce each syllable distinctly.

**7. Review basic spelling rules.** Your college library or learning lab may have manuals, workbooks, or computer programs that cover basic rules and provide guided practice.

**8. Be sure to have a dictionary readily available when you write.**

**9. Read your final draft through once, checking only for spelling errors.** Look at each word carefully, and check the spelling of those words of which you are uncertain.

## F.6 Six Useful Spelling Rules

The following six rules focus on common spelling trouble spots.

**1. Is it *ei* or *ie*?**

   *Rule:* Use *i* before *e*, except after *c* or when the syllable is pronounced *ay* as in the word *weigh*.

      EXAMPLE:  *i* before *e*: bel<u>ie</u>ve, n<u>ie</u>ce

             except after *c*: re<u>ce</u>ive, conce<u>i</u>ve

             or when pronounced *ay*: neighbor, sl<u>ei</u>gh

   *Exceptions:*

| either | neither | foreign | forfeit |
|--------|---------|---------|---------|
| height | leisure | weird   | seize   |

2. **When adding an ending, do you keep or drop the final *e*?**

   *Rules:*　a. Keep the final *e* when adding an ending that begins with a consonant. (Vowels are *a, e, i, o, u,* and sometimes *y*; all other letters are consonants.)

   hope → hopeful　　　aware → awareness
   live → lively　　　　force → forceful

   b. Drop the final *e* when adding an ending that begins with a vowel.

   hope → hoping　　　file → filing
   note → notable　　　write → writing

   *Exceptions:*　argument　　truly　　　changeable
   　　　　　　　　awful　　　　manageable　courageous
   　　　　　　　　judgment　　noticeable　outrageous
   　　　　　　　　acknowledgment

3. **When adding an ending, do you keep the final *y*, change it to *i*, or drop it?**

   *Rules:*　a. Keep the *y* if the letter before the *y* is a vowel.

   delay → delaying　　buy → buying　　prey → preyed

   b. Change the *y* to *i* if the letter before the *y* is a consonant, but keep the *y* for the *-ing* ending.

   defy → defiance　　　marry → married
   　　→ defying　　　　　→ marrying

4. **When adding an ending to a one-syllable word, when do you double the final letter if it is a consonant?**

   *Rules:*　a. In one-syllable words, double the final consonant when a single vowel comes before it.

   drop → dropped　　shop → shopped　　pit → pitted

   b. In one-syllable words, *don't* double the final consonant when two vowels or a consonant comes before it.

   repair → repairable　　sound → sounded
   real → realize

5. **When adding an ending to a word with more than one syllable, when do you double the final letter if it is a consonant?**

   *Rules:*　a. In multisyllable words, double the final consonant when a single vowel comes before it *and* the stress falls on the last syllable. (Vowels are *a, e, i, o, u,* and sometimes *y.* All other letters are consonants.)

begin´ → beginning     transmit´ → transmitted
repel´ → repelling

b. In multisyllable words, do *not* double the final consonant (a) when two vowels or a vowel and another consonant come before it *or* (b) when the stress is not on the last syllable.

despair → despairing     ben´efit → benefited
conceal → concealing

6. **To form a plural, do you add -*s* or -*es*?**

*Rules:*   a. For most nouns, add -*s.*

cat → cats     house → houses

b. Add -*es* to words that end in -*o* if the -*o* is preceded by a consonant.

hero → heroes     potato → potatoes

*Exceptions: zoos, radios, ratios,* and other words ending with two vowels.

c. Add -*es* to words ending in -*ch,* -*sh,* -*ss,* -*x,* or -*z.*

church → churches     fox → foxes     dish → dishes

# G

# Documenting Sources

Whenever you use the words or ideas of other people, you must *document* the source. You must give credit to whom or where you borrowed the material and include full information about it in a list of references so your reader can locate it easily. Failure to provide documentation of a source is called "plagiarism." It means using an author's words or ideas without acknowledging that you have done so. Plagiarism is a serious ethical error and legal violation. In many colleges, students who plagiarize may fail the course in which the plagiarized paper was submitted or be dismissed from the college.

There are a number of different documentation formats (these are often called *styles*) that are used by scholars and researchers. Members of a particular academic discipline usually use the same format. For example, biologists follow a format described in *Scientific Style and Format: A Manual for Authors, Editors, and Publishers,* and social scientists follow guidelines given in *Publication Manual of the American Psychological Association.* Style manuals exist for other disciplines as well, including mathematics, medicine, and chemistry.

The most widely used documentation style is that of the Modern Language Association. The MLA style, as it is called, is used in English and the humanities. In this section, this style is discussed briefly. For a comprehensive review of the MLA style, consult the following:

Gibaldi, Joseph. MLA Handbook for Writers of Research Papers. 4th ed. New York: MLA, 1995.

## G.1 An Overview of the MLA Style

### MLA In-Paper (In-Text) Citations

In your paper, if you refer to, summarize, paraphrase, quote, or in any other way use another author's words or ideas, you must indicate the source from which you took them. You do this by inserting a reference called an *in-text citation*. It refers your reader to your source list, which you include at the end of your paper. This list of sources is called "Works Cited." An in-text citation identifies the name and page number of your source and looks like this:

> One researcher concludes that women "who work with men might find it useful to learn something about sports to take part in those conversations" (Tannen 65).

The in-text citation "(Tannen 65)" refers the reader to the entry in the Works Cited list that gives full information about Tannen's book:

Tannen, Deborah. Talking from 9 to 5. New York: Morrow, 1994.

Here are the answers to a few common questions about preparing in-text citations.

**1. Where should I place the citation?** Place your citation at the end of the sentence in which you refer to, summarize, paraphrase, or quote a source. It should follow a quotation mark, but come before punctuation that ends the last sentence. If a question mark ends the sentence, place the question mark before the citation and a period after the citation.

**2. What information should the citation contain?** If you have not mentioned the author's name in your sentence, the citation should include both the author's name and date. If you did name the author when you introduced the quotation or material to be acknowledged, you do not need to repeat it in the citation. Simply give the page number.

**3. What if I use two or more works by the same author?** If you have used two or more works by the same author, either include the title in your sentence or include an abbreviated title in your citation.

> In Talking from 9 to 5, Tannen concludes . . . (67).

or

> Tannen concludes . . . (Talking 67).

**4. What if my source has more than one author?** If there are two or three authors, include the last names of all of them. If there are four or more, include only the first author's last name and follow it with *et al.*, which means "and others."

McCleary, West, and Rodriguez (1989) argue that . . .

Thompson et al. (1995) conclude that . . .

## MLA Works Cited

Your list of works cited should include all the sources you referred to, summarized, paraphrased, or quoted in your paper. The list appears on a separate page at the end of your paper and is titled "Works Cited." Arrange these entries alphabetically by each author's last name. If an author is not named (as in an editorial), then alphabetize the item by title. Single-space the entries, and indent any continuing lines.

**1. What format is used for books?** The basic format for a book can be illustrated as follows:

```
                                                            place of
           ┌───── author ─────┐ ┌────────── title ──────────┐ ┌─publication─┐
           Tannen, Deborah. You Just Don't Understand. New York:
           Morrow, 1990.
           └─name of─┘ └─ date ─┘
             publisher
```

Special cases are handled as follows:

a. **Two or more authors.** If there are two or three authors, include all names in the order in which they appear in the source. If there are four or more, give the first author's name only and follow it with "et al."

b. **Two or more works by the same author.** If your list contains two or more works by the same author, list the author's name only once. For additional entries, substitute three hyphens in place of the name.

Tannen, Deborah. Talking from 9 to 5. New York: Morrow, 1994.

———. You Just Don't Understand. New York: Morrow, 1990.

c. **Editor.** If the book has an editor instead of an author, list the editor's name at the beginning of the entry and follow it with "ed."

Ruttenberg, Francis, ed. Perceptions of History. New York: Harper, 1995.

d. **Edition.** If the book has an edition number, include it after the title.

Bernstein, Douglas A., et al. <u>Psychology</u>. 2d ed. Boston: Houghton, 1991.

    **e. Publisher.** The entire name of the publisher is not used. For example, Houghton Mifflin Company is listed as "Houghton."

**2. What format is used for articles?** The basic format for a periodical can be illustrated as follows:

Maccoby, Eleanor E. "Gender and Relationships: A Developmental Account." American Psychologist 45 (1990): 513–20.

*(labels: author — article title — name of periodical — volume — year — pages)*

Special cases are handled as follows:

    **a. Newspaper articles.** Include the author, article title, name of the newspaper, date, section letter or number, and page(s).

Zurawik, David. "It's Not the Job." <u>Buffalo News</u> 9 Mar. 1996, sec. C: 7.

    **b. An article in a weekly magazine.** List the author, article title, name of the magazine, date, and page(s). Abbreviate all months except May, June, and July, and place the day before the month.

Purvis, Andrew. "Where does the Ebola Hide?" <u>Time</u> 4 Mar. 1996: 59.

    **c. Electronic Sources.** List the author's name, title, source or service, and date of publication (or date you found the information if your source is an on-line service). Here are a few examples:

<u>Random House Unabridged Dictionary</u>. CD-ROM. New York: Random, 1993.

"Boeing Co." <u>Disclosure Database</u>. Dialog. 26 March 1996.

# G.2 Sample Documented Paper—MLA Style

Melinda Lawson

Professor Applegate

English 099-02

24 January 1996

Some Pros and Cons of Legalizing Drugs

The question of whether or not to legalize drugs has become a major issue in the United States within the past decade. Since either resolution of the drug problem has both advantages and disadvantages, it is useful to understand the consequences of each in order to take a position on the issue.

Those arguing for drug legalization believe that making illegal drugs legally available to the public will solve many drug-related problems. One of these problems is burglary, for it is a fact that some people who use certain illegal drugs become chemically addicted to such drugs and then have to support their drug habit by stealing money (or property to be sold for money) from others. This leads to a rise in burglary. However, if drugs were legalized, burglary would no longer be necessary because drugs would be sold at cost. This means that drug users, especially addicts, would not need to commit crimes in order to support their drug use. Gore Vidal states that if drugs were made legal, "there would be no friendly playground for pushers, and addicts would not commit crimes to pay for the next fix" (174).

On the other side of the issue, there are people who believe that decriminalizing drugs will not only not solve the

Lawson 2

drug problem but make it worse. It is logical to assume that if drugs were to become legally available, there would be an increase in the number of drug users. Legalization has been tried in England and Switzerland, and Schmoke and Roques report that both countries suffered: drug use actually increased instead of decreased (17). In countries such as Iran and Thailand, where drugs have long been cheap and available, the rate of addiction is higher than in other countries in which drugs are not as accessible (Courtwright 50).

If addictions increase, so will health problems and, consequently, health costs. As Schmoke and Roques state, "The increase in drug use that would accompany decriminalization/legalization would cause a dramatic rise in health damage and the associated health costs" (17). Possible health risks include low birth weight and birth defects of infants born to users, as well as increased health problems of the drug users themselves.

Public safety is the basis for another argument against the legalization of drugs. People who drive buses, fly airplanes, fight fires, and work in hospitals all would have easy access to drugs and would use them on the job. Drunk drivers would become drugged drivers, increasing the risk of accidents. Random drug testing would be necessary, and costs and regulations would multiply.

In summary, there does not seem to be any easy solution to the drug problem in the United States. Legalizing drugs might result in a decreased crime rate, but it would also result in increased national health and safety problems. Not legalizing drugs might continue to force drug users to commit crimes to support their drug habits. Perhaps a compromise is needed. Controlled or government-regulated drug availability, rather than an open drug market, is an option worth exploring.

## Works Cited

Courtwright, David T. "Should We Legalize Drugs? No." American Heritage May/June 1993: 42–48.

Schmoke, Kurt L. and Wayne J. Roques. "Would Decriminalizing Drugs Reduce Crime and Violence?" CQ Researcher 6 Jan. 1995: 17–18.

Vidal, Gore. Homage to Daniel Shays: Collected Essays. New York: Random, 1970.

# Error Correction Exercises

Revise each of the following paragraphs. Look for errors in sentence structure, grammar, punctuation, mechanics, and spelling. Rewrite these paragraphs with corrections.

### Paragraph 1

Jazz is a type of music, originating in New orleans in the early Twenties, and contained a mixture of Afro-American and European musical elements. There are a wide variety of types of jazz including: the blues, swing, bop and modern. Jazz includes both hard and soft music and it doesn't get to radical. Unlike rock music, rock it does not goes to extremes. Rock bands play so loud you can't understand half of the words. As a result, jazz is more relacking and enjoyable.

### Paragraph 2

every one thinks vacations are great fun but that isnt allways so. Some people are too hyper to relax when their on vaccation. My sister Sally is like that. She has to be on the move at alltimes. She can never slow down and take it easy. She goes from activity to activity at a wild pace. When Sally does have a spare moment between activities, she spends her freetime thinking about work problems and her family and their problems and what she should do about them when she gets back. Consequently, when Sally gets back from a vacation she is exhausted and more tense and upset then when she left home.

### Paragraph 3

Soap operas are usually serious eposodes of different people in the world of today. There about fictuous people whom are supposed to look real. But each character has their unique prblems, crazzy relationships and nonrealistical quirks and habits.In real live, it would never happen.The actors are always getting themself into wiered and unusall situation that are so of the wall that they could never be real. Its just to unreal to have 20 looney people all good frinds.

*Paragraph 4*

Here are two forms of music, we have rock music and we have country music. First, these two sound differen. Rock music is very loud and with a high base sound, sometimes you can't even understand the words that the singer is singing. On the other hand, country music is a bit softer with a mellow but up beat sound. Although country music sometimes sounds boring, at least you can understand the lyrics when listening to it. Country singers usually have a country western accent also unlike rock singers.

*Essay 1*

### What A Good Friend Is

I have this friend Margaret who is really not too intelligent. It took awhile before I could accept her limitations. But, I had to get to know Margaret and her feelings. We are like two hands that wash each other. I help her, she helps me. when I need her to babysit for me while I'm at work it's done. If she needs a ride to the dentist she's got it. All I need is to be given time to do them. We help each other and that is why we are friends.

Good friends; Friends that do for one another. To tell the friend the truth about something that is asked of them. And for the other to respect your views as you would theirs. A friend is there to listen if you have a problem and to suggest something to help solve the problem but, yet not telling you just what to do. Or just to be the shoulder to cry on. Good friends go places and do things together. Good Friends are always there when you need them.

*Essay 2*

### Putting Labels on People

People tend to label someone as stupid if they are slower and takes more time in figuring out an assignment or just trying to understand directions. My friend Georgette is a good example. People make fun of her. When a person has to deal with this type of ridicule by her fellow students or friend she start to feel insecure in speaking up. She start to think she is slower mentally, she gets extremely paranoid when asked to give answer in class. She feels any answer out of her mouth will be wrong. Her self-image shoots down drastically, like a bottom less pit. that She will avoyd in answering all answers even when she's almost positive she's right. It's the possibility of being wrong that will keep her from speaking. Then when some one else gives the answer she seess she was right, she would become extremely anoid at herself for not answering the question. As a result, she start to run away from all challenges, even the slightest challenge will frighten her away. Do from the teasing of her friends, Georgette will lock herself away from trying to understand and her famous words when facing to a challenge will be I can't do it!

Therefore, when a person makes a mistake, you should think of what you say before you say it and be sure it's not going to hurt the person. You comments may help destroy that person self confidence.

# SKILL REFRESHER SCORE CHART

| Skill Refresher | Score (%) | *Where to Get Help in Part Five: Reviewing the Basics* |
|---|---|---|
| Sentence Fragments *(page 52)* | _____ | C.1 *(page 400)* |
| Run-on Sentences *(page 70)* | _____ | C.2 *(page 405)* |
| Subject-Verb Agreement *(page 90)* | _____ | C.7 *(page 417)* |
| Pronoun-Antecedent Agreement *(page 110)* | _____ | C.8 *(page 421)* |
| Pronoun Reference *(page 128)* | _____ | C.9 *(page 423)* |
| Dangling Modifiers *(page 152)* | _____ | D.1 *(page 432)* |
| Misplaced Modifiers *(page 173)* | _____ | D.1 *(page 433)* |
| Coordinate Sentences *(page 190)* | _____ | D.3 *(page 436)* |
| Subordinate Clauses *(page 215)* | _____ | D.4 *(page 438)* |
| Parallelism *(page 244)* | _____ | D.5 *(page 440)* |
| When to Use Commas *(page 264)* | _____ | E.2, E.3 *(pages 452, 454)* |
| Using Colons and Semicolons *(page 286)* | _____ | E.4 *(page 456)* |
| When to Use Capital Letters *(page 309)* | _____ | F.1 *(page 462)* |

# Skill Refresher Answer Key

## SKILL REFRESHER—CHAPTER 3

### Sentence Fragments (page 52)

Answers may vary.

1. Correct
2. Correct
3. Because we're good friends, I remembered her birthday.
   I remembered her birthday because we're good friends.
4. After I left the classroom, I realized I forgot my book.
   I realized I forgot my book after I left the classroom.
5. Before the professor moved on to the next topic, Jason asked a question about centrifugal force.
   Jason asked a question about centrifugal force before the professor moved on to the next topic.
6. The phone rang, and the answering machine answered. The phone rang; the answering machine answered.
7. I was hoping I would do well on the test.
   I studied fervently, hoping I would do well on the test.
8. Martha scheduled a conference with her art history professor to discuss the topic for her final paper.
9. I got a "B" on the quiz because I reread my notes.
   Because I reread my notes, I got a "B" on the quiz.
10. Marcus was interested in the course that focused on the rise of communism.
    Marcus was interested in the course because it focused on the rise of communism.

## SKILL REFRESHER—CHAPTER 4

### Run-On Sentences (page 70)

Answers may vary.

1. The Civil War ended in 1865; the period of Reconstruction followed.
   The Civil War ended in 1865, and the period of Reconstruction followed.

2. Although light and sound both emit waves, they do so in different ways.

3. Correct

4. Archaeologists study the physical remains of cultures; anthropologists study the cultures themselves.
   Archaeologists study the physical remains of cultures, while anthropologists study the cultures themselves.

5. The body's nervous system carries electrical and chemical messages. These messages tell parts of the body how to react and what to do.
   The body's nervous system carries electrical and chemical messages that tell parts of the body how to react and what to do.

6. Neil Armstrong was the first human to walk on the moon. This event occurred in 1969.
   Neil Armstrong was the first human to walk on the moon; this event occurred in 1969.

7. Robert Frost is a well-known American poet; his most famous poem is "The Road Not Taken."
   Robert Frost is a well-known American poet. His most famous poem is "The Road Not Taken."

8. Algebra and geometry are areas of study of mathematics; calculus and trigonometry are other branches.

9. Correct

10. Since it is easy to become distracted by other thoughts and responsibilities while studying, it helps to make a list of these distractions
    It is easy to become distracted by other thoughts and responsibilities while studying. It helps to make a list of these distractions.

## SKILL REFRESHER—CHAPTER 5

### Subject-Verb Agreement (page 90)

1. wants
2. are
3. agrees
4. swim
5. knows
6. are
7. are
8. Candy
9. Sabrina
10. were

## SKILL REFRESHER—CHAPTER 6

### Pronoun-Antecedent Agreement (page 110)

1. our
2. his
3. his or her
4. it
5. his or her
6. their
7. he or she
8. his or her
9. their
10. he or she

## SKILL REFRESHER—CHAPTER 7

### Pronoun Reference (page 128)

Answers may vary.

1. Marissa told Kristin, "My car wouldn't start."
2. In the trunk, Brian found a book that his mother owned.
   Brian found a book in his mother's trunk.
3. Naomi put the cake on the table, and Roberta moved it to the counter after she noticed the cake was still hot.
4. The professor asked the student to loan him a book.
   The professor asked the student, "Could I borrow that book?"
5. Our waiter, who was named Burt, described the restaurant's specials.
6. Aaron's sister was injured in a car accident, but she would heal.
7. Correct
8. Another car, which was swerving crazily, hit mine.
   The car that was swerving crazily hit mine.
9. In hockey games, the players frequently injure each other in fights.
10. The hunting lodge had lots of deer and moose antlers hanging on its walls, and Ryan said he had killed some of the deer.
    The hunting lodge had lots of deer and moose antlers hanging on its walls, and Ryan said he had killed some of these animals.

## SKILL REFRESHER—CHAPTER 8

### Dangling Modifiers (page 152)

Answers may vary.

1. While standing on the ladder, Harvey patched the roof with tar paper.
2. Since I was nervous, the test seemed more difficult than it was.
   The test seemed more difficult than it was because I was nervous.
3. I was waiting to drop a class at the Records Office; the line seemed to go on forever.
   Everyone was waiting to drop a class at the Records Office; thus, the line seemed to go on forever.
4. Correct
5. The elevator was, of course, out of order while I was moving the couch.
   We discovered, while moving the couch, that the elevator was, of course, out of order.
6. While we were watching the evening news, the power went out.
   The power went out while Marge was watching the evening news.
7. After I decided to mow the lawn, it began to rain.
8. Since I was very tired, the long wait was unbearable.
   The long wait was unbearable because I was very tired.
9. While I was skiing downhill, the wind picked up.
   Skiing downhill, we noticed that the wind picked up.
10. The phone company hired me at the age of eighteen.

## SKILL REFRESHER—CHAPTER 9

### Misplaced Modifiers (page 173)

Answers may vary.

1. Marietta studiously previewed the test before she began answering the questions.
2. The book that Mark had returned late was checked out by another student.
3. Correct
4. The shocking article about the large donations political candidates receive from interest groups caused Lily to reconsider how she viewed candidates and their campaign promises.
   The article about the large donations political candidates receive shocked Lily, causing her to reconsider how she viewed candidates and their campaign promises.

5. Bryant cashed the student loan check that he desperately needed.
6. The angry crowd booed the referee when he finally arrived.
   Angry with the delay, the crowd booed the referee when he finally arrived.
7. Correct
8. The poetry of Emily Dickinson, a young, unhappy, and love-lorn woman, reveals a particular kind of misery and pain.
   The poetry of the young, unhappy, and love-lorn Emily Dickinson reveals a particular kind of misery and pain.
9. The governors of all the states met to discuss homelessness, a national problem.
10. Because health care workers are concerned about the risk of being exposed to the virus, they refuse treatment to many AIDS patients.

## SKILL REFRESHER—CHAPTER 10

### Coordinate Sentences (page 190)

Answers will vary.

1. A field study observes subjects in their natural settings; therefore, only a small number of subjects can be studied at one time.
2. The Grand Canyon is an incredible sight; it was formed less than ten million year ago.
3. Alaska and Siberia used to be connected twenty-five thousand years ago; consequently, many anthropologists believe that Native Americans migrated to North and South America from Asia.
4. Neon, argon, and helium are called inert gases, and they are never found in chemical compounds.
5. The professor returned the tests, but he did not comment on them.
6. Ponce de Leon was successful because he was the first European to "discover" Florida; however, he did not succeed in finding the fountain of youth he was searching for.
7. The lecture focused on the cardio-pulmonary system; therefore, the students needed to draw diagrams in their notes.
8. Rudy had never read Hamlet, nor had Rufus ever read Hamlet.
9. Presidents Lincoln and Kennedy did not survive assassination attempts, but President Ford escaped two assassination attempts.
10. Marguerite might write her paper about Moll Flanders, or she might write her paper about its author, Daniel Defoe.

# SKILL REFRESHER—CHAPTER 11

### Subordinate Clauses (page 215)

Answers will vary.

1. Although mushrooms are a type of fungus, some types are safe to eat.
2. When grape juice is fermented, it becomes wine.
3. It is important for children to be immunized since children who are not immunized are vulnerable to many dangerous diseases.
4. After a poem is read carefully, it should be analyzed.
5. Although the Vikings were probably the first Europeans to set foot in North America, Columbus "discovered" America much later.
6. While I was giving a speech in my communications class, Carl Sagan was giving a speech on campus.
7. When I started my assignment for French class, I was relieved that it was very easy.
8. Although infants may seem unaware and oblivious to their surroundings, they are able to recognize their mother's voice and smell from birth.
9. Because Neo-Freudians disagreed with Freud's focus on biological instincts and sexual drive, they formed new theories.
10. Although the hypothalamus is a tiny part of the brain, it has many very important functions, including the regulation of hormones, body temperature, and hunger.

# SKILL REFRESHER—CHAPTER 12

### Parallelism (page 244)

Answers may vary.

1. Melinda's professor drew an organizational chart of the human nervous system on the board, passed out a handout of it, and lectured about the way the nervous system is divided into subcategories.
2. Correct
3. Ski jumping, speed skating, and hang gliding are sports that require consideration and manipulation of velocity and wind resistance.
4. Professor Bargo's poetry class read famous poets, analyzed their poetry, and researched their lives.
   Professor Bargo's poetry class reads famous poets, analyzes their poetry and researches their lives.
5. Clams, oysters, and mussels are examples of mollusks.
   The clam, the oyster, and the mussel are examples of mollusks.

6. Correct
7. The United Nations was formed in 1945 to renounce war, uphold personal freedoms, and bring about worldwide peace and well-being.
8. In the 1980's Sandra Day O'Connor was appointed the first female Supreme Court Justice, Geraldine Ferraro became the first female presidential candidate, and the Equal Rights Amendment was defeated.
9. The Eighteenth Amendment to the Constitution implemented Prohibition, but the Twenty-First Amendment, ratified fourteen years later, repealed it.
10. Correct

## SKILL REFRESHER—CHAPTER 13

### When to Use Commas (page 264)

1. Although I was late, my sister was still waiting for me at the restaurant.
2. Tom invited Marie, Ted, Leah, and Pete.
3. Following the movie, we had a late lunch.
4. I bumped into a beautiful woman, Lisa's mother, on my way into the grocery store.
5. The phone rang, but I was outside.
6. My niece began to yell, "I'm Tarzan, king of the jungle."
7. Bill, a friend from school, sent me a postcard from Florida.
8. When I entered the room, everyone was watching television.
9. I heard her call, "Wait for me."
10. Although I have visited Vancouver, I have never been to Vancouver Island.

## SKILL REFRESHER—CHAPTER 14

### Using Colons and Semicolons (page 286)

1. Anthropologists believe human life began in the Middle East; skeletons that have been found provide evidence for this.
2. The natural sciences include botany, the study of plants; chemistry, the study of elements that compose matter; and biology, the study of all living things.
3. The courses I am taking cover a wide range of subjects: linguistics, racquetball, calculus, anatomy, and political science.

4. Introductory courses tend to be broad in scope; they do give a good overview of the subject matter.

5. The poet, John Milton, tells how Eve must have felt when she was created: "That day I remember, when from sleep / I first awaked, and found myself reposed / under a shade on flowers, much wond'ring where / and what I was, whence thither brought, and how."

6. Trigonometry incorporates many other math skills: geometry, algebra, and logic.

7. I enjoy a variety of sports: tennis, which is my favorite; golf, because it is relaxing; basketball, because it is a team sport; and racquetball, because it is a good workout.

8. When a skull is dug up by a gravedigger, Hamlet begins what is now a famous meditation on mortality: "Alas, poor Yorick, I knew him, Horatio."

9. Spanish is important to learn because many Americans speak it exclusively; it is also useful to understand another culture.

10. My botany text has a section about coniferous trees: pines, firs, cedars, and spruces.

## SKILL REFRESHER—CHAPTER 15

### When to Use Capital Letters (page 309)

1. Because I spent last Sunday in Pittsburgh, I missed my favorite television show—*60 Minutes*.

2. This summer I plan to visit the Baltic states—Estonia, Latvia, Lithuania—former Republics of the Soviet Union.

3. This May, Professor Gilbert will give us our final exam.

4. Last week I rented my favorite movie from the video rental store on Elmwood Avenue.

5. One of Shakespeare's most famous plays is *Hamlet*.

6. I live next door to Joe's Mobile gas station.

7. My brother will only eat Rice Krispies for breakfast.

8. Jean Griffith is a senator who lives in Washington County.

9. I love to vacation in California because the Pacific Ocean is so beautiful.

10. My neighbors, Mr. and Mrs. Wilson, have a checking account at the Lincoln Bank.

# TEXT AND ART CREDITS

**Chapter 1**  PHOTO OF STUDENTS Michael Kagan/Monkmeyer Press.

**Chapter 2**  CITIBANK AD Courtesy of Citibank.

**Chapter 3**  FRED MOODY From "Divorce: Sometimes a Bad Notion." *Seattle Weekly*, Nov. 22, 1989. Used with permission.

**Chapter 4**  STUART W. HYDE From *Television and Radio Announcing*, Seventh Edition. Copyright © 1995 by Houghton Mifflin Company. Used by permission.

**Chapter 5**  E.B. WHITE Reprinted courtesy of Cornell University Library, Department of Rare Books; PHOTO OF FIRST FLAG ON THE MOON Bettman-Corbis.

**Chapter 6**  L. RUST HILLS From "How to Eat an Ice-Cream Cone," *How to Do Things Right: The Revelations of a Fussy Man* (New York: Doubleday, 1972). Reprinted by permission of the author; GORDON PARKS From *Voices in the Mirror* by Gordon Parks. Copyright © 1990 by Gordon Parks. Used by permission of Doubleday, a division of Bantam Doubleday Dell Publishing Group, Inc; PHOTO OF ELLA WATSON Roy Stryker Collection, Photographic Archives, University of Louisville.

**Chapter 7**  GAIL Y. MIYASAKI "Obachan," *Asian Women's Journal*, 1971. Every attempt has been made to locate the rightsholder of this work. If the rightsholder should read this, please contact Houghton Mifflin Company, College Permissions, 222 Berkeley Street, Boston, MA 02116-3764; PHOTO OF CHIMP AND DOG George Mars/The Picture Cube; PHOTO OF COUPLE WITH BABY STROLLER Nancy Bates/The Picture Cube.

**Chapter 8**  STEPHANIE ERICSSON Excerpted from "The Ways We Lie." Copyright © 1992 by Stephanie Ericsson. Originally published in the *Utne Reader*. Used by permission of the Rhoda Weyr Agency, New York.

**Chapter 9**  SAUL KASSIN From *Psychology*. Copyright © 1995 by Houghton Mifflin Company. Used by permission.

**Chapter 10**  JO CLARE HARTSIG AND WALTER WINK Reprinted by permission of *Fellowship*, the magazine of the Fellowship of Reconciliation (January/February 1995), Box 271, Nyack, NY 10960; "NOT IN OUR TOWN" PHOTO James Woodcock/The Billings Gazette.

**Chapter 11**  JOHN CASSIDY Excerpted from "Who Killed the Middle Class?" by John Cassidy, *The New Yorker*, October 16, 1995. Used by permission of the author; PHOTO FROM "FATHER KNOWS BEST" Photofest; PHOTO FROM "ROSEANNE" Photofest.

**Chapter 12**  BREHM/KASSIN From *Social Psychology*, Third Edition. Copyright © 1996 by Houghton Mifflin Company. Used by permission; BARBARA EHRENREICH From "In Defense of Talk Shows," *Time*, December 4, 1995. © 1995 Time, Inc. Reprinted by permission; ELAYNE RAPPING From "Daytime Inquiries." Reprinted by permission from *The Progressive*, 409 East Main Street, Madison, WI 53703; ZICK RUBIN, ANNE PEPLAN, AND PETER SALOVEY From "What's in a Label: 'Black' or 'African American'?" from *Psychology*, Copyright © 1993 by Houghton Mifflin Company. Reprinted by permission; RICHARD P. APPELBAUM Excerpt, "Who Has the Right to Name?" from *Sociology* by Richard P. Appelbaum and William J. Chambliss. Copyright © 1995 by HarperCollins College Publishers. Reprinted by permission of Addison Wesley Longman Higher Education Publishing Group; JOHN HEILEMANN From "Black Is Back," by John Heilemann, The Talk of the Town, *The New Yorker*, October 30, 1995. Reprinted by permission. © 1995 The New Yorker Magazine, Inc. All rights reserved.

**Chapter 13**     ELLEN GOODMAN "A High Cost for a Small Hope," by Ellen Goodman from *The Boston Globe,* January 25, 1996. Copyright © 1996, The Boston Globe Newspaper Co./Washington Post Writers Group. Reprinted with permission; GEOFFREY COWLEY Excerpts from "Living Longer With HIV," by Geoffrey Cowley from *Newsweek,* February 12, 1996, copyright © 1996, Newsweek, Inc. All rights reserved. Reprinted by permission.

**Chapter 14**     MICHAEL CASTLEMAN "Flesh Wounds" by Michael Castleman from *Sierra,* March/April 1995, p. 26. Reprinted by permission of the author; BRENDA PETERSON *credit line to come*

**Chapter 15**     ELAINE MARIEB Excerpted from *Human Anatomy and Physiology*, Second Edition, by Elaine Marieb. Copyright © 1992 by Benjamin/Cummings Publishing Company. Reprinted by permission; PHOTO OF NEWSROOM Margaret Miller/Photo Researchers.

**Additional Readings**     ARMIN A BROTT "Taken for a Stranger" by Armin A. Brott, *New York Times Magazine,* November 21, 1993. Copyright © 1993 by The New York Times Co. Reprinted by permission; CASTLE FREEMAN JR. From "Stuck With Strangers" by Castle Freeman Jr. Copyright © 1996 Castle Freeman Jr., as first published in *The Atlantic Monthly,* January 1996. Reprinted by permission; BARBARA LAZEAR ASCHER "Hers: A Brother's Death," *New York Times Magazine,* November 19, 1989. Copyright © 1989 by The New York Times Company. Reprinted by permission; GERRI HIRSHEY "Toddler Terrorism," *New York Woman,* Sept. 1990. Reprinted by permission of Sterling Lord Literistic, Inc. Copyright 1990 by Gerri Hirshey; DOUGLAS A. BERNSTEIN ET AL. From *Psychology,* Second Edition. Copyright © 1991 by Houghton Mifflin Company. Used with permission; JOE SCHWARTZ AND THOMAS MILLER From "The Earth's Best Friends," *American Demographics,* Feb. 1991, pp. 26–35. Excerpt used with permission © *American Demographics,* February 1991; JEFF ISEMINGER Excerpts from "All in the Family," by Jeff Iseminger in *Wisconsin,* Sept/Oct. 1995. Used by permission; SCOTT RUSSELL SANDERS From *Secrets of the Universe* by Scott Russell Sanders. Copyright © 1991 by Scott Russell Sanders. Reprinted by permission of Beacon Press, Boston; MICHAEL POWELL Excerpted from "Wanted: 10 Things You Can Do to Make a Difference," by Michael Powell, from *Rolling Stone,* October 5, 1995. Straight Arrow Publishing Company, L. P. 1995. All rights reserved. Reprinted by permission; PETE HAMILL From "Crack in the Box." Permission granted by International Creative Management, Inc. Copyright © 1990 by Pete Hamill. Article first appeared in *Esquire;* MICHAEL W. FOX From *Inhumane Society: The American Way of Exploiting Animals* by Michael W. Fox. Copyright © 1990 St. Martin's Press, Inc., New York, NY. Reprinted with permission of St. Martin's Press; MARC PEYSER "Predators on the Prowl," by Marc Peyser. From *Newsweek,* January 1996 and © 1996, Newsweek, Inc. All rights reserved. Reprinted by permission; PHOTO OF CAR STUCK IN SNOW Goodwin/Monkmeyer Press; CARTOON Illustration by Ellwood Smith; PHOTO OF MOUNTAIN LION Victoria Hurst/Tom Stack & Associates.

# INDEX

# Correction and Editing Marks

Note: For help with some of these topics, see page number(s) following *Meaning*.

| Abbreviation | Meaning | Page |
|---|---|---|
| ab or abbr | abbreviation error | 463 |
| adj | adjective | 430 |
| adv | adverb | 430 |
| agr | faulty agreement | 417, 421 |
| awk | awkward | |
| ca or case | case | 426 |
| cap | capital letter | 462 |
| coord | coordination | 436 |
| cs | comma splice | 405 |
| d | diction | 448 |
| dm | dangling modifier | 433 |
| frag | fragment | 400 |
| fs | fused sentence | 405 |
| hyph | hyphenation | 464 |
| irreg | error in irregular verb | 368 |
| jar | jargon | |
| lc | use lowercase letter | 462 |
| mm | misplaced modifer | 432 |
| ms | manuscript form | 474 |
| nonst | nonstandard usage | 449 |
| num | faulty use of numbers | 465 |
| pass | ineffective passive voice | 414 |
| ref | pronoun reference error | 423 |
| sp | misspelled word | 467 |
| sub | subordination | 438 |
| t | verb tense error | 413 |
| trans | transition | 203 |
| s-v agr | subject-verb agreement | 417 |
| v or vb | verb error | 367 |
| w | wordy | 446 |
| wc | word choice error | 63 |
| ww | wrong word | |
| ?? | unclear or illegible | |
| ¶ or par | new paragraph | |
| no ¶ | no new paragraph | |
| // | parallelism | 440 |
| ⌒ | close up space | |
| # | add space | |
| ^ | insert | |
| ℮ | delete | |
| tr | transpose | |
| x | obvious error | |